Self, Symbols, and Society

Self, Symbols, and Society

Classic Readings in Social Psychology

Edited by
Nathan Rousseau

ROWMAN & LITTLEFIELD PUBLISHERS, INC.
Lanham • Boulder • New York • Oxford

To Gloria and Gerald Rotter

ROWMAN & LITTLEFIELD PUBLISHERS, INC.

Published in the United States of America
by Rowman & Littlefield Publishers, Inc.
An Imprint of the Rowman & Littlefield Publishing Group
4720 Boston Way, Lanham, Maryland 20706
www.rowmanlittlefield.com

12 Hid's Copse Road
Cumnor Hill, Oxford OX2 9JJ, England

Copyright © 2002 by Rowman & Littlefield Publishers, Inc.

British Library Cataloguing in Publication Information Available

Library of Congress Cataloging-in-Publication Data

Rousseau, Nathan, 1957–
    Self, symbols, and society : classic readings in social psychology / edited by Nathan Rousseau.
        p. cm.
    Includes bibliographical references and index.
    ISBN 0-7425-1630-X (alk. paper) — ISBN 0-7425-1631-8 (alk. paper)
    1. Social psychology. 2. Self. 3. Symbolic interactionism. I. Title.
HM1033 .R68 2002
302—dc21   2001058744

Printed in the United States of America

♾ ™ The paper used in this publication meets the minimum requirements of
American National Standard for Information Sciences—Permanence of Paper for
Printed Library Materials, ANSI/NISO Z39.48-1992.

~

Contents

Introduction   1

Part I: European Influences

Chapter 1   Emile Durkheim on the Division of Labor in Society   9

Chapter 2   Max Weber on Social Action   25

Chapter 3   Georg Simmel on the Social Development
              of Individualism   52

Part II: Early- to Mid-Twentieth-Century Developments

Chapter 4   Charles Horton Cooley's Concept of the
              Looking-Glass Self and Its Applications   85

Chapter 5   William I. Thomas on the Definition of the
              Situation   103

Chapter 6   George Herbert Mead on Self and Society   116

Chapter 7   Alfred Schutz on Society and Intersubjectivity   143

Chapter 8   Karl Mannheim on Self, Society, and the Sociology
              of Knowledge   168

Part III: Mid-Century Critiques and Refinements

Chapter 9   David Riesman on Social Character   187

Chapter 10   Erving Goffman on the Presentation of Self   209

Chapter 11   Peter Berger and Thomas Luckmann on the Social
              Construction of Self and Society   230

Chapter 12   Herbert Blumer on Symbolic Interactionism   249

Chapter 13   Harold Garfinkel on Ethnomethodology   264

Part IV: The Last Quarter Century

Chapter 14   Arlie Russell Hochschild on the Management
              of Emotion   297

Chapter 15   Robert Bellah et al. on Individualism and
              Community in America   317

Where Do We Go from Here? Toward a Theory of the Cycle
of Individualism   345

Glossary   355

Bibliography   359

Index   363

Credits   369

About the Editor   373

Introduction

"In the beginning is the relation."

—Martin Buber, *I and Thou*

Sociology emerged in the nineteenth century as scholars attempted to understand the changes taking place in society due to the Industrial Revolution. The term "sociology" was coined by the French philosopher Auguste Comte (1798–1857), and it literally means the study of society. As the discipline developed, sociologists became increasingly divided in terms of how they studied society. Some scholars (like Georg Simmel, who is discussed in chapter 3) argued that the best way to understand society is by examining the interactions that occur between the persons that comprise society (an approach now called microsociology). However, other scholars (like Emile Durkheim, who is discussed in chapter 1) argued that examining the relationships among social institutions such as politics, economy, and religion is the best way to understand society (an approach now called macrosociology). While both perspectives have merit, this book focuses on the microsociological approach.

Given microsociology's emphasis on face-to-face interaction, it places greater weight on understanding the roles of individuals in society than does macrosociology. In this way, microsociology looks somewhat like the discipline of psychology. Indeed, microsociology, which takes into account the development of individualism as well as the role of individualism in society, is commonly referred to as social psychology. While the disciplines of psychology and sociology each contain an area of study called social psychology, these disciplines approach the subject area in different ways. Psychological social psychology (PSP) tends to view individuals in social interaction as independent entities who affect one another. PSP tends to emphasize quantitative methods in analyzing the personal experience of individuals

1

who are engaged in social interaction. However, from a sociological social psychology (SSP) point of view, this emphasis on the individual contains a bias—the bias being an emphasis on the individual. Newcomers to sociology sometimes find this difficult to understand. From a sociological point of view, we live in a psychological society. We place great emphasis on individual experience, and while this may seem natural and normal, sociologists recognize that placing individual experience ahead of a shared experience is a product of our current culture. At other times in history and in other places in the world, individual experience has not been primary—shared community experience has been. The point is not whether one perspective is right and the other is wrong. Rather, viewing the individual as a distinct entity apart from his or her environment is a relative point of view based upon the shared experiences of the individuals comprising a given culture. Newcomers to sociology are sometimes perplexed by the sociological perspective because they first have to understand that their view of themselves as self-interested individuals is not a reflection of some absolute principle—though it seems that way because it is reinforced throughout their cultural experience— but rather a product of the time and place in which they live. Once you are able to take into consideration the role of the social factors that contribute significantly to the definition of personal preferences and identity, you can better appreciate the sociological study of individualism (what I like to call the sociology of psychology), as well as come to see the dynamic social forces that occur between individuals who reinforce or alter these social forces as they participate in social interaction. The investigation of the social forces that affect social interaction and identity and the study of the social factors operating between individuals participating in social interaction represent two branches of study within SSP.

Sociological social psychology is divided roughly between theoretical and methodological approaches called Symbolic Interactionism and Personality and Social Structure. Symbolic Interactionism has a multimethod approach employing both qualitative and quantitative procedures, while Personality and Social Structure tends to emphasize a comparative-historical approach. This book focuses on the development of SSP as it has occurred in both the areas of Symbolic Interactionism and Personality and Social Structure, showing the significant contributions made in these areas and demonstrating how these two branches share a common intellectual history. As you progress through the book, you will see that the convergence of these two currently distinct branches has synergistic results.

While Symbolic Interactionism tends to emphasize the interaction itself that occurs between participants, and Personality and Social Structure tends to emphasize the historical, cultural, and institutional factors (what were called "social forces" above) affecting social interaction and identity, both branches of SSP are concerned with the nature of social interaction. Generally speaking, sociological social psychology focuses on the empirical factors (such as gestures) occurring between individuals that orient the process of interaction. Sociological social psychology also focuses on what sociologist Peter Berger called the paradox of social existence: while society creates individuals, individuals create society. While society provides the history and the language that individuals use to orient their thoughts and actions, society is maintained or changed by individuals in social interaction. When the members of society follow the roles, scripts, and attitudes of the society they were born into, those members reinforce the continuation of the norms of that society; conversely, when the members of society engage in social interactions that redefine their roles, scripts, and attitudes, then the members of society change their society. Whether tendencies towards stasis or tendencies towards social change prevail is contingent upon the density and intensity of the innovative actions. As you can see, there is much potential power in the hands of individuals in interaction for shaping the destiny of their society.

One of the issues that will be addressed in this book, particularly in the conclusion, is the degree to which individuals in interaction realize that they have this much power. Despite how much we value individualism in our society, individuals frequently experience frustrations and failures as they try to navigate through the social institutions that comprise society. Our sense of personal power seems to be limited within a narrow circle of power.

The value of studying sociology, and sociological social psychology in particular, is that you acquire a greater appreciation of not only yourself (because, how can you know yourself unless you are clear about the social factors that affect your individual decision-making?), but also of how your behavior is affected by, and affects, social interaction and society itself. Once you see how personal thoughts and behaviors contribute to the social forces that affect your life, you are in a better position to affect those forces in a more positive direction. I liken this situation to that of caring for plants. In a psychologically oriented society, it is as if there is an assumption that watering one's houseplants will automatically take care of the plants outside of one's house as well. We tend to focus on inner processes, assuming that this will take care of the world around us. But the fact is that unless you go outside and water and trim the plants in your yard, your yard is not going to take care of itself. Sociological social psychology emphasizes both inner and outer processes—both the houseplants, which represent your sense of self, and the plants in your yard, which represent the shared experience of social life.

Now, let's discuss the book itself. Each introductory section provides a biographical as well as theoretical context that bridges the intellectual developments in each chapter and orients the reader to the material ahead. Important persons and terms that are not sufficiently addressed in the reading selections or expanded upon in the introductory sections may be found in the glossary. Any anthology is, by definition, selective. In editing this volume, I did not want to present readers with short excerpts from the "best of." The selections are longer than those that are found in many anthologies today. Why include long passages by a bunch of dead guys (though certainly not all of the authors represented here are deceased, and not all are men)? What relevance can readings that are fifty to one hundred years old have for us today? Look at it this way: unless people kept records so that we could look to the past, how would anyone know the point at which Mark McGwire or Barry Bonds broke the home run record? Because of historical records, life today has context and meaning, and we have goals to work toward for the future. Understanding the past informs the present and guides us intelligently into the future. So why read a bunch of mostly dead sociologists? The works in this book are classic pieces; they convey unique innovations and timeless struggles in our understanding of ourselves, of each other, and of the society that we all share. Why have longer pieces than what are commonly found? If you are only exposed to snippets of the "best of," you are denied the opportunity of discovering for yourself how rich in thinking these pieces are. You are denied access to how these innovative thinkers came to their conclusions. By being exposed to some of the processes by which these thinkers came to their conclusions, you will become a better, perhaps an innovative, thinker yourself. Reading these works will give you a better appreciation of where we have been, where we are, and what our choices are (what your choices are) concerning the future direction of important aspects of social life.

The book is divided into four sections tracing the chronological development of sociological social psychology from some of the founders of sociology in Europe in the late nineteenth century to the late twentieth century in the United States. Part I begins with Emile Durkheim, because his research, which gave academic legitimacy to the discipline of sociology, represents a foundation from which many reacted. The theoretical and empirical study of the self as an active participant in either maintaining or changing the social order is, in part, the result of moving away from the once dominating sociological theory (rooted in Durkheim's work, and reinforced later by Talcott Parsons, 1902–1979, who will be discussed in some detail in the conclusion of this book) that selves are the product of society. It is in the second and third chapters of the book, however, that we begin to see the roots of sociological social psychology. Chapter 2 is on Max Weber's theory of social action, and chapter 3 concerns Georg Simmel's work on social development, particularly the work related to modernity and individualism.

Part II is composed principally of the early- to mid-twentieth century key social psychological developments in the United States. Chapter 4 is a relatively in-depth look at Charles Horton Cooley's concept of the looking-glass self; the chapter contains extended excerpts from his brilliant (though sometimes certainly dated) book *Human Nature and the Social Order*. A popular and influential book in its day, today many students are exposed to only the few pages of the book that outline the looking-glass self. Chapter 5 is not only on William I. Thomas's concept of the definition of the situation, but it contextualizes Thomas's concerns at the time he was writing. Thomas discusses the definition of the situation in order to point out that the deviance in girls that was causing some concern among people in 1923 was a product of the changing roles for women in society. Moreover, while Thomas was concerned about delinquent behavior because of the harm it may do to self and society, he also recognized that the definition of a deviant act is contingent upon time and place. Sociological social psychology would not be what it is today without the brilliant work of George Herbert Mead. Because of the widely held belief that he did not publish very much and because of contemporary unfamiliarity with his social activism, chapter 6 contains primary readings on some of Mead's most significant contributions to the development of social psychology as well as a primary reading on social reform. Part II continues by outlining some of Alfred Schutz's contributions to social psychology. Schutz's blending of the work of mathematician-turned-philosopher Edmund Husserl (1859–1938) and Max Weber results in a perceptive theory concerning the relationship between selves in social interaction (a dynamic relationship called intersubjectivity, which means relation between subjects). Karl Mannheim is the last figure represented in this section. His unique contributions to the study of self and society lay in his insights concerning the sociology of knowledge. In particular, Mannheim's work asks us to examine the impact of historical and cultural trends in shaping self-knowledge.

Part III (chapters 9 through 13) concerns mid-century critiques and refinements in the study of social interaction and, more generally, the relationship between self and society. The first chapter in this section presents excerpts from David Riesman's *The Lonely Crowd*. This book had such a social impact that it landed Riesman on the cover of *Time* magazine. Chapter 9's focus on the relationship between social change and character remains an interesting and timely topic. Chapter 10 presents Erving Goffman's dramaturgical perspective in *The Presentation of Self in Everyday Life*. Goffman describes the dynamics of social interaction as a theatrical performance. Chapter 11 presents Peter Berger and Thomas Luckmann's "treatise," *The Social Construction of Reality*. Berger and Luckmann describe in some detail how society constructs selves and how selves either reinforce or change existing constructions of how society defines reality. Chapter 12 presents a key article on Symbolic Interactionism by the man who coined the term, Herbert Blumer. The final chapter in this section is on Harold Garfinkel's work in ethnomethodology (literally, "people's methods"). Garfinkel's blending of Schutz's unique approach with Parsons's influential sociological work produces a theory that incorporates the power of language, the subtle effects of institutionalized or routinized practices in guiding moral choices (for example, the specific behavior that we expect while attending a funeral differs from the behavior we see at ball games), and the freedom of selves to make choices while participating in social interaction. This chapter includes a brief discussion of Garfinkel's famous case study on Agnes, the individual who, Garfinkel notes, carefully observed the social practices of gender in order to legitimate a sex-change operation in 1958.

The final section of the book takes us to the end of the twentieth century. Chapter 14 contains extended excerpts from Arlie Russell Hochschild's (Cooley Award–winning) book *The Managed Heart*. This chapter discusses the management of emotion and social inequalities based upon gender. The final chapter is taken from Robert Bellah et al.'s best-selling book *Habits of the Heart*. The chapter focuses on the cultural development of individualism in the United States. The chapter also includes some discussion of the debate between stressing greater personal autonomy (as noted by Riesman) versus a greater sense of community in resolving social problems.

The conclusion, entitled "Where Do We Go from Here? Toward a Theory of the Cycle of Individualism," summarizes and integrates the various themes that have been discussed in the book. It summarizes where sociological social psychology has been, where it is presently, and makes recommendations for the future. The conclusion provides a context within which to analyze how far the discipline has progressed theoretically, and it confronts how far the discipline, in its varying forms, has progressed in terms of resolving in any kind of real, practical way some of the social issues that it has been studying for a century, i.e., promoting an awareness of the social factors that impact self-knowledge and thereby affect social interactions; contributing to the amelioration of the social inequalities related to gender that exist in social interactions and thereby exist in society at large. As you will see, despite one hundred years of study, we still have a long way to go in terms of implementing social practices that would empower more of our citizens.

I hope that the reader will come away from this book with a greater appreciation of social history, a more thorough awareness of the social factors that affect self-understanding, a deeper insight into self-knowledge, a greater sense of responsibility for one's participation in society, and an invigorated commitment to work on the social inequalities that continue to undermine the creation of a genuine spirit of community (where self-interest is balanced by civic concern).

PART ONE

EUROPEAN INFLUENCES

CHAPTER ONE

Emile Durkheim on the Division of Labor in Society

∼ Introduction ∼

Emile Durkheim (1858–1917) grew up in the small French town of Epinal. In 1879, after his third attempt, Durkheim was admitted to France's most prestigious college, the Ecole Normale Supérieure. Although his studies focused on Latin, Greek, literature, philosophy, and history, Durkheim was more interested in opportunities to learn systematically about the social and political issues that were creating tensions in contemporary France. Rapid social changes and political unrest following the French Revolution resulted in a number of social ills, including family breakdown, suicide, and crime.

Durkheim was influenced by the works of such people as Auguste Comte (1798–1857), who coined the term "sociology," and Herbert Spencer (1820–1895), who wrote *Principles of Sociology*, when he set out to devise a systematic social theory to explain the social changes that he observed taking place. The product of his efforts led to innovative ways of explaining social life. In 1902 Durkheim accepted an appointment as professor of education at the prestigious University of Paris, Sorbonne. Eleven years later a permanent position in sociology was created for him there. More than anyone else, Durkheim's efforts gave legitimacy to the discipline of sociology in France.

Durkheim's varied interests are highlighted by the titles of his most influential books: *The Division of Labor in Society, The Rules of the Sociological Method, Suicide: A Study of Sociology*, and *The Elementary Forms of the Religious Life*. Regardless of topic, though, Durkheim always set out to establish the relevance of sociology as a systematic method of explaining social life (Durkheim emphasizes in *The Rules* that only sociological analyses can explain social phenomena), and he strived to work out theories of social order upon which to put to rest the social conflicts that he observed. These points are exemplified in Durkheim's first book, *The Division of Labor in Society*, and it is from this work that you will read.

Like many of his contemporaries, Durkheim's thinking was affected by the works of Adam Smith and Charles Darwin, and you will be able to observe those influences. In this work Durkheim postulates that early or primitive society was held together by strong social bonds or a dominating common or collective consciousness that limited individual expression. Because of the machine-like operations of the clearly defined, interconnected roles of this form of social organization, Durkheim refers to this type of social order as mechanical solidarity. However, Durkheim argues, as society becomes more complex due to such factors as the moral or dynamic density of society (that is, population growth and increasingly complex social interaction), the division of labor in society results in individual specialization. The tasks necessary for society to function at a more sophisticated level require that individuals fulfill roles that are more complex and specialized, and in order to fulfill the increasing diversity of specialized tasks, individuals must have greater independence. Hence, personal independence and the division of labor advance as a result of increasing specialization in society.

Because Durkheim makes the analogy between the functioning of society and that of a living organism (consistent with the Functionalist perspective that society consists of interrelated, supportive parts or organs), he refers to this more complex type of social organization as organic solidarity. It is important to note that as individuals gain independent functions in society, the nature of the collective consciousness changes: it becomes less of a determining influence in defining individual roles. While this sounds thoroughly positive, there is a negative consequence: as the collective consciousness weakens, individuals may feel a sense of normlessness (that is, feel directionless, aimless, and with no ties or connection to something larger than oneself). Durkheim demonstrates that in extreme forms such normlessness, or anomie, can lead to suicide. Durkheim argues that, while anomie can arise with the increasing complexity of the division of labor, it is not a necessary consequence of it. Durkheim views anomie as an avoidable pathology in society. As such, when anomie arises in society it must be remedied.

We have discussed mechanical and organic solidarity. Durkheim states that these represent two types of positive solidarity or forms of moral bonds that connect people to each other. Within a social order, individuals may be connected in a way that emphasizes their differences; in other words, specializations in society make people different from but also dependent upon each other. Due to the complex nature of a society based upon organic solidarity, the underlying bonds of positive solidarity may be overshadowed by the bonds of negative solidarity— the social boundaries that allow for individual expression. When negative solidarity overshadows positive solidarity, we fail to see that we participate in maintaining the boundaries that allow us each to express ourselves. This, then, is the source of much of the anomie that exists in complex societies.

In order to resolve the problem of anomie, society must be structured in such a way that individuals clearly recognize the moral bonds that connect them with others. Durkheim suggests the proliferation of associations such as community, religious, and business organizations as the way to facilitate the connection of individuals in reciprocal give-and-take. The result would be a strengthened moral order and a healthy society.

⌒ The Division of Labor ⌒

Although the division of labour is not of recent origin, it was only at the end of the last century that societies began to become aware of this law, to which up to then they had submitted almost unwittingly. Undoubtedly even from antiquity several thinkers had perceived its importance. Yet Adam Smith was the first to attempt to elaborate the theory of it. Moreover, it was he who first coined the term, which social science later lent to biology.

Nowadays the phenomenon has become so widespread that it catches everyone's attention. We can no longer be under any illusion about the trends in modern industry. It involves increasingly powerful mechanisms, large-scale groupings of power and capital, and consequently an extreme division of labour. Inside factories, not only are jobs demarcated, becoming extremely specialised, but each product is itself a specialty entailing the existence of others. Adam Smith and John Stuart Mill persisted in hoping that agriculture at least would prove an exception to the rule, seeing in it the last refuge of small-scale ownership. Although in such a matter we must guard against generalising unduly, nowadays it appears difficult to deny that the main branches of the agricultural industry are increasingly swept along in the general trend. Finally, commerce itself contrives ways to follow and reflect, in all their distinctive nuances, the boundless diversity of industrial undertakings. Although this evolution occurs spontaneously and unthinkingly, those economists who study its causes and evaluate its results, far from condemning such diversification or attacking it, proclaim its necessity. They perceive in it the higher law of human societies and the condition for progress.

Yet the division of labour is not peculiar to economic life. We can observe its increasing influence in the most diverse sectors of society. Functions, whether political, administrative or judicial, are becoming more and more specialised. The same is true in the arts and sciences. The time lies far behind us when philosophy constituted the sole science. It has become fragmented into a host of special disciplines, each having its purpose, method and ethos. 'From one half-century to another the men who have left their mark upon the sciences have become more specialized.' . . .

. . . However richly endowed we may be, we always lack something, and the best among us feel our own inadequacy. This is why we seek in our friends those qualities we lack, because in uniting with them we share in some way in their nature, feeling ourselves then less incomplete. In this way small groups of friends grow up in which each individual plays a role in keeping with his character, in which a veritable exchange of services occurs. The one protects, the other consoles; one advises, the other executes, and it is this distribution of functions or, to use the common expression, this division of labour, that determines these relations of friendship.

We are therefore led to consider the division of labour in a new light. In this case, indeed, the economic services that it can render are insignificant compared with the moral effect that it produces, and its true function is to create between two or more people a feeling of solidarity. . . .

If exchange alone has often been held to constitute the social relationships that arise from the division of labour, it is because we have failed to recognise what exchange implies and what results from it. It presumes that two beings are mutually dependent upon each other because they are both incomplete, and it does no more than interpret externally this mutual dependence. Thus it is only the superficial expression of an internal and deeper condition. Precisely because this condition remains constant, it gives rise to a whole system of images which function with a continuity that is lacking in exchange. The image of the one who complements us becomes inseparable within us from our own, not only because of the frequency with which it is associated with it, but above all because it is its natural complement. Thus it becomes an integral, permanent part of our consciousness to such a degree that we can no longer do without it. We seek out everything that can increase the image's strength. This is why we like the company of the one the image represents, because the presence of the object whose expression it is, by causing it to pass to the state of perception here and now, gives it greater vividness. By contrast, we suffer in any circumstance where, such as in absence or death, the effect can be to prevent its return or to lessen its intensity. . . .

The totality of beliefs and sentiments common to the average members of a society forms a determinate system with a life of its own. It can be termed the collective or common consciousness. Undoubtedly the substratum of this consciousness does not consist of a single organ. By definition it is diffused over society as a whole, but nonetheless possesses specific characteristics that make it a distinctive reality. In fact it is independent of the particular conditions in which individuals find themselves. Individuals pass on, but it abides. It is the same in north and south, in large towns and in small, and in different professions. Likewise it does not change with every generation but, on the contrary, links successive generations to one another. Thus it is something totally different from the consciousnesses of individuals, although it is only realised in individuals. . . .

. . . Two consciousnesses exist within us: the one comprises only states that are personal to each one of us, characteristic of us as individuals, whilst the other comprises states that are common to the whole of society. The former represents only our individual personality, which it constitutes; the latter represents the collective type and consequently the society without which it would not exist. When it is an element of the latter determining our behaviour, we do not act with an eye to our own personal interest, but are pursuing collective ends. Now, although distinct, these two consciousnesses are linked to each other, since in the end they constitute only one entity, for both have one and the same organic basis. Thus they are solidly joined together. This gives rise to a solidarity *sui generis* which, deriving from resemblances, binds the individual directly to society. . . .

· . . . [T]he rules relating to 'real' rights and personal relationships that are established by virtue of them form a definite system whose function is not to link together the different parts of society, but on the contrary to detach them from one another, and mark out clearly the barriers separating them. Thus they do not correspond to any positive social tie. The very expression 'negative solidarity' that we have employed is not absolutely exact. It is not a true solidarity, having its own life and being of a special nature, but rather the negative aspects of every type of solidarity. The first condition for an entity to become coherent is for the parts that form it not to clash discordantly. But such an external harmony does not bring about cohesion. On the contrary, it presumes it. Negative solidarity is only possible where another kind is present, positive in nature, of which it is both the result and the condition.

Indeed the rights that individuals possess both over themselves and things can only be determined by means of compromise and mutual concessions, for everything that is granted to some is necessarily given up by others. It is sometimes stated that the level of normal development in an individual could be deduced either from the concept of human personality (Kant), or from the idea of the individual organism (Spencer). This is possible, although the rigour in this reasoning is very questionable. In any case what is certain is that, in historical reality, it is not upon these abstract considerations that the moral order was founded. In fact, for a man to acknowledge that others have rights, not only as a matter of logic, but as one of daily living, he must have agreed to limit his own. . . .

Since negative solidarity on its own brings about no integration, and since, moreover, there is nothing specific in it, we shall identify only two kinds of positive solidarity, distinguished by the following characteristics:

(1) The first kind links the individual directly to society without any intermediary. With the second kind he depends upon society because he depends upon the parts that go to constitute it.
(2) In the two cases, society is not viewed from the same perspective. In the first, the term is used to denote a more or less organised society composed of beliefs and sentiments common to all the members of the group: this is the collective type. On the contrary, in the second case the society to which we are solidly joined is a system of different and special functions united by definite relationships. Moreover, these two societies are really one. They are two facets of one and the same reality, but which none the less need to be distinguished from each other.
(3) From this second difference there arises another which will serve to allow us to characterise and delineate the features of these two kinds of solidarity.

The first kind can only be strong to the extent that the ideas and tendencies common to all members of the society exceed in number and intensity those that appertain personally to each one of those members. The greater this excess, the more active this kind of society is. Now what constitutes our personality is that which each one of us possesses that is peculiar and characteristic, what distinguishes it from others. This solidarity can therefore only increase in inverse relationship to the personality. As we have said, there is in the consciousness of each one of us two consciousnesses: one that we share in common with our group in its entirety, which is consequently not ourselves, but society living and acting within us; the other that, on the contrary, represents us alone in what is personal and distinctive about us, what makes us an individual. The solidarity that derives from similarities is at its *maximum* when the collective consciousness completely envelops our total consciousness, coinciding with it at every point. At that moment our individuality is zero. That individuality cannot arise until the community fills us less completely. Here there are two opposing forces, the one centripetal, the other centrifugal, which cannot increase at the same time. We cannot ourselves develop simultaneously in two so opposing directions. If we have a strong inclination to think and act for ourselves we cannot be strongly inclined to think and act like other people. If the ideal is to create for ourselves a special, personal image, this cannot mean to be like everyone else. Moreover, at the very moment when this solidarity exerts its effect, our personality, it may be said by definition, disappears, for we are no longer ourselves, but a collective being.

The social molecules that can only cohere in this one manner cannot therefore move as a unit save in so far as they lack any movement of their own, as do the molecules of inorganic bodies. This is why we suggest that this kind of solidarity should be called mechanical. The word does not mean that the solidarity is produced by mechanical and artificial means. We only use this term for it by analogy with the cohesion that links together the elements of raw materials, in contrast to that which encompasses the unity of living organisms. What finally justifies the use of this term is the fact that the bond that thus unites the individual with society is completely analogous to that which links the thing to the person. The individual consciousness, considered from this viewpoint, is simply a dependency of the collective type, and follows all its motions, just as the object possessed follows those which its owner imposes upon it. In societies where this solidarity is highly developed the individual, as we shall see later, does not belong to himself; he is literally a thing at the disposal of society. Thus, in these same social types, personal rights are still not yet distinguished from 'real' rights.

The situation is entirely different in the case of solidarity that brings about the division of labour. Whereas the other solidarity implies that individuals resemble one another, the latter assumes that they are different from one another. The former type is only possible in so far as the individual personality is absorbed into the collective personality; the latter is only possible if each one of us has a sphere of action that is peculiarly our own, and consequently a personality. Thus the collective consciousness leaves uncovered a part of the individual consciousness, so that there may be established in it those special functions that it cannot regulate. The more extensive this free area is, the stronger the cohesion that arises from this solidarity. Indeed, on the one hand each one of us depends more intimately upon society the more labour is divided up, and on the other, the activity of each one of us is correspondingly more specialised, the more personal it is. Doubtless, however circumscribed that activity may be, it is never completely original. Even in the exercise of our profession we conform to usages and practices that are common to us all within our corporation. Yet even in this case, the burden that we bear is in a different way less heavy than when the whole of society bears down upon us, and this leaves much more room for the free play of our initiative. Here, then, the individuality of the whole grows at the same time as that of the parts. Society becomes more effective in moving in concert, at the same time as each of its elements has more movements that are peculiarly its own. This solidarity resembles that observed in the higher animals. In fact each organ has its own special characteristics and autonomy, yet the greater the unity of the organism, the more marked the individualisation of the parts. Using this analogy, we propose to call 'organic' the solidarity that is due to the division of labour. . . .

Thus on the whole the common consciousness comprises ever fewer strong and well-defined sentiments. This is therefore the case because the average intensity and degree of determinateness of the collective states of feeling continue still to diminish, as we have just stated. Even the very limited increase that we have just observed only confirms this result. Indeed it is very remarkable that the sole collective sentiments that have gained in intensity are those that relate, not to social matters, but to the individual. For this to be so the individual personality must have become a much more important factor in the life of society. For it to have been able to acquire such importance it is not enough for the personal consciousness of each individual to have increased in absolute terms; it must have increased more than the common consciousness. The personal consciousness must have thrown off the yoke of the common consciousness, and consequently the latter must have lost its power to dominate and that determining action that it exerted from the beginning. If indeed the relationship between these two elements had remained unchanged, if both had developed in extent and vitality in the same proportion, the collective sentiments that relate to the individual would likewise have remained unchanged. Above all, they would not have been the sole sentiments to have grown. This is because they depend solely on the social value of the individual factor, which in turn is determined not by any absolute development of that factor, but by the relative size of the share that falls to him within the totality of social phenomena.

This proposition could be verified by utilising a method that we shall only sketch out briefly.

At the present time we do not possess any scientific conception of what religion is. In order to do so we would need to have dealt with the problem using the same comparative method that we have applied to the question of crime, and such an attempt has not yet been made. It has often been stated that at any moment in history religion has consisted of the set of beliefs and sentiments of every kind concerning man's links with a being or beings whose nature he regards as superior to his own. But such a definition is manifestly inadequate. In fact there are a host of rules of conduct or ways of thinking that are certainly religious and that, however, apply to relationships of a totally different kind. Religion prohibits the Jew from eating certain kinds of meat and lays down that he must dress in a prescribed fashion. It imposes upon him this or that view regarding the nature of men and things, and regarding the origin of the world. Often it regulates legal, moral and economic relationships. Its sphere of action thus extends far beyond man's communication with the divine. We are assured, moreover, that there exists at least one religion without a god. This single fact alone, were it firmly established, would suffice to demonstrate that we have no right to define religion as a function of the notion of God. Finally, if the extraordinary authority that the believer attributes to the divinity can account for the special prestige attached to everything that is religious, it remains to be explained how men have been led to ascribe such an authority to being who, on the admission of everybody, is in many, if not all cases, a figment of their imagination. Nothing proceeds from nothing. Thus the force that the being possesses must come from somewhere, and consequently the above formula does not inform us about the essence of the phenomenon.

Yet, setting this element on one side, the sole characteristic that is apparently shared equally by all religious ideas and sentiments is that they are common to a certain number of individuals living together. Moreover, their average intensity is fairly high. Indeed it is invariably the fact that when a somewhat strong conviction is shared by a single community of people it inevitably assumes a religious character. It inspires in the individual consciousness the same reverential respect as religious beliefs proper. Thus it is extremely probable—but this brief outline doubtless cannot constitute a rigorous proof—that likewise religion corresponds to a very central domain of the common consciousness. It is true that such a domain would have to be mapped out, distinguishing it from the area that corresponds to penal law, with which, moreover, it frequently wholly or partly overlaps. These are problems that have to be studied, but whose solution is not directly relevant to the very feasible conjecture we have just made.

Yet if there is one truth that history has incontrovertibly settled, it is that religion extends over an ever diminishing area of social life. Originally, it extended to everything; everything social was religious—the two words were synonymous. Then gradually political, economic and scientific functions broke free from the religious function, becoming separate entities and taking on more and more a markedly temporal character. God, if we may express it in such a way, from being at first present in every human relationship, has progressively withdrawn. He leaves the world to men and their quarrels. At least, if He continues to rule it, it is from on high and afar off, and the effect that He exercises, becoming more general and indeterminate, leaves freer rein for human forces. The individual thus feels, and he is in reality, much less *acted upon*; he becomes more a source of spontaneous activity. In short, not only is the sphere of religion not increasing at the same time as that of the temporal world, nor in the same proportion, but it is continually diminishing. This regression did not begin at any precise moment in history, but one can follow the phases of its development from the very origins of social evolution. It is therefore bound up with the basic conditions for the development of societies and thus demonstrates that there is a constantly decreasing number of beliefs and collective sentiments that are both sufficiently collective and strong enough to assume a religious character. This means that the average intensity of the common consciousness is itself weakening.

This demonstration has one advantage over the previous one: it allows it to be established that the same law of regression applies to the representative element in the common consciousness as it does to the affective element. Through the penal law we can reach only phenomena that relate to the sensibility, whereas religion embraces not only feelings but also ideas and doctrines.

The decrease in the number of proverbs, adages and sayings as societies develop is still further proof that the collective representations are also becoming less determinate.

Among primitive peoples, in fact, maxims of this kind are very numerous. According to Ellis, 'The Ewe-speaking peoples like most races of West Africa, have a large collection of proverbs, one, at least, being provided for almost every circumstance in life; a peculiarity which is common to most peoples who have made but little progress in civilization.'

More advanced societies are only slightly fertile in this way during the preliminary phases of their existence. Later not only are no new proverbs coined, but the old ones gradually fade away, lose their proper meaning, and end up by not being understood at all. This clearly shows that it is above all in lower societies that they are most favoured, and that today they only succeed in maintaining their currency among the lower classes. But a proverb is the concentrated expression of a collective idea or feeling, relating to a determinate class of objects. Beliefs and feelings of this kind cannot even exist without their crystallising in this form. As every thought tends to find the expression that is most adequate for it, if it is common to a certain number of individuals it necessarily ends up by being encapsulated in a formula that is equally common to them all. Any lasting function fashions an organ for itself in its own image. Thus it is wrong to have adduced our inclination for realism and our scientific outlook to explain the decline in proverbs. In conversational language we do not pay much attention to precision nor so disdain imagery. On the contrary, we relish greatly the old proverbs that we have preserved. Moreover, the image is not an element inherent in a proverb. It is one of the ways—yet not the only one—in which the thought of the collectivity is epitomised. Yet these brief formulas end up by being too constricting to contain the diversity of individual sentiments. Their unity no longer chimes with the divergences that have occurred. Thus they only sustain their existence successfully by taking on a more general meaning, and gradually die out. The organ becomes atrophied because the function is no longer exercised, that is, because there are fewer collective representations sufficiently well-defined to be enclosed within any determinate form.

Thus everything goes to prove that the evolution of the common consciousness proceeds along the lines we have indicated. Very possibly it progresses less than does the individual consciousness. In any case it becomes weaker and vaguer as a whole. The collective type loses some of its prominence, its forms become more abstract and imprecise. Undoubtedly, if this decline were, as we are often inclined to believe, an original product of our most recent civilisation and a unique event in the history of societies, we might ask whether it would last. But in fact it has continued uninterruptedly from earliest times. This is what we set out to demonstrate. Individualism and free thinking are of no recent date, neither from 1789, the Reformation, scholasticism, the collapse of Graeco-Latin polytheism, nor the fall of oriental theocracies. They are a phenomenon that has no fixed starting point but one that has developed unceasingly throughout history. Their development is undoubtedly not linear. The new societies that replace extinct social types never embark on their course at the very spot where the others came to a halt. How could that be possible? What the child continues is not the old age or the years of maturity of his parents, but their own childhood. Thus if we wish to take stock of the course that has been run we must consider successive societies only at the same stage of their existence. We must, for example, compare the Christian societies of the Middle Ages with primitive Rome, and the latter with the original Greek cities, etc. We then find that this progress or, if you like, this regression, has been accomplished, so to speak, without any break in continuity. Thus an iron law exists against which it would be absurd to revolt.

Moreover, this is not to say that the common consciousness is threatened with total disappearance. But it increasingly comprises modes of thinking and feeling of a very general, indeterminate nature, which leave room for an increasing multitude of individual acts of dissent. There is indeed one area in which the common consciousness has grown stronger, becoming more clearly delineated, viz., in its view of the individual. As all the other beliefs and practices assume less and less religious a character, the individual becomes the object of a sort of religion. We carry on the worship of the dignity of the human person, which, like all strong acts of worship, has already acquired its superstitions. If you like, therefore it is indeed a common faith. Yet first of all, it is only possible because of the collapse of other faiths and consequently it cannot engender the same results as that multiplicity of extinct beliefs. There is no compensation. Moreover, if the faith is common because it is shared among the community, it is individual in its object. If it impels every will towards the same end, that end is not a social one. Thus it holds a wholly exceptional position within the collective consciousness. It is indeed from society that it draws all this strength, but it is not to society that it binds us; it is to ourselves. Thus it does not constitute a truly social link. This is why theorists have been justly reproached with effecting the dissolution of society, because they have made this sentiment the exclusive basis for their moral doctrine. We may therefore conclude by affirming that all those social links resulting from similarity are growing progressively weaker.

This law alone suffices to demonstrate the absolute grandeur of the part played by the division of labour. Indeed, since mechanical solidarity is growing ever weaker, social life proper must either diminish or another form of solidarity must emerge gradually to take the place of the one that is disappearing. We have to choose. In vain is it maintained that the collective consciousness is growing and becoming stronger with that of individuals. We have just proved that these two factors vary in inverse proportion to each other. Yet social progress does not consist in a process of continual dissolution—quite the opposite: the more we evolve, the more societies develop a profound feeling of themselves and their unity. Thus there must indeed be some other social link to bring about this result. And there can be no other save that which derives from the division of labour.

If, moreover, we recall that even where it is most resistant, mechanical solidarity does not bind men together with the same strength as does the division of labour, and also that its sphere of action does not embrace most of present-day social phenomena, it will become even more evident that social solidarity is tending to become exclusively organic. It is the division of labor that is increasingly fulfilling the role that once fell to the common consciousness. This is mainly what holds together social entities in the higher types of society.

This is a function of the division of labour that is important, but in a different way from that normally acknowledged by economists.

A corollary of everything that has gone before is that the division of labour cannot be carried out save between the members of a society already constituted.

Indeed when competition opposes isolated individuals not known to one another, it can only separate them still more. If they have ample space at their disposal, they will flee from one another. If they cannot go beyond set limits, they will begin to differentiate, but in a way so that they become still more independent of one another. We can cite no case where relationships of open hostility have been transformed into social relationships, without the intervention of any other factor. Thus, as there is generally no bond between individuals or creatures of the same vegetable or animal species, the war they wage upon one another serves only to diversify them, to give rise to dissimilar varieties that increasingly grow further apart. It is this progressive disjunction that Darwin has called the law of the divergence of characteristics. Yet the division of labour unites at the same time as it sets at odds; it causes the activities that it differentiates to converge; it brings closer those that it separates. Since competition cannot have determined their coming together, it must indeed have already pre-existed. The individuals between whom the conflict is joined must already be solidly linked to one another and feel so, that is, they belong to the same society. This is why, where this sentiment of solidarity is too weak to resist the centrifugal influence of competition, the latter produces completely different effects from the division of labour. In countries where existence is too difficult because of the extreme density of the population, the inhabitants, instead of specialising, withdraw permanently or provisionally from society by emigrating to other areas.

Moreover, it is enough to represent to ourselves what the division of labour is to make us understand that things cannot be otherwise. It consists in the sharing out of functions that up till then were common to all. But such an allocation cannot be effected according to any preconceived plan. We cannot say beforehand where the line of demarcation is drawn between tasks, once they have been separated. In the nature of things that line is not marked out so self-evidently, but on the contrary depends upon a great number of circumstances. The division must therefore come about of itself, and progressively. Consequently, in these conditions for a function to be capable of being shared out in two exactly complementary fractions, as the nature of the division of labour requires, it is indispensable that the two parties specialising should be in constant communication over the whole period that this dissociation is occurring. There is no other way for one part to take over from the other the whole operation that the latter is surrendering, and for them to adapt to each other. Now, just as an animal colony, the tissue of whose members is a continuum, constitutes an individual, so every aggregate of individuals in continuous contact forms a society. The division of labour can therefore only occur within the framework of an already existing society. By this we do not just simply mean that individuals must cling materially to one another, but moral ties must also exist between them. Firstly, material continuity alone gives rise to links of this kind, provided that it is lasting. Moreover, they are directly necessary. If the relationships beginning to be established during the period of uncertainty were not subject to any rule, if no power moderated the clash of individual interests, chaos would ensue from which no new order could emerge. It is true that we imagine that everything occurs by means of private agreements freely argued over. All social action therefore seems to be absent. But we forget that contracts are only possible where a legal form of regulation, and consequently a society, already exists.

Thus it has been wrong sometimes to see in the division of labour the basic fact of all social life. Work is not shared out between independent individuals who are already differentiated from one another, who meet and associate together in order to pool their different abilities. It would be a miracle if these differences, arising from chance circumstances, could be so accurately harmonised as to form a coherent whole. Far from their preceding collective life, they derive from it. . . .

If this important truth failed to be realised by the Utilitarians, it is an error springing from the manner in which they conceived the genesis of society. They supposed that originally there were isolated and independent individuals who thus could only enter into relationships with one another in order to co-operate, for they had no other reason to bridge the empty gap separating them, and to associate together. But this theory, which is so widely held, postulates a veritable creation *ex nihilo.*

It consists, in fact, of deducing society from the individual. But we possess no knowledge that gives grounds for believing in the possibility of such a spontaneous generation. On Spencer's admission, for society to be able to be formed on such an hypothesis, 'the units [must] pass from the state of perfect independence to that of a mutual dependence.' But what can have determined them to make so complete a transformation? The prospect of the advantages that social life offers? But these are balanced, and even unduly so, by the loss of independence, because for creatures destined by nature for a free and solitary life, such a sacrifice is the most intolerable of all. In addition, in the first social types, the sacrifice was as absolute as possible, because nowhere is the individual more completely absorbed within the group. How could man, if he were born an individualist, as we suppose, have resigned himself to an existence that goes so violently against his most fundamental inclination? How very pallid the problematic utility of co-operation must have appeared to him in comparison with such a surrender! From autonomous individualities, like those we imagine, nothing can therefore emerge save what is individual; consequently co-operation itself, which is a social fact, subject to social rules, cannot arise. It is in this way that the psychologist who begins to shut himself up within his own self can no longer emerge from it, to find again the non-self.

Collective life did not arise from individual life; on the contrary, it is the latter that emerged from the former. On this condition alone can we explain how the personal individuality of social units was able to form and grow without causing society to disintegrate. Indeed, since in this case it developed from within a pre-existing social environment, it necessarily bears its stamp. It is constituted in such a way as not to ruin that collective order to which it is solidly linked. It remains adapted to it, whilst detaching itself from it. There is nothing antisocial about it, because it is a product of society. . . .

The more general the common consciousness becomes, the more scope it leaves for individual variations. When God is remote from things and men, His action does not extend to every moment of time and to every thing. Only abstract rules are fixed, and these can be freely applied in very different ways. Even then they have neither the same ascendancy nor the same strength of resistance. Indeed, if usages and formulas, when they are precise, determine thought and action with a compulsion analogous to that of the reflexes, by contrast these general principles can only be translated into facts with the assistance of the intelligence. Yet once reflective thinking has been stimulated, it is not easy to set bounds to it. When it has gathered strength, it spontaneously develops beyond the limits assigned to it. At the beginning certain articles of faith are stipulated to be beyond discussion, but later the discussion extends to them. There is a desire to account for them, the reason for their existence is questioned, and however they fare in this examination, they relinquish some part of their strength. For ideas arising from reflection have never the same constraining power as instincts. Thus actions that have been deliberated upon have not the instant immediacy of involuntary acts. Because the collective consciousness becomes more rational, it therefore becomes less categorical and, for this reason again, is less irksome to the free development of individual variations. . . .

. . . It [the division of labour] has often been accused of diminishing the individual by reducing him to the role of a machine. And indeed, if he is not aware of where the operations required of him are leading, if he does not link them to any aim, he can no longer perform them save out of routine. Every day he repeats the same movements with monotonous regularity, but without having any interest or understanding of them. He is no longer the living cell of a living organism, moved continually by contact with neighbouring cells, which acts upon them and responds in turn to their action, extends itself, contracts, yields and is transformed according to the needs and circumstances. He is no more than a lifeless cog, which an external force sets in motion and impels always in the same direction and in the same fashion. Plainly, no matter how one represents the moral ideal, one cannot remain indifferent to such a debasement of human nature. If the aim of morality is individual perfection, it cannot allow the individual to be so utterly ruined, and if it has society as its end, it cannot let the very source of social life dry up. The evil not only threatens economic functions, but all the social functions, no matter how elevated these may be. 'If,' says Comte, 'we have often rightly deplored on the material plane the fact of the worker exclusively occupied throughout his life in making knife handles or pinheads, a healthy philosophy must not, all in all, cause us to regret any the less on the intellectual plane the exclusive and continual use of the human brain to resolve a few equations or classify a few insects: the moral effect, in both cases, is unfortunately very similar.'

Occasionally the remedy has been proposed for workers, that besides their technical and special knowledge, they should receive a general education. But even assuming that in this way some of the bad effects attributed to the division of labour can be redeemed, it is still not a means of preventing them. The division of labour does not change its nature because it has been preceded by a liberal education. It is undoubtedly good for the worker to be able to interest himself in artistic and literary matters, etc. But it remains none the less wrong that throughout the day he should be treated like a machine. Moreover, who can fail to see that these two types of existence are too opposing to be reconciled or to be able to be lived by the same man! If one acquires the habit of contemplating vast horizons, overall views, and fine generalisations, one can no longer without impatience allow oneself to be confined within the narrow limits of a special task. Such a remedy would therefore only make specialisation inoffensive by making it intolerable, and in consequence more or less impossible.

What resolves this contradiction is the fact that, contrary to what has been said, the division of labour does not produce these consequences through some imperative of its own nature, but only in exceptional and abnormal circumstances. For it to be able to develop without having so disastrous an influence on the human consciousness, there is no need to mitigate it by means of its opposite. It is necessary and sufficient for it to be itself, for nothing to come from outside to deform its nature. For normally the operation of each special function demands that the individual should not be too closely shut up in it, but should keep in constant contact with neighbouring functions, becoming aware of their needs and the changes that take place in them, etc. The division of labour supposes that the worker, far from remaining bent over his task, does not lose sight of those co-operating with him, but acts upon them and is acted upon by them. He is not therefore a machine who repeats movements the sense of which he does not perceive, but he knows that they are tending in a certain direction, towards a goal that he can conceive of more or less distinctly. He feels that he is of some use. For this he has no need to take in very vast areas of the social horizon; it is enough for him to perceive enough of it to understand that his actions have a goal beyond themselves. Thenceforth, however specialised, however uniform his activity may be, it is that of an intelligent being, for he knows that his activity has a meaning. The economists would not have left this essential characteristic of the division of labour unclarified and as a result would not have lain it open to this undeserved reproach, if they had not reduced it to being only a way of increasing the efficiency of the social forces, but had seen it above all as a source of solidarity. . . .

. . . As evolution advances, the bonds that attach the individual to his family, to his native heath, to the traditions that the past has bequeathed him, to the collective practices of the group—all these become loosened. Being more mobile, the individual changes his environment more easily, leaves his own people to go and live a more autonomous life elsewhere, works out for himself his ideas and sentiments. Doubtless all trace of common consciousness does not vanish because of this. At the very least there will always subsist that cult of the person and individual dignity about which we have just spoken, which today is already the unique rallying-point for so many minds. But how insignificant this is if we consider the ever-increasing scope of social life and, consequently, of the individual consciousness! As the latter becomes more expansive, as the intelligence becomes even better equipped, and activity more varied, for morality to remain unchanged, that is, for the individual to be bound to the group even so strongly as once he was, the ties that bind him must be reinforced, becoming more numerous. Thus if only those ties were forged that were based on similarities, the disappearance of the segmentary type of society would be accompanied by a steady decline in morality. Man would no longer be held adequately under control. He would no longer feel around him and above him that salutary pressure of society that moderates his egoism, making of him a moral creature. This it is that constitutes the moral value of the division of labour. Through it the individual is once more made aware of his dependent state *vis-à-vis* society. It is from society that proceed those forces that hold him in check and keep him within bounds. In short, since the division of labour becomes the predominant source of social solidarity, at the same time it becomes the foundation of the moral order.

We may thus state literally that in higher societies our duty lies not in extending the range of our activity but in concentrating it, in making it more specialised. We must limit our horizons, select a definite task, and involve ourselves utterly, instead of making ourselves, so to speak, a finished work of art, one that derives all its value from itself rather than from the services it renders. Finally, this specialisation must be carried the farther the more society is of a higher species. No other limits can be placed upon it. Undoubtedly we must also work towards realising within ourselves the collective type, in so far as it exists. There are common sentiments and ideas without which, as one says, one is not a man. The rule prescribing that we should specialise remains limited by the opposite rule. We conclude that it is not good to push specialisation as far as possible, but only as far as necessary. The weight to be given to these two opposing necessities is determined by experience and cannot be calculated *a priori*. It suffices for us to have shown that the latter is no different in nature from the former, but that it is also moral and that, moreover, this duty becomes ever more important and urgent, because the general qualities we have discussed suffice less and less to socialise the individual. . . .

Indeed to be a person means to be an autonomous source of action. Thus man only attains this state to the degree that there is something within him that is his and his alone, that makes him an individual, whereby he is more than the mere embodiment of the generic type of his race and group. It will in any case be objected that he is endowed with free will, and that this is sufficient upon which to base his personality. But whatever this freedom may consist of—and it is the subject of much argument—it is not this impersonal, invariable, metaphysical attribute that can serve as the sole basis for the empirical, variable and concrete personality of individuals. . . .

. . . [T]he advance of the individual personality and that of the division of labour depend on one and the same cause. Thus also it is impossible to will the one without willing the other.

CHAPTER TWO

~

Max Weber on Social Action

~ Introduction ~

Max Weber (1864–1920) was a lawyer, economist, historian, and one of the founders of the discipline of sociology. Weber held teaching appointments at Freiburg University, the University of Heidelberg, and the University of Munich. In addition to being politically active, Weber, along with Georg Simmel, helped to found the German Sociological Society. He published numerous articles on a wide variety of topics including law, religion, and music and published a number of books, including the widely read and influential *The Protestant Ethic and the Spirit of Capitalism.*

During Weber's lifetime, Germany was transformed from a loose confederation of states into a powerful nation. This transformation occurred as a result of the Industrial Revolution and the rise of bureaucratic structures under the leadership of Kaiser William I and Chancellor Otto von Bismarck. While Weber observed the value of the efficient organization of large-scale human activity, he worried about efficiency becoming an end in itself. A part of the problem was that, while more and more people in Germany were enjoying the rewards of economic expansion, the leadership nevertheless maintained a tight grip on the functioning of the nation. Tensions such as these, in addition to the periods of psychological depression that sometimes slowed his otherwise prolific output, most likely contributed to the statement by Weber in *Economy and Society* (as noted by Guenther Roth in the introduction to the English translation):

> Rational calculation . . . reduces every worker to a cog in this [bureaucratic] machine and, seeing himself in this light, he will merely ask how to transform himself from a little into a somewhat bigger cog, . . . an attitude you find, just as in the

Egyptian *papyri*, increasingly among our civil servants and especially their successors, our students. The passion for bureaucratization at this meeting drives us to despair. (lix)

This comment highlights an important aspect of Weber's approach to studying social life: It drew from comparative and historical analyses and it considered both individuals and institutions in their dynamic relationship. What this comment does not make clear, however, was Weber's commitment to value neutrality. While Weber demonstrated value neutrality in terms of his research, he was not hesitant to express his own (not always popular) views within the political domain. Weber believed that research should inform one's political judgments, but that one's value system should not impinge upon scholarly conclusions. Weber's approach to citizenship and scholarship established a precedent that is respected to this day.

It is important to note that the political, social, and economic revolutions of the eighteenth and nineteenth centuries, including the Industrial Revolution and the American and French Revolutions, set in motion a series of reforms that slowly but steadily increased the individual freedoms of more and more people. As a result, nineteenth-century thought tended to emphasize individual reflection or be quite subjectivist in nature. This emphasis contributed significantly to the rise of individual critiques of society. Sociology arose to fulfill an intellectual need to understand systematically the important social changes taking place, including changes in the way individuals viewed themselves.

The selection you are about to read by Weber comes from his monumental work *Economy and Society*. In two volumes Weber discusses the range of topics that concerned him: history, economy, rationalization, bureaucracy, law, politics, and religion. Weber begins his analysis by defining his theory of social action. He postlates that "[a]ction is 'social' insofar as its subjective meaning takes account of the behavior of others and is thereby oriented in its course." Social action refers to individual acts that occur in response to others. When I behave in particular ways *because* I have thought about others, I have engaged in social action. For example, when I put on a tie because I feel that I have to look professional in the eyes of others, I am engaging in social action. When I am walking my dog and cross the street in order to avoid passing by the neighbor who hates my dog, then I am engaging in social action. When our actions result from having others in mind (and others may be real or imagined, and they may constitute persons, groups, or even society), then I am engaging in social action. While Durkheim argues that we may understand individualism as a social product, Weber inserts individualism into his analysis of social relations. Individuals are a basic building block of the structures of society; however, individuals tend to orient their actions in accordance to these structures. In this way, Weber could emphasize individual actors but at the same time suggest that the structures of society tend to orient individual actions. Moreover, he would assert that psychological analysis of subjective behavior is limited because we cannot have full access to the recesses of the subjective mind; hence, the way to interpret the meaning and motivation of individual behavior is through the analysis of the actions of individuals, in particular their social actions. In the reading, Weber says:

> It is held that everything which is not physical is *ipso facto* psychic. However, the *meaning* of a train of mathematical reasoning which a person carries out is not in the relevant sense 'psychic.' Similarly the rational deliberation of an actor as to whether the results of a given proposed course of action will or will not promote certain specific interests, and the corresponding decision, do not become one bit more understandable by taking 'psychological' considerations into account.

What Weber is alluding to here is that our individual actions take into account the actual and potential reactions of others, thereby guiding our individual actions more than we realize. And this phenomenon of subjective experience in relation to the world can be studied systematically.

Social action is so central a theme to Weber that he defines sociology as "the interpretive understanding of social action"—"interpretive" because social action is meaningful, but variously so. As you will read, after Weber defines sociology in terms of social action, he proceeds to discuss meaning. Meaning may refer to some actual case involving particular persons or to theoretically derived scenarios involving hypothetical actors or persons. Weber emphasizes that all interpretation of meaning strives for clarity and may be based on either rational or emotional understanding. In order to understand irrational actions clearly and systematically, Weber suggests analyzing these reactions in terms of a "conceptually pure type of rational action" or ideal type of action. He writes:

> Only in this way is it possible to assess the causal significance of irrational factors as accounting for the deviations from this type. The construction of a purely rational course of action in such cases serves the sociologist as a type (ideal type) which has the merit of clear understandability and lack of ambiguity. By comparison with this it is possible to understand the ways in which actual action is influenced by irrational factors of all sorts, such as affects and errors, in that they account for the deviation from the line of conduct which would be expected on the hypothesis that the action were purely rational.

It is important to emphasize that Weber does not infer from this that there is necessarily an "objectively correct meaning or one which is 'true' in some metaphysical sense." He clearly emphasizes that there is always a danger that rationalistic interpretations of actions will be applied "where they are out of place." Weber's analysis incorporates this valuable insight regarding the relationship between rational action and efficient activity. He suggests that irrational modes of action (action derived from noncalculable means), such as mystical states or religious faith, also convey meaning in social action and warrant sociological analysis.

Elaborating on his analysis of meaningful action, Weber states that under-standing may be either direct, where there is a "direct rational understanding of ideas or emotions," or where there is understanding based upon motive and in-tended meaning. He is quick to add that analysis of intended meaning is ex-tremely complex because the actual motives of action may not be clear even to those who are engaged in the action. In Weber's words, "[T]he 'conscious mo-tives' may well, even to the actor himself, conceal the various 'motives' and 're-pressions' which constitute the real driving force of his action." He concludes that, under these circumstances, analysis of social action requires "comparing the largest possible number of historical or contemporary processes which, while otherwise similar, differ in the one decisive point of their relation to the partic-ular motive . . . being investigated. This is a fundamental task of comparative sociology." Comparative, historical analysis informs analysis of social action. Relatedly, in any given situation, an act is "adequate" when it is "recognized to constitute a 'typical' complex of meaning." We tend to understand each other's actions when they conform to "habitual modes of thought and feeling." Weber points out that "typical" or "habitual modes of thought and action" are usually considered to be the "correct" modes of thought and action. In other words, ac-tions frequently reflect the norms of a given culture. Now, a typified act is not necessarily an instance of social action. Weber cites this example: "[A] mere collision of two cyclists may be compared to a natural event. On the other hand, their attempt to avoid hitting each other . . . would constitute 'social action.'" As a further example of the difference between social action and mere habitu-alized or imitative action, Weber notes, "[I]f at the beginning of a shower a number of people on the street put up their umbrellas at the same time, this would not ordinarily be a case of action mutually oriented to that of each other." He also notes that the borderline here may sometimes be quite thin: "On the other hand, if the action of others is imitated because it is fashionable or tradi-tional or exemplary, or lends social distinction . . . it is meaningfully oriented." This statement suggests that social action may be based on a number of factors, or that there are different types of social action. Weber points out four some-times overlapping types: (1) social action based upon rational calculation; (2) social action based upon value orientation; (3) social action based upon af-fect or emotion; and, (4) social action based upon traditional behavior. As one might expect, Weber places the latter two on the borderline between social ac-tion and mere action.

Finally, social action may be guided by "the belief in the existence of a legiti-mate order." Social action may be guided by the sanctions of group members. We-ber also points out that the same group may abide by a "plurality of contradictory systems of order [that] may all be recognized as valid. . . . Indeed, it is even possi-ble for the same individual to orient his action to contradictory systems of order" (32). While this may create problems such as role conflict and, generally, conflicts in society, this does not create problems for the analysis of society; if anything, it makes studying social life that much more intriguing and invaluable.

⌇ Social Action ⌇

The Definition of Sociology and of Social Action

Sociology (in the sense in which this highly ambiguous word is used here) is a science concerning itself with the interpretive understanding of social action and thereby with a causal explanation of its course and consequences. We shall speak of "action" insofar as the acting individual attaches a subjective meaning to his behavior—be it overt or covert, omission or acquiescence. Action is "social" insofar as its subjective meaning takes account of the behavior of others and is thereby oriented in its course.

Methodological Foundations

1. "Meaning" may be of two kinds. The term may refer first to the actual existing meaning in the given concrete case of a particular actor, or to the average or approximate meaning attributable to a given plurality of actors; or secondly to the theoretically conceived *pure type* of subjective meaning attributed to the hypothetical actor or actors in a given type of action. In no case does it refer to an objectively "correct" meaning or one which is "true" in some metaphysical sense. It is this which distinguishes the empirical sciences of action, such as sociology and history, from the dogmatic disciplines in that area, such as jurisprudence, logic, ethics, and esthetics, which seek to ascertain the "true" and "valid" meanings associated with the objects of their investigation.

2. The line between meaningful action and merely reactive behavior to which no subjective meaning is attached, cannot be sharply drawn empirically. A very considerable part of all sociologically relevant behavior, especially purely traditional behavior, is marginal between the two. In the case of some psychophysical processes, meaningful, i.e., subjectively understandable, action is not to be found at all; in others it is discernible only by the psychologist. Many mystical experiences which cannot be adequately communicated in words are, for a person who is not susceptible to such experiences, not fully understandable. At the same time the ability to perform a similar action is not a necessary prerequisite to understanding; "one need not have been Caesar in order to understand Caesar." "Recapturing an experience" is important for accurate understanding, but not an absolute precondition for its interpretation. Understandable and non-understandable components of a process are often intermingled and bound up together.

3. All interpretation of meaning, like all scientific observations, strives for clarity and verifiable accuracy of insight and comprehension (*Evidenz*). The basis for certainty in understanding can be either rational, which can be further subdivided into logical and mathematical, or it can be of an emotionally empathic or artistically appreciative quality. Action is rationally evident chiefly when we attain a completely clear intellectual grasp of the action-elements in their intended context of meaning. Empathic or appreciative accuracy is attained when, through sympathetic participation, we can adequately grasp the emotional context in

which the action took place. The highest degree of rational understanding is attained in cases involving the meanings of logically or mathematically related propositions; their meaning may be immediately and unambiguously intelligible. We have a perfectly clear understanding of what it means when somebody employs the proposition $2 \times 2 = 4$ or the Pythagorean theorem in reasoning or argument, or when someone correctly carries out a logical train of reasoning according to our accepted modes of thinking. In the same way we also understand what a person is doing when he tries to achieve certain ends by choosing appropriate means on the basis of the facts of the situation, as experience has accustomed us to interpret them. The interpretation of such rationally purposeful action possesses, for the understanding of the choice of means, the highest degree of verifiable certainty. With a lower degree of certainty, which is, however, adequate for most purposes of explanation, we are able to understand errors, including confusion of problems of the sort that we ourselves are liable to, or the origin of which we can detect by sympathetic self-analysis.

On the other hand, many ultimate ends or values toward which experience shows that human action may be oriented, often cannot be understood completely, though sometimes we are able to grasp them intellectually. The more radically they differ from our own ultimate values, however, the more difficult it is for us to understand them empathically. Depending upon the circumstances of the particular case we must be content either with a purely intellectual understanding of such values or when even that fails, sometimes we must simply accept them as given data. Then we can try to understand the action motivated by them on the basis of whatever opportunities for approximate emotional and intellectual interpretation seem to be available at different points in its course. These difficulties confront, for instance, people not susceptible to unusual acts of religious and charitable zeal, or persons who abhor extreme rationalist fanaticism (such as the fanatic advocacy of the "rights of man").

The more we ourselves are susceptible to such emotional reactions as anxiety, anger, ambition, envy, jealousy, love, enthusiasm, pride, vengefulness, loyalty, devotion, and appetites of all sorts, and to the "irrational" conduct which grows out of them, the more readily can we empathize with them. Even when such emotions are found in a degree of intensity of which the observer himself is completely incapable, he can still have a significant degree of emotional understanding of their meaning and can interpret intellectually their influence on the course of action and the selection of means.

For the purposes of a typological scientific analysis it is convenient to treat all irrational, affectually determined elements of behavior as factors of deviation from a conceptually pure type of rational action. For example a panic on the stock exchange can be most conveniently analysed by attempting to determine first what the course of action would have been if it had not been influenced by irrational affects; it is then possible to introduce the irrational components as accounting for the observed deviations from this hypothetical course. Similarly, in analysing a political or military campaign it is convenient to determine in the first place what would have been a rational course, given the ends of the participants and adequate knowledge of all the circumstances. Only in this way is it possible to assess the causal significance of irrational factors as accounting for the deviations from this type. The construction of a purely rational course of action in such cases serves the sociologist as a type (ideal type) which has the merit of clear understandability and lack of ambiguity. By comparison with this it is possible to understand the ways in which actual action is influenced by irrational factors of all sorts, such as affects and errors, in that they account for the deviation from the line of conduct which would be expected on the hypothesis that the action were purely rational.

Only in this respect and for these reasons of methodological convenience is the method of sociology "rationalistic." It is naturally not legitimate to interpret this procedure as involving a rationalistic bias of sociology, but only as a methodological device. It certainly does not involve a belief in the actual predominance of rational elements in human life, for on the question of how far this predominance does or does not exist, nothing whatever has been said. That there is, however, a danger of rationalistic interpretations where they are out of place cannot be denied. All experience unfortunately confirms the existence of this danger.

4. In all the sciences of human action, account must be taken of processes and phenomena which are devoid of subjective meaning, in the role of stimuli, results, favoring or hindering circumstances. To be devoid of meaning is not identical with being lifeless or non-human; every artifact, such as for example a machine, can be understood only in terms of the meaning which its production and use have had or were intended to have; a meaning which may derive from a relation to exceedingly various purposes. Without reference to this meaning such an object remains wholly unintelligible. That which is intelligible or understandable about it is thus its relation to human action in the role either of means or of end; a relation of which the actor or actors can be said to have been aware and to which their action has been oriented. Only in terms of such categories is it possible to "understand" objects of this kind. On the other hand processes or conditions, whether they are animate of inanimate, human or non-human, are in the present sense devoid of meaning in so far as they cannot be related to an intended purpose. That is to say they are devoid of meaning if they cannot be related to action in the role of means or ends but constitute only the stimulus, the favoring or hindering circumstances. It may be that the flooding of the Dollart [at the mouth of the Ems river near the Dutch-German border] in 1277 had historical significance as a stimulus to the beginning of certain migrations of considerable importance. Human mortality, indeed the organic life cycle from the helplessness of infancy to that of old age, is naturally of the very greatest sociological importance through the various ways in which human action has been oriented to these facts. To still another category of facts devoid of meaning belong certain psychic or psychophysical phenomena such as fatigue, habituation, memory, etc.; also certain typical states of euphoria under some conditions of ascetic mortification; finally, typical variations in the reactions of individuals according to reaction-time, precision, and other modes. But in the last analysis the same principle applies to these as to other phenomena which are devoid of

meaning. Both the actor and the sociologist must accept them as data to be taken into account.

It is possible that future research may be able to discover non-interpretable uniformities underlying what has appeared to be specifically meaningful action, though little has been accomplished in this direction thus far. Thus, for example, differences in hereditary biological constitution, as of "races," would have to be treated by sociology as given data in the same way as the physiological facts of the need of nutrition or the effect of senescence on action. This would be the case if, and insofar as, we had statistically conclusive proof of their influence on sociologically relevant behavior. The recognition of the causal significance of such factors would not in the least alter the specific task of sociological analysis or of that of the other sciences of action, which is the interpretation of action in terms of its subjective meaning. The effect would be only to introduce certain non-interpretable data of the same order as others which are already present, into the complex of subjectively understandable motivation at certain points. (Thus it may come to be known that there are typical relations between the frequency of certain types of teleological orientation of action or of the degree of certain kinds of rationality and the cephalic index or skin color or any other biologically inherited characteristic.)

5. Understanding may be of two kinds: the first is the direct observational understanding of the subjective meaning of a given act as such, including verbal utterances. We thus understand by direct observation, in this case, the meaning of the proposition $2 \times 2 = 4$ when we hear or read it. This is a case of the direct rational understanding of ideas. We also understand an outbreak of anger as manifested by facial expression, exclamations or irrational movements. This is direct observational understanding of irrational emotional reactions. We can understand in a similar observational way the action of a woodcutter or of somebody who reaches for the knob to shut a door or who aims a gun at an animal. This is rational observational understanding of actions.

Understanding may, however, be of another sort, namely explanatory understanding. Thus we understand in terms of *motive* the meaning an actor attaches to the proposition twice two equals four, when he states it or writes it down, in that we understand what makes him do this at precisely this moment and in these circumstances. Understanding in this sense is attained if we know that he is engaged in balancing a ledger or in making a scientific demonstration, or is engaged in some other task of which this particular act would be an appropriate part. This is rational understanding of motivation, which consists in placing the act in an intelligible and more inclusive context of meaning. Thus we understand the chopping of wood or aiming of a gun in terms of motive in addition to direct observation if we know that the woodchopper is working for a wage or is chopping a supply of firewood for his own use or possibly is doing it for recreation. But he might also be working off a fit of rage, an irrational case. Similarly we understand the motive of a person aiming a gun if we know that he has been commanded to shoot as a member of a firing squad, that he is fighting against an enemy, or that he is doing it for revenge. The last is affectually determined and thus in a certain sense irrational. Finally we have a motivational understanding of the outburst of anger if we know that it has been provoked by jealousy, injured pride, or an insult. The last examples are all affectually determined and hence derived from irrational motives. In all the above cases the particular act has been placed in an understandable sequence of motivation, the understanding of which can be treated as an explanation of the actual course of behavior. Thus for a science which is concerned with the subjective meaning of action, explanation requires a grasp of the complex of meaning in which an actual course of understandable action thus interpreted belongs. In all such cases, even where the processes are largely affectual, the subjective meaning of the action, including that also of the relevant meaning complexes, will be called the intended meaning. (This involves a departure from ordinary usage, which speaks of intention in this sense only in the case of rationally purposive action.)

6. In all these cases understanding involves the interpretive grasp of the meaning present in one of the following contexts: (a) as in the historical approach, the actually intended meaning for concrete individual action; or (b) as in cases of sociological mass phenomena, the average of, or an approximation to, the actually intended meaning; or (c) the meaning appropriate to a scientifically formulated pure type (an ideal type) of a common phenomenon. The concepts and "laws" of pure economic theory are examples of this kind of ideal type. They state what course a given type of human action would take if it were strictly rational, unaffected by errors or emotional factors and if, furthermore, it were completely and unequivocally directed to a single end, the maximization of economic advantage. In reality, action takes exactly this course only in unusual cases, as sometimes on the stock exchange; and even then there is usually only an approximation to the ideal type. . . .

Every interpretation attempts to attain clarity and certainty, but no matter how clear an interpretation as such appears to be from the point of view of meaning, it cannot on this account claim to be the causally valid interpretation. On this level it must remain only a peculiarly plausible hypothesis. In the first place the "conscious motives" may well, even to the actor himself, conceal the various "motives" and "repressions" which constitute the real driving force of his action. Thus in such cases even subjectively honest self-analysis has only a relative value. Then it is the task of the sociologist to be aware of this motivational situation and to describe and analyse it, even though it has not actually been concretely part of the conscious intention of the actor; possibly not at all, at least not fully. This is a borderline case of the interpretation of meaning. Secondly, processes of action which seem to an observer to be the same or similar may fit into exceedingly various complexes of motive in the case of the actual actor. Then even though the situations appear superficially to be very similar we must actually understand them or interpret them as very different, perhaps, in terms of meaning, directly opposed. (Simmel, in his *Probleme der Geschichtsphilosophie*, gives a number of examples.) Third, the actors in any given situation are often subject to opposing and conflicting impulses, all of which we are able to understand. In a large number of cases we know from experience it is not possible to arrive at even an approximate estimate of the relative strength of conflicting motives and very often we cannot be certain of our interpretation. Only the actual outcome of the conflict gives a solid basis of judgment.

More generally, verification of subjective interpretation by comparison with the concrete course of events is, as in the case of all hypotheses, indispensable. Unfortunately this type of verification is feasible with relative accuracy only in the few very special cases susceptible of psychological experimentation. In very different degrees of approximation, such verification is also feasible in the limited number of cases of mass phenomena which can be statistically described and unambiguously interpreted. For the rest there remains only the possibility of comparing the largest possible number of historical or contemporary processes which, while otherwise similar, differ in the one decisive point of their relation to the particular motive or factor the role of which is being investigated. This is a fundamental task of comparative sociology. Often, unfortunately, there is available only the uncertain procedure of the "imaginary experiment" which consists in thinking away certain elements of a chain of motivation and working out the course of action which would then probably ensue, thus arriving at a causal judgment.

For example, the generalization called Gresham's Law is a rationally clear interpretation of human action under certain conditions and under the assumption that it will follow a purely rational course. How far any actual course of action corresponds to this can be verified only by the available statistical evidence for the actual disappearance of under-valued monetary units from circulation. In this case our information serves to demonstrate a high degree of accuracy. The facts of experience were known before the generalization, which was formulated afterwards; but without this successful interpretation our need for causal understanding would evidently be left unsatisfied. On the other hand, without the demonstration that what can here be assumed to be a theoretically adequate interpretation also is in some degree relevant to an actual course of action, a "law," no matter how fully demonstrated theoretically, would be worthless for the understanding of action in the real world. In this case the correspondence between the theoretical interpretation of motivation and its empirical verification is entirely satisfactory and the cases are numerous enough so that verification can be considered established. But to take another example, Eduard Meyer has advanced an ingenious theory of the causal significance of the battles of Marathon, Salamis, and Platea for the development of the cultural peculiarities of Greek, and hence, more generally, Western civilization. This is derived from a meaningful interpretation of certain symptomatic facts having to do with the attitudes of the Greek oracles and prophets towards the Persians. It can only be directly verified by reference to the examples of the conduct of the Persians in cases where they were victorious, as in Jerusalem, Egypt, and Asia Minor, and even this verification must necessarily remain unsatisfactory in certain respects. The striking rational plausibility of the hypothesis must here necessarily be relied on as a support. In very many cases of historical interpretation which seem highly plausible, however, there is not even a possibility of the order of verification which was feasible in this case. Where this is true the interpretation must necessarily remain a hypothesis.

7. A motive is a complex of subjective meaning which seems to the actor himself or to the observer an adequate ground for the conduct in question. The interpretation of a coherent course of conduct is "subjectively adequate" (or "adequate on the level of meaning"), insofar as, according to our habitual modes of thought and feeling, its component parts taken in their mutual relation are recognized to constitute a "typical" complex of meaning. It is more common to say "correct." The interpretation of a sequence of events will on the other hand be called *causally* adequate insofar as, according to established generalizations from experience, there is a probability that it will always actually occur in the same way. An example of adequacy on the level of meaning in this sense is what is, according to our current norms of calculation or thinking, the correct solution of an arithmetical problem. On the other hand, a causally adequate interpretation of the same phenomenon would concern the statistical probability that, according to verified generalizations from experience, there would be a correct or an erroneous solution of the same problem. This also refers to currently accepted norms but includes taking account of typical errors or of typical confusions. Thus causal explanation depends on being able to determine that there is a probability, which in the rare ideal case can be numerically stated, but is always in some sense calculable, that a given observable event (overt or subjective) will be followed or accompanied by another event.

A correct causal interpretation of a concrete course of action is arrived at when the overt action and the motives have both been correctly apprehended and at the same time their relation has become meaningfully comprehensible. A correct causal interpretation of typical action means that the process which is claimed to be typical is shown to be both adequately grasped on the level of meaning and at the same time the interpretation is to some degree causally adequate. If adequacy in respect to meaning is lacking, then no matter how high the degree of uniformity and how precisely its probability can be numerically determined, it is still an incomprehensible statistical probability, whether we deal with overt or subjective processes. On the other hand, even the most perfect adequacy on the level of meaning has causal significance from a sociological point of view only insofar as there is some kind of proof for the existence of a probability that action in fact normally takes the course which has been held to be meaningful. For this there must be some degree of determinable frequency of approximation to an average or a pure type.

Statistical uniformities constitute understandable types of action, and thus constitute sociological generalizations, only when they can be regarded as manifestations of the understandable subjective meaning of a course of social action. Conversely, formulations of a rational course of subjectively understandable action constitute sociological types of empirical process only when they can be empirically observed with a significant degree of approximation. By no means is the actual likelihood of the occurrence of a given course of overt action always directly proportional to the clarity of subjective interpretation. Only actual experience can prove whether this is so in a given case. There are statistics of processes devoid of subjective meaning, such as death rates, phenomena of fatigue, the production rate of machines, the amount of rainfall, in exactly the same sense as there are statistics of meaningful phenomena. But only when the phenomena are meaningful do we speak of sociological statistics. Examples are such cases as crime rates, occupational distributions, price statistics, and statistics of crop acreage. Naturally there are many cases where both components are involved, as in crop statistics.

8. Processes and uniformities which it has here seemed convenient not to designate as sociological phenomena or uniformities because they are not "understandable," are naturally not on that account any the less important. This is true even for sociology in our sense which is restricted to subjectively understandable phenomena—a usage which there is no intention of attempting to impose on anyone else. Such phenomena, however important, are simply treated by a different method from the others; they become conditions, stimuli, furthering or hindering circumstances of action.

9. Action in the sense of subjectively understandable orientation of behavior exists only as the behavior of one or more *individual* human beings. For other cognitive purposes it may be useful or necessary to consider the individual, for instance, as a collection of cells, as a complex of bio-chemical reactions, or to conceive his psychic life as made up of a variety of different elements, however these may be defined. Undoubtedly such procedures yield valuable knowledge of causal relationships. But the behavior of these elements, as expressed in such uniformities, is not subjectively understandable. This is true even of psychic elements because the more precisely they are formulated from a point of view of natural science, the less they are accessible to subjective understanding. This is never the road to interpretation in terms of subjective meaning. On the contrary, both for sociology in the present sense, and for history, the object of cognition is the subjective meaning-complex of action. The behavior of physiological entities such as cells, or of any sort of psychic elements, may at least in principle be observed and an attempt made to derive uniformities from such observations. It is further possible to attempt, with their help, to obtain a causal explanation of individual phenomena, that is, to subsume them under uniformities. But the subjective understanding of action takes the same account of this type of fact and uniformity as of any others not capable of subjective interpretation. (This is true, for example, of physical, astronomical, geological, meteorological, geographical, botanical, zoological, and anatomical facts, of those aspects of psycho-pathology which are devoid of subjective meaning, or of the natural conditions of technological processes.)

For still other cognitive purposes—for instance, juristic ones—or for practical ends, it may on the other hand be convenient or even indispensable to treat social collectivities, such as states, associations, business corporations, foundations, as if they were individual persons. Thus they may be treated as the subjects of rights and duties or as the performers of legally significant actions. But for the subjective interpretation of action in sociological work these collectivities must be treated as *solely* the resultants and modes of organization of the particular acts of individual persons, since these alone can be treated as agents in a course of subjectively understandable action. Nevertheless, the sociologist cannot for his purposes afford to ignore these collective concepts derived from other disciplines. For the subjective interpretation of action has at least three important relations to these concepts. In the first place it is often necessary to employ very similar collective concepts, indeed often using the same terms, in order to obtain an intelligible terminology. Thus both in legal terminology and in everyday speech the term "state" is used both for the legal concept of the state and for the phenomena of social action to which its legal rules are relevant. For sociological purposes, however, the phenomenon "the state" does not consist necessarily or even primarily of the elements which are relevant to legal analysis; and for sociological purposes there is no such thing as a collective personality which "acts." When reference is made in a sociological context to a state, a nation, a corporation, a family, or an army corps, or to similar collectivities, what is meant is, on the contrary, *only* a certain kind of development of actual or possible social actions of individual persons. Both because of its precision and because it is established in general usage the juristic concept is taken over, but is used in an entirely different meaning.

Secondly, the subjective interpretation of action must take account of a fundamentally important fact. These concepts of collective entities which are found both in common sense and in juristic and other technical forms of thought, have a meaning in the minds of individual persons, partly as of something actually existing, partly as something with normative authority. This is true not only of judges and officials, but of ordinary private individuals as well. Actors thus in part orient their action to them, and in this role such ideas have a powerful, often a decisive, causal influence on the course of action of real individuals. This is above all true where the ideas involve normative prescription or prohibition. Thus, for instance, one of the important aspects of the existence of a modern state, precisely as a complex of social interaction of individual persons, consists in the fact that the action of various individuals is oriented to the belief that it exists or should exist, thus that its acts and laws are valid in the legal sense. This will be further discussed below. Though extremely pedantic and cumbersome, it would be possible, if purposes of sociological terminology alone were involved, to eliminate such terms entirely, and substitute newly-coined words. This would be possible even though the word "state" is used ordinarily not only to designate the legal concept but also the real process of action. But in the above important connexion, at least, this would naturally be impossible.

Thirdly, it is the method of the so-called "organic" school of sociology—classical example: Schäffle's brilliant work, *Bau und Leben des sozialen Körpers*—to attempt to understand social interaction by using as a point of departure the "whole" within which the individual acts. His action and behavior are then interpreted somewhat in the way that a physiologist would treat the role of an organ of the body in the "economy" of the organism, that is from the point of view of the survival of the latter. (Compare the famous dictum of a well-known physiologist: "Sec. 10. The spleen. Of the spleen, gentlemen, we know nothing. So much for the spleen." Actually, of course, he knew a good deal about the spleen—its position, size, shape, etc.; but he could say nothing about its function, and it was his inability to do this that he called "ignorance.") How far in other disciplines this type of functional analysis of the relation of "parts" to a "whole" can be regarded as definitive, cannot be discussed here; but it is well known that the bio-chemical and bio-physical modes of analysis of the organism are on principle opposed to stopping there. For purposes of sociological analysis two things can be said. First this functional frame of reference is convenient for purposes of practical illustration and for provisional orientation. In these respects it is not only useful but indispensable. But at the same time if its cognitive value is overestimated and its concepts illegitimately "reified," it can be highly dangerous. Secondly, in certain circumstances this is the only available way of determining just what processes of social action it is important to understand in order to explain a given phenomenon. But this is only the beginning of sociological analysis as here understood. In the case of social collectivities, precisely as distinguished from organisms, we are in a position to go beyond merely demonstrating functional relationships and uniformities. We can accomplish something which is never attainable in the natural sciences, namely the subjective understanding of the action of the component individuals. The natural sciences on the other hand cannot do this, being limited to the formulation of causal uniformities in objects and events and the explanation of individual facts by applying them. We do not "understand" the behavior of cells, but can only observe the relevant functional relationships and generalize on the basis of these observations. This additional achievement of explanation by interpretive understanding, as distinguished from external observation, is of course attained only at a price—the more hypothetical and fragmentary character of its results. Nevertheless, subjective understanding is the specific characteristic of sociological knowledge. . . .

The various works of Othmar Spann [1878–1950] are often full of suggestive ideas though at the same time he is guilty of occasional misunderstandings and above all of arguing on the basis of pure value judgments which have no place in an empirical investigation. But he is undoubtedly correct in doing something to which, however, no one seriously objects, namely, emphasizing the sociological significance of the functional point of view for preliminary orientation to problems. This is what he calls the "universalistic method." It is true that we must know what kind of action is functionally necessary for "survival," but even more so for the maintenance of a cultural type and the continuity of the corresponding modes of social action, before it is possible even to inquire how this action has come about and what motives determine it. It is necessary to know what a "king," an "official," an "entrepreneur," a "procurer," or a "magician" does, that is, what kind of typical action, which justifies classifying an individual in one of these categories, is important and relevant for an analysis, before it is possible to undertake the analysis itself. (This is what Rickert means by *Wertbezogenheit*.) But it is only this analysis itself which can achieve the sociological understanding of the actions of typically differentiated human (and only human) individuals, and which hence constitutes the specific function of sociology. It is a tremendous misunderstanding to think that an "individualistic" *method* should involve what is in any conceivable sense an individualistic system of *values*. It is as important to avoid this error as the related one which confuses the unavoidable tendency of sociological concepts to assume a rationalistic character with a belief in the predominance of rational motives, or even a positive valuation of rationalism. Even a socialistic economy would have to be understood sociologically in exactly the same kind of "individualistic" terms; that is, in terms of the action of individuals, the types of officials found in it, as would be the case with a system of free exchange analysed in terms of the theory of marginal utility or a "better," but in this respect similar theory. The real empirical sociological investigation begins with the question: What motives determine and lead the individual members and participants in this socialistic community to behave in such a way that the community came into being in the first place and that it continues to exist? Any form of functional analysis which proceeds from the whole to the parts can accomplish only a preliminary preparation for this investigation— a preparation, the utility and indispensability of which, if properly carried out, is naturally beyond question.

10. It is customary to designate various sociological generalizations, as for example "Gresham's Law," as "laws." These are in fact typical probabilities confirmed by observation to the effect that under certain given conditions an expected course of social action will occur, which is understandable in terms of the typical motives and typical subjective intentions of the actors. These generalizations are both understandable and definite in the highest degree insofar as the typically observed course of action can be understood in terms of the purely rational pursuit of an end, or where for reasons of methodological convenience such a theoretical type can be heuristically employed. In such cases the relations of means and ends will be clearly understandable on grounds of experience, particularly where the choice of means was "inevitable." In such cases it is legitimate to assert that insofar as the action was rigorously rational it could not have taken any other course because for technical reasons, given their clearly defined ends, no other means were available to the actors. This very case demonstrates how erroneous it is to regard any kind of psychology as the ultimate foundation of the sociological interpretation of action. The term psychology, to be sure, is today understood in a wide variety of senses. For certain quite specific methodological purposes the type of treatment which attempts to follow the procedures of the natural sciences employs a distinction between "physical" and "psychic" phenomena which is entirely foreign to the disciplines concerned with human

action, at least in the present sense. The results of a type of psychological investigation which employs the methods of the natural sciences in any one of various possible ways may naturally, like the results of any other science, have outstanding significance for sociological problems; indeed this has often happened. But this use of the results of psychology is something quite different from the investigation of human behavior in terms of its subjective meaning. Hence sociology has no closer relationship on a general analytical level to this type of psychology than to any other science. The source of error lies in the concept of the "psychic." It is held that everything which is not physical is *ipso facto* psychic. However, the *meaning* of a train of mathematical reasoning which a person carries out is not in the relevant sense "psychic." Similarly the rational deliberation of an actor as to whether the results of a given proposed course of action will or will not promote certain specific interests, and the corresponding decision, do not become one bit more understandable by taking "psychological" considerations into account. But it is precisely on the basis of such rational assumptions that most of the laws of sociology, including those of economics, are built up. On the other hand, in explaining the irrationalities of action sociologically, that form of psychology which employs the method of subjective understanding undoubtedly can make decisively important contributions. But this does not alter the fundamental methodological situation.

11. We have taken for granted that sociology seeks to formulate type concepts and generalized uniformities of empirical process. This distinguishes it from history, which is oriented to the causal analysis and explanation of individual actions, structures, and personalities possessing cultural significance. The empirical material which underlies the concepts of sociology consists to a very large extent, though by no means exclusively, of the same concrete processes of action which are dealt with by historians. An important consideration in the formulation of sociological concepts and generalizations is the contribution that sociology can make toward the causal explanation of some historically and culturally important phenomenon. As in the case of every generalizing science the abstract character of the concepts of sociology is responsible for the fact that, compared with actual historical reality, they are relatively lacking in fullness of concrete content. To compensate for this disadvantage, sociological analysis can offer a greater precision of concepts. This precision is obtained by striving for the highest possible degree of adequacy on the level of meaning. It has already been repeatedly stressed that this aim can be realized in a particularly high degree in the case of concepts and generalizations which formulate rational processes. But sociological investigation attempts to include in its scope various irrational phenomena, such as prophetic, mystic, and affectual modes of action, formulated in terms of theoretical concepts which are adequate on the level of meaning. In *all* cases, rational or irrational, sociological analysis both abstracts from reality and at the same time helps us to understand it, in that it shows with what degree of approximation a concrete historical phenomenon can be subsumed under one or more of these concepts. For example, the same historical phenomenon may be in

one aspect feudal, in another patrimonial, in another bureaucratic, and in still another charismatic. In order to give a precise meaning to these terms, it is necessary for the sociologist to formulate pure ideal types of the corresponding forms of action which in each case involve the highest possible degree of logical integration by virtue of their complete adequacy on the level of meaning. But precisely because this is true, it is probably seldom if ever that a real phenomenon can be found which corresponds exactly to one of these ideally constructed pure types. The case is similar to a physical reaction which has been calculated on the assumption of an absolute vacuum. Theoretical differentiation (*Kasuistik*) is possible in sociology only in terms of ideal or pure types. It goes without saying that in addition it is convenient for the sociologist from time to time to employ average types of an empirical statistical character, concepts which do not require methodological discussion. But when reference is made to "typical" cases, the term should always be understood, unless otherwise stated, as meaning *ideal* types, which may in turn be rational or irrational as the case may be (thus in economic theory they are always rational), but in any case are always constructed with a view to adequacy on the level of meaning.

It is important to realize that in the sociological field as elsewhere, averages, and hence average types, can be formulated with a relative degree of precision only where they are concerned with differences of degree in respect to action which remains qualitatively the same. Such cases do occur, but in the majority of cases of action important to history or sociology the motives which determine it are qualitatively heterogeneous. Then it is quite impossible to speak of an "average" in the true sense. The ideal types of social action which for instance are used in economic theory are thus unrealistic or abstract in that they always ask what course of action would take place if it were purely rational and oriented to economic ends alone. This construction can be used to aid in the understanding of action not purely economically determined but which involves deviations arising from traditional restraints, affects, errors, and the intrusion of other than economic purposes or considerations. This can take place in two ways. First, in analysing the extent to which in the concrete case, or on the average for a class of cases, the action was in part economically determined along with the other factors. Secondly, by throwing the discrepancy between the actual course of events and the ideal type into relief, the analysis of the non-economic motives actually involved is facilitated. The procedure would be very similar in employing an ideal type of mystical orientation, with its appropriate attitude of indifference to worldly things, as a tool for analysing its consequences for the actor's relation to ordinary life—for instance, to political or economic affairs. The more sharply and precisely the ideal type has been constructed, thus the more abstract and unrealistic in this sense it is, the better it is able to perform its functions in formulating terminology, classifications, and hypotheses. In working out a concrete causal explanation of individual events, the procedure of the historian is essentially the same. Thus in attempting to explain the campaign of 1866, it is indispensable both in the case of Moltke and of Benedek to attempt to construct imaginatively how each, given fully adequate knowledge both of his own situation and of that of his opponent, would have acted. Then it is possible to compare with this the actual course of action and to arrive at a causal explanation of the observed deviations, which will be attributed to such factors as misinformation, strategical errors, logical fallacies, personal temperament, or considerations outside the realm of strategy. Here, too, an ideal-typical construction of rational action is actually employed even though it is not made explicit.

The theoretical concepts of sociology are ideal types not only from the objective point of view, but also in their application to subjective processes. In the great majority of cases actual action goes on in a state of inarticulate half-consciousness or actual unconsciousness of its subjective meaning. The actor is more likely to "be aware" of it in a vague sense than he is to "know" what he is doing or be explicitly self-conscious about it. In most cases his action is governed by impulse or habit. Only occasionally and, in the uniform action of large numbers, often only in the case of a few individuals, is the subjective meaning of the action, whether rational or irrational, brought clearly into consciousness. The ideal type of meaningful action where the meaning is fully conscious and explicit is a marginal case. Every sociological or historical investigation, in applying its analysis to the empirical facts, must take this fact into account. But the difficulty need not prevent the sociologist from systematizing his concepts by the classification of possible types of subjective meaning. That is, he may reason as if action actually proceeded on the basis of clearly self-conscious meaning. The resulting deviation from the concrete facts must continually be kept in mind whenever it is a question of this level of concreteness, and must be carefully studied with reference both to degree and kind. It is often necessary to choose between terms which are either clear or unclear. Those which are clear will, to be sure, have the abstractness of ideal types, but they are none the less preferable for scientific purposes. . . .

Social Action

1. Social action, which includes both failure to act and passive acquiescence, may be oriented to the past, present, or expected future behavior of others. Thus it may be motivated by revenge for a past attack, defence against present, or measures of defence against future aggression. The "others" may be individual persons, and may be known to the actor as such, or may constitute an indefinite plurality and may be entirely unknown as individuals. (Thus, money is a means of exchange which the actor accepts in payment because he orients his action to the expectation that a large but unknown number of individuals he is personally unacquainted with will be ready to accept it in exchange on some future occasion.)

2. Not every kind of action, even of overt action, is "social" in the sense of the present discussion. Overt action is non-social if it is oriented solely to the behavior of inanimate objects. Subjective attitudes constitute social action only so far as they are oriented to the behavior of others. For example, religious behavior is not social if it is simply a matter of contemplation or of solitary prayer. The

economic activity of an individual is social only if it takes account of the behavior of someone else. Thus very generally it becomes social insofar as the actor assumes that others will respect his actual control over economic goods. Concretely it is social, for instance, if in relation to the actor's own consumption the future wants of others are taken into account and this becomes one consideration affecting the actor's own saving. Or, in another connexion, production may be oriented to the future wants of other people.

3. Not every type of contact of human beings has a social character; this is rather confined to cases where the actor's behavior is meaningfully oriented to that of others. For example, a mere collision of two cyclists may be compared to a natural event. On the other hand, their attempt to avoid hitting each other, or whatever insults, blows, or friendly discussion might follow the collision, would constitute "social action."

4. Social action is not identical either with the similar actions of many persons or with every action influenced by other persons. Thus, if at the beginning of a shower a number of people on the street put up their umbrellas at the same time, this would not ordinarily be a case of action mutually oriented to that of each other, but rather of all reacting in the same way to the like need of protection from the rain. It is well known that the actions of the individual are strongly influenced by the mere fact that he is a member of a crowd confined within a limited space. Thus, the subject matter of studies of "crowd psychology," such as those of Le Bon, will be called "action conditioned by crowds." It is also possible for large numbers, though dispersed, to be influenced simultaneously or successively by a source of influence operating similarly on all the individuals, as by means of the press. Here also the behavior of an individual is influenced by his membership in a "mass" and by the fact that he is aware of being a member. Some types of reaction are only made possible by the mere fact that the individual acts as part of a crowd. Others become more difficult under these conditions. Hence it is possible that a particular event or mode of human behavior can give rise to the most diverse kinds of feeling—gaiety, anger, enthusiasm, despair, and passions of all sorts—in a crowd situation which would not occur at all or not nearly so readily if the individual were alone. But for this to happen there need not, at least in many cases, be any meaningful relation between the behavior of the individual and the fact that he is a member of a crowd. It is not proposed in the present sense to call action "social" when it is merely a result of the effect on the individual of the existence of a crowd as such and the action is not oriented to that fact on the level of meaning. At the same time the borderline is naturally highly indefinite. In such cases as that of the influence of the demagogue, there may be a wide variation in the extent to which his mass clientele is affected by a meaningful reaction to the fact of its large numbers; and whatever this relation may be, it is open to varying interpretations.

But furthermore, mere "imitation" of the action of others, such as that on which Tarde has rightly laid emphasis, will not be considered a case of specifically social action if it is purely reactive so that there is no meaningful orientation to the actor imitated. The borderline is, however, so indefinite that it is often hardly possible to discriminate. The mere fact that a person is found to employ some apparently useful procedure which he learned from someone else does not, however, constitute, in the present sense, social action. Action such as this is not oriented to the action of the other person, but the actor has, through observing the other, become acquainted with certain objective facts; and it is these to which his action is oriented. His action is then *causally* determined by the action of others, but not meaningfully. On the other hand, if the action of others is imitated because it is fashionable or traditional or exemplary, or lends social distinction, or on similar grounds, it is meaningfully oriented either to the behavior of the source of imitation or of third persons or of both. There are of course all manner of transitional cases between the two types of imitation. Both the phenomena discussed above, the behavior of crowds and imitation, stand on the indefinite borderline of social action. The same is true, as will often appear, of traditionalism and charisma. The reason for the indefiniteness of the line in these and other cases lies in the fact that both the orientation to the behavior of others and the meaning which can be imputed by the actor himself, are by no means always capable of clear determination and are often altogether unconscious and seldom fully self-conscious. Mere "influence" and meaningful orientation cannot therefore always be clearly differentiated on the empirical level. But conceptually it is essential to distinguish them, even though merely reactive imitation may well have a degree of sociological importance at least equal to that of the type which can be called social action in the strict sense. Sociology, it goes without saying, is by no means confined to the study of social action; this is only, at least for the kind of sociology being developed here, its central subject matter, that which may be said to be decisive for its status as a science. But this does not imply any judgment on the comparative importance of this and other factors.

Types of Social Action

Social action, like all action, may be oriented in four ways. It may be:

(1) *instrumentally rational (zweckrational)*, that is, determined by expectations as to the behavior of objects in the environment and of other human beings; these expectations are used as "conditions" or "means" for the attainment of the actor's own rationally pursued and calculated ends;

(2) *value-rational (wertrational)*, that is, determined by a conscious belief in the value for its own sake of some ethical, aesthetic, religious, or other form of behavior, independently of its prospects of success;

(3) *affectual* (especially emotional), that is, determined by the actor's specific affects and feeling states;

(4) *traditional*, that is, determined by ingrained habituation.

1. Strictly traditional behavior, like the reactive type of imitation discussed above, lies very close to the borderline of what can justifiably be called mean-

ingfully oriented action, and indeed often on the other side. For it is very often a matter of almost automatic reaction to habitual stimuli which guide behavior in a course which has been repeatedly followed. The great bulk of all everyday action to which people have become habitually accustomed approaches this type. Hence, its place in a systematic classification is not merely that of a limiting case because, as will be shown later, attachment to habitual forms can be upheld with varying degrees of self-consciousness and in a variety of senses. In this case the type may shade over into value rationality (*Wertrationalität*).

2. Purely affectual behavior also stands on the borderline of what can be considered "meaningfully" oriented, and often it, too, goes over the line. It may, for instance, consist in an uncontrolled reaction to some exceptional stimulus. It is a case of sublimation when affectually determined action occurs in the form of conscious release of emotional tension. When this happens it is usually well on the road to rationalization in one or the other or both of the above senses.

3. The orientation of value-rational action is distinguished from the affectual type by its clearly self-conscious formulation of the ultimate values governing the action and the consistently planned orientation of its detailed course to these values. At the same time the two types have a common element, namely that the meaning of the action does not lie in the achievement of a result ulterior to it, but in carrying out the specific type of action for its own sake. Action is affectual if it satisfies a need for revenge, sensual gratification, devotion, contemplative bliss, or for working off emotional tensions (irrespective of the level of sublimation).

Examples of pure value-rational orientation would be the actions of persons who, regardless of possible cost to themselves, act to put into practice their convictions of what seems to them to be required by duty, honor, the pursuit of beauty, a religious call, personal loyalty, or the importance of some "cause" no matter in what it consists. In our terminology, value-rational action always involves "commands" or "demands" which, in the actor's opinion, are binding on him. It is only in cases where human action is motivated by the fulfillment of such unconditional demands that it will be called value-rational. This is the case in widely varying degrees, but for the most part only to a relatively slight extent. Nevertheless, it will be shown that the occurrence of this mode of action is important enough to justify its formulation as a distinct type; though it may be remarked that there is no intention here of attempting to formulate in any sense an exhaustive classification of types of action.

4. Action is instrumentally rational (*zweckrational*) when the end, the means, and the secondary results are all rationally taken into account and weighed. This involves rational consideration of alternative means to the end, of the relations of the end to the secondary consequences, and finally of the relative importance of different possible ends. Determination of action either in affectual or in traditional terms is thus incompatible with this type. Choice between alternative and conflicting ends and results may well be determined in a value-rational manner. In that case, action is instrumentally rational only in respect to the choice of means. On the other hand, the actor may, instead of deciding between alternative

and conflicting ends in terms of a rational orientation to a system of values, simply take them as given subjective wants and arrange them in a scale of consciously assessed relative urgency. He may then orient his action to this scale in such a way that they are satisfied as far as possible in order of urgency, as formulated in the principle of "marginal utility." Value-rational action may thus have various different relations to the instrumentally rational action. From the latter point of view, however, value-rationality is always irrational. Indeed, the more the value to which action is oriented is elevated to the status of an absolute value, the more "irrational" in this sense the corresponding action is. For, the more unconditionally the actor devotes himself to this value for its own sake, to pure sentiment or beauty, to absolute goodness or devotion to duty, the less is he influenced by considerations of the consequences of his action. The orientation of action wholly to the rational achievement of ends without relation to fundamental values is, to be sure, essentially only a limiting case.

5. It would be very unusual to find concrete cases of action, especially of social action, which were oriented *only* in one or another of these ways. Furthermore, this classification of the modes of orientation of action is in no sense meant to exhaust the possibilities of the field, but only to formulate in conceptually pure form certain sociologically important types to which actual action is more or less closely approximated or, in much the more common case, which constitute its elements. The usefulness of the classification for the purposes of this investigation can only be judged in terms of its results.

The Concept of Social Relationship

The term "social relationship" will be used to denote the behavior of a plurality of actors insofar as, in its meaningful content, the action of each takes account of that of the others and is oriented in these terms. The social relationship thus consists entirely and exclusively in the existence of a probability that there will be a meaningful course of social action—irrespective, for the time being, of the basis for this probability.

1. Thus, as a defining criterion, it is essential that there should be at least a minimum of mutual orientation of the action of each to that of the others. Its content may be of the most varied nature: conflict, hostility, sexual attraction, friendship, loyalty, or economic exchange. It may involve the fulfillment, the evasion, or the violation of the terms of an agreement; economic, erotic, or some other form of "competition"; common membership in status, national or class groups (provided it leads to social action). Hence, the definition does not specify whether the relation of the actors is cooperative or the opposite.

2. The "meaning" relevant in this context is always a case of the meaning imputed to the parties in a given concrete case, on the average, or in a theoretically formulated pure type—it is never a normatively "correct" or a metaphysically "true" meaning. Even in cases of such forms of social organization as a state, church, association, or marriage, the social relationship consists exclu-

sively in the fact that there has existed, exists, or will exist a probability of action in some definite way appropriate to this meaning. It is vital to be continually clear about this in order to avoid the "reification" of those concepts. A "state," for example, ceases to exist in a sociologically relevant sense whenever there is no longer a probability that certain kinds of meaningfully oriented social action will take place. This probability may be very high or it may be negligibly low. But in any case it is only in the sense and degree in which it does exist that the corresponding social relationship exists. It is impossible to find any other clear meaning for the statement that, for instance, a given "state" exists or has ceased to exist.

3. The subjective meaning need not necessarily be the same for all the parties who are mutually oriented in a given social relationship; there need not in this sense be "reciprocity." "Friendship," "love," "loyalty," "fidelity to contracts," "patriotism," on one side, may well be faced with an entirely different attitude on the other. In such cases the parties associate different meanings with their actions, and the social relationship is insofar objectively "asymmetrical" from the points of view of the two parties. It may nevertheless be a case of mutual orientation insofar as, even though partly or wholly erroneously, one party presumes a particular attitude toward him on the part of the other and orients his action to this expectation. This can, and usually will, have consequences for the course of action and the form of the relationship. A relationship is objectively symmetrical only as, according to the typical expectations of the parties, the meaning for one party is the same as that for the other. Thus the actual attitude of a child to its father may be at least approximately that which the father, in the individual case, on the average or typically, has come to expect. A social relationship in which the attitudes are completely and fully corresponding is in reality a limiting case. But the absence of reciprocity will, for terminological purposes, be held to exclude the existence of a social relationship only if it actually results in the absence of a mutual orientation of the action of the parties. Here as elsewhere all sorts of transitional cases are the rule rather than the exception.

4. A social relationship can be of a very fleeting character or of varying degrees of permanence. In the latter case there is a probability of the repeated recurrence of the behavior which corresponds to its subjective meaning and hence is expected. In order to avoid fallacious impressions, let it be repeated that it is *only* the existence of the probability that, corresponding to a given subjective meaning, a certain type of action will take place which constitutes the "existence" of the social relationship. Thus that a "friendship" or a "state" exists or has existed means this and only this: that we, the observers, judge that there is or has been a probability that on the basis of certain kinds of known subjective attitude of certain individuals there will result in the average sense a certain specific type of action. For the purposes of legal reasoning it is essential to be able to decide whether a rule of law does or does not carry legal authority, hence whether a legal relationship does or does not "exist." This type of question is not, however, relevant to sociological problems.

5. The subjective meaning of a social relationship may change, thus a political relationship once based on solidarity may develop into a conflict of interests. In that case it is only a matter of terminological convenience and of the degree of continuity of the change whether we say that a new relationship has come into existence or that the old one continues but has acquired a new meaning. It is also possible for the meaning to be partly constant, partly changing.

6. The meaningful content which remains relatively constant in a social relationship is capable of formulation in terms of maxims which the parties concerned expect to be adhered to by their partners on the average and approximately. The more rational in relation to values or to given ends the action is, the more is this likely to be the case. There is far less possibility of a rational formulation of subjective meaning in the case of a relation of erotic attraction or of personal loyalty or any other affectual type than, for example, in the case of a business contract.

7. The meaning of a social relationship may be agreed upon by mutual consent. This implies that the parties make promises covering their future behavior, whether toward each other or toward third persons. In such cases each party then normally counts, so far as he acts rationally, in some degree on the fact that the other will orient his action to the meaning of the agreement as he (the first actor) understands it. In part he orients his action rationally (*zweckrational*) to these expectations as given facts with, to be sure, varying degrees of subjectively "loyal" intention of doing his part. But in part also he is motivated value-rationally by a sense of duty, which makes him adhere to the agreement as he understands it. This much may be anticipated. . . .

Types of Action Orientation: Usage, Custom, Self-Interest

Within the realm of social action certain empirical uniformities can be observed, that is, courses of action that are repeated by the actor or (simultaneously) occur among numerous actors since the subjective meaning is meant to be the same. Sociological investigation is concerned with these typical modes of action. Thereby it differs from history, the subject of which is rather the causal explanation of important individual events; important, that is, in having an influence on human destiny.

If an orientation toward social action occurs regularly, it will be called "usage" (*Brauch*) insofar as the probability of its existence within a group is based on nothing but actual practice. A usage will be called a "custom" (*Sitte*) if the practice is based upon long standing. On the other hand, a uniformity of orientation may be said to be "determined by self-interest," if and insofar as the actors' conduct is instrumentally (*zweckrational*) oriented toward identical expectations.

1. Usage also includes "fashion" (*Mode*). As distinguished from custom and in direct contrast to it, usage will be called fashion so far as the mere fact of the *novelty* of the corresponding behavior is the basis of the orientation of ac-

tion. Its locus is in the neighborhood of "convention," since both of them usually spring from a desire for social prestige. Fashion, however, will not be further discussed here.

2. As distinguished from both "convention" and "law," "custom" refers to rules devoid of any external sanction. The actor conforms with them of his own free will, whether his motivation lies in the fact that he merely fails to think about it, that it is more comfortable to conform, or whatever else the reason may be. For the same reasons he can consider it likely that other members of the group will adhere to a custom.

Thus custom is not "valid" in anything like the legal sense; conformity with it is not "demanded" by anybody. Naturally, the transition from this to validly enforced convention and to law is gradual. Everywhere what has been traditionally handed down has been an important source of what has come to be enforced. Today it is customary every morning to eat a breakfast which, within limits, conforms to a certain pattern. But there is no obligation to do so, except possibly for hotel guests, and it has not always been customary. On the other hand, the current mode of dress, even though it has partly originated in custom, is today very largely no longer customary alone, but conventional. . . .

3. Many of the especially notable uniformities in the course of social action are not determined by orientation to any sort of norm which is held to be valid, nor do they rest on custom, but entirely on the fact that the corresponding type of social action is in the nature of the case best adapted to the normal interests of the actors as they themselves are aware of them. This is above all true of economic action, for example, the uniformities of price determination in a "free" market, but is by no means confined to such cases. The dealers in a market thus treat their own actions as means for obtaining the satisfaction of the ends defined by what they realize to be their own typical economic interests, and similarly treat as conditions the corresponding typical expectations as to the prospective behavior of others. The more strictly rational (*zweckrational*) their action is, the more will they tend to react similarly to the same situation. In this way there arise similarities, uniformities, and continuities in their attitudes and actions which are often far more stable than they would be if action were oriented to a system of norms and duties which were considered binding on the members of a group. This phenomenon—the fact that orientation to the situation in terms of the pure self-interest of the individual and of the others to whom he is related can bring about results comparable to those which imposed norms prescribe, very often in vain—has aroused a lively interest, especially in economic affairs. Observation of this has, in fact, been one of the important sources of economics as a science. But it is true in all other spheres of action as well. This type, with its clarity of self-consciousness and freedom from subjective scruples, is the polar antithesis of every sort of unthinking acquiescence in customary ways as well as of devotion to norms consciously accepted as absolute values. One of the most important aspects of the process of

"rationalization" of action is the substitution for the unthinking acceptance of ancient custom, of deliberate adaptation to situations in terms of self-interest. To be sure, this process by no means exhausts the concept of rationalization of action. For in addition this can proceed in a variety of other directions; positively in that of a deliberate formulation of ultimate values (*Wertrationalisierung*); or negatively, at the expense not only of custom, but of emotional values; and, finally, in favor of a morally sceptical type of rationality, at the expense of any belief in absolute values. The many possible meanings of the concept of rationalization will often enter into the discussion. . . .

4. The stability of merely customary action rests essentially on the fact that the person who does not adapt himself to it is subjected to both petty and major inconveniences and annoyances as long as the majority of the people he comes in contact with continue to uphold the custom and conform with it.

Similarly, the stability of action in terms of self-interest rests on the fact that the person who does not orient his action to the interests of others, does not "take account" of them, arouses their antagonism or may end up in a situation different from that which he had foreseen or wished to bring about. He thus runs the risk of damaging his own interests.

Legitimate Order

Action, especially social action which involves a social relationship, may be guided by the belief in the existence of a legitimate order. The probability that action will actually be so governed will be called the "validity" (*Geltung*) of the order in question.

1. Thus, the validity of an order means more than the mere existence of a uniformity of social action determined by custom or self-interest. If furniture movers regularly advertise at the time many leases expire, this uniformity is determined by self-interest. If a salesman visits certain customers on particular days of the month or the week, it is either a case of customary behavior or a product of self-interested orientation. However, when a civil servant appears in his office daily at a fixed time, he does not act only on the basis of custom or self-interest which he could disregard if he wanted to; as a rule, his action is also determined by the validity of an order (viz., the civil service rules), which he fulfills partly because disobedience would be disadvantageous to him but also because its violation would be abhorrent to his sense of duty (of course, in varying degrees).

2. Only then will the content of a social relationship be called an order if the conduct is, approximately or on the average, oriented toward determinable "maxims." Only then will an order be called "valid" if the orientation toward these maxims occurs, among other reasons, also because it is in some appreciable way regarded by the actor as in some way obligatory or exemplary for him. Naturally, in concrete cases, the orientation of action to an order involves a wide variety of motives. But the circumstance that, along with the other sources of conformity, the order is also held by at least part of the actors to define a model or

to be binding, naturally increases the probability that action will in fact conform to it, often to a very considerable degree. An order which is adhered to from motives of pure expediency is generally much less stable than one upheld on a purely customary basis through the fact that the corresponding behavior has become habitual. The latter is much the most common type of subjective attitude. But even this type of order is in turn much less stable than an order which enjoys the prestige of being considered binding, or, as it may be expressed, of "legitimacy." The transitions between orientation to an order from motives of tradition or of expediency to the case where a belief in its legitimacy is involved are empirically gradual.

3. It is possible for action to be oriented to an order in other ways than through conformity with its prescriptions, as they are generally understood by the actors. Even in the case of evasion or disobedience, the probability of their being recognized as valid norms may have an effect on action. This may, in the first place, be true from the point of view of sheer expediency. A thief orients his action to the validity of the criminal law in that he acts surreptitiously. The fact that the order is recognized as valid in his society is made evident by the fact that he cannot violate it openly without punishment. But apart from this limiting case, it is very common for violation of an order to be confined to more or less numerous partial deviations from it, or for the attempt to be made, with varying degrees of good faith, to justify the deviation as legitimate. Furthermore, there may exist at the same time different interpretations of the meaning of the order. In such cases, for sociological purposes, each can be said to be valid insofar as it actually determines the course of action. The fact that, in the same social group, a plurality of contradictory systems of order may all be recognized as valid, is not a source of difficulty for the sociological approach. Indeed, it is even possible for the same individual to orient his action to contradictory systems of order. This can take place not only at different times, as is an everyday occurrence, but even in the case of the same concrete act. A person who fights a duel follows the code of honor; but at the same time, insofar as he either keeps it secret or conversely gives himself up to the police, he takes account of the criminal law. To be sure, when evasion or contravention of the generally understood meaning of an order has become the rule, the order can be said to be "valid" only in a limited degree and, in the extreme case, not at all. Thus for sociological purposes there does not exist, as there does for the law, a rigid alternative between the validity and lack of validity of a given order. On the contrary, there is a gradual transition between the two extremes; and also it is possible, as it has been pointed out, for contradictory systems of order to exist at the same time. In that case each is "valid" precisely to the extent that there is a probability that action will in fact be oriented to it.

CHAPTER THREE

$\sim$

Georg Simmel on the Social
Development of Individualism

$\sim$ Introduction $\sim$

Like Weber, Georg Simmel (1858–1918) witnessed tremendous social changes taking place in Germany during his lifetime. Simmel was particularly interested in the cultural changes, due to such factors as population and economic growth, that were transforming Berlin into an important European city. Upon completing his doctoral studies in philosophy at the University of Berlin, Simmel sought a teaching position at his alma mater. Unfortunately, anti-Semitism prevented him from earning a professorship (until late in his career at the University of Strasbourg), so he taught as a lecturer, a lower-paying, lower-status job, for most of his professional life in Berlin.

Simmel's far-reaching interests led him beyond his training as a philosopher into the study of social interaction. For example, he contributed significantly to our understanding of the impact of group size on the nature of the associations between members. Simmel pointed out that the larger a group becomes (from dyad to triad to groups of four or more), the less its members engage in face-to-face interactions and the more its members become dependent upon formal rules and procedures for their association. Moreover, while a two-person group may be less formal or more intimate, this association tends to come with more member-to-member responsibilities, and thereby fewer freedoms, than association within large groups. Simmel (1950) observes in his widely-read, influential essay "The Metropolis and Mental Life" that population growth, particularly population density, loosens the bonds of association, thereby providing each member with greater individual movement. However, what goes with this increased freedom is an anonymity that may contribute significantly to alienation. Simmel adds:

[M]an is tempted to adopt the most tendentious peculiarities, that is, the specifically metropolitan extravagances of mannerism, caprice, and preciousness. Now, the meaning of these extravagances does not at all lie in the contents of such behavior, but rather in its form of 'being different,' of standing out in a striking manner and thereby attracting attention. For many character types, ultimately the only means of saving for themselves some modicum of self-esteem and the sense of filling a position is indirect, through the awareness of others. . . . On the one hand, life is made infinitely easy for the personality in that stimulations, interests, uses of time and consciousness are offered to it from all sides. They carry the person as if in a stream, and one needs hardly to swim for oneself. On the other hand, however, life is composed more and more of these impersonal contents and offerings which tend to displace the genuine personal colorations and incomparabilities. This results in the individual's summoning the utmost in uniqueness and particularization, in order to preserve his most personal core. He has to exaggerate this personal element in order to remain audible even to himself. (421–422)

Although Simmel discusses the impact of group size, density, and diversity on associative bonds and self-expression, it is important to realize that his approach is attuned to the nature of interaction itself to effect these changes (i.e., as the members grow in number and in the complexity of social interaction, the nature of associative bonds change, and complex interaction reinforces diverse expression with sometimes creative and/or alienating consequences).

The selections from Simmel that you will be reading not only have particular relevance to the study of sociological social psychology; they also highlight a number of the key themes with which he wrestled: the tension between self and society, the relationship between equality and freedom, the impact of the money economy and increasing social complexity on social interaction and self-relationship. The first selection, entitled "Individual and Society in Eighteenth- and Nineteenth-Century Views of Life: An Example of Philosophical Sociology," is from Simmel's volume *Fundamental Questions of Sociology*, published in 1917. In this essay, Simmel's insights pertaining to social interaction frequently draw from ideas developed by influential German philosophers such as Friedrich Nietzsche (1844–1900) and Immanuel Kant (1724–1804). As you begin to read the essay, the main point to remember is this: society reflects human activity and aspiration, but society also limits expression of individual activity and aspiration. While individuals comprise the institutions that make up society, society requires individuals to specialize in a given activity, to fulfill a role with a particular function. According to Simmel, this undermines the individual's striving to be well-rounded and whole. While society and the individual depend upon each other, they have opposing needs. A part of what Simmel is addressing is one of the consequences of the growing complexity of social life on individuation.

In the eighteenth century the need of the individual to realize him- or herself apart from society took the form of the abstract pursuit of individual freedom, which led to the revolutionary movements for freedom. Simmel discusses abstract freedom because, contrary to conventional understanding, freedom does not mean the absence of social obligations and bonds. The freedom to develop as an individual only has meaning within the context of social relationships. In everyday life freedom means playing a role in choosing those bonds. (For example, most individuals need to work in order to survive, but they are free if they have choices regarding career, employer, etc.) Moreover, freedom is only a positive value when one knows what to do with it. As Simmel (402) writes in *The Philosophy of Money*, "[W]e learn by experience that peace from specific things is valuable or even bearable only if it is, at the same time, peace to engage in specific things."

Despite the fact that freedom always inheres in a type of dependency, in the eighteenth century, abstract freedom became the vehicle through which the individual sought to free himself from the restraint of "institutions which had lost their inner justifications" (64–65). A fascinating idea that Simmel develops throughout *The Philosophy of Money* is that the individual pursuit of liberty was fueled by the confluence of the money economy (an abstract form of exchange), the modern state (as opposed to small-scale autonomous communities), advances in technology, and the growing belief in the value of science. All of these forces converged to improve the individual's quality of life to a point where conventional institutional restraints and morality could no longer serve as binding. It was believed that by removing coercive institutional controls as they existed within religious and feudal systems, individuals would achieve freedom and equality. The problem with this development, as Simmel notes, is that unrestrained freedom, practically speaking, translates into differential treatment of individuals. Since individuals always seem to vary in privilege and capacity, unrestrained freedom creates the social legitimacy of the stronger to prey upon the weaker, obviating the opportunity for equality. Simmel argues that only a form of socialism that would suspend the particular freedoms of some in order to create the opportunity of freedom for others could result in the ideal of freedom for all. Yet Simmel is doubtful that socialism, in practice, could successfully synthesize equality and freedom.

Simmel points out that another "deeper historical current" contributed significantly to the rise of the social movements and psychological changes being discussed here. The Enlightenment thinkers (notably Kant) legitimized the notion of a type of egoism (already in embryonic development) that would become self-contained individualism for future generations. The notion was that each person's ego stemmed from the same source, making people the same underneath, but in order for the ego to understand itself, all distorting "entanglements" must be removed. Implicit in this idea is that individuals are free and have the responsibility to understand and overcome the forces that limit them. Of course, what is missing here is an acknowledgement that people vary in privilege and capacity. Simmel observes in the selection, "Thus, the eighteenth-century conception of individuality, with its emphasis on personal freedom that does not exclude, but includes, equality, because the 'true person' is the same in every accidental man, has found its abstract perfection in Kant."

The *seemingly* symbiotic relationship between freedom and equality gave way to a unique emphasis on the ego in the nineteenth century. From an attempted synthesis of freedom and equality based upon a notion of a common core, arrived, in the nineteenth century, a form of "individualization" that strove to distinguish itself; each self was now a universe unto itself. Moreover, as Simmel states in the selection, "the idea that the absolute only lives in the form of the individual, and that individuality is not a restriction of the infinite but its expression and mirror, makes the principle of the social division of labor part of the metaphysical ground of reality itself" (81). The new emphasis on self due to social developments, such as the money economy, population growth and density, innovations in technology, and the growing reliance on science, reinforces the Christian idea of the spiritual individual (Jesus as synthesis of God and man) and legitimates one's station as determined by one's own relative success or failure in the eyes of God (that is, class is God-made not man-made).

As Simmel points out, the irony here is that the eighteenth-century ideal of freedom and equality led to either equality without freedom or freedom without equality. Attempts to synthesize the two resulted in ideals and social conditions that did not fulfill the eighteenth-century ideal, but rather led to definitions of self that accommodated the socially restrictive realities taking shape; that is, self-contained individualism seemed to "work" or make sense within the social interactions of unlimited competition and thereby reinforced both self-contained individualism and unlimited competition. In essence, Simmel is saying that we have created and continue to reinforce a system of relations that do not adequately harmonize the needs of the individual with that of society. Using the metropolis as an example of this point, Simmel (420) in "The Metropolis and Mental Life," says, "It is decisive that city life has transformed the struggle with nature for livelihood into an inter-human struggle for gain, which here is not granted by nature but by other men." In fact, Simmel sees the whole modern trend (greater reliance on abstract scientific formulations and technologies; greater reliance on the abstract exchange of goods: coins and credit; the increasing number of impersonal relations; and, the increasingly abstract and reductionistic theoretical formulations of self) as a consistent movement that places a greater cultural and psychological emphasis on "quantitative determinations" as opposed to qualitative ones. This whole train of thought is particularly evident in Simmel's discussion of objective and subjective culture. The chapter concludes on this theme with excerpts from *The Philosophy of Money*.

~ Social Development of Individualism ~

Individual Life as the Basis of the Conflict between Individual and Society

The really practical problem of society is the relation between its forces and forms and the individual's own life. The question is not whether society exists only in the individuals or also outside of them. For even if we attribute "life," properly speaking, only to individuals, and identify the life of society with that of its individual members, we must still admit the existence of conflict between the two. One reason for this conflict is the fact that, in the individuals themselves, social elements fuse into the particular phenomenon called "society." "Society" develops its own vehicles and organs by whose claims and commands the individual is confronted as by an alien party. A second reason results from another aspect of the inherency of society in the individual. For man has the capacity to decompose himself into parts and to feel any one of these as his proper self. Yet each part may collide with any other and may struggle for the dominion over the individual's actions. This capacity places man, insofar as he feels himself to be a social being, into an often contradictory relation with those among his impulses and interests that are *not* preempted by his social character. In other words, the conflict between society and individual is continued in the individual himself as the conflict among his component parts. Thus, it seems to me, the basic struggle between society and individual inheres in the general form of individual life. It does not derive from any single, "anti-social," individual interest.

Society strives to be a whole, an organic unit of which the individuals must be mere members. Society asks of the individual that he employ all his strength in the service of the special function which he has to exercise as a member of it; that he so modify himself as to become the most suitable vehicle for this function. Yet the drive toward unity and wholeness that is characteristic of the individual himself rebels against this role. The individual strives to be rounded out in himself, not merely to help to round out society. He strives to develop his full capacities, irrespective of the shifts among them that the interest of society may ask of him. This conflict between the whole, which imposes the one-sidedness of partial function upon its elements, and the part, which itself strives to be a whole, is insoluble. No house can be built of houses, but only of specially formed stones; no tree can grow from trees, but only from differentiated cells.

Individual Egoism vs. Individual
Self-Perfection as an Objective Value

The formulation presented seems to me to describe the contrast between the two parties much more comprehensively than does its customary reduction to the egoism-altruism dichotomy. On the one hand, the individual's striving for wholeness appears as egoism, which is contrasted with the altruism of his ordering himself into society as a selectivity formed social member of it. Yet on the other hand, the very quest of society is an egoism that does violence to the individual for the benefit and utility of the many, and that often makes for an extremely one-sided individual specialization, and even atrophy. Finally, the individual's urge toward self-perfection is not necessarily an expression of egoism. It may also be an objective ideal whose goal is by no means success in terms of happiness and narrowly personal interests but a super-personal value realized in the personality.

What has just been suggested—and what will be elaborated presently— appears to me to exemplify a very significant stage in the development of cultural-philosophical consciousness. It also throws new light on the ethics of the individual and, indirectly, on the ethics of society. It is popularly held that all intentions which do not break through the orbit of the individual existence and interest are of an egoistic nature, and that egoism is overcome only when concern shifts toward the welfare of the Thou or of society. Yet it is already some time that a deeper reflection on the values of life has ascertained a third alternative, most impressively perhaps in the figures of Goethe and Nietzsche (though not in any abstract formula). It is the possibility that the perfection of the individual as such constitutes an objective value, quite irrespective of its significance for any other individuals, or in merely accidental connection with it. This value, moreover, may exist in utter disregard for the happiness or unhappiness of this individual himself, or may even be in conflict with them. What a person represents in terms of strength, nobility of character, achievement, or harmony of life, is very often quite unrelated to what he or others "get out" of these qualities. All that can be said about them is that the world is enriched by the existence in it of a valuable human being who is perfect in himself. Certainly, his value often consists in his practical devotion to other individuals or groups; but to limit it to this would be to proceed by an arbitrary moralistic dogma. For, beauty and perfection of life, the working upon oneself, the passionate efforts to obtain ideal goods, do not always result in happiness. These efforts and aims are inspired by certain *world* values, and may have no other effect than to create and maintain a particular attitude in the individual consciousness.

Countless times, the individual craves situations, events, insights, achievements, in whose particular existence or general nature he simply sees ultimately satisfactory aims. Occasionally the content of such cravings may be the improvement or well-being of others. But not necessarily: the aim is striven after for the sake of its own realization; and, therefore, to sacrifice others or even oneself may not be too high a price. *"Fiat justitia, pereat mundus"*; the fulfillment of divine will merely because it is divine; the fanaticism of the artist, completion of whose work makes him forget any other consideration, altruistic or egoistic; the political idealist's enthusiasm for a constitutional reform that renders him entirely indifferent to the question of how the citizens would fare under it—these are examples of purely objective valuations that permeate even the most trivial contents. The acting individual feels himself to be only the object or executor—who at bottom is accidental—of the task his cause puts to him. The passion for this cause is as little concerned with the I, Thou, or society as the value of the state of the world can be measured in terms of the world's pleasure or suffering (although it can, of course, be partly so measured). Yet, evidently, the claims made by individuals or groups, insofar as they, too, are agents of ultimate values, do not necessarily coincide with the individual's striving after such objective values. Particularly if he tries to realize a value either in himself or in an accomplishment that is unappreciated socially, the super-egoistic nature of his procedure is not rewarded by society. Society claims the individual for itself. It wants to make of him a form that it can incorporate into its own structure. And this societal claim is often so incompatible with the claim imposed on the individual by his striving after an objective value, as only a purely egoistic claim can be incompatible with a purely social one.

The Social vs. the Human

The stage reached by the interpretation presented certainly goes beyond the customary contrast between egoism and altruism, as I have already pointed out. But even this interpretation cannot resolve the basic contrast between individual and society. And a related contrast that deals with the same content but springs from another ultimate world view is suggested by the modern analysis of certain sociological concepts.

Society—and its representative in the individual, social-ethical conscience— very often imposes a specialization upon him. I have already called attention to the fact that this specialization not only leaves undeveloped, or destroys, his harmonious wholeness. What is more, it often foists contents on the individual that are wholly inimical to the qualities usually called general-human. Nietzsche seems to have been the first to feel, with fundamental distinctness, the difference between the interest of humanity, of mankind, and the interest of society. Society is but one of the forms in which mankind shapes the contents of its life, but it is neither essential to all forms nor is it the only one in which human development is realized. All purely objective realms in which we are involved in whatever way—logical cognition or metaphysical imagination, the beauty of life or its image in the sovereignty of art, the realms of religion or of nature—none of these, to the extent to which they become our intimate possessions, has intrinsically and essentially anything whatever to do with "society." The human values that are measured by our greater or smaller stakes in these ideal realms have a merely accidental relation to social values, however often they intersect with them.

On the other hand, purely personal qualities—strength, beauty, depth of thought, greatness of conviction, kindness, nobility of character, courage, purity of heart—have their autonomous significance which likewise is entirely independent of their social entanglements. They are values of human existence. As such they are profoundly different from social values, which always rest upon the individual's *effects*. At the same time, they certainly are elements, both as effects and causes, of the social process. But this is only one side of their significance— the other is the intrinsic fact of their existence in the personality. For Neitzsche, this, strictly speaking, *immediate* existence of man is the criterion by which the level of mankind must be gauged at any given moment. For him, all social institutions, all giving and receiving by which the individual becomes a social being, are mere preconditions or consequences of his own nature. It is by virtue of this intrinsic nature that he constitutes a stage in the development of mankind.

Yet utilitarian-social valuation does not entirely depend on this intrinsic nature. It also depends on other individuals' responses to it. Thus, the individual's value does not wholly reside in himself: part of it he receives as the reflection of processes and creations in which his own nature has fused with beings and circumstances outside of him. It is on the basis of this relation between him and others that ethics (above all, Kantian ethics) has shifted the ground on which to appraise man, from his deeds to his attitude. Our value lies in our good will—a certain quality of the ultimate springs of our action that must be left undefined. It lies behind all appearance of our actions which, along with the effects they may have, are its mere consequences. They sometimes express it correctly, sometimes distort it—since they are mere "phenomena," they have but an accidental relationship to this fundamental value, good will itself.

Kant's position was expanded, or conceived more profoundly, by Nietzsche. He translated the Kantian contrast between attitude and success of external action (which already had freed the value of the individual from its social dependence) into the contrast between the existence and the effect of man in general. For Nietzsche, it is the qualitative *being* of the personality which marks the stage that the development of mankind has reached; it is the highest exemplars of a given time that carry humanity beyond its past. Thus Nietzsche overcame the limitations of merely social existence, as well as the valuation of man in terms of his sheer effects. It thus is not only quantitatively that mankind is more than society. Mankind is not simply the sum of all societies: it is an entirely different synthesis of the same elements that in other syntheses result in societies. Mankind and societies are two different vantage points, as it were, from which the individual can be viewed. They measure him by different standards, and their claims on him may be in violent conflict. What ties us to mankind and what we may contribute to the development of mankind—religious and scientific contributions, inter-family and international interests, the aesthetic perfection of personality, and purely objective production that aims at no "utility"—all this, of course, may on occasion also help develop the historical society of which we are members. But, essentially, it is rooted in claims that go far beyond any given society and that serve the elevation and objective enrichment of the type "man" itself. They may even be in pointed conflict with the more specific claims of the group that for any given man represents "his society."

In many other respects, however, society promotes a leveling of its members. It creates an average and makes it extremely difficult for its members to go beyond this average merely through the individual excellence in the quantity or quality of life. Society requires the individual to differentiate himself from the humanly general, but forbids him to stand out from the socially general. The individual is thus doubly oppressed by the standards of society: he may not transcend them either in a more general or in a more individual direction. In recent historical periods, these conflicts into which he falls with his political group, with his family, with his economic association, with his party, with his religious community, etc., have eventually become sublimated into the abstract need, as it were, for individual freedom. This is the general category that came to cover what was common in the various complaints and self-assertions of the individual against society.

The Eighteenth Century

The Freedom of the Individual

The need for freedom in general, for the severance of the ties between society as such and individual as such, found its most highly developed consciousness and its strongest effects in the eighteenth century. This fundamental quest can be observed, in its economic form, in the Physiocrats' praise of free competition of individual interests as the natural order of things; in its sentimental elaboration, in Rousseau's notion of the rape of man by historical society as the origin of all corruption and evil; in its political aspect, in the French Revolution's intensification of the idea of individual liberty to the point of prohibiting workers from associating even for the protection of their own interests; in its philosophical sublimation, in Kant's and Fichte's conceptions of the ego as the bearer of the cognizable world and of its absolute autonomy as the moral value as such. The inadequacy of the socially accepted forms of life of the eighteenth century, in contrast with its material and intellectual productions, struck the consciousness of the individual as an unbearable limitation of his energies. Examples of these restrictive forms of life are the privileges of the higher estates, the despotic control of commerce and life in general, the still potent survivals of the guilds, the intolerant coercion by the church, the feudal obligations of the peasantry, the political tutelage dominating the life of the state, and the weakness of municipal constitutions. The oppressiveness of these and similar institutions which had lost their inner justifications, resulted in the ideal of the mere liberty of the individual. It was believed that the removal of these ties, which pressed the forces of the personality into unnatural grooves, would result in the unfolding of all the inner and outer values (that were there potentially, but whose free action was paralyzed politically, economically, and religiously), and would lead society out of the epoch of historical unreason into that of natural reason. Since nature did not know any of these ties, the ideal of freedom appeared as that of the "natural" state. If nature is conceived as the original existence of our species, as well as of each individual, as the starting point of the cultural process (irrespective of the ambiguity of "original," which may stand for "first in time" or for "essential and basic"), the eighteenth century tried to reconnect, in a gigantic synthesis, the end or peak of this process with its starting point. The freedom of the individual was too empty and weak to carry his existence; since historical forces no longer filled and supported it, it could now be filled and supported by the idea that it was merely necessary to gain this freedom as purely and completely as possible to recapture the original basis of the existence of our species and of our personality, a basis which was as certain and fruitful as nature itself.

The Antinomy between Freedom and Equality

Yet this need for the freedom of the individual who feels himself restricted and deformed by historical society results in a self-contradiction once it is put into practice. For evidently, it can be put into practice permanently only if society exclusively consists of individuals who externally as well as internally are equally strong and equally privileged. Yet this condition exists nowhere. On the contrary, the power-giving and rank-determining forces of men are, in principle, unequal, both qualitatively and quantitatively. Therefore, complete freedom necessarily leads to the exploitation of this inequality by the more privileged, to the exploitation of the stupid by the clever, of the weak by the strong, of the timid by the grasping. The elimination of all external impediments must result in the expression of different inner potentialities in correspondingly different external positions. Institutionalized freedom is made illusory by personal relations. Furthermore, since in all power relations an advantage once gained facilitates the gaining of additional advantages (the "accumulation of capital" is merely a specific instance of this general proposition), power inequality is bound to expand in quick progression, and the freedom of the privileged always and necessarily develops at the expense of the freedom of the oppressed.

For this reason it was quite legitimate to raise the paradoxical question whether the socialization of all means of production is not the only condition of free competition. For, only by forcibly taking from the individual the possibility of fully exploiting his superiority over the weaker, can an equal measure of freedom reign throughout society. Therefore, if it is this ideal that is aimed at, "socialism" does not refer to the suspension of freedom. Rather, socialism suspends only that which, at any given degree of freedom, becomes the means for suppressing the freedom of some in favor of others. This means is private property. It is more than the expression of individual differences; it multiplies them; it intensifies them to the point, to put it radically, where at one pole of the society a maximum of freedom has developed, and at the other, a minimum. Full freedom of each can obtain only if there is full equality with everybody else. But as long as the economic set-up permits the exploitation of personal superiorities, this equality is unattainable both in strictly personal and in economic matters. Only when this exploitation is eliminated; when, that is, the private ownership of the means of production is suspended, is economic equality possible. Only then is there no longer a barrier to freedom—a barrier which is inseparable from inequality. It is precisely this possibility of exploiting personal superiorities which conclusively shows the deep antinomy between freedom and equality: the antinomy can be resolved only if both are dragged down to the negative level of propertylessness and powerlessness.

In the eighteenth century, only Goethe seems to have seen this antinomy with full clarity. Equality, he said, demands submission to a general norm; freedom "strives toward the unconditional." "Legislators or revolutionaries," he pointed out, "who promise at the same time equality and freedom are fantasts or charlatans." Perhaps it was an instinctive intuition of this condition which made for the addition, to freedom and equality, of a third requirement: fraternity. For the rejection of coercion as a means of resolving the contradiction between freedom and equality leaves as this means only emphatic altruism. Equality, after being destroyed by freedom, can be re-established only through the ethical renunciation to utilize natural gifts. Except for this notion, however, the typical individualism of the eighteenth century is completely blind to the intrinsic difficulty of freedom. The intellectual limitations and the restrictions by estates, guilds, and the church, against which it fought, had created innumerable inequalities whose injustices were deeply felt but were seen to derive from merely external-historical origins. The removal of these institutions, which was bound to eliminate the inequalities caused by *them,* was therefore thought to eliminate *all* inequalities. Freedom and equality thus appeared as self-evidently harmonious aspects of the same human ideal.

"Natural Man"

This ideal was carried by still another and deeper historical current, the peculiar contemporaneous conception of nature. In its theoretical interests, the eighteenth century was decisively oriented toward the natural sciences. Continuing the work of the seventeenth, it established the modern concept of natural law as the highest ideal of cognition. This concept, however, eliminates individuality, properly speaking. There no longer exist the incomparability and indissolubility of the single existence, but only the general law. Any phenomenon, be it an individual or a nebula in the Milky Way, is merely one of its instances. In spite of the utter unrepeatability of its form, the individual is a mere crosspoint and a resolvable pattern of fundamentally general laws. This, at least, was the understanding of "nature" of the time—only poets understood it differently. For this reason, man in general, man as such, is the central interest of the period; not historically given, particular, differentiated man. Concrete man is reduced to general man: he is the essence of each individual person, just as the universal laws of matter in general are embodied in any fragment of matter, however specifically it be formed. This argument gives one the right to see freedom and equality together from the beginning. For, the general-human man, the natural-law man, exists as the essential core in each empirical man, who is individualized by virtue of particular qualities, social position, and contingencies. Therefore, all that is needed to make appear what is common to all men, or man's essence, or man as such, is to *free* the individual from all these historical influences and distortions which merely hide his deepest nature.

Thus, the crucial point of this conception of individuality—which is one of the great conceptions of intellectual history—is this: if man is freed from all that he is not purely himself, if man has found himself, there emerges as the proper substance of his being, man-as-such or humanity. This humanity lives in all individuals. It is their constant, fundamental nature which only empirically and historically is disguised, made smaller, distorted. Freedom is the expression without restrictions or residues and in all domains of existence, of this essence of man, of this central ego, of this unconditioned self, which alone reigns over man's existence. In terms of the pure concept of mankind, all men are essentially alike. Compared with this general element, all *differentiated* individuality is something external and accidental. It is the significance of this general element that makes the literature of the revolutionary period continuously speak of the "people," the "tyrant," "freedom" in general. It is for this reason that the "natural religion" contains providence "as such," justice "as such," divine education "as such," but does not recognize the right of any specific elaborations or manifestations of these ideas. It is for this reason that "natural law" is based on the fiction of isolated and similar individuals. Commonness in the sense of collective unity has disappeared—whether this unity be economic or of the church or of the estate or of the state itself. (The only function of which the state has not been deprived is the negative function of protection, of the prevention of disturbances.) Only the free, self-contained individual is left. Historical-social units have yielded to the conviction of generality of human nature, which subsists as the essential, inalienable, and always traceable characteristic of each individual, and which must only be found and pointed out in him to make him perfect. This generality of human nature attenuates and makes bearable the isolation of the individual. At the same time, it makes freedom possible as an ethical concept, for it appears to eradicate the very development of inequality (which nevertheless is the inevitable consequence of freedom). In this sense it was possible for Frederick the Great to speak of the prince as "the first judge, the first financier, the first minister of society," but in the same breath, as "a *man* like the least among his subjects." Thus, eighteenth-century individualism made the sociological antinomy between freedom and inequality, with which I began my discussion, into an ethical paradox, too: the antinomy was conceived as the innermost spring of man's nature, and yet as imposing the renunciation of the self. And it also makes it into a religious paradox that is expressed in the axiom, "He who loses his soul shall find it."

Individualism in Kant
It is in the philosophy of Kant that this conception of individuality attains its highest intellectual sublimation. All cognition, Kant taught, results from the fact that the intrinsically heterogeneous variety of sense impressions is formed into units. This unification is possible because the mind, in which it occurs, itself is a unit, an *ego*. The fact that instead of fleeting sensations we have a consciousness of *objects* is the expression of the unification which the ego brings about in these sensations. The object is the counterpart of the subject. Thus the ego—not the accidental, psychological, individual ego, but the fundamental, creative, unchangeable ego—becomes the vehicle and producer of objectivity. Cognition is objectively true and necessary in the measure in which it is formed by this pure ego, the ultimate legislator of the cognizing mind. From this unshakable assumption of *one* truth, of *one objective* world, it follows that in all men the ego which forms or could form this world, must always be identical. Kantian idealism thus makes the knowable world the product of the ego. At the same time, it insists on

the oneness and perpetual identity of true cognition. This idealism is the expression of an individualism which sees in all that is human an unconditionally identical core. It is forced to hold that, just as the cognized world is the same for all men, so the deepest productive element in all men is homogeneous, even if it is not always equally developed or manifest.

Thus, for Kant, the identity of the egos results in the identity of their worlds. It is in this notion that he also discovers the root of freedom. The world can be given only as the representation of the idealistic ego, which embodies the absolute independence of the person from all extrinsic conditions and determinations. Inasmuch as the ego creates all conscious contents of existence—and among them, the empirical ego itself—it cannot in turn be created by any of them. In Kantian philosophy, the ego has wrested its absolute sovereignty from all possible entanglements with nature, Thou, society. It stands so much on itself alone that even its world, *the* world, can stand on it. It is no use for the powers of history to interfere with this ego since there is nothing above or even beside it: by definition, it can go no other road than that prescribed to it by its own nature. Kant and his epoch make abstract man, the individuality that is freed from all ties and specificities and is therefore always identical, the ultimate substance of personality and, thereby, the ultimate *value* of personality. However unholy man may be, Kant says, humanity in him is holy. And Schiller: "The idealist thinks so highly of mankind that he runs the risk of despising single men."

The Dual Role of "Nature"

Even for Rousseau, who certainly was sensitive to individual differences, these differences, nevertheless, are superficial. He argues that the more completely man returns to his own heart and grasps his inner absoluteness instead of mere external relations, the more forcefully flows in him, that is, in each individual equally, the fountain of goodness and happiness. When man thus really is himself, he possesses a sustained strength that is abundant for more than his own maintenance. He can make it flow over to others, as it were; it is sufficient to absorb others in himself and to identify himself with them. We are ethically the more valuable, charitable, and good, the more each of us is purely himself; the more, that is, one allows that innermost core to become sovereign in himself in which all men are identical in spite of all social ties and accidental guises. Inasmuch as he is more than sheer empirical individuality, the true individual has in this "more" the possibility to give of himself and thus to overcome his empirical egoism.

We realize how the peculiar eighteenth-century conception of nature establishes a close relation to ethics; and in all of the eighteenth century, the double role of nature finds its strongest expression in Rousseau. I already called attention to the significance of nature for the problem of individuality: nature not only is what really alone exists—the substance of all historical oscillations and shifts—but also, at the same time, it is what ought to be, the ideal with whose growing realization all men must be concerned. To say that what truly exists is, at the same time, an aim that must yet be reached, sounds contradictory. Yet actually, these two propositions are the two sides of a consistent psychological position which is taken in regard to more than one value complex. We can simply not express it otherwise than in this logically contradictory dualism. And it is precisely in its specific stand on the problem of the ego that the dual significance of the "natural" becomes most readily plausible. We feel in ourselves an ultimate reality which forms the essence of our nature, but which is yet only very imperfectly represented by our empirical reality. But it is by no means merely a fantasy-like ideal which hovers above this empirical reality; for, in some shape it already exists, traced in ideal lines, as it were, into our existence; and yet it contains the *norm* for this existence, and only requires to be fully worked out and elaborated in the material of our existence. That the ego which we already are, nevertheless is something yet to be achieved because we are it not yet purely and absolutely but only in the disguise and distortion of our historical-social destinies—this argument became an extremely powerful feeling in the eighteenth century. The ego's setting-of-norms for the ego is ethically justified because the ideal ego is real in a higher sense of the word: it is the generally human ego. When it is attained, the true equality of all that is man is also attained. This thought was expressed most exhaustively by Schiller: "Every individual man carries a pure and ideal man in himself, as disposition and destination. It is the great task of his life, in all his changes, to coincide with the unchangeable unity of this ideal man. This pure man makes himself manifest, more or less distinctly, in every individual."

Kant's "Categorical Imperative":
Individuality as the Synthesis of Freedom and Equality

The formula of the "categorical imperative," in which Kant epitomized man's moral task, is the most profound elaboration of this concept of individuality. It bases man's whole moral value upon freedom. As long as we are mere parts of the mechanism of the world, including the social world, we have as little "value" as the passing cloud or the withering stone. Only when we cease being a mere product and crosspoint of external forces and become a being that develops out of his own ego, can we be *responsible*. Only then can we acquire the possibility of both guilt and moral value. Within the natural-social cosmos, "being-for-oneself" or "personality" do not exist. Only when we are rooted in absolute freedom (the metaphysical counterpart of *laissez-faire*) do we gain both personality and the dignity of the moral. And what this morality is, is expressed by the categorical imperative as follows: "Act in such a way that the principle governing your will could at the same time be valid as the principle of a general legislation." With the categorical imperative, the ideal of equality has become the meaning of every Ought. Self-flattering arrogance has been made impossible: the individual can no longer feel himself entitled to indulge in special actions and enjoyments because he fancies that he is "different from the others." Moral trial "without regard to person," equality before the moral law, is perfected in the requirement that it must be possible to think consistently of one's own action as of everybody's necessary manner of acting. Equality supplies freedom, which is the mainspring of all ethics, with its content. The absolutely self-dependent and self-responsible personality is precisely the personality whose action is ethically justified by the identical claim to this action on the part of all others. Not merely, only the man who is free is moral, but also, only the man who is moral is free because only *his* action possesses the character of the general law that is real exclusively in the uninfluenced and self-based ego. Thus, the eighteenth-century conception of individuality, with its emphasis on personal freedom that does not exclude, but includes, equality, because the "true person" is the same in every accidental man, has found its abstract perfection in Kant.

The Nineteenth Century

In the nineteenth century, this conception splits up into two ideals. Crudely and without regard for many necessary qualifications, these ideals may be identified as the tendencies toward equality without freedom, and toward freedom without equality.

Socialism

The former is characteristic of socialism. Although it does not, of course, exhaustively define socialism, it is yet more profoundly a part of it than is admitted by the majority of its adherents. In energetically rejecting mechanical equalization, the socialists are mistaken about the central role that the idea of equality will always play in the formation of socialist ideals. Socialization of the means of production may, as I have already stressed, bring out many individual differences which in the present social system are atrophied because of their disappearance into class levels, and because of imperfect education, overwork, indigence, and worry. Nevertheless, the elimination of undeserved advantages and disadvantages due to birth, fluctuation of the stock market, accumulation of capital, differential evaluation of identical quantities of work, etc., would certainly lead to a very considerable leveling of economic conditions as compared with the present state of affairs. And according to the close dependence which precisely in socialist theory exists between the economic and the general cultural situation, the relative economic equilibration is bound to be paralleled by a comprehensive personal equilibration. Yet the crucial point is that the various measures of leveling (which differ with different socialist programs) only concern the oscillations in the *theory* of the ideal of equality—an ideal which is one of the great character traits of human nature. There will always be a type of person whose notions regarding social values are contained in the idea of the equality of all, however nebulous and unthinkable in the concrete this idea may be. And there will also be a type to whom individual differences and distances constitute an ultimate, irreducible, and self-justified value of the social form of existence. One of the leading socialists asserts that all socialist measures, including those which superficially strike one as coercive, actually aim at the development and security of the free personality. Thus, the institution of maximum hours of work is merely a prohibition to give up personal freedom for more than a particular number of hours. It is thus basically the same as the prohibition to sell oneself permanently into personal servitude. But this sort of argument shows our particular socialist to think in terms of eighteenth-century individualism with its schematic conception of freedom.

Perhaps no empirical man is guided exclusively by any one of these two tendencies, freedom and equality. Perhaps, too, the exclusive realization of either of them is entirely impossible. Yet this does not prevent them from socially manifesting themselves as fundamental types of character differences. Once one of them exists, the individual who is dominated by it, will not be swayed by rational argument. For in spite of any retrospective rationalizations to the contrary, such a tendency does not originate in its appraisal as a means for the attainment of an ultimate end, such as general happiness or personal perfection or the rationalization of life. It rather itself is the ultimate ground on which all intentions, decisions, and deductions are built. It expresses the existence of man, the substance of his essence. His relation to his fellowmen is something very important, grave, and basic to him. Hence his decision as to whether he is, or wants, or ought to be, like or unlike them (individually, as well as in principle) is bound to come from the very depth of his being. It seems to me that socialism recruits most of its adherents, at any rate its most fanatic adherents, from individuals who tend in the manner suggested toward this quite general ideal of equality.

The relation between the relative equality of a socialized system, and freedom is very complex. It is characterized by the typical ambiguity which class differentiation commonly inflicts upon general influences or modifications that concern the whole of a given society. For, since the development and the life conditions of the various parts of a society are extremely different, any general modification must result in extremely different, even diametrically opposed consequences for these various parts. The same measure of general equalization that would give a great deal of freedom to the laborer who is constantly exposed to the threat of hunger and the hardships of wage work, would entail at least an equal limitation of freedom for the entrepreneur, the *rentier*, the artist, the scholar, and other leaders of the present order. A formally corresponding sociological ambiguity characterizes the woman question. The freedom to engage in economic production is sought after by the women of the higher classes in an effort to secure their solid independence and a satisfactory demonstration of their ability. Yet, for the woman factory worker, this same freedom constitutes a terrible obstacle to the fulfillment of her duties and to her happiness as wife and mother. As it hits two different classes, the elimination of domestic and family restrictions results in totally different values. To recapitulate, in the socialist movement, the synthesis of freedom and equality has been modified by the emphasis upon equality. And only because the class, whose interests are represented by socialism, would feel equality *as* freedom (at least during the initial period of socialist equalization), can socialism overlook the antagonism between the two ideals.

One might suggest that the loss of freedom which socialism would impose on certain layers of the society, will be only transitional, will last only as long as the aftereffects of present conditions still allow for sensitivity to individual differences. In fact, in view of the difficulties of reconciling freedom and equality, touched upon above, socialism has been forced to resort to an *adjustment* to equality which, as an overall satisfaction, is supposed to reduce the desires for freedom that go beyond it. Yet this resort to such a panacea of adjustment is a questionable device, if only because it can be used with equal readiness by any contrary position. For, one could assert no less plausibly that the drives toward freedom which are based on social *differences* could adjust to any degree of reduction in the absolute quantity of these differences. But the fact is that the nature of our sensitivity depends on *differences in stimulus*. Therefore, after a brief period of adjustment, the individual differences would base their utterly inevitable passions of greed and envy, of domination and feeling of oppression, on the slight differences in social position that have remained because they cannot be removed in even the most socialized situation. By virtue of this psychological structure of man, the exercise of freedom at the expense of others would find a fertile field of expansion, even if the extreme degree of equality attainable were actually attained.

One might, however, understand equality only in the sense of equal justice. One might hold, that is, that the social institutions should give each individual a certain quantity of freedom, not on the basis of some mechanical and constant criterion, but in exact proportion to his qualitative importance. Yet even this conception could not be acted upon in practice. The reason is a largely neglected fact which, nevertheless, is of the greatest significance for an understanding of the relation between individual and society. Any social order requires a hierarchy of superordinations and subordinations, even if only for technical reasons. Therefore, equality in the sense of justice can only be the exact correspondence of personal qualification with position in this hierarchy. Yet, this harmonious correspondence is in principle impossible for the very simple reason that there always are more persons qualified for superior positions than there are superior positions. Among the million subjects of a prince, there surely is a large number who would make equally good or better princes. A good many factory workers could as well be entrepreneurs or at least foremen. A large portion of the common soldiers have full officer qualifications, even if only latently. Here lies the observational truth of the proverb, "If God gives somebody an office, he also gives him the mind necessary for it." Many people presumably have the qualifications required for the filling of higher positions, but they demonstrate, develop, and make them manifest only once they occupy these positions. Let us only remember the often grotesque accidents by which men in all spheres attain their positions. Is it not an incomprehensible miracle that there should not be an incomparably greater amount of incompetence than there actually is? No—precisely because we must assume that competence is actually very widely diffused.

This incommensurability between the quantity of superior competence and its possible use can perhaps be explained on the basis of the difference (discussed earlier) between the character of man as group member and as individual. The group as such is on a low level and is in need of leadership because its members generally contribute to it only those aspects of their personalities that are common to all. These aspects always are the coarser, more primitive, and more "subordinate" aspects. Hence, whenever men associate in groups, it serves the purpose of the group to organize in the form of subordination to a few. But this does not prevent any single member from individually possessing higher and finer qualities. But these are, precisely, individual qualities. They diverge in different directions, all of them irrelevant to any common group possession. They do not therefore raise the low level of the qualities in which all securely meet. It follows that the group as a whole needs a leader—that there are bound to be many subordinates and only few superordinates. It further follows that each individual group member is more highly qualified or more often capable of occupying a leading position than he is able to make use of in his capacity as a group member. The axiom, "Many are called but few are chosen," also applies to social structures. The antinomy is met by a priori limiting the number of persons who are considered "qualified" to occupy leading positions. Both the principle of estates and the contemporary social order implement this limitation by building classes one on top of the other in the form of a pyramid which contains increasingly fewer members as it approaches its top. The equal right of all to occupy all positions obviously makes it impossible to satisfy any justified claim whatever. Therefore, an estate or class arrangement of the social order intrinsically exerts a limiting selection. This selection is far from being determined by considering the individuals but on the contrary, shapes them.

It is questionable whether a socialist order could eventually do without such a priori super-subordination. Socialism postulates that any accidental chance be eliminated from the determination of positions to be occupied, and that individual qualification alone decide the attainment of positions. On the other hand, it also postulates that any talent develop "freely," that is, that it find the position commensurate with it. From this and from what has been pointed out before, it follows that in socialism there would be more superordinates than subordinates, more persons who command than execute commands. If freedom in the social sense refers to the adequate expression of any measure of individual strength and importance in the configuration of leading and following within the group, then freedom is here excluded from the start. We have seen that the conflict between man's individual wholeness and his nature as a group member, makes the harmonious proportion between personal qualification and social position impossible; and thus makes impossible the synthesis, on the basis of justice, between freedom and equality. And this conflict cannot be eliminted even by a socialist order, because it may be called a *logical* presupposition of society itself.

The New Individualism: The Incomparability of the Individual
I must limit myself to presenting these fragments in the field of the much-discussed
relation of socialism to individual freedom. I shall now sketch the peculiar form of
individualism that dissolved the eighteenth-century synthesis which based equality upon freedom, and freedom upon equality. In place of the equality which (it will
be recalled) expressed the deepest nature of man and which, at the same time, had
yet to be realized, it puts inequality. Just as equality in the eighteenth century, so
now inequality in the nineteenth, only needs freedom to emerge from its mere la-
tency and potentiality and to dominate all of human life. Freedom remains the
general denominator even if its correlate is the opposite of what it had been. It
seems that, as soon as the ego had become sufficiently strengthened by the feeling
of equality and generality, it fell back into the search for inequality. Yet this new
inequality was posited from within. First, there had been the thorough liberation
of the individual from the rusty chains of guild, birth right, and church. Now, the
individual that had thus become independent also wished to distinguish himself
from other individuals. The important point no longer was the fact that he was a free
individual as such, but that he was this specific, irreplaceable, given individual.

In this development, the modern tendency toward differentiation attains an
intensification that leads it away from the form it had just reached in the preceding century. But in stressing this contrast, one must not overlook the fact that
the fundamental direction, which actually pervades all of the modern period, remains identical. This direction may be expressed by stating that the individual
seeks his *self* as if he did not yet have it, and yet, at the same time, is certain that
his only fixed point is this self. In the light of the unbelievable expansion of theoretical and practical horizons, it is understandable that the individual should
ever more urgently seek such a fixed point, but that he should be no longer capable of finding it in anything external to himself. The double need for unquestionable clarity and for enigmatic unfathomableness—a need whose two components have been diverging ever further in the course of the development of
modern man—is satisfied, as if it were one homogeneous need, in the idea of the
ego and in the feeling of personality. Yet even socialism receives psychological
help from both a conceptually demonstrated rationalism and from very obscure,
possibly atavistic-communistic instincts. Thus, in the end, all relations to others
are merely stations on the road on which the ego arrives at itself. His relations
may be such stations in two respects. Either the ego may ultimately come to feel
that it is like the others because, living as it does on nothing but its own forces,
it may still need this encouraging and supporting consciousness. Or, on the contrary, it may be strong enough to bear the loneliness of its own quality, and may
hold that the only reason for a multitude of individuals to exist at all is the possibility of each component individual to measure his own incomparability and
the individuality of his own world by those of the others.

Historically, then, the tendency toward individualization, as I have already
suggested, leads from one ideal to a very different ideal. The first is the ideal of
fundamentally equal, even if wholly free and self-responsible personalities. The

other is that of the individuality which, precisely in its innermost nature, is incomparable and which is called upon to play an irreplaceable role. Intimations of the later ideal are already found in the eighteenth century, in Lessing, Herder, and Lavater. Lavater's Christ cult has been ascribed to his desire to individualize even God, and the intensification of this cult, to his quest for ever new images of Christ. Yet it is in a work of art that this form of individualism finds its first full elaboration—in Goethe's *Wilhem Meister*. *Wilhem Meister's Apprenticeship*, for the first time, shows a world which is based exclusively on the individual peculiarities of its protagonists and which is organized and developed only on this basis, quite irrespective of the fact that these protagonists are designed as types. For, however often they may be repeated in reality, it still is the essential significance of each of them that, in his ultimate ground, he is different from the other with whom fate has thrown him together. The *accent* of life and development does not lie on similarity but on absolute peculiarity. In *Wilhelm Meister's Travels*, the interest shifts from the individual to mankind—not in the sense of eighteenth-century abstract man-in-general, but of the collective, of the concrete totality of the living species. It is most remarkable to note how this individualism with its emphasis on individual incomparability and uniqueness, comes to the fore even on the basis of this interest in mankind. The individualistic requirement of specificity does not make for the valuation of total personality within society, but for the personality's objective achievement for the benefit of society. "Your general culture and all its institutions," Goethe says in the *Travels*, "are fooleries. Any man's task is to do *something* extraordinarily well, as no other man in his immediate environment can." This is the absolute opposite of the ideal of free and equal personalities that Fichte had compressed into this one sentence: "A rational being must simply be an individual—but precisely, *not* this or that particular individual." The older ideal had resulted in the imperative that the individual differentially characterized ego develop itself, through the moral process, into the pure, absolute ego, which was the philosophical crystalization of eighteenth-century "general man." In pointed antithesis to this position, Frederick Schlegel formulated the new individualism thus: "It is precisely individuality that is the original and eternal aspect of man; personality is less important. To see one's noblest calling in the cultivation and development of this individuality would be divine egoism."

The new individualism found its philosophical expression in Schleiermacher. For Schleiermacher, the moral task consists in each individual's *specific* representation of mankind. Each individual is a "compendium" of mankind; what is more, he is a synthesis of the forces that constitute the universe. Yet out of this material that is common to all, each individual creates an entirely unique form. And here, too, as in the earlier conception of individualism, reality also is the blueprint of what *ought* to be. Not only as something already existing is man incomparable, placed into a framework which can be filled out only by him. There also is another aspect: the realization of this incomparability, the filling-out of this framework, is a man's *moral* task. Each individual is *called* or destined to realize his own, incomparable image.

The great world-historical idea that not only the equality of men but also their differentiation represents a moral challenge, becomes the core of a new world view in Schleiermacher. The idea that the absolute only lives in the form of the individual, and that individuality is not a restriction of the infinite but its expression and mirror, makes the principle of the social division of labor part of the metaphysical ground of reality itself. To be sure, a differentiation that thus penetrates the last depths of the individual nature, easily exhibits a mystical-fatalistic character. ("This is the way thou hast to be; thou canst not escape thyself. *Sibyls and prophets have always said this*.") For this reason, it remained foreign to the bright rationalism of the Enlightenment and, on the other hand, recommended itself to Romanticism, with which Scheiermacher was very closely connected.

The new individualism might be called qualitative, in contrast with the quantitative individualism of the eighteenth century. Or it might be labeled the individualism of uniqueness [*Einzigkeit*] as against that of singleness [*Einzelheit*]. At any rate, Romanticism perhaps was the broadest channel through which it reached the consciousness of the nineteenth century. Goethe had created its artistic, and Schleiermacher its metaphysical basis: Romanticism supplied its sentimental, experiential foundation. After Herder (in whom therefore one of the mainsprings of qualitative individualism must be sought), the Romanticists were the first to absorb and to emphasize the particularity and uniqueness of historical realities. They deeply felt the important claim and the fascinating beauty of the Middle Ages, which had been neglected, and of the Orient, which had been despised by the activistic culture of a liberal Europe. In this sense, Novalis wanted his "one spirit" to transform itself into infinitely many alien spirits; the "one spirit inheres, as it were, in all objects it contemplates, and it feels the infinite, simultaneous sensations of a harmonious plurality." Above all, the Romanticists experienced the inner rhythm of the incomparability, of the specific claim, of the sharp qualitative differentiation of the single element, which the new individualism also sees in the *social* element, among the components of *society*. Here, too, Lavater is an interesting predecessor. Occasionally, his physiognomy so stubbornly pursues the special characteristics of man's visible and inner traits that he cannot find his way back to man's total individuality, but remains arrested in his interest in the completely individual and single. The Romantic mind, too, feels its way through an endless series of contrasts. At the instant it is being lived and experienced, each of them appears as something absolute, completed, self-contained, but at the next moment it is left behind. The Romanticist enjoys the very essence of each of these contrasts only in its difference from every other. "He who is glued to only one point," Frederick Schlegel says, "is nothing but a rational oyster." In the protean succession of its contrasts of mood and task and conviction and sentiment, the life of the Romanticist reflects the social scene in which each individual finds the sense of his existence— individual no less than social—only in contrast with others, in the personal uniqueness of his nature and his activities.

In its purely societal version, this conception of the task of the individual evidently points toward the constitution of a more comprehensive whole that is composed of the differentiated elements. The more specific the achievements (but also the needs) of the individuals, the more urgent becomes their reciprocal supplementation. In the same measure, the total organism which has grown out of the individuals engaged in the division of labor and which includes and mediates their interrelated effects and countereffects, shifts, so to speak, into a location high above them. The specificity of the individual thus requires a powerful political constitution which allocates his place to him, but in this fashion also becomes his master. It is for this reason that this individualism, which restricts freedom to a purely inward sense of the term, easily acquires an anti-liberal tendency. It thus is the complete antithesis of eighteenth-century individualism which, in full consistency with its notion of atomized and basically undifferentiated individuals, could not even conceive the idea of a collective as an organism that unifies heterogeneous elements. The eighteenth-century collective holds its elements together exclusively by means of the *law* that is above all of them. The function of this law is to restrict the freedom of the individual to the point where this freedom can coexist with that of every other individual. The godfathers of this law were, on the one hand, the laws of a mechanically construed nature and, on the other, law in the Roman-legal sense. By virtue of these two origins, the social scene in its concreteness entirely escapes eighteenth-century individualism. For, the social scene cannot be put together through the mere addition of isolated and equal individuals. It only arises from individual interactions within a division of labor. And it rises above these interactions as a unit which cannot be found in the individual, not even as some sort of proportionate quantity.

In terms of intellectual history, the doctrine of freedom and equality is the foundation of free competition; while the doctrine of differentiated personality is the basis of the division of labor. Eighteenth-century liberalism put the individual on his own feet: in the nineteenth, he was allowed to go as far as they would carry him. According to the new theory, the natural order of things saw to it that the unlimited competition of all resulted in the harmony of all interests, that the unrestricted striving after individual advantages resulted in the optimum welfare of the whole. This is the metaphysics with which the nature-optimism of the eighteenth century socially justified free competition. The metaphysical foundation of the division of labor was discovered with the individualism of difference, with the deepening of individuality to the point of the individual's incomparability, to which he is "called" both in his nature and in his achievement. The two great principles which operate, inseparably, in nineteenth-century economic theory and practice— competition and division of labor—thus appear to be the economic projections of the philosophical aspects of social individualism. Or inversely, these philosophical aspects appear to be the sublimations of the concrete economic forms of production of the period. Or, finally and more correctly, and thus suggesting the very possibility of this mutual interdependence: they both derive from one of the profound transformations of history which we cannot know in their essential nature and motivation but only in the manifestations they engender, as it were, when fusing with particular, contentually determined spheres of life.

To be sure, unlimited competition and individual specialization through division of labor have affected individual culture in a way that shows them not to be its most suitable promoters. Perhaps, however, beyond the economic form of cooperation between the two great sociological themes, individual and society (the only sociological themes that have thus far been realized), there yet exists a higher form that might be the latent ideal of our culture. I should prefer to believe, however, that the ideas of free personality as such and of unique personality as such, are not the last words of individualism. I should like to think that the efforts of mankind will produce ever more numerous and varied forms for the human personality to affirm itself and to demonstrate the value of its existence. In fortunate periods, these varied forms may order themselves into harmonious wholes. In doing so, their contradictions and conflicts will cease to be mere obstacles to mankind's efforts: they will also stimulate new demonstrations of the strength of these efforts and lead them to new creations.

〜 The Style of Life 〜

. . . If one compares our culture with that of a hundred years ago, then one may surely say—subject to many individual exceptions—that the things that determine and surround our lives, such as tools, means of transport, the products of science, technology and art, are extremely refined. Yet individual culture, at least in the higher strata, has not progressed at all to the same extent; indeed, it has even frequently declined. This does not need to be shown in detail. I only wish, therefore, to emphasize some aspects of it. Linguistic possibilities for expression, in German as well as in French, have become much more refined and subtle in the last hundred years. Not only do we now have Goethe's language, but in addition we have a large number of refinements, subtleties and individual modes of expression. Yet, if one looks at the speech and writing of individuals, they are on the whole increasingly less correct, less dignified and more trivial. In terms of content, the scope of objects of conversation has been widened during that time through advances in theory and practice, yet, none the less, it seems that conversation, both social as well as intimate and in the exchange of letters, is now more superficial, less interesting and less serious than at the end of the eighteenth century. The fact that machinery has become so much more sophisticated than the worker is part of this same process. How many workers are there today, even within large-scale industry, who are able to understand the machine with which they work, that is the mental effort invested in it? The same applies to military culture. The work of the individual soldier has essentially remained the same for a long time, and in some respects has even been reduced through modern methods of warfare. In contrast, not only the material instruments but, above all, the completely impersonal organization of the army have become extremely sophisticated and a real triumph of objective culture. In the purely intellectual sphere, even the best informed and most thoughtful persons work with a growing number of ideas, concepts and statements, the exact meaning and content of which they are not fully aware. The tremendous expansion of objective, available material of knowledge allows or even enforces the use of expressions that pass from hand to hand like sealed containers without the condensed content of thought actually enclosed within them being unfolded for the individual user. Just as our everyday life is surrounded more and more by objects of which we cannot conceive how much intellectual effort is expended in their production, so our mental and social communication is filled with symbolic terms, in which a comprehensive intellectuality is accumulated, but of which the individual mind need make only minimal use. The preponderance of objective over subjective culture that developed during the nineteenth century is reflected partly in the fact that the eighteenth century pedagogic ideal was focused upon the formation of man, that is upon a personal internal value, which was replaced during the nineteenth century, however, by the concept of 'education' in the sense of a body of objective knowledge and behavioural patterns. This discrepancy seems to widen steadily. Every day and from all sides, the wealth of objective culture increases, but the individual mind can enrich the forms and contents of its own development only by distancing itself still further from that culture and developing its own at a much slower pace.

How can we explain this phenomenon? If all the culture of things is, as we saw, nothing but a culture of people, so that we develop ourselves only by developing things, then what does that development, elaboration and intellectualization of objects mean, which seems to evolve out of these objects' own powers and norms without correspondingly developing the individual mind? This implies an accentuation of the enigmatic relationship which prevails between the social life and its products on the one hand and the fragmentary life-contents of individuals on the other. The labour of countless generations is embedded in language and custom, political constitutions and religious doctrines, literature and technology as objectified spirit from which everyone can take as much of it as they wish to or are able to, but no single individual is able to exhaust it all. Between the amount of this treasure and what is taken from it, there exists the most diverse and fortuitous relationships. The insignificance or irrationality of the individual's share leaves the substance and dignity of mankind's ownership unaffected, just as any physical entity is independent of its being individually perceived. Just as the content and significance of a book remains indifferent to a large or small, understanding or unresponsive, group of readers, so any cultural product confronts its cultural audience, ready to be absorbed by anyone but in fact taken up only sporadically. This concentrated mental labour of a cultural community is related to the degree to which it comes alive in individuals just as the abundance of possibilities is related to the limitations of reality. . . .

. . . The entire life-style of a community depends upon the relationship between the objectified culture and the culture of the subjects. I have already mentioned the significance of numerical factors. In the small community of a lower culture, this relationship will be almost one of perfect equality; the objective cultural possibilities will not extend much beyond the subjective cultural reality. An increase in the cultural level—particularly if it coincides with an enlargement of the group—will favour a discrepancy between both. The unique situation of the golden age of Athens was due to the fact that it was able to avoid this, except perhaps with reference to philosophy at its peak. Yet the size of the social circle does not yet in itself fully explain the divergence of the subjective and the objective factor. On the contrary, we must now search for the concrete, effective causes of this phenomenon.

. . . If we wish to confine the cause and its present magnitude in a single concept, then it is that of the division of labour, in terms of its importance within production as well as consumption. With regard to production, it has been emphasized often enough that the product is completed at the expense of the development of the producer. The increase in psycho-physical energies and skills, which is the result of specialized activity, is of little value for the total personality, which often even becomes stunted because of the diversion of energies that are indispensable for the harmonious growth of the self. In other cases, it develops as if cut off from the core of the personality, as a province with unlimited autonomy whose fruits do not flow back to the centre. Experience seems to show that the inner wholeness of the self basically evolves out of interaction with the uniformity and the completion of our life task.

The unity of an object is realized for us only by projecting our self into the object in order to shape it according to our image, so that the diversity of determinations grows into the unity of the 'ego.' In the same manner, the unity or lack of unity of the object that we create affects, in a psychological-practical sense, the corresponding formation of our personality. Whenever our energies do not produce something whole as a reflection of the total personality, then the proper relationship between subject and object is missing. The internal nature of our achievement is bound up with parts of achievements accomplished by others which are a necessary part of the totality, but it does not refer back to the producer. As a result, the inadequacy that develops between the worker's existential form and that of his product because of greater specialization easily serves to completely divorce the product from the labourer. Its meaning is not derived from the mind of the producer but from its relationship with products of a different origin. Because of its fragmentary character, the product lacks the spiritual determinacy that can be easily perceived in a product of labour that is wholly the work of a *single* person. The significance of the product is thus to be sought neither in the reflection of a subjectivity nor in the reflex of a creative spirit, but is to be found only in the objective achievement that leads away from the subject. . . .

. . . Modern man is so surrounded by nothing but impersonal objects that he becomes more and more conditioned into accepting the idea of an antiindividualistic social order—though, of course, he may also oppose it. Cultural objects increasingly evolve into an interconnected enclosed world that has increasingly fewer points at which the subjective soul can interpose its will and feelings. And this trend is supported by a certain autonomous mobility on the part of the objects. It has been pointed out that the merchant, the craftsman and the scholar are today much less mobile than they were at the time of the Reformation. Both material and intellectual objects today move independently, without personal representatives or transport. Objects and people have become separated from one another. Thought, work effort and skill, through their growing embodiment in objective forms, books and commodities, are able to move independently; recent progress in the means of transportation is only the realization or expression of this. By their independent, impersonal mobility, objects complete the final stage of their separation from people. The slot machine is the ultimate example of the mechanical character of the modern economy, since by means of the vending machine the human relationship is completely eliminated even in the retail trade where, for so long, the exchange of commodities was carried out between one person and another. The money equivalent is now exchanged against the commodity by a mechanical device. At another level, the same principle is also at work in the five cents store and in similar stores where the psycho-economic process runs not from the commodity to the price, but from the price to the commodity. The *a priori* equivalence of prices for all commodities will eliminate the numerous deliberations and examinations of the buyer, the numerous efforts and elucidations of the seller, so that the economic transaction will very quickly and indifferently pass through its personal channels.

This concurrent differentiation has the same effect as consecutive differentiation. Changes in fashion disrupt that inner process of acquisition and assimilation between subject and object which usually does not tolerate a discrepancy between the two. Fashion is one of those social forms which combines, to a particular degree, the attraction of differentiation and change with that of similarity and conformity. Every fashion is essentially the fashion of a social class; that is, it always indicates a social stratum which uses similarity of appearance to assert both its own inner unity and its outward differentiation from other social strata. As soon as the lower strata attempt to imitate the upper strata and adopt their fashion, the latter create a new one. Wherever fashions have existed they have sought to express social differences. Yet the social changes of the last hundred years have accelerated the pace of changes in fashion, on the one hand through the weakening of class barriers and frequent upward social mobility of individuals and sometimes even of whole groups to a higher stratum, and on the other through the predominance of the third estate. The first factor makes very frequent changes of fashion necessary on the part of leading strata because imitation by the lower strata rapidly robs fashions of their meaning and attraction. The second factor comes into operation because the middle class and the urban population are, in contrast to the conservatism of the highest strata and the peasantry, the groups in which there is great variability. Insecure classes and individuals, pressing for change, find in fashion, in the changing and contrasting forms of life, a pace that mirrors their own psychological movements. If contemporary fashions are much less extravagant and expensive and of much shorter duration than those of earlier centuries, then this is due partly to the fact that it must be made much easier for the lower strata to emulate these fashions and partly because fashion now originates in the wealthy middle class. Consequently, the spreading of fashion, both in breadth as well as speed, appears to be an independent movement, an objective and autonomous force which follows its own course independently of the individual. As long as fashions, and we are talking here not only of dress fashions, lasted longer and held relatively restricted social circles together, it was possible for a personal relationship to exist, as it were, between the individual and the particular content of the fashion. But the speed of change, that is its consecutive differentiation, and the growing extension of fashion dissolve this connection. What has happened to some other social shibboleths in recent times has also happened to fashion: it becomes less dependent upon the individual and the individual becomes less dependent upon fashion. Both develop like separate evolutionary worlds.

The concurrent and consecutive differentiation of omnipresent aspects of culture helps to establish their independent objectivity. I wish now to elaborate on one of the factors that brings about this development. I refer to the multitude of styles that confronts us when we view the objects that surround us, from the construction of buildings to the format of books, from sculptures to gardens and furniture with their juxtaposition of Renaissance and Japanese styles, Baroque and Empire, the style of Pre-Raphaelites and realistic functionalism. This is the result of the enlargement of our historical knowledge, which in turn is associated with modern man's penchant for change mentioned earlier. All historical understanding requires a flexibility of the mind, a capacity to empathize with and reconstruct casts of mind altogether different from one's own. For all history, however much it may deal with the visible, has meaning and becomes intelligible only as the history of the basic interests, emotions and strivings that lie at its roots. Even historical materialism is nothing but a psychological hypothesis. In order to grasp the content of history, a plasticity and pliability of the perceiving mind, a sublimated liking for change is necessary. The historicizing preference of our century, its unique ability to reproduce and bring back to life the most remote entities, both in time as well as in space, is only the internal aspect of the general development of its adaptability and its wide-ranging mobility. This is the root of the bewildering plurality of styles that are absorbed, presented and appreciated by our culture. If every style is like a language unto itself, with specific sounds, inflexions and syntax for expressing life, than as long as we know only a single style that forms our environment we are not aware of style as an autonomous factor with an independent life. No one speaking his mother tongue naively senses the objective law-like regularities that he has to consult, like something outside of his own subjectivity, in order to borrow from them resources for expressing his feelings—resources that obey independent norms. Rather, what one wants to express and what one expresses are, in this case, one and the same, and we experience not only our mother tongue but language as such as an independent entity only if we come to know foreign languages. In the same way, people who know only one uniform style which permeates their whole life will perceive this style as being identical with its *contents*. Since everything they create or contemplate is naturally expressed in this style, there are no psychological grounds for distinguishing it from the material of the formative and contemplative process or for contrasting the style as a form independent of the self. Only where a variety of given styles exists will one detach itself from its content so that its independence and specific significance gives us the freedom to choose between the one or the other. Through the differentiation of styles each individual style, and thus style in general, becomes something objective whose validity is independent of human subjects and their interests, activities, approval or disapproval. The fact that the entire visible environment of our cultural life has disintegrated into a plurality of styles dissolves that original relationship to style where subject and object are not yet separated. Instead, we are confronted with a world of expressive possibilities each developed according to their own norms, with a host of forms within which to express life as a whole. Thus these forms on the one side, and our subjectivity on the other, are like two parties between whom a purely fortuitous relationship of contacts, harmonies and disharmonies prevails.

Broadly speaking, this is the orbit in which the major process of objectification of modern culture is carried out through the division of labour and specialization in both its personal and objective sense. The total picture is composed of all these phenomena, in which the cultural content becomes an increasingly conscious *objective mind* in relation not only to recipients but also to producers. To the extent to which this objectification increases, the strange phenomenon from which we started our investigation becomes more comprehensible, namely that the cultural growth of the individual can lag considerably behind the cultural growth of tangible as well as functional and intellectual objects. . . .

The relationship between objectified mind and its evolution to the subjective mind is of extreme importance to every cultural community and especially with reference to its style of life. For if the importance of style lies in its ability to express any number and variety of contents in related forms, then the relationship between objective and subjective mind with reference to quantity, size and pace of development can be the same, even for quite different *contents* of the cultural mind. The general way of living, the framework that the social culture offers to individual impulses, is circumscribed by the following questions: is the inner life of the individual close to or estranged from the objective cultural evolution of his age? Does the individual experience this evolution, of which he has only a marginal comprehension, as superior, or does he consider his personal value to be higher than that of all reified mind? Are the objective, historically given elements an autonomous power within his own mental life, so that they and the specific core of his personality develop independently of each other? Is the soul, so to speak, master in its own house, or is there at least a harmony with regard to standards, meaning and rhythm established between its innermost life and what it has to absorb into that life as impersonal contents? These abstract formulations indicate the outline of innumerable concrete daily and life-long interests and moods, and in so doing also denote the extent to which the relationships between objective and subjective culture determine the style of life. . . .

. . . The nature of this relationship [objective and subjective culture] is clearly revealed by the fact that money transactions represent the preponderance of objective over subjective mind, as well as the reverse, independent enhancement and autonomous development of the subjective mind. The superior power of the culture of objects over the culture of individuals is the result of the unity and autonomous self-sufficiency that the objective culture has accomplished in modern times. Production, with its technology and its achievements, seems to be a cosmos with definite and, as it were, logical determinations and developments which confront the individual in the same way as fate confronts the instability and irregularity of our will. This formal autonomy, this inner compulsion, which unifies cultural contents into a mirror-image of the natural context, can be realized only through money. On the one hand, money functions as the system of articulations in this organism, enabling its elements to be shifted, establishing a relationship of mutual dependence of the elements, and transmitting all impulses through the system. On the other hand, money can be compared to the bloodstream whose continuous circulation permeates all the intricacies of the body's organs and unifies their functions by feeding them all to an equal extent. Thus money, as an intermediate link between man and thing, enables man to have, as it were, an abstract existence, a freedom from direct concern with things and from a direct relationship to them, without which our inner nature would not have the same chances of development. If modern man can, under favourable circumstances, secure an island of subjectivity, a secret, closed-off sphere of privacy—not in the social but in a deeper metaphysical sense—for his most personal existence, which to some extent compensates for the religious style of life of former times, then this is due to the fact that money relieves us to an ever-increasing extent of direct contact with things, while at the same time making it infinitely easier for us to dominate them and select from them what we require.

These counter-tendencies, once started, may press forward to an ideal of completely pure separation in which all the material contents of life become increasingly objective and impersonal, so that the remainder that cannot be reified becomes all the more personal, all the more the indisputable property of the self. A typical individual instance of this trend is the typewriter. Writing, an external concrete activity but one that still has a typically individual form, can now abandon this form in favour of mechanical uniformity. On the other hand, this has a dual advantage: first, the written page now conveys only its pure content without any support or disturbance from its written form, and second, it avoids revealing the most personal element which is so often true of handwriting, in superficial and unimportant as well as in the most intimate communications. No matter how socialistic all such mechanical contrivances may be, the remaining private property of the intellectual self becomes all the more jealously guarded. Clearly the expulsion of subjective spirituality from everything external is as hostile to the aesthetic ideal of life as it may be favourable to pure introspectiveness. Such a combination may explain why it is that aesthetically minded people despair of the world today as well as why a slight tension develops in subterranean forms—quite unlike those in the age of Savonarola—between these people and those who are concerned only with inner salvation. In so far as money is the symbol as well as the cause of making everything indifferent and of the externalization of everything that lends itself to such a process, it also becomes the gatekeeper of the most intimate sphere, which can then develop within its own limits.

Whether this will lead to personal refinement, distinctiveness and introspection or whether, on the contrary, the subjugated objects, in view of the ease with which they may be acquired, will gain control over men, depends no longer upon money but upon man himself. Here again the money economy reveals its formal affinity to a socialist society. For what is expected of socialism—release from the individual struggle for survival, secure access to life's necessities and access to the higher economic values—would probably exercise the same differentiating effect, such that a certain sector of society might rise to unprecedented heights of spirituality far removed from earthly concerns, while another sector might plunge into a correspondingly unprecedented practical materialism.

Money, by and large, is most influential in those parts of our life whose style is determined by the preponderance of objective over subjective culture. That it may also support its converse places the nature and extent of its historical power in the clearest light. In some respects, money may be compared to language, which also lends itself to the most divergent directions of thought and feeling. Money belongs to those forces whose peculiarity lies in a lack of peculiarity, but which, none the less, may colour life very differently because their mere formal, functional and quantitative nature is confronted with qualitatively determined contents and directions of life, and induces them to generate qualitatively new formations. The significance of money for the style of life is not negated but enhanced, not refuted but demonstrated by the fact that it favours *both* possible relations between the objective and the subjective mind.

PART TWO

EARLY- TO
MID-TWENTIETH-CENTURY
DEVELOPMENTS

~

CHAPTER FOUR

Charles Horton Cooley's Concept of the Looking-Glass Self and Its Applications

~ Introduction ~

Charles Horton Cooley (1864–1929) was born in Ann Arbor, Michigan, where he was to spend almost his entire life. As one of six children and the shy son of an ambitious and energetic father (Thomas McIntyre Cooley, who served on the Supreme Court of Michigan), Charles developed his own introspective style of achieving a successful life. Although Cooley studied engineering as an undergraduate at the University of Michigan, he had strong interests in history, philosophy, political economy, and sociology. As a result, he returned to the University of Michigan in 1890 for graduate study in political economy and sociology, although there was no formal instruction in sociology at Michigan at the time. In 1892, Cooley was hired as an instructor of sociology at the University of Michigan. Cooley's solid presence for thirty-five years at Michigan contributed to the new disciplines of sociology and social psychology. Cooley also participated in the formation of the American Sociological Society in 1905 and became its president in 1918.

The intellectual influences of the day—a philosophical and psychological approach to describing and analyzing behavior, Pragmatism, and Darwinism—all are apparent in Cooley's work. While Cooley and Weber observed similar dynamics operating in social interaction, Cooley's examination was more psychologically focused than Weber's (for example, compare Weber's theory of social action with Cooley's notion of the looking-glass self, described below). Cooley was well read in both the social sciences and literature, and his writing easily moves from one to the other. Another notable feature of his writing is that he describes the behavior of his own children when explaining processes of the self and social interaction; while we may regard this approach today as unscientific, his work nevertheless displays a respectable holism and keen observation of human behavior. Cooley's few but popular works include: *Human Nature and the Social Order* (1902); *Social Organization* (1909), in which he introduces the idea of the primary group; and *Social Process* (1918).

Within sociological social psychology, Cooley's most significant contribution is his idea of the looking-glass self, which you will be reading about in excerpts from his 1922 revised edition of *Human Nature and the Social Order*. The concept of the looking-glass self demonstrates that self-relation, or how one views oneself, is not a solitary phenomenon, but rather includes others. For example, if I think that I am a funny person but no one ever laughs at my jokes, then my view of myself as funny is likely to undergo revision. If I tell a particular joke that others find offensive, then I am likely to withdraw that joke in favor of another that gets my desired result—laughter—which indicates to me that others are enjoying my company and finding me humorous, which I find self-gratifying. Self-relation and self-expression are tied to others. The looking-glass self represents a bridge that overcomes the dualism between each person's sense of self in interaction. Along this train of thought, Cooley states in the reading, "'[S]ociety' and 'individuals' do not denote separable phenomena, but are simply collective and distributive aspects of the same thing."

Developmentally, Cooley theorizes that human beings possess an inherent tendency to reach out, interact, or socialize with those people and objects that surround them. What emerges from this process is a phenomenon that leads an infant increasingly to define him- or herself as distinct from other people and objects. Cooley states in the reading, "[T]here is nothing about personal feeling which sharply marks it off from other feeling; here as elsewhere we find no fences, but gradual transition, progressive differentiation." This process, he notes, is facilitated significantly by the act of communication:

> Where there is no communication there can be no nomenclature and no developed thought. What we call 'me,' 'mine,' or 'myself,' is, then, not something separate from the general life, but . . . a part whose interest arises from the very fact that it is both general and individual. That is, we care for it just because it is that common life, trying to impress itself upon the minds of others. 'I' is a militant social tendency, working to hold and enlarge its place in the general current of tendencies. (181)

From the beginning, and throughout one's life, the differentiated self is always in reference to a common ground. Whether it is in terms of defining oneself as distinct from others, noting differences of opinion, or whether one is harboring a secret place or project, all of these significant instances of differentiation include a shared foundation.

Since a unique sense of self, or self-feeling, is tied to relations with others who, in toto, comprise society, and society is a multilayered phenomenon of time and space, then self-feeling will also be affected by such influences as the history and class structure of society. Cooley observes that this bond is so strong that "[o]nly the imaginative student, in his best hours, can really free himself—and that only in some respects—from the limitations of his time. . . . We can scarcely rid ourselves of the impression that the way of life we are used to is the normal" (73). Cooley goes on to say that it is not unusual for an existing generation to look back upon those of a previous era and view them as "eccentric" and impressionable. The point is not only that hindsight is 20/20; the point is that every generation seems to have difficulty seeing beyond practices that may be presently interpreted as reasonable, but may actually be oppressive. In order to try to gain insight into this contradiction, Cooley (309) suggests that "[s]elf-feeling and social feeling must be harmonized and made to go abreast." Since self-feeling and social life are two sides of the same phenomenon, then personal freedom is tied to the relations that comprise society. The concept of the looking-glass self may inform the selves that comprise a society that freedom is not merely the individualistic "absence of constraint"; rather, the degree of freedom available to all is defined by the type of social order that is maintained by the collective activities of interacting selves. Cooley's comment about harmonizing self-feeling with social feeling is not intended to suggest that people should lose themselves in society, but rather that they should examine responsibly the effects of their actions on others.

Cooley's *Human Nature and the Social Order* not only orients the reader toward thinking in pragmatically nondualistic terms, but in its democratic vision, it is hopeful that humankind, with thoughtfulness and perseverance, will make progress along the lines of achieving freedom for more and more people.

～ Human Nature and the Social Order ～

A separate individual is an abstraction unknown to experience, and so likewise is society when regarded as something apart from individuals. The real thing is Human Life, which may be considered either in an individual aspect or in a social, that is to say a general, aspect; but is always, as a matter of fact, both individual and general. In other words, "society" and "individuals" do not denote separable phenomena, but are simply collective and distributive aspects of the same thing. . . .

. . . [A]ll the principal epochs of European history might be, and most of them are, spoken of as individualistic on one ground or another, and without departing from current usage of the word. The decaying Roman Empire was individualistic if a decline of public spirit and an every-man-for-himself feeling and practice constitute individualism. So also was the following period of political confusion. The feudal system is often regarded as individualistic, because of the relative independence and isolation of small political units—quite a different use of the word from the preceding—and after this come the Revival of Learning, the Renaissance, and the Reformation, which are all commonly spoken of, on still other grounds, as assertions of individualism. Then we reach the seventeenth and eighteenth centuries, sceptical, transitional, and, again, individualistic; and so to our own time, which many hold to be the most individualistic of all. . . .

. . . [W]herever you find life as society there you will find life as individuality, and *vice versa*.

I think, then, that the antithesis, society *versus* the individual, is false and hollow whenever used as a general or philosophical statement of human relations. Whatever idea may be in the minds of those who set these words and their derivatives over against each other, the notion conveyed is that of two separable entities or forces; and certainly such a notion is untrue to fact.

Most people not only think of individuals and society as more or less separate and antithetical, but they look upon the former as antecedent to the latter. That persons make society would be generally admitted as a matter of course; but that society makes persons would strike many as a startling notion, though I know of no good reason for looking upon the distributive aspect of life as more primary or causative than the collective aspect. The reason for the common impression appears to be that we think most naturally and easily of the individual phase of life, simply because it is a tangible one, the phase under which men appear to the senses, while the actuality of groups, of nations, of mankind at large, is realized only by the active and instructed imagination. We ordinarily regard society, so far as we conceive it at all, in a vaguely material aspect, as an aggregate of physical bodies, not as the vital whole which it is; and so, of course, we do not see that it may be as original or causative as anything else. . . .

. . . [T]he view which I regard as sound, is that individuality is neither prior in time nor lower in moral rank than sociality; but that the two have always existed side by side as complementary aspects of the same thing, and that the line of progress is from a lower to a higher type of both, not from the one to the other. If the word social is applied only to the higher forms of mental life it should, as already suggested, be opposed not to individual, but to animal, sensual, or some other word implying mental or moral inferiority. If we go back to a time when the state of our remote ancestors was such that we are not willing to call it social, then it must have been equally undeserving to be described as individual or personal; that is to say, they must have been just as inferior to us when viewed separately as when viewed collectively. To question this is to question the vital unity of human life.

The life of the human species, like that of other species, must always have been both general and particular, must always have had its collective and distributive aspects. The plane of this life has gradually risen, involving, of course, both the aspects mentioned. . . .

Can we separate the individual from society? Only in an external sense. If you go off alone into the wilderness you take with you a mind formed in society, and you continue social intercourse in your memory and imagination, or by the aid of books. This, and this only, keeps humanity alive in you, and just in so far as you lose the power of intercourse your mind decays. Long solitude, as in the case of sheepherders on the Western plains, or prisoners in solitary confinement, often produces imbecility. This is especially likely to happen with the uneducated, whose memories are not well stored with material for imaginative intercourse.

At times in the history of Christianity, and of other religions also, hermits have gone to dwell in desert places, but they have usually kept up some communication with one another and with the world outside, certain of them, like St. Jerome, having been famous letter-writers. Each of them, in fact, belonged to a social system from which he drew ideals and moral support. We may suspect that St. Simeon Stylites, who dwelt for years on top of a pillar, was not unaware that his austerity was visible to others.

A castaway who should be unable to retain his imaginative hold upon human society might conceivably live the life of an intelligent animal, exercising his mind upon the natural conditions about him, but his distinctively human faculties would certainly be lost, or in abeyance.

Is the individual in any sense free, or is he a mere piece of society?

Yes, he is free, as I conceive the matter, but it is an organic freedom, which he works out in co-operation with others, not a freedom to do things independently of society. It is team-work. He has freedom to function in his own way, like the quarter-back, but, in one way or another, he has to play the game as life brings him into it.

The evolutionary point of view encourages us to believe that life is a creative process, that we are really building up something new and worth while, and that the human will is a part of the creative energy that does this. Every individual has his unique share in the work, which no one but himself can discern and perform. Although his life flows into him from the hereditary and social past, his being as a whole is new, a fresh organization of life. Never any one before had the same powers and opportunities that you have, and you are free to use them in your own way.

It is, after all, only common sense to say that we exercise our freedom through co-operation with others. If you join a social group—let us say a dramatic club— you expect that it will increase your freedom, give your individual powers new stimulus and opportunity for expression. And why should not the same principle apply to society at large? It is through a social development that mankind has emerged from animal bondage into that organic freedom, wonderful though far from complete, that we now enjoy. . . .

There appears to be quite a general impression that children are far more subject to control through suggestion or mechanical imitation than grown-up people are; in other words, that their volition is less active. I am not at all sure that this is the case: their choices are, as a rule, less stable and consistent than ours, their minds have less definiteness of organization, so that their actions appear less rational and more externally determined; but on the other hand they have less of the mechanical subjection to habit that goes with a settled character. . . .

. . . [A]dults imitate at longer range, as it were, so that the imitative character of their acts is not so obvious. They come into contact with more sorts of persons, largely unknown to one another, and have access to a greater variety of suggestions in books. Accordingly they present a deceitful appearance of independence simply because we do not see their models.

Though we may be likely to exaggerate the difference between children and adults as regards the sway of suggestive influences, there is little danger of our overestimating the importance of these in the life of mankind at large. The common impression among those who have given no special study to the matter appears to be that suggestion has little part in the mature life of a rational being; and though the control of involuntary impulses is recognized in tricks of speech and manner, in fads, fashions, and the like, it is not perceived to touch the more important points of conduct. The fact, however, is that the main current of our thought is made up of impulses absorbed without deliberate choice from the life about us, or else arising from hereditary instinct, or from habit; while the function of higher thought and of will is to organize and apply these impulses. To revert to an illustration already suggested, the voluntary is related to the involuntary very much as the captain of a ship is related to the seamen and subordinate officers. Their work is not altogether of a different sort from his, but is of a lower grade in a mental series. He supplies the higher sort of co-ordination, but the main bulk of the activity is of the mentally lower order.

The chief reason why popular attention should fix itself upon voluntary thought and action, and tend to overlook the involuntary, is that choice is acutely conscious, and so must, from its very nature, be the focus of introspective thought. Because he *is* an individual, a specialized, contending bit of psychical force, a man very naturally holds his will, in its individual aspect, to be of supreme moment. If we did not feel a great importance in the things we do we could not will to do them. And in the life of other people voluntary action seems supreme, for very much the same reasons that it does in our own. It is always in the foreground, active, obvious, intrusive, the thing that creates differences and so fixes the attention. We notice nothing except through contrast; and accordingly the mechanical control of suggestion, affecting all very much alike, is usually unperceived. As we do not notice the air, precisely because it is always with us, so, for the same reason, we do not notice a prevailing mode of dress. In like manner we are ignorant of our local accent and bearing, and are totally unaware, for the most part, of all that is common to our time. . . .

. . . So long as an idea is uncontradicted, not felt to be in any way inconsistent with others, we take it as a matter of course. It is a truth, though hard for us to realize, that if we had lived in Dante's time we should have believed in a material Hell, Purgatory, and Paradise, as he did, and that our doubts of this, and of many other things which his age did not question, have nothing to do with our natural intelligence, but are made possible and necessary by competing ideas which the growth of knowledge has enabled us to form. Our particular minds or wills are members of a slowly growing whole, and at any given moment are limited in scope by the state of the whole, and especially of those parts of the whole with which they are in most active contact. Our thought is never isolated, but always some sort of a response to the influences around us, so that we can hardly have thoughts that are not in some way aroused by communication. Will—free will if you choose—is thus a co-operative whole, not an aggregation of disconnected fragments, and the freedom of the individual is freedom under law, like that of the good citizen, not anarchy. We learn to speak by the exercise of will, but no one, I suppose, will assert that an infant who hears only French is free to learn English. . . .

. . . [N]ational habits and sentiments, . . . so completely envelop us that we are for the most part unaware of them. The more thoroughly American a man is the less he can perceive Americanism. He will embody it; all he does, says, or writes, will be full of it; but he can never truly see it, simply because he has no exterior point of view from which to look at it. If he goes to Europe he begins to get by contrast some vague notion of it, though he will never be able to see just what it is that makes futile his attempts to seem an Englishman, a German, or an Italian. Our appearance to other peoples is like one's own voice, which one never hears quite as others hear it. . . .

. . . Only the imaginative student, in his best hours, can really free himself—and that only in some respects—from the limitations of his time and see things from a height. For the most part the people of other epochs seem strange, outlandish, or a little insane. We can scarcely rid ourselves of the impression that the way of life we are used to is the normal, and that other ways are eccentric. Doctor Sidis holds that the people of the Middle Ages were in a quasi-hypnotic state, and instances the crusades, dancing manias, and the like. But the question is, would not our own time, viewed from an equal distance, appear to present the signs of abnormal suggestibility? Will not the intense preoccupation with material production, the hurry and strain of our cities, the draining of life into one channel, at the expense of breadth, richness, and beauty, appear as mad as the crusades, and perhaps of a lower type of madness? . . .

. . . When a child is, say, five months old, no doubt can remain, in most cases, that the smile has become an expression of pleasure in the movements, sounds, touches, and general appearance of other people. It would seem, however, that personal feeling is not at first clearly differentiated from pleasures of sight, sound, and touch of other origin. . . . Indeed, there is nothing about personal feeling which sharply marks it off from other feeling; here as elsewhere we find no fences, but gradual transition, progressive differentiation. . . .

. . . It is the same throughout life; alone one is like fireworks without a match: he cannot set himself off, but is a victim of *ennui*, the prisoner of some tiresome train of thought that holds his mind simply by the absence of a competitor. A good companion brings release and fresh activity, the primal delight in a fuller existence. So with the child: what excitement when visiting children come! He shouts, laughs, jumps about, produces his playthings and all his accomplishments. He needs to express himself, and a companion enables him to do so. The shout of another boy in the distance gives him the joy of shouting in response.

But the need is for something more than muscular or sensory activities. There is also a need of feeling, an overflowing of personal emotion and sentiment, set free by the act of communication. By the time a child is a year old the social feeling that at first is indistinguishable from sensuous pleasure has become much specialized upon persons, and from that time onward to call it forth by reciprocation is a chief aim of his life. . . .

I take it that the child has by heredity a generous capacity and need for social feeling, rather too vague and plastic to be given any specific name like love. It is not so much any particular personal emotion or sentiment as the undifferentiated material of many: perhaps sociability is as good a word for it as any.

And this material, like all other instinct, allies itself with social experience to form, as time goes on, a growing and diversifying body of personal thought, in which the phases of social feeling developed correspond, in some measure, to the complexity of life itself. It is a process of organization, involving progressive differentiation. . . .

. . . It is by intercourse with others that we expand our inner experience. In other words, and this is the point of the matter, the personal idea consists at first and in all later development, of a sensuous element or symbol with which is connected a more or less complex body of thought and sentiment; the whole social in genesis, formed by a series of communications. . . .

. . . [W]e do not think "I" except with reference to a complementary thought of other persons; it is an idea developed by association and communication. . . .

. . . The idea of a division on this line appears to flow from a vague presumption that personal ideas must have a separateness answering to that of material bodies. . . .

Opposition between one's self and some one else is also a very real thing; but this opposition, instead of coming from a separateness like that of material bodies, is, on the contrary, dependent upon a measure of community between one's self and the disturbing other, so that the hostility between one's self and a social person may always be described as hostile sympathy. And the sentiments connected with opposition, like resentment, pertain neither to myself, considered separately, nor to the symbol of the other person, but to ideas including both. I shall discuss these matters at more length in subsequent chapters; the main thing here is to note that personal opposition does not involve mechanical separateness, but arises from the emphasis of inconsistent elements in ideas having much in common. . . .

It is well to say at the outset that by the word "self" in this discussion is meant simply that which is designated in common speech by the pronouns of the first person singular, "I," "me," "my," "mine," and "myself." "Self" and "ego" are used by metaphysicians and moralists in many other senses, more or less remote from the "I" of daily speech and thought, and with these I wish to have as little to do as possible. What is here discussed is what psychologists call the empirical self, the self that can be apprehended or verified by ordinary observation. I qualify it by the word social not as implying the existence of a self that is not social—for I think that the "I" of common language always has more or less distinct reference to other people. . . .

. . . The distinctive thing in the idea for which the pronouns of the first person are names is apparently a characteristic kind of feeling which may be called the my-feeling or sense of appropriation. Almost any sort of ideas may be associated with this feeling, and so come to be named "I" or "mine," but the feeling, and that alone it would seem, is the determining factor in the matter. . . .

I do not mean that the feeling aspect of the self is necessarily more important that any other, but that it is the immediate and decisive sign and proof of what "I" is; there is no appeal from it; if we go behind it it must be to study its history and conditions. . . .

The emotion or feeling of self may be regarded as instinctive, and was doubtless evolved in connection with its important function in stimulating and unifying the special activities of individuals. It is thus very profoundly rooted in the history of the human race and apparently indispensable to any plan of life at all similar to ours. It seems to exist in a vague though vigorous form at the birth of each individual, and, like other instinctive ideas or germs of ideas, to be defined and developed by experience, becoming associated, or rather incorporated, with muscular, visual, and other sensations; with perceptions, apperceptions, and conceptions of every degree of complexity and of infinite variety of content; and, especially, with personal ideas. Meantime the feeling itself does not remain unaltered, but undergoes differentiation and refinement just as does any other sort of crude innate feeling. Thus, while retaining under every phase its characteristic tone of flavor, it breaks up into innumerable self-sentiments. . . .

. . . [I]nstinctive self-feeling is doubtless connected in evolution with its important function in stimulating and unifying the special activities of individuals. It appears to be associated chiefly with ideas of the exercise of power, of being a cause, ideas that emphasize the antithesis between the mind and the rest of the world. The first definite thoughts that a child associates with self-feeling are probably those of his earliest endeavors to control visible objects—his limbs, his playthings, his bottle, and the like. Then he attempts to control the actions of the persons about him, and so his circle of power and of self-feeling widens without interruption to the most complex objects of mature ambition. Although he does not say "I" or "my" during the first year or two, yet he expresses so clearly by his actions the feeling that adults associate with these words that we cannot deny him a self even in the first weeks. . . .

That the "I" of common speech has a meaning which includes some sort of reference to other persons is involved in the very fact that the word and the ideas it stands for are phenomena of language and the communicative life. It is doubtful whether it is possible to use language at all without thinking more or less distinctly of some one else, and certainly the things to which we give names and which have a large place in reflective thought are almost always those which are impressed upon us by our contact with other people. Where there is no communication there can be no nomenclature and no developed thought. What we call "me," "mine," or "myself" is, then, not something separate from the general life, but the most interesting part of it, a part whose interest arises from the very fact that it is both general and individual. That is, we care for it just because it is that phase of the mind that is living and striving in the common life, trying to impress itself upon the minds of others. "I" is a militant social tendency, working to hold and enlarge its place in the general current of tendencies. . . .

If a thing has no relation to others of which one is conscious he is unlikely to think of it at all, and if he does think of it he cannot, it seems to me, regard it as emphatically *his*. The appropriative sense is always the shadow, as it were, of the common life, and when we have it we have a sense of the latter in connection with it. Thus, if we think of a secluded part of the woods as "ours," it is because we think, also, that others do not go there. As regards the body I doubt if we have a vivid my-feeling about any part of it which is not thought of, however vaguely, as having some actual or possible reference to some one else. Intense self-consciousness regarding it arises along with instincts or experiences which connect it with the thought of others. Internal organs, like the liver, are not thought of as peculiarly ours unless we are trying to communicate something regarding them, as, for instance, when they are giving us trouble and we are trying to get sympathy.

"I," then, is not all of the mind, but a peculiarly central, vigorous, and well-knit portion of it, not separate from the rest but gradually merging into it, and yet having a certain practical distinctness, so that a man generally shows clearly enough by his language and behavior what his "I" is as distinguished from thoughts he does not appropriate. It may be thought of, as already suggested, under the analogy of a central colored area on a lighted wall. It might also, and perhaps more justly, be compared to the nucleus of a living cell, not altogether separate from the surrounding matter, out of which indeed it is formed, but more active and definitely organized.

The reference to other persons involved in the sense of self may be distinct and particular, as when a boy is ashamed to have his mother catch him at something she has forbidden, or it may be vague and general, as when one is ashamed to do something which only his conscience, expressing his sense of social responsibility, detects and disapproves; but it is always there. There is no sense of "I," as in pride or shame, without its correlative sense of you, or he, or they. Even the miser gloating over his hidden gold can feel the "mine" only as he is aware of the world of men over whom he has secret power; and the case is very similar with all kinds of hid treasure. Many painters, sculptors, and writers have loved to withhold their work from the world, fondling it in seclusion until they were quite done with it; but the delight in this, as in all secrets, depends upon a sense of the value of what is concealed.

I remarked above that we think of the body as "I" when it comes to have social function or significance, as when we say "I am looking well to-day," or "I am taller than you are." We bring it into the social world, for the time being, and for that reason put our self-consciousness into it. Now it is curious, though natural, that in precisely the same way we may call any inanimate object "I" with which we are identifying our will and purpose. This is notable in games, like golf or croquet, where the ball is the embodiment of the player's fortunes. You will hear a man say, "I am in the long grass down by the third tee," or "I am in position for the middle arch." So a boy flying a kite will say "I am higher than you," or one shooting at a mark will declare that he is just below the bullseye.

In a very large and interesting class of cases the social reference takes the form of a somewhat definite imagination of how one's self—that is any idea he appropriates—appears in a particular mind, and the kind of self-feeling one has is determined by the attitude toward this attributed to that other mind. A social self of this sort might be called the reflected or looking-glass self:

> "Each to each a looking-glass
> Reflects the other that doth pass."

As we see our face, figure, and dress in the glass, and are interested in them because they are ours, and pleased or otherwise with them according as they do or do not answer to what we should like them to be; so in imagination we perceive in another's mind some thought of our appearance, manners, aims, deeds, character, friends, and so on, and are variously affected by it.

A self-idea of this sort seems to have three principal elements: the imagination of our appearance to the other person; the imagination of his judgment of that appearance; and some sort of self-feeling, such as pride or mortification. The comparision with a looking-glass hardly suggests the second element, the imagined judgment, which is quite essential. The thing that moves us to pride or shame is not the mere mechanical reflection of ourselves, but an imputed sentiment, the imagined effect of this reflection upon another's mind. This is evident from the fact that the character and weight of that other, in whose mind we see ourselves, makes all the difference with our feeling. We are ashamed to seem evasive in the presence of a straightforward man, cowardly in the presence of a brave one, gross in the eyes of a refined one, and so on. We always imagine, and in imagining share, the judgments of the other mind. A man will boast to one person of an action—say some sharp transaction in trade—which he would be ashamed to own to another.

It should be evident that the ideas that are associated with self-feeling and form the intellectual content of the self cannot be covered by any simple description, as by saying that the body has such a part in it, friends such a part, plans so much, etc., but will vary indefinitely with particular temperaments and environments. The tendency of the self, like every aspect of personality, is expressive of far-reaching hereditary and social factors, and is not to be understood or predicted except in connection with the general life. Although special, it is in no way separate—speciality and separateness are not only different but contradictory, since the former implies connection with a whole. The object of self-feeling is affected by the general course of history, by the particular development of nations, classes, and professions, and other conditions of this sort.

The truth of this is perhaps most decisively shown in the fact that even those ideas that are most generally associated or colored with the "my" feeling, such as one's idea of his visible person, of his name, his family, his intimate friends, his property, and so on, are not universally so associated, but may be separated from the self by peculiar social conditions. Thus the ascetics, who have played so large a part in the history of Christianity and of other religions and philosophies, endeavored not without success to divorce their appropriative thought from all material surroundings, and especially from their physical persons, which they sought to look upon as accidental and degrading circumstances of the soul's earthly sojourn. In thus estranging themselves from their bodies, from property and comfort, from domestic affections—whether of wife or child, mother, brother or sister—and from other common objects of ambition, they certainly gave a singular direction to self-feeling, but they did not destroy it: there can be no doubt that the instinct, which seems imperishable so long as mental vigor endures, found other ideas to which to attach itself; and the strange and uncouth forms which ambition took in those centuries when the solitary, filthy, idle, and sense-tormenting anchorite was a widely accepted ideal of human life, are a matter of instructive study and reflection. Even in the highest exponents of the ascetic ideal, like St. Jerome, it is easy to see that the discipline, far from effacing the self, only concentrated its energy in lofty and unusual channels. The self-idea may be that of some great moral reform, of a religious creed, of the destiny of one's soul after death, or even a cherished conception of the deity. Thus devout writers, like George Herbert and Thomas à Kempis, often address my God, not at all conventionally as I conceive the matter, but with an intimate sense of appropriation. And it has been observed that the demand for the continued and separate existence of the individual soul after death is an expression of self-feeling. . . .

. . . The view that "self" and the pronouns of the first person are names which the race has learned to apply to an instinctive attitude of mind, and which each child in turn learns to apply in a similar way, was impressed upon me by observing my child M. at the time when she was learning to use these pronouns. When she was two years and two weeks old I was surprised to discover that she had a clear notion of the first and second persons when used possessively. When asked, "Where is your nose?" she would put her hand upon it and say "my." She also understood that when some one else said "my" and touched an object, it meant something opposite to what was meant when she touched the same object and used the same word. Now, any one who will exercise his imagination upon the question how this matter must appear to a mind having no means of knowing anything about "I" and "my" except what it learns by hearing them used, will see that it should be very puzzling. Unlike other words, the personal pronouns have, apparently, no uniform meaning, but convey different and even opposite ideas when employed by different persons. It seems remarkable that children should master the problem before they arrive at considerable power of abstract reasoning. . . .

It seemed to me that she might have learned the use of these pronouns about as follows. The self-feeling had always been there. From the first week she had wanted things and cried and fought for them. She had also become familiar by observation and opposition with similar appropriative activities on the part of R. Thus she not only had the feeling herself, but by associating it with its visible expression had probably divined it, sympathized with it, resented it, in others. Grasping, tugging, and screaming would be associated with the feeling in her own case and would recall the feeling when observed in others. They would constitute a language, precedent to the use of first-personal pronouns, to express the self-idea. All was ready, then, for the word to name this experience. She now observed that R., when contentiously appropriating something, frequently exclaimed, *"my," "mine," "give it to me," "I* want it," and the like. Nothing more natural, then, than that she should adopt these words as names for a frequent and vivid experience with which she was already familiar in her own case and had learned to attribute to others. Accordingly it appeared to me, as I recorded in my notes at the time, that "'my' and 'mine' are simply names for concrete images of appropriativeness," embracing both the appropriative feeling and its manifestation. If this is true the child does not at first work out the I-and-you idea in an abstract form. The first-personal pronoun is a sign of a concrete thing after all, but that thing is not primarily the child's body, or his muscular sensations as such, but the phenomenon of aggressive appropriation, practised by himself, witnessed in others. . . .

. . . [T]he meaning of "I" and "mine" is learned in the same way that the meanings of hope, regret, chagrin, disgust, and thousands of other words of emotion and sentiment are learned: that is, by having the feeling, imputing it to others in connection with some kind of expression, and hearing the word along with it. As to its communication and growth the self-idea is in no way peculiar that I see, but essentially like other ideas. In its more complex forms, such as are expressed by "I" in conversation and literature, it is a social sentiment, or type of sentiments, defined and developed by intercourse. . . .

. . . And, as I have suggested, even in adult life, "I," "me," and "mine" are applied with a strong sense of their meaning only to things distinguished as peculiar to us by some sort of opposition or contrast. They always imply social life and relation to other persons. That which is most distinctively mine is very private, it is true, but it is that part of the private which I am cherishing in antithesis to the rest of the world, not the separate but the special. The aggressive self is essentially a militant phase of the mind, having for its apparent function the energizing of peculiar activities, and, although the militancy may not go on in an obvious, external manner, it always exists as a mental attitude. . . .

. . . The process by which self-feeling of the looking-glass sort develops in children may be followed without much difficulty. Studying the movements of others as closely as they do they soon see a connection between their own acts and changes in those movements; that is, they perceive their own influence or power over persons. The child appropriates the visible actions of his parent or nurse, over which he finds he has some control, in quite the same way as he appropriates one of his own members or a plaything, and he will try to do things with this new possession, just as he will with his hand or his rattle. A girl six months old will attempt in the most evident and deliberate manner to attract attention to herself, to set going by her actions some of those movements of other persons that she has appropriated. She has tasted the joy of being a cause, of exerting social power, and wishes more of it. She will tug at her mother's skirts, wriggle, gurgle, stretch out her arms, etc., all the time watching for the hoped-for effect. . . .

The young performer soon learns to be different things to different people, showing that he begins to apprehend personality and to foresee its operation. If the mother or nurse is more tender than just she will almost certainly be "worked" by systematic weeping. . . .

Progress from this point is chiefly in the way of a greater definiteness, fulness, and inwardness in the imagination of the other's state of mind. A little child thinks of and tries to elicit certain visible or audible phenomena, and does not go back of them; but what a grown-up person desires to produce in others is an internal, invisible condition which his own richer experience enables him to imagine, and of which expression is only the sign. Even adults, however, make no separation between what other people think and the visible expression of that thought. They imagine the whole thing at once, and their idea differs from that of a child chiefly in the comparative richness and complexity of the elements that accompany and interpret the visible or audible sign. There is also a progress from the naïve to the subtle in socially self-assertive action. A child obviously and simply, at first, does things for effect. Later there is an endeavor to suppress the appearance of doing so; affection, indifference, contempt, etc., are simulated to hide the real wish to affect the self-image. It is perceived that an obvious seeking after good opinion is weak and disagreeable.

I doubt whether there are any regular stages in the development of social self-feeling and expression common to the majority of children. The sentiments of self develop by imperceptible gradations out of the crude appropriative instinct of new-born babes, and their manifestations vary indefinitely in different cases. . . .

. . . In so far as a man amounts to anything, stands for anything, is truly an individual, he has an ego about which his passions cluster, and to aggrandize which must be a principal aim with him. But the very fact that the self is the object of our schemes and endeavors makes it a centre of mental disturbance: its suggestions are of effort, responsibility, doubt, hope, and fear. Just as a man cannot enjoy the grass and trees in his own grounds with quite the peace and freedom that he can those abroad, because they remind him of improvements that he ought to make and the like; so any part of the self is, in its nature, likely to be suggestive of exertion rather than rest. Moreover, it would seem that self-feeling, though pleasant in normal duration and intensity, is disagreeable in excess, like any other sort of feeling. One reason why we get tired of ourselves is simply that we have exhausted our capacity of experiencing with pleasure a certain kind of emotion. . . .

. . . [T]he passion of self-aggrandizement is persistent but plastic; it will never disappear from a vigorous mind, but may become morally higher by attaching itself to a larger conception of what constitutes the self. . . .

. . . Persons of great ambitions, or of peculiar aims of any sort, lie open to disorders of self-feeling, because they necessarily build up in their minds a self-image which no ordinary social environment can understand or corroborate, and which must be maintained by hardening themselves against immediate influences, enduring or repressing the pains of present depreciation, and cultivating in imagination the approval of some higher tribunal. If the man succeeds in becoming indifferent to the opinions of his neighbors he runs into another danger, that of a distorted and extravagant self of the pride sort, since by the very process of gaining independence and immunity from the stings of depreciation and misunderstanding, he has perhaps lost that wholesome deference to some social tribunal. . . .

. . . It is true that the self has great adaptability. Hardship does not necessarily impair it; in fact strenuous occupation is one of its needs. But there are other needs, equally essential, whose gratification is often denied by the conditions of life. Leaving aside individual peculiarities, the additional needs shared by all of us may perhaps be summed up in three, self-expression, appreciation, and a reasonable security. No man can or ought to be content unless he has a chance to work out his personality, to form, strive for, and gratify reasonable ambitions. In connection with this, indeed really as a part of it, he needs fellowship and that appreciation by others which gives his self social corroboration and support. And, finally, he cannot take much satisfaction in life unless he feels that he is not at the mercy of chance or of others' wills, but has a fair prospect, if he strives steadily, of maintaining his position. No one can study sympathetically the actual state of men and women in our social order without being convinced that large numbers of them are denied some or all of these fundamentals of human living.

We find, for example, workmen who have no security in their work, but are hired and fired arbitrarily, or perhaps lose their occupation altogether for reasons having no apparent relation to their merit. Very commonly their work itself does not admit of that exercise of the will and growth in skill and power which keeps the sense of self alive and interested. And if there is nothing in the work itself, or in appreciation by his employer, to gratify the self-feeling of the worker, it may well be that resentment and occasional rebellion are the only way to preserve his self-respect. One of the great reasons for the popularity of strikes is that they give the suppressed self a sense of power. For once the human tool knows itself a man, able to stand up and speak a word or strike a blow. Many occupations, also, are of an irregular or nomadic character which makes it impossible for men and women to have that primary self-expression which we get from a family and a settled home.

The immigrant has for the most part been treated purely as a source of labor, with little or no regard to the fact that he is a human being, with a self like the rest of us. There is nothing less to our credit than our neglect of the foreigner and his children, unless it be the arrogance most of us betray when we set out to "americanize" him.

The negro question includes a similar situation. There is no understanding it without realizing the kind of self-feeling a race must have who, in a land where men are supposed to be equal, find themselves marked with indelible inferiority. And so with many other classes; with offenders against the law, for example, whom we often turn into hardened criminals by a treatment which destroys their self-respect—or rather convinces them that their only chance of self-respect is in defiance of authority. The treatment of children, in and out of school, involves similar questions, and so of domestic workers, married women, and other sorts of people more or less subject to the arbitrary will of others. In general only a resolute exercise of sympathetic imagination, informed by study of the facts, will give us a right point of view. . . .

. . . The trouble with our industrial relations is not the mere extent of competition, but the partial lack of established laws, rules, and customs, to determine what is right and fair in it. This partial lack of standards is connected with the rapid changes in industry and industrial relations among men, with which the development of law and of moral criteria has by no means kept pace. Hence there arises great uncertainty as to what some persons and classes may rightly and fairly require of other persons and classes; and this uncertainty lets loose angry imaginations. . . .

An ideal social system . . . would be one in which the work of individuals in each occupation, the work of occupations in relation to one another, that of class in relation to class and of nation in relation to nation, should be motivated by a desire to excel, this desire being controlled and subordinated by allegiance to common social ideals.

I have little faith in any system of motives which does not leave room for personal and group ambitions. Self-feeling and social feeling must be harmonized and made to go abreast. . . .

The question of right and wrong, as it presents itself to any particular mind, is, then, a question of the completest practicable organization of the impulses with which that mind finds itself compelled to deal. The working out of the right conclusion may be compared to the process by which a deliberative body comes to a conclusion upon some momentous public measure. Time must be given for all the more important passions, prejudices, traditions, interests, and the like, to be urged upon the members with such cogency as their advocates can give them, and for attempts to harmonize these conflicting forces so that a measure can be framed which the body can be induced to pass. And when a decision is finally reached there is a sense of relief, the greater in proportion as the struggle has been severe, and a tendency, even on the part of the opposition, to regard the matter as settled. Those people who cannot achieve moral unity, but have always a sense of two personalities warring within them, may be compared to certain countries in whose assemblies political parties are so embittered that they never come to an understanding with one another.

The mental process is, of course, only the proximate source of the idea of right, the conflict by which the competitive strength of the various impulses is measured, and some combination of them achieved; behind it is the whole history of the race and of the individual, in which impulses are rooted. Instinctive passions, like love, ambition, and revenge; the momentum of habit, the need of change, personal ascendencies, and the like, all have their bearing upon the final synthesis. . . .

. . . Those who think as I do will reject the opinion that the right is, in any general sense, the social as opposed to the individual. As already stated, I look upon this antithesis as false when used to imply a radical opposition. All our human thought and activity is either individual or social, according to how you look at it, the two being no more than phases of the same thing, which common thought, always inclined to confuse words with things, attempts to separate. This is as true in the ethical field as in any other. The consideration of other persons usually enters largely into questions of right and wrong; but the ethical decision is distinctly an assertion of a private, individualized view of the matter. . . .

In short, ethical thinking and feeling, like all our higher life, has its individual and social aspects, with no peculiar emphasis on either. If the social aspect is here at its highest, so also is the individual aspect. . . .

The common notion of freedom is negative, that is, it is a notion of the absence of constraint. Starting with the popular individualistic view of things, the social order is thought of as something apart from, and more or less a hindrance to, a man's natural development. There is an assumption that an ordinary person is self-sufficient in most respects, and will do very well if he is only left alone. But there is, of course, no such thing as the absence of restraint, in the sense of social limitations; man has no existence apart from a social order, and can develop his personality only through the social order, and in the same degree that it is developed. A freedom consisting in the removal of limiting conditions is inconceivable. If the word is to have any definite meaning in sociology, it must therefore be separated from the idea of a fundamental opposition between society and the individual, and made to signify something that is both individual and social. . . .

. . . If instead of contrasting what a particular man is with what he might be, we do the same for mankind as a whole, we have the notion of progress. Progress which does not involve liberation is evidently no progress at all; and, on the other hand, a freedom that is not part of the general onward movement of society is not free in the largest sense. . . .

. . . A child born in a slum, brought up in a demoralized family, and put at some confining and mentally deadening work when ten or twelve years old, is no more free to be healthy, wise, and moral than a Chinese child is free to read Shakespeare. Every social ill involves the enslavement of individuals.

This idea of freedom is quite in accord with a general, though vague, sentiment among us; it is an idea of fair play, of giving every one a chance; and nothing arouses more general and active indignation among our people than the belief that some one or some class is not getting a fair chance. There seems, however, to be too great complacency in the way in which the present state of things is interpreted, a tendency to assume that freedom has been achieved once for all by the Declaration of Independence and popular suffrage, and that little remains but to let each person realize the general blessing to the best of his ability. It is well to recognize that the freedom which we nominally worship is never more than partly achieved, and is every day threatened by new encroachments, that the right to vote is only one phase of it, and possibly, under present conditions, not the most important phase, and that we can maintain and increase it only by a sober and determined application of our best thought and endeavor.

CHAPTER FIVE

~

William I. Thomas on the Definition of the Situation

~ Introduction ~

William Isaac Thomas (1893–1947) was born in a rural area of Virginia and grew up in Knoxville, Tennessee. As an undergraduate attending the University of Tennessee, he studied literature and the classics and was also very interested in the natural sciences. Thomas stayed on as an instructor at Tennessee until he had the opportunity to study in Berlin and Goettingen, Germany, in 1888. While in Germany, he became very interested in psychological research, and particularly, ethnographic research.

Returning to the United States, Thomas accepted a professorship in English at Oberlin College. However, he gave up his teaching position in order to become a graduate student at the first American department of sociology, located at the University of Chicago. After completing his doctoral studies, Thomas became an assistant professor of sociology at Chicago at about the same time that George Herbert Mead accepted a position in philosophy there. In addition to his scholarly work, Thomas was involved in social reform efforts in Chicago. In 1908 he received funding from Helen Culver, affiliated with Hull House, to study problems associated with immigration. He focused on the Polish community because it was the largest ethnic group in Chicago experiencing difficulties.

Thomas developed the life-history method of analysis as a result of this research. Along with Florian Znaniecki (whom Thomas met in Poland), Thomas published the influential book *The Polish Peasant in Europe and America*. This sociological work documents the difficult transition involved in changing cultures. While it would seem that Thomas's professional life was set, the public scandal of an extramarital affair resulted in his dismissal from the University of Chicago. Thereafter, he taught for a number of years at the fledgling New School for Social

Research. He also lectured for a short time at Harvard University, became president of the American Sociological Society, and, throughout his career, continued his research.

An important concept in Thomas's analysis of social problems is the notion of the definition of the situation. This concept became an important social psychological tool for examining how individuals create and reinforce meanings in social situations. For example, what is a deviant act? Sociologically speaking, it is an act that violates a norm. A norm is maintained by how persons define appropriate behavior in a particular situation. Individuals respond not only to the objective features of a situation but also to the meaning they impart onto it, or the meaning the situation has for them. The definition of the situation reinforces order when interacting persons or groups agree on the habitualized behavior; it identifies problems of meaning when interacting persons or groups disagree on appropriate behavior. At one point in American history (not that long ago), women were denied the right to vote. The suffragettes involved themselves in a number of activities in order to change this law. Were the suffragettes wrong to go against the norm that suggested that women did not have the reasoning skills necessary to vote? These women looked at the objective conditions of the situation and defined it in a way that violated the *hitherto* definition of the situation.

In studying social problems, Thomas concluded that social factors must be considered in defining individual or group activities as deviant. Why? Because deviance is defined by the interaction of individual and social factors. What is deviant at one time and place (or situation) may not be considered deviant at another. Moreover, individual behavior is based upon adjustments to a given situation. Therefore, one cannot understand another's behavior until one understands how he or she defines the situation. This point is forcefully made by Thomas's well-known statement, "If men define situations as real, they are real in their consequences." Individual factors (such as a particular intellectual or physical skill or appearance) and social factors (such as fads, family, and political economy) interact to create or reinforce a definition of a situation. How these individual and social factors play out (or create meaning) result in how we define our lives. As Thomas notes in the reading, "[G]radually a whole life-policy . . . follows from a series of such definitions" (42).

The reading for this chapter comes from Thomas's 1923 publication, *The Unadjusted Girl*. Prior to explaining the concept of the definition of the situation, Thomas classifies human motivation or wishes into four types: the desire for experience, the desire for security, the desire for response, and the desire for recognition. Reducing motivation to these four general types is Thomas's way of creating a conceptual scheme through which to explain individual and social habitualization and deviance. It should be pointed out, however, that as the book proceeds, the framework of wishes ultimately becomes less significant to his argument than the dynamic process of the definition of the situation. Regardless, Thomas makes it clear that the same wish can have varying consequences, depending upon individual and social definitions. For example, the desire for new experience can become manifest as thrill seeker, scientist, venture capitalist, or criminal depending upon individual tendencies, family dynamics, and cultural factors (e.g., the stability or instability of values, politics, and the economy). If the wishes can manifest discrepant consequences, how is social order maintained? Thomas argues that "organized society seeks . . . to regulate the conflict and competition inevitable between its members in the pursuit of their wishes" (43). Successive definitions of the situation regulate the expression of wishes. Such regulation may be understood also as a moral code. Morality and the generally accepted definition of the situation reinforce each other and may appear as synonymous. The "situation" constitutes varying and overlapping levels of social order—from family to community to the variety of institutions that make up a nation. We are born into a situation that has already been defined. Individuals then adapt (either in an individually and socially defined positive or negative way) to the situation we are in. Of course, certain types of adaptation can result in innovation. (Certainly, inventors fit this description; they take the materials available to them and create something entirely new: Think of Philo Farnsworth's invention of the television picture tube.)

What happens when cultural definitions of the situation such as morality become vague? On the one hand, restoring social order is essential for the maintenance of individual and cultural meaning, purpose, and direction. On the other hand, it is at these times that individual exploration and variation is at its highest peak; that is, each person must continually define his or her situation. Moreover, while habituation provides order, it may also contain norms that are oppressive to the general population or particularly oppressive for certain groups. Social order is in decline when its standards are no longer adequate to define situations. At this point, individual expression proliferates as a result of individually unique attempts to define the situations of one's life. Social order is restored when definitions are socially created that embody in a meaningful way the changes that led to the decay of order in the first place. Individualism is a phenomenon that evolves and recedes due to social circumstances or situations. Thomas believed, as did others we have discussed, that the sources of the social changes that he was observing were the rapid social, intellectual, and technological upheavals brought forth by the Industrial Revolution. Thomas's goal was to have a social order that finds valuable applications for those who seem to be making maladjusted definitions of situations. This would increase social responsibility and decrease maladjustedness (and thereby reinforce social order). He refers to this as the sublimation of the wish. Thomas's work conveys an ideal that has yet to be reached and represents a radical strand that many would probably find as disturbing today as they found it in 1923.

⌒ The Unadjusted Girl ⌒

The Wishes

. . . It is only as we understand behavior as a whole that we can appreciate the failure of certain individuals to conform to the usual standards. . . .

. . . The variety of expressions of behavior is as great as the variety of situ-ations arising in the external world, while the nervous system represents only a general mechanism for action. We can however approach the problem of be-havior through the study of the forces which impel to action, namely, the wishes, and we shall see that these correspond in general with the nervous mechanism.

The human wishes have a great variety of concrete forms but are capable of the following general classification:

1. The desire for new experience.
2. The desire for security.
3. The desire for response.
4. The desire for recognition.

. . . Men crave excitement, and all experiences are exciting which have in them some resemblance to the pursuit, flight, capture, escape, death which characterized the earlier life of mankind. Behavior is an adaptation to envi-ronment, and the nervous system itself is a developmental adaptation. It rep-resents, among other things, a hunting pattern of interest. "Adventure" is what the young boy wants, and stories of adventure. Hunting trips are entic-ing; they are the survival of natural life. All sports are of the hunting pattern; there is a contest of skill, daring, and cunning. It is impossible not to admire the nerve of a daring burglar or highwayman. A fight, even a dog fight, will draw a crowd. In gambling or dice throwing you have the thrill of success or the chagrin of defeat. The organism craves stimulation and seeks expansion and shock even through alcohol and drugs. "Sensations" occupy a large part of the space in newspapers. Courtship has in it an element of "pursuit." Nov-els, theaters, motion pictures, etc., are partly an adaptation to this desire, and their popularity is a sign of its elemental force. . . .

Vagabondage secures a maximum of new experience by the avoidance of the routine of organized society and the irksomeness at labor to which I will refer presently. In the constitutional vagabond the desire for new experience predom-inates over the other wishes and is rather contemplative and sensory, while in the criminal it is motor. . . .

. . . The modern scientific man uses the same mental mechanism but with a different application. He spends long months in his laboratory on an invention in anticipation of his final "achievement." . . .

The craftsman, the artist, the scientist, the professional man, and to some ex-tent the business man make new experience the basis of organized activity. . . .

. . . The desire for security is opposed to the desire for new experience. The desire for new experience is, as we have seen, emotionally related to anger, which tends to invite death, and expresses itself in courage, advance, attack, pursuit. The desire for new experience implies, therefore, motion, change, danger, instability, social irresponsibility. The individual dominated by it

·shows a tendency to disregard prevailing standards and group interests. He may be a social failure on account of his instability, or a social success if he converts his experiences into social values—puts them into the form of a poem, makes of them a contribution to science. The desire for security, on the other hand, is based on fear, which tends to avoid death and expresses itself in timidity, avoidance, and flight. The individual dominated by it is cautious, conservative, and apprehensive, tending also to regular habits, systematic work, and the accumulation of property.

The social types known as "bohemian" and "philistine" are determined respectively by the domination of the desire for new experience and the desire for security. The miser represents a case where the means of security has become an end in itself. . . .

. . . The desire for response, on the other hand, is primarily related to the instinct of love, and shows itself in the tendency to seek and to give signs of appreciation in connection with other individuals. . . .

In some natures this wish, both to receive and to give response, is out of proportion to the other wishes, "over-determined," so to speak, and interferes with a normal organization of life. . . .

. . . This wish is expressed in the general struggle of men for position in their social group, in devices for securing a recognized, enviable, and advantageous social status. . . . Veblen's volume, "Theory of the Leisure Class," points out that the status of men is established partly through the show of wealth made by their wives. Distinction is sought also in connection with skillful and hazardous activities, as in sports, war, and exploration. Playwriters and sculptors consciously strive for public favor and "fame." In the "achievement" of Pasteur and of similar scientific work there is not only the pleasure of the "pursuit" itself, but the pleasure of public recognition. Boasting, bullying, cruelty, tyranny, "the will to power" have in them a sadistic element allied to the emotion of anger and are efforts to compel a recognition of the personality. The frailty of women, their illness, and even feigned illness, is often used as a power-device, as well as a device to provoke response. On the other hand, humility, self-sacrifice, saintliness, and martyrdom may lead to distinction. The showy motives connected with the appeal for recognition we define as "vanity"; the creative activities we call "ambition."

The importance of recognition and status for the individual and for society is very great. The individual not only wants them but he needs them for the development of his personality. The lack of them and the fear of never obtaining them are probably the main source of those psychopathic disturbances which the Freudians treat as sexual in origin.

On the other hand society alone is able to confer status on the individual and in seeking to obtain it he makes himself responsible to society and is forced to regulate the expression of his wishes. His dependence on public opinion is perhaps the strongest factor impelling him to conform to the highest demands which society makes upon him. . . .

From the foregoing description it will be seen that wishes of the same general class—those which tend to arise from the same emotional background—may be totally different in moral quality. The moral good or evil of a wish depends on the social meaning or value of the activity which results from it. Thus the vagabond, the adventurer, the spendthrift, the bohemian are dominated by the desire for new experience, but so are the inventor and the scientist; adventures with women and the tendency to domesticity are both expressions of the desire for response; vain ostentation and creative artistic work both are designed to provoke recognition; avarice and business enterprise are actuated by the desire for security.

Moreover, when a concrete wish of any general class arises it may be accompanied and qualified by any or all of the other classes of wishes. . . . The immigrant who comes to America may wish to see the new world (new experience), make a fortune (security), have a higher standing on his return (recognition), and induce a certain person to marry him (response).

The general pattern of behavior which a given individual tends to follow is the basis of our judgment of his character. Our appreciation (positive or negative) of the character of the individual is based on his display of certain wishes as against others and on his modes of seeking their realization. Whether given wishes tend to predominate in this or that person is dependent primarily on what is called temperament. . . . Individuals are certainly temperamentally predisposed toward certain classes of the wishes. But we know also . . . that the expression of the wishes is profoundly influenced by the approval of the man's immediate circle and of the general public. . . .

The significant point about the wishes as related to the study of behavior is that they are the motor element, the starting point of activity. Any influences which may be brought to bear must be exercised on the wishes. . . .

. . . One of the most important powers gained during the evolution of animal life is the ability to make decisions from within instead of having them imposed from without. Very low forms of life do not make decisions, as we understand this term, but are pushed and pulled. . . .

On the other hand, the higher animals, and above all man, have the power of refusing to obey a stimulation which they followed at an earlier time. Response to the earlier stimulation may have had painful consequences and so the rule or habit in this situation is changed. We call this ability the power of inhibition, and it is dependent on the fact that the nervous system carries memories or records of past experiences. At this point the determination of action no longer comes exclusively from outside sources but is located within the organism itself.

Preliminary to any self-determined act of behavior there is always a stage of examination and deliberation which we may call *the definition of the situation*. And actually not only concrete acts are dependent on the definition of the situation, but gradually a whole life-policy and the personality of the individual himself follow from a series of such definitions.

But the child is always born into a group of people among whom all the general types of situation which may arise have already been defined and corresponding rules of conduct developed, and where he has not the slightest chance of making his definitions and following his wishes without interference. . . .

There is therefore always a rivalry between the spontaneous definitions of the situation made by the member of an organized society and the definitions which his society has provided for him. The individual tends to a hedonistic selection of activity, pleasure first; and society to a utilitarian selection, safety first. . . . [O]rganized society seeks also to regulate the conflict and competition inevitable between its members in the pursuit of their wishes. The desire to have wealth, for example, or any other socially sanctioned wish, may not be accomplished at the expense of another member of the society—by murder, theft, lying, swindling, blackmail, etc.

It is in this connection that a moral code arises, which is a set of rules or behavior norms, regulating the expression of the wishes, and which is built up by successive definitions of the situation. In practice the abuse arises first and the rule is made to prevent its recurrence. Morality is thus the generally accepted definition of the situation, whether expressed in public opinion and the unwritten law, in a formal legal code, or in religious commandments and prohibitions.

The family is the smallest social unit and the primary defining agency. As soon as the child has free motion and begins to pull, tear, pry, meddle, and prowl, the parents begin to define the situation through speech and other signs and pressures. . . .

In addition to the family we have the community as a defining agency. . . .

In this whole connection fear is used by the group to produce the desired attitudes in its member. Praise is used also but more sparingly. And the whole body of habits and emotions is so much a community and family product that disapproval or separation is almost unbearable. . . .

At the best no society has ever succeeded in regulating the behavior of all its members satisfactorily all the time. There are crimes of passion, of avarice, of revenge, even in face-to-face communities where the control is most perfect. . . . And the sexual passions have never been completely contained within the framework of marriage. But communities have been so powerful that all members have acknowledged the code and have been ready to repent and be forgiven. . . . And as long as the offender wishes to be forgiven and restored the code is working. The code is failing only if the sinner does not recognize it and does not repent. . . .

. . . From the foregoing it appears that the face-to-face group (family-community) is a powerful habit-forming mechanism. The group has to provide a system of behavior for many persons at once, a code which applies to everybody and lasts longer than any individual or generation. Consequently the group has two interests in the individual—to suppress wishes and activities which are in conflict with the existing organization, or which seem the starting point of social disharmony, and to encourage wishes and actions which are required by the existing social system. And if the group performs this task successfully, as it does among savages, among Mohammedans, and as it did until recently among European peasants, no appreciable change in the moral code or in the state of culture is observable from generation to generation. In small and isolated communities there is little tendency to change or progress because the new experience of the individual is sacrificed for the sake of the security of the group.

But by a process, an evolution, connected with mechanical inventions, facilitated communication, the diffusion of print, the growth of cities, business organization, the capitalistic system, specialized occupations, scientific research, doctrines of freedom, the evolutionary view of life, etc., the family and community influences have been weakened and the world in general has been profoundly changed in content, ideals, and organization.

Young people leave home for larger opportunities, to seek new experience, and from necessity. Detachment from family and community, wandering, travel, "vagabondage" have assumed the character of normality. Relationships are casualized and specialized. Men meet professionally, as promoters of enterprises, not as members of families, communities, churches. Girls leave home to work in factories, stores, offices, and studios. Even when families are not separated they leave home for their work.

Every new invention, every chance acquaintanceship, every new environment, has the possibility of redefining the situation and of introducing change, disorganization or different type of organization into the life of the individual or even of the whole world. . . .

In the small and spatially isolated communities of the past, where the influences were strong and steady, the members became more or less habituated to and reconciled with a life of repressed wishes. The repression was demanded of all, the arrangement was equitable, and while certain new experiences were prohibited, and pleasure not countenanced as an end in itself, there remained satisfactions, not the least of which was the suppression of the wishes of others. On the other hand the modern world presents itself as a spectacle in which the observer is never sufficiently participating. The modern revolt and unrest are due to the contrast between the paucity of fulfillment of the wishes of the individual and the fullness, or apparent fullness, of life around him. . . .

The world has become large, alluring, and confusing. Social evolution has been so rapid that no agency has been developed in the larger community of the state for regulating behavior which would replace the failing influence of the community and correspond completely with present activities. There is no universally accepted body of doctrines or practices. . . .

The definition of the situation is equivalent to the determination of the vague. In the Russian *mir* and the American rural community of fifty years ago nothing was left vague, all was defined. But in the general world movement to which I have referred, connected with free communication in space and free communication of thought, not only particular situations but the most general situations have become vague. Some situations were once defined and have become vague again; some have arisen and have never been defined. Whether this country shall participate in world politics, whether America is a refuge for the oppressed of other nationalities, whether the English should occupy India or the Belgians Africa, whether there shall be Sunday amusements, whether the history of the world is the unfolding of the will of God, whether men may drink wine, whether evolution may be taught in schools, whether marriage is indissoluble, whether sex life outside of marriage is permissible, whether children should be taught the facts of sex, whether the number of children born may be voluntarily limited—these questions have become vague. There are rival definitions of the situation, and none of them is binding. . . .

. . . There is no question that a more rational and adequate control in the field of human behavior is very desirable. And there are no powers of the human mind necessary to the formation of a science in this field which have not already been employed in the development of a science and a corresponding practice in the material world. The chief obstacle to the growth of a science of behavior has been our confidence that we had an adequate system for the control of behavior in the customary and common sense regulation of the wishes of the individual by family, community, and church influences, . . . if only we applied the system successfully. And the old forms of control based on the assumption of an essential stability of the whole social framework were real so long as this stability was real.

But this stability is no longer a fact. Precisely the marvelous development of the physical and biological sciences, as expressed in communication in space and in the industrial system has made the world a different place. The disharmony of the social world is in fact due to the disproportionate rate of advance in the mechanical world. The evolution of the material world, based on science, has been so rapid as to disorganize the social world, based on common sense. If there had been no development of mechanical inventions community life would have remained stable. But even so, the life of the past was nothing we wish to perpetuate.

Another cause of the backwardness of the science of society is our emotional attachment to the old community standards or "norms." I described [previously] how much emotion enters into the formation of everyday habits. It is well known that men have always objected to change of any kind. There was strong condemnation, for example, of the iron plow, invented late in the eighteenth century, on the ground that it was an insult to God and therefore poisoned the ground and caused weeds to grow. The man who first built a water-driven sawmill in England was mobbed; the man who first used an umbrella in Philadelphia was arrested. There was opposition to the telegraph, the telephone, the illumination of city streets by gas, the introduction of stoves and organs in churches, and until recent years it would be difficult to find a single innovation that has not encountered opposition and ridicule.

This emotional prepossession for habitual ways of doing things enters into and controls social investigations, particularly social reforms. The Vice Commission of Chicago, for example, which undertook an investigation of prostitution, was composed of thirty representative men, including ministers, physicians, social workers, criminologists, business men and university professors. In the introduction to its report it was at pains to state that it was anxious to make no discoveries and no recommendations which did not conform to standards accepted by society. "[The Commission] has kept constantly in mind that to offer a contribution of any value such an offering must be, first, moral; second, reasonable and practical; third, possible under the constitutional powers of our courts; fourth, that which will square with the public conscience of the American people." This commission made, in fact, a very valuable report. . . . [B]ut it had determined beforehand the limitations and character of its investigation and results, and excluded the possibility of a new determination of behavior norms in this field.

A method of investigation which seeks to justify and enforce any given norm of behavior ignores the fact that a social evolution is going on in which not only activities are changing but the norms which regulate the activities are also changing. Traditions and customs, definitions of the situation, morality, and religion are undergoing an evolution, and a society going on the assumption that a certain norm is valid and that whatever does not comply with it is abnormal finds itself helpless when it realizes that this norm has lost social significance and some other norm has appeared in its place. Thus fifty years ago we recognized, roughly speaking, two types of women, the one completely good and the other completely bad—what we now call the old-fashioned girl and the girl who had sinned and been outlawed. At present we have several intermediate types—the occasional prostitute, the charity girl, the demi-virgin, the equivocal flapper, and in addition girls with new but social behavior norms who have adapted themselves to all kinds of work. And some of this work is surprisingly efficient. Girls of twenty and thereabouts are successfully competing in literature with the veteran writers. But no one of these girls, neither the orderly nor the disorderly, is conforming with the behavior norms of her grandmother. All of them represent the same movement, which is a desire to realize their wishes under the changing social conditions. The movement contains disorganization and reorganization, but it is the same movement in both cases. It is the release of important social energies which could not find expression under the norms of the past. Any general movement away from social standards implies that these standards are no longer adequate.

A successful method of study will be wide and objective enough to include both the individual and the norms as an evolving process, and such a study must be made from case to case, comparatively and without prejudice or indignation. Every new movement in society implies some disorder, some random, exploratory movements preliminary to a different type of organization answering to new conditions. Individualism is a stage of transition between two types of social organization. No part of the life of the individual should be studied as dissociated from the whole of his life, the abnormal as separated from the normal, and abnormal groups should be studied in comparison with the remaining groups which we call normal. There is no break in continuity between the normal and the abnormal in actual life that would permit the selection of any exact bodies of corresponding materials, and the nature of the normal and the abnormal can be understood only with the help of comparison. When we have sufficiently determined causal relations we shall probably find that there is no individual energy, no unrest, no type of wish, which cannot be sublimated and made socially useful. From this standpoint the problem is not the right of society to protect itself from the disorderly and anti-social person, but the right of the disorderly and anti-social person to be made orderly and socially valuable.

But while we have prepossessions which have stood in the way of an objective study of behavior there is no doubt that the main difficulty at present is the lack of a concrete method of approach. This method will have to be developed in detail in the course of many particular investigations, as has been the case in the physical sciences, but the approach to the problem of behavior lies in the study of the wishes of the individual and of the conditions under which society, in view of its power to give recognition, response, security, and new experience, can limit and develop these wishes in socially desirable ways. . . .

The problem of society is to produce the right attitudes in its members, so that the activity will take a socially desirable form. . . . [S]ociety is more or less successful to the degree that it makes its definitions of situations valid. If the members of a certain group react in an identical way to certain values, it is because they have been socially trained to react thus, because the traditional rules of behavior predominant in the given group impose upon every member certain ways of defining and solving the practical situations which he meets in his life.

It is, of course, precisely in this connection that the struggle between the individual and his society arises. Society is indispensable to the individual because it possesses at a given moment an accumulation of values, of plans and materials which the child could never accumulate alone. For example, a boy can now construct a wireless plant or build an engine, but he could never in his life accumulate the materials, devise the principles alone. These are the results of the experience of the entire past of a cultural society. But the individual is also indispensable to society because by his activity and ingenuity he creates all the material values, the whole fund of civilization. The conflict arises from the fact that the individual introduces other definitions of the situation and assumes other attitudes toward values than the conventionalized ones and consequently tends to change plans of action and introduce disorder, to derange the existing norms. A new plan may be merely destructive of values and organization, as when a counterfeiter imitates a bank note or a girl destroys her value and that of her family by prostituting herself, or it may be temporarily disorganizing but eventually organizing, as when an inventor displaces the hand-loom by the power-loom or the biologist introduces a theory of evolution which contradicts the theory of special creation. Society desires stability and the individual desires new experience and introduces change. But eventually all new values, all the new cultural elements of a society are the result of the changes introduced by the individual.

If we now examine the plans of action carried out by children and men with reference to social values, whether they are good or mischievous, we find that the general intellectual pattern of the plan, the quality of ingenuity, is pretty much the same in any case. When, for example, children have escapades, run away, lie, steal, plot, etc., they are following some plan, pursuing some end, solving some problem as a result of their own definition of the situation. The naughtiness consists in doing something which is not allowed, or in ways which are not allowed. The intellectual pattern is the same whether they are solving a problem in arithmetic, catching a fish, building a dog house, or planning some deviltry. . . .

The moral good or evil of a wish lies therefore not in the cleverness or elaboration of the mental scheme through which it is expressed but in its regard or disregard for existing social values. The same wish and the same quality of mind may lead to totally different results. A tendency to phantasy may make of the subject a scientist, a swindler, or simply a liar. The urge to wandering and adventure may stop at vagabondage, the life of a cowboy, missionary, geologist, or ethnologist. The sporting interest may be gratified by shooting birds, studying them with a camera, or pursuing a scientific theory. The desire for response may be expressed in the Don Juan type of life, with many love adventures, in stable family life, in love lyrics, or in the relation of the prostitute to her pimp. The desire for recognition may seek its gratification in ostentatious dress and luxury or in forms of creative work. That is to say, a wish may have various psychologically equivalent expressions. The problem is to define situations in such ways as to produce attitudes which direct the action exclusively toward fields yielding positive social values. The transfer of a wish from one field of application to another field representing a higher level of values is called the sublimation of the wish. This transfer is accomplished by the fact of public recognition which attaches a feeling of social sacredness to some schemes of action and their application in comparison with others—the activities of the scientist, physician, or craftsman on the one hand and the activities of the adventurer, the criminal, or the prostitute on the other. This feeling of sacredness actually arises only in groups, and an individual can develop the feeling only in association with a group which has definite standards of sacredness. Practically, any plan which gets favorable public recognition is morally good—for the time being. And this is the only practical basis of judgment of the moral quality of an act—whether it gets favorable or unfavorable recognition.

The problem of the desirable relation of individual wishes to social values is thus twofold, containing (1) the problem of the dependence of the individual upon social organization and culture, and (2) the problem of the dependence of social organization and culture upon the individual. In practice the first problem means: What social values and how presented will produce the desirable mental attitudes in the members of the social group? And the second problem means: What schematizations of the wishes of the individual members of the group will produce the desirable social values, promote the organization and culture of the society?

The problem of the individual involves in its details the study of all the social influences and institutions—family, school, church, the law, the newspaper, the story, the motion picture, the occupations, the economic system, the unorganized personal relationships, the division of life into work and leisure time, etc. But the human wish underlies all social happenings and institutions, and human experiences constitute the reality beneath the formal social organization and behind the statistically formulated mass-phenomena. Taken in themselves statistics are nothing more than symptoms of unknown causal processes. A social institution can be understood and modified only if we do not limit ourselves to the study of its formal organization but analyze the way in which it appears in the personal experience of various members of the group and follow the influence which it has on their lives. And an individual can be understood only if we do not limit ourselves to a cross-section of his life as revealed by a given act, a court record or a confession, or to the determination of what type of life-organization *exists*, but determine the means by which a certain life-organization is *developed*. . . .

. . . [V]ery rapid and positive gains are being made in the treatment of delinquency, but for a fundamental control and the prevention of anti-social behavior a change in the general attitudes and values of society will be necessary. . . .

The modern division and organization of labor brings a continually growing quantitative prevalence of occupations which are almost completely devoid of stimulation and therefore present little interest for the workman. This fact affects human behavior and happiness profoundly, and the restoration of stimulation to labor is among the most important problems confronting society. The present industrial organization tends also to develop a type of human being as abnormal in its way as the opposite type of individual who gets the full amount of occupational stimulation by taking a line of interest destructive of social order— the criminal or vagabond.

The moralist complains of the materialization of men and expects a change of the social organization to be brought about by moral or religious preaching; the economic determinist considers the whole social organization as conditioned fundamentally and necessarily by economic factors and expects an improvement exclusively from a possible historically necessary modification of the economic organization itself. From the viewpoint of behavior the problem is much more serious and objective than the moralist conceives it, but much less limited and determined that it appears to the economic determinist. The economic interests are only one class of human attitudes among others, and every attitude can be modified by an adequate social technic. . . . In other words, with the appropriate change of attitudes and values all work may become artistic work. And with the appropriate change of attitudes and values the recognition of economic success may be subordinated to the recognition of human values.

CHAPTER SIX

George Herbert Mead
on Self and Society

~ Introduction ~

George Herbert Mead (1863–1931) was born in South Hadley, Massachusetts, to Hiram Mead, a Congregationalist minister, and Elizabeth Storrs Billings Mead, who, after her husband's death in 1881, served as president of Mount Holyoke College. When Mead was seven, the family moved to Ohio where his father had accepted a position as professor of homiletics (preaching) at Oberlin College. Mead entered Oberlin at the age of sixteen and graduated four years later with a B.A. degree. At Oberlin, Mead was exposed to a mix of ideas—from a conservative Protestant orientation to social activism and liberal politics to the influence of Darwin via the natural sciences.

After completing his undergraduate studies, Mead worked for several years as a surveyor with the Wisconsin Central Rail Road Company. In 1887 he followed his college friend Henry Castle to Harvard University to study philosophy. At Harvard, Mead was exposed to the influential thinking of Josiah Royce and William James, among others. At that time, physiological psychology was a branch of philosophy, and it was this area that really sparked his interest. After completing his master's degree at Harvard, Mead began studying toward a Ph.D. in philosophy and physiological psychology at the University of Leipzig in Germany with Wilhelm Wundt and G. Stanley Hall. Before he could complete his graduate studies, however, he accepted an offer from the University of Michigan to teach philosophy and psychology.

At Michigan, Mead became acquainted with Charles Horton Cooley and John Dewey. Mead and Dewey became good friends, and after Dewey accepted the position of chair of philosophy at the new, up-and-coming University of Chicago, both Dewey and Mead moved to Chicago. With Mead, Dewey, and

James H. Tufts, the University of Chicago became an important center for the study and advancement of the philosophical movement of pragmatism. The idea of pragmatism is to test the value of ideas in the real world for their consequences; ideas that help solve problems are judged to be valid. In addition to the voices of influential pragmatic thinkers whom Mead had met during his graduate school years, the pragmatic movement must have had a familiar and powerful ring in his ears, echoing back to the mix of Christian values, social activism, and Darwinian thought co-existing at Oberlin. In addition to becoming a leading figure in pragmatism himself and writing many articles that appeared in a variety of journals, Mead was also a member of a socially active civic group called the City Club, which advocated policies to improve living conditions for all of the citizens of Chicago. He was particularly involved in programs to improve the education of poor people living in the city. Mead was also a supporter of women's suffrage and worked with Jane Addams, who won the Nobel Peace Prize in 1931 for her service to many people, particularly women, at Hull House.

While Mead himself was always modest about his contributions, his students recognized in his work a significant train of thought that would lead to a school of thinking that would blend, in an observable way, language, the psychological, and social interaction. In particular, Mead's synthesis of pragmatic philosophy and physiological psychology produced an innovative approach to the study of self and society. In an essay entitled, "Social Psychology As Counterpart to Physiological Psychology," Mead (1909) pointed out that: (1) consciousness is a product of physiological processes that require biological investigation; (2) self-consciousness is a product of social processes that require social scientific investigation; and, (3) psychology tends to deny the need of studying the self (for example, Watson's behaviorism), and, in any case, psychology or self-consciousness is itself the product of physiological and social processes. Mead (407) writes, "There must be other selves if one's own is to exist. Psychological analysis, retrospection, and the study of children . . . give no inkling of situations in which a self could have existed in consciousness except as the counterpart of other selves."

While Mead never presented his ideas systematically in a book, he wrote a number of insightful articles. Four of these are reprinted here. In the first article, "The Mechanism of Social Consciousness," Mead asserts that we are objects to each other that call out responses. Human beings are social animals that interact. Interaction involves action that contains a series of acts or gestures. We are objects or stimuli that gesture to others. Others are objects or stimuli that gesture to us. Interaction occurs when the stimulation (stemming from a gesture) of one party results in a response from another. As Mead (402) writes, this interaction "does not simply relate the individual to other individuals as physical objects, but puts him *en rapport.* . . ." This exchange leads to a sort of dance of gestures and attitudes, both parties adjusting and readjusting themselves to the other. In this dance, I am not only adjusting myself or responding to the other as a stimulus; I am readjusting or formulating an act that will call for a response in the other. There is nothing passive about this exchange. The power of this exchange of gesturing in relation to consciousness lies in the fact that my act calls out a response not only in the other, but also in myself. Gestures communicate to the self as they communicate to another (that is, a nod or a smile in interaction is a response of another to an act I have initiated, and it is a stimulus to me that I have been acknowledged and understood). My reading of another's response to my acts turns me into an object to myself that I may then read. My reading of others' responses to me builds up a sense of self. The vocal gesturing involved in speech constitutes a particularly sophisticated form of exchange.

Mead (405) argues that without speech, human consciousness would be different from our experience of it. Just think about this! How are you thinking about it? You are using words in your mind to consider this question. Language and thinking are intricately linked. Language creates common meanings through a symbol system of words, which allows for the acquisition of understanding. The acquisition of understanding also builds up the unique sense of self. A unique sense of self is realized in interaction with others through the exchange of physical and vocal gestures, particularly language. As you can see, Mead's pragmatic approach demonstrates the series of observable processes that give rise to a unique sense of self.

The second article, entitled "The Social Self," elaborates on a theme raised in the first article, namely, Mead's notion of the self as an "I" and a "me" or "me's." The "me" or "me's" represent the importation of our perceptions of ourselves through others (through others' responses to our acts). The importation of the "me's" comes to represent how we present ourselves to ourselves. Now, the organizing force of the "me's" is the "I." The activity of the "me's" (one's inner voice that has been acquired via interaction) is constituted by, and itself constitutes, the experience of an "I" that we cannot experience directly. Upon reflection (which involves the "I" in rapport with a "me"), we cannot be present to ourselves in the act of reflecting upon what we have done. When the "I" is conversing, it is always doing so with a "me" after the fact. Our awareness of what we are doing is a watching and an evaluating of the "me's" in action. This is so, in part, because, as Mead states in this article, "[I]t is only as the individual finds himself acting with reference to himself as he acts towards others, that he becomes a subject to himself." That which even permits for self-conversation, language, is a social phenomenon. Without others, the "I" could not converse. And if the "I" could not converse, it could not be aware of itself. While individuals experience reflexivity as their own, it nevertheless is derived from physiological and social factors. Mead seems to suggest that while individuals can make unique contributions to the world, the contributions they make are a product of the degree to which the self has addressed itself with the contents learned from others. It should be emphasized here that Mead is not saying that the self is a mirror image of others or that the self merely engages in imitation in order to know how to behave. Rather, what Mead is suggesting is that physiological and social development, motivated by the need to overcome problems or conflicts, has created a complex phenomenon of self-relationship.

In his article "What Social Objects Must Psychology Presuppose?" Mead (1910, 178) argues that "[h]uman conduct is distinguished from animal conduct by that increase in inhibition which is an essential phase of voluntary attention, and increased inhibition means an increase in gesture in the signs of activities which are not carried out." Problems create a pause in action that results in various degrees of deliberation (self-talk between an "I" and a "me"). Without such inhibition and deliberation, conduct is habitual. It is here that Mead seems to see the locale for creativity and innovation, but its springboard is always others. Once conduct resumes, the habitualization of the new act is contingent upon our reading of the response of another's reaction to our act. Examination of the self as an island distorts the objective realities pertaining to the conduct of the self. One cannot understand the self in isolation from the social and physical factors that continuously impinge upon it.

In a 1925 article, "The Genesis of the Self and Social Control," Mead described the development of self-consciousness in children in terms of play and the game. During play, children take on the roles of others in society: parent, teacher, policeman, etc. In the game, there are rules and procedures that all participants must follow. In this way, the self is not only playing a particular role, but is also acquiring a common system of regulations. Generally speaking, in the transition from "play" to "the game," we acquire the roles preexisting in society and make them our own. As our social circle enlarges and becomes more complex, we take on the general attitude, or what Mead calls the generalized other, of this social milieu.

In the third article you will be reading, "A Behavioristic Account of the Significant Symbol," Mead elaborates on gestures and interaction. In particular, Mead uses the term "symbol" when a gesture leads to a particular response in another. Moreover, the symbol becomes significant when the person who elicits the gesture responds in the same way. Morris (1967) notes:

> [W]hen the tendency to call out "Fire!" affects the individual as it affects others, and is itself controlled in terms of these effects, the vocal gesture has become a significant symbol; the individual is conscious of what he is about; he has reached the stage of genuine language instead of unconscious communication. . . . (xxi)

This common response may be generalized beyond a particular situation. Significant symbols of a universal nature reflect the attitudes of the generalized other. It is in the exchange of significant symbols that a role that I am taught becomes my own, and, in the process, I become a part of a social order.

Mead's social psychology is consistent with his politics. He understands morality to be the product of human association. Human beings create the moral order by which they abide. Mead (1923) concludes his essay, "Scientific Method and the Moral Sciences" this way:

> The order of the universe that we live in is the moral order. It has become the moral order by becoming the self-conscious method of the members of a human society. We are not pilgrims and strangers. We are at home in our own world, but it

is not ours by inheritance but by conquest. The world that comes to us from the past possesses and controls us. We possess and control the world that we discover and invent. And thus is the world of the moral order. (247)

As a pragmatist, Mead displays his belief in democracy and in the use of a scientific attitude for achieving democratic goals. However, he is quick to note in his writings that the institutions that represent a democratic society can become self-serving instead of progressing toward the fulfillment of democratic liberty and equality for all. In the above essay, Mead writes:

Our institutions are in so far democratic that when a public sentiment is definitely formed and expressed it is authoritative. But an authoritative public sentiment upon a public issue is very infrequent. . . . In the meantime . . . we are governed by minorities, and the relatively intelligent minorities are swayed by the import of the issue to these minorities. (239)

Institutions governed by such minorities undermine the ideals of a democratic society. While persons acquire a sense of self from others, they may make judgments apart from their habitualized routines, and in this instance, they should do so because their habitualized routines undermine the progress of a democratic and moral order.

Despite appearances Mead does not believe that we should be working toward some distant idealized goal. His thinking is pragmatic. He sees a society of selves. These selves have become selves via interaction. Selves seek satisfaction from that which they are inherently a part. To undermine this realization is to undermine democratic progress. While Mead hesitates to predict where human progress will take us, he does not hesitate to state explicitly that current means either contribute to, or undermine, democracy. In "National-Mindedness and International-Mindedness," Mead (1929) suggests that self-fulfillment may be derived from a disinterested attitude about personally profiting from a moral order that one comes from and shapes. Mead suggests looking at continuing conflicts as the areas that need our intelligence. Again in "Scientific Method and the Moral Sciences," Mead (1923, 245) says, "The task of intelligence is to use this growing intelligence of interdependence to formulate the problems of all, in terms of the problems of every one." Ultimately, Mead seeks a resolution to the continuing conflicts of impulses that drive people away from that which connects them: each other. This chapter concludes with a fourth essay of Mead's, entitled "The Philosophical Basis of Ethics," permitting the reader the opportunity to engage Mead in his own terms on these issues pertaining to morality and ethics.

~ The Mechanism of Social Consciousness ~

The organization of consciousness may be regarded from the standpoint of its objects and the relation of these objects to conduct. I have in mind to present somewhat schematically the relation of social objects or selves to the form of social conduct, and to introduce this by a statement of the relation of the physical object to the conduct within which it appears.

A physical object or percept is a construct in which the sensuous stimulation is merged with imagery which comes from past experience. This imagery on the cognitive side is that which the immediate sensuous quality stands for, and in so far satisfies the mind. The reason for this satisfaction is found in the fact that this imagery arises from past experience of the result of an act which this stimulus has set going. Thus the wall as a visual stimulus tends to set free the impulse to move toward it and push against it. The perception of the wall as distant and hard and rough is related to the visual experience as response to stimulation. A peculiar stimulus value stands for a certain response value. A percept is a collapsed act in which the result of the act to which the stimulus incites is represented by imagery of the experience of past acts of a like nature.

In so far as our physical conduct involves movements toward or away from distant objects and their being handled when we come into contact with them, we perceive all things in terms of distance sensation—color, sound, odor—which stand for hard or soft, big or little, objects of varying forms, which actual contact will reveal.

Our conduct in movement and manipulation, with its stimulations and responses, gives the framework within which objects of perception arise—and this conduct is in so far responsible for the organization of our physical world. Percepts—physical objects—are compounds of the experience of immediate stimulation and the imagery of the response to which this stimulation will lead. The object can be properly stated in terms of conduct.

I have referred to percepts as objects which arise in physical experience because it is a certain phase of conduct which, with its appropriate stimuli and responses, gives rise to such products, i.e., movement under the influence of distant stimuli leading to contact experiences of manipulation.

Given a different type of conduct with distinguishable stimulations and responses, and different objects would arise—such a different field is that of social conduct. By social conduct I refer simply to that which is mediated by the stimulations of other animals belonging to the same group of living forms, which lead to responses which again affect these other forms—thus fighting, reproduction, parental care, much of animal play, hunting, etc., are the results of primitive instincts or impulses which are set going by the stimulation of one form by another, and these stimulations again lead to responses which affect other forms.

It is of course true that a man is a physical object to the perception of another man, and as really as is a tree or a stone. But a man is more than a physical object, and it is this more which constitutes him a social object or self, and it is this self which is related to that peculiar conduct which may be termed social conduct.

Most social stimulation is found in the beginnings or early stages of social acts which serve as stimuli to other forms whom these acts would affect. This is the field of gestures, which reveal the motor attitude of a form in its relation to others; an attitude which psychologists have conceived of as predominantly emotional, though it is emotional only in so far as an ongoing act is inhibited. That certain of these early indications of an incipient act have persisted, while the rest of the act has been largely suppressed or has lost its original value, e.g., the baring of the teeth or the lifting of the nostrils, is true, and the explanation can most readily be found in the social value which such indications have acquired. It is an error, however, to overlook the relation which these truncated acts have assumed toward other forms of reactions which complete them as really as the original acts, or to forget that they occupy but a small part of the whole field of gesture by means of which we are apprised of the reactions of others toward ourselves. The expressions of the face and attitudes of body have the same functional value for us that the beginnings of hostility have for two dogs, who are maneuvering for an opening to attack.

This field of gesture does not simply relate the individual to other individuals as physical objects, but puts him *en rapport* with their actions, which are as yet only indicated, and arouses instinctive reactions appropriate to these social activities. The social response of one individual, furthermore, introduces a further complication. The attitude assumed in response to the attitude of another becomes a stimulus to him to change his attitude, thus leading to that conversation of attitudes which is so vividly illustrated in the early stages of a dog fight. We see the same process in courting and mating, and in the fondling of young forms by the mother, and finally in much of the play of young animals.

It has been recognized for some time that speech belongs in its beginnings, at least, to this same field of gesture, so-called vocal gesture. Originally indicating the preparation for violent action, which arises from a sudden change of breathing and circulation rhythms, the articulate sounds have come to elaborate and immensely complicate this conversation of attitudes by which social forms so adjust themselves to each other's anticipated action that they may act appropriately with reference to each other.

Articulate sounds have still another most important result. While one feels but imperfectly the value of his own facial expression or bodily attitude for another, his ear reveals to him his own vocal gesture in the same form that it assumes to his neighbor. One shakes his fist primarily only at another, while he talks to himself as really as he talks to his *vis-à-vis*. The genetic import of this has long been recognized. The young child talks to himself, i.e., uses the elements of articulate speech in response to the sounds he hears himself make, more continuously and persistently than he does in response to the sounds he hears from those about him, and displays greater interest in the sounds he himself makes than in those of others. We know also that this fascination of one's own vocal gestures continues even after the child has learned to talk with others, and that the child will converse for hours with himself, even constructing imaginary companions, who function in the child's growing self-consciousness as the processes of inner speech—of thought and imagination—function in the consciousness of the adult.

To return to the formula given above for the formation of an object in consciousness, we may define the social object in terms of social conduct as we defined the physical object in terms of our reactions to physical objects. The object was found to consist of the sensuous experience of the stimulation to an act plus the imagery from past experience of the final result of the act. The social object will then be the gestures, *i.e.*, the early indications of an ongoing social act in another plus the imagery of our own response to that stimulation. To the young child the frowns and smiles of those about him, the attitude of body, the outstretched arms, are at first simply stimulations that call out instinctive responses of his own appropriate to these gestures. He cries or laughs, he moves toward his mother, or stretches out his arms. When these gestures in others bring back the images of his own responses and their results, the child has the material out of which he builds up the social objects that form the most important part of his environment. We are familiar with this phase of a baby's development, being confident that he recognizes the different members of the group about him. He acts then with confidence toward them since their gestures have come to have meaning for him. His own response to their stimulations and its consequences are there to interpret the facial expressions and attitudes of body and tones of voice. The awakening social intelligence of the child is evidenced not so much through his ready responses to the gestures of others, for these have been in evidence much earlier. It is the inner assurance of his own readiness to adjust himself to the attitudes of others that looks out of his eyes and appears in his own bodily attitudes.

If we assume that an object arises in consciousness through the merging of the imagery of experience of the response with that of the sensuous experience of the stimulation, it is evident that the child must merge the imagery of his past responses into the sensuous stimulation of what comes to him through distance senses. His contact and kinesthetic experiences must be lodged in the sensuous experiences that call them out if they are to achieve objective character in his consciousness.

It will be some time before he can successfully unite the different parts of his own body, such as hands and feet, which he sees and feels, into a single object. Such a step must be later than the formation of the physical objects of his environment. The form of the object is given in the experience of things, which are not his physical self. When he has synthesized his various bodily parts with the organic sensations and affective experiences, it will be upon the model of objects about him. The mere presence of experiences of pleasure and pain, together with organic sensations, will not form an object unless this material can fall into the scheme of an object—that of sensuous stimulation plus the imagery of the response.

In the organization of the baby's physical experience the appearance of his body as a unitary thing, as an object, will be relatively late, and must follow upon the structure of the objects of his environment. This is as true of the object that appears in social conduct, the self. The form of the social object must be found first of all in the experience of other selves. The earliest achievement of social consciousness will be the merging of the imagery of the baby's first responses and their results with the stimulations of the gestures of others. The child will not succeed in forming an object of himself—of putting the so-called subjective material of consciousness within such a self—until he has recognized about him social objects who have arisen in his experience through this process of filling out stimulations with past experiences of response. And this is indeed our uniform experience with children. The child's early social percepts are of others. After these arise incomplete and partial selves—or "me's"—which are quite analogous to the child's percepts of his hands and feet, which precede his perception of himself as a whole. The mere presence of affective experience, of imagery, of organic sensations, does not carry with it consciousness of a self to which these experiences belong. Nor does the unitary character of the response which tends to synthesize our objects of perception convey that same unitary character to the inner experience until the child is able to experience himself as he experiences other selves.

It is highly probable that lower animals never reach any such objective reference of what we term subjective experiences to selves, and the question presents itself—what is there in human social conduct that give rise to a "me," a self which is an object? Why does the human animal transfer the form of a social object from his environment to an inner experience?

The answer to the question is already indicated in the statement of vocal gesture. Certainly the fact that the human animal can stimulate himself as he stimulates others and can respond to his stimulations as he responds to the stimulations of others, places in his conduct the form of a social object out of which may arise a "me" to which can be referred so-called subjective experiences.

Of course the mere capacity to talk to oneself is not the whole of self-consciousness, otherwise the talking birds would have souls or at least selves. What is lacking to the parrot are the social objects which can exist for the human baby. Part of the mechanism for transferring the social objects into an inner experience the parrot possesses, but he has nothing to import into such an inner world. Furthermore, the vocal gesture is not the only form which can serve for the building up of a "me," as is abundantly evident from the building-up gestures of the deaf mutes. Any gesture by which the individual can himself be affected as others are affected, and which therefore tends to call out in him a response as it would call it out in another, will serve as a mechanism for the construction of a self. That, however, a consciousness of a self as an object would ever have arisen in man if he had not had the mechanism of talking to himself, I think there is every reason to doubt.

If this statement is correct the objective self of human consciousness is the merging of one's responses with the social stimulation by which he affects himself. The "me" is a man's reply to his own talk. Such a me is not then an early formation, which is then projected and ejected into the bodies of other people to give them the breadth of human life. It is rather an importation from the field of social objects into an amorphous, unorganized field of what we call inner experience. Through the organization of this object, the self, this material is itself organized and brought under the control of the individual in the form of so-called self-consciousness.

It is a commonplace of psychology that it is only the "me"—the empirical self—that can be brought into the focus of attention—that can be perceived. The "I" lies beyond the range of immediate experience. In terms of social conduct this is tantamount to saying that we can perceive our responses only as they appear as images from past experience, merging with the sensuous stimulation. We can not present the response while we are responding. We can not use our responses to others as the materials for construction of the self—this imagery goes to make up other selves. We must socially stimulate ourselves to place at our own disposal the material out of which our own selves as well as those of others must be made.

The "I" therefore never can exist as an object in consciousness, but the very conversational character of our inner experience, the very process of replying to one's own talk, implies an "I" behind the scenes who answers to the gestures, the symbols, that arise in consciousness. The "I" is the transcendental self of Kant, the soul that James conceived behind the scene holding on to the skirts of an idea to give it an added increment of emphasis.

The self-conscious, actual self in social intercourse is the objective "me" or "me's" with the process of response continually going on and implying a fictitious "I" always out of sight of himself.

Inner consciousness is socially organized by the importation of the social organization of the outer world.

⌒ The Social Self ⌒

Recognizing that the self can not appear in consciousness as an "I," that it is always an object, i.e., a "me," I wish to suggest an answer to the question, What is involved in the self being an object? The first answer may be that an object involves a subject. Stated in other words, that a "me" is inconceivable without an "I." And to this reply must be made that such an "I" is a pre-supposition, but never a presentation of conscious experience, for the moment it is presented it has passed into the objective case, presuming, if you like, an "I" that observes— but an "I" that can disclose himself only by ceasing to be the subject for whom the object "me" exists. It is, of course, not the Hegelism of a self that becomes another to himself in which I am interested, but the nature of the self as revealed by introspection and subject to our factual analysis. This analysis does reveal, then, in a memory process an attitude of observing oneself in which both the observer and the observed appear. To be concrete, one remembers asking himself how he could undertake to do this, that, or the other, chiding himself for his short-comings or pluming himself upon his achievements. Thus, in the redintegrated self of the moment passed, one finds both a subject and an object, but it is a subject that is now an object of observation, and has the same nature as the object self whom we present as in intercourse with those about us. In quite the same fashion we remember the questions, admonitions, and approvals addressed to our fellows. But the subject attitude which we instinctively take can be presented only as something experienced—as we can be conscious of our acts only through the sensory processes set up after the act has begun.

The contents of this presented subject, who thus has become an object in being presented, but which still distinguish him as the subject of the passed experience from the "me" whom he addressed, are those images which initiated the conversation and the motor sensations which accompany the expression, plus the organic sensations and the response of the whole system to the activity initiated. In a word, just those contents which go to make up the self which is distinguished from the others whom he addresses. The self appearing as "I" is the memory image of the self who acted toward himself and is the same self who acts toward other selves.

On the other hand, the stuff that goes to make up the "me" whom the "I" addresses and whom he observes, is the experience which is induced by this action of the "I." If the "I" speaks, the "me" hears. If the "I" strikes, the "me" feels the blow. Here again the "me" consciousness is of the same character as that which arises from the action of the other upon him. That is, it is only as the individual finds himself acting with reference to himself as he acts towards others, that he becomes a subject to himself rather than an object, and only as he is affected by his own social conduct in the manner in which he is affected by that of others, that he becomes an object to his own social conduct.

The differences in our memory presentations of the "I" and the "me" are those of the memory images of the initiated social conduct and those of the sensory responses thereto.

It is needless, in view of the analysis of Baldwin, of Royce and of Cooley and many others, to do more than indicate that these reactions arise earlier in our social conduct with others than in introspective self-consciousness, i.e., that the infant consciously calls the attention of others before he calls his own attention by affecting himself and that he is consciously affected by others before he is conscious of being affected by himself.

The "I" of introspection is the self which enters into social relations with other selves. It is not the "I" that is implied in the fact that one presents himself as "me." And the "me" of introspection is the same "me" that is the object of the social conduct of others. One presents himself as acting toward others—in this presentation he is presented in indirect discourse as the subject of the action and is still an object—and the subject of this presentation can never appear immediately in conscious experience. It is the same self who is presented as observing himself, and he affects himself just in so far as he can address himself by the means of social stimulation which affect others. The "me" whom he addresses is the "me," therefore, that is similarly affected by the social conduct of those about him.

This statement of the introspective situation, however, seems to overlook a more or less constant feature of our consciousness, and that is that running current of awareness of what we do which is distinguishable from the consciousness of the field of stimulation, whether that field be without or within. It is this "awareness" which has led many to assume that it is the nature of the self to be conscious both of subject and of object—to be subject of action toward an object world and at the same time to be directly conscious of this subject as subject—"Thinking its non-existence along with whatever else it thinks." Now, as professor James pointed out, this consciousness is more logically conceived of as sciousness—the thinker being an implication rather than a content, while the "me" is but a bit of object content within the stream of sciousness. However, this logical statement does not do justice to the findings of consciousness. Besides the actual stimulations and responses and the memory images of these, within which lie perforce the organic sensations and responses which make up the "me," there accompanies a large part of our conscious experience, indeed all that we call self-conscious, an inner response to what we may be doing, saying, or thinking. At the back of our heads we are a large part of the time more or less clearly conscious of our own replies to the remarks made to others, of innervations which would lead to attitudes and gestures answering our gestures and attitudes towards others.

The observer who accompanies all our self-conscious conduct is then not the actual "I" who is responsible for the conduct in *propria persona*—he is rather the response which one makes to his own conduct. The confusion of this response of ours, following upon our social stimulations of others with the implied subject of our action, is the psychological ground for the assumption that the self can be directly conscious of itself as acting and acted upon. The actual situation is this: The self acts with reference to others and is immediately conscious of the objects about it. In memory it also redintegrates the self acting as well as the others acted upon. But besides these contents, the action with reference to the others calls out responses in the individual himself—there is then another "me" criticizing, approving, and suggesting, and consciously planning, *i.e.*, the reflective self.

It is not to all our conduct toward the objective world that we thus respond. Where we are intensely preoccupied with the objective world, this accompanying awareness disappears. We have to recall the experience to become aware that we have been involved as selves, to produce the self-consciousness which is a constituent part of a large part of our experience. As I have indicated elsewhere, the mechanism for this reply to our own social stimulation of others follows as a natural result from the fact that the very sounds, gestures, especially vocal gestures, which man makes in addressing others, call out or tend to call out responses from himself. He can not hear himself speak without assuming in a measure the attitude which he would have assumed if he had been addressed in the same words by others.

The self which consciously stands over against other selves thus becomes an object, an other to himself, through the very fact that he hears himself talk, and replies. The mechanism of introspection is therefore given in the social attitude which man necessarily assumes toward himself, and the mechanism of thought, in so far as thought uses symbols which are used in social intercourse, is but an inner conversation.

Now it is just this combination of the remembered self which acts and exists over against other selves with the inner response to his action which is essential to the self-conscious ego—the self in the full meaning of the term—although neither phase of self-consciousness, in so far as it appears as an object of our experience, is a subject.

It is also to be noted that this response to the social conduct of the self may be in the rôle of another—we present his arguments in imagination and do it with his intonations and gestures and even perhaps with his facial expression. In this way we play the rôles of all our group; indeed, it is only in so far as we do this that they become part of our social environment—to be aware of another self as a self implies that we have played his rôle or that of another with whose type we identify him for purposes of intercourse. The inner response to our reaction to others is therefore as varied as is our social environment. Not that we assume the rôles of others toward ourselves because we are subject to a mere imitative instinct, but because in responding to ourselves we are in the nature of the case taking the attitude of another than the self that is directly acting, and into this reaction there naturally flows the memory images of the responses of those about us, the memory images of those responses of others which were in answer to like actions. Thus the child can think about his conduct as good or bad only as he reacts to his own acts in the remembered words of his parents. Until this process has been developed into the abstract process of thought, self-consciousness remains dramatic, and the self which is a fusion of the remembered actor and this accompanying chorus is somewhat loosely organized and very clearly social. Later the inner stage changes into the forum and workshop of thought. The features and intonations of the *dramatis personæ* fade out and the emphasis falls upon the meaning of the inner speech, the imagery becomes merely the barely necessary cues. But the mechanism remains social, and at any moment the process may become personal.

It is fair to say that the modern western world has lately done much of its thinking in the form of the novel, while earlier the drama was a more effective but equally social mechanism of self-consciousness. And, in passing, I may refer to that need of filling out the bare spokesman of abstract thought, which even the most abstruse thinker feels, in seeking his audience. The import of this for religious self-consciousness is obvious.

There is one further implication of this nature of the self to which I wish to call attention. It is the manner of its reconstruction. I wish especially to refer to it, because the point is of importance in the psychology of ethics.

As a mere organization of habit the self is not self-conscious. It is this self which we refer to as character. When, however, an essential problem appears, there is some disintegration in this organization, and different tendencies appear in reflective thought as different voices in conflict with each other. In a sense the old self has disintegrated, and out of the moral process a new self arises. The specific question I wish to ask is whether the new self appears together with the new object or end. There is of course a reciprocal relation between the self and its object, the one implies the other and the interests and evaluations of the self answer exactly to the content and values of the object. On the other hand, the consciousness of the new object, its values and meaning, seems to come earlier to consciousness than the new self that answers to the new object.

The man who has come to realize a new human value is more immediately aware of the new object in his conduct than of himself and his manner of reaction to it. This is due to the fact to which reference has already been made, that direct attention goes first to the object. When the self becomes an object, it appears in memory, and the attitude which it implies has already been taken. In fact, to distract attention from the object to the self implies just that lack of objectivity which we criticize not only in the moral agent, but in the scientist.

Assuming as I do the essentially social character of the ethical end, we find in moral reflection a conflict in which certain values find a spokesman in the old self or a dominant part of the old self, while other values answering to other tendencies and impulses arise in opposition and find other spokesmen to present their cases. To leave the field to the values represented by the old self is exactly what we term selfishness. The justification for the term is found in the habitual character of conduct with reference to these values. Attention is not claimed by the object and shifts to the subjective field where the affective responses are identified with the old self. The result is that we state the other conflicting ends in subjective terms of other selves and the moral problem seems to take on the form of the sacrifice either of the self or of the others.

Where, however, the problem is objectively considered, although the conflict is a social one, it should not resolve itself into a struggle between selves, but into such a reconstruction of the situation that different and enlarged and more adequate personalities may emerge. Attention should be centered on the objective social field.

In the reflective analysis, the old self should enter upon the same terms with the selves whose rôles are assumed, and the test of the reconstruction is found in the fact that all the personal interests are adequately recognized in a new social situation. The new self that answers to this new situation can appear in consciousness only after this new situation has been realized and accepted. The new self can not enter into the field as the determining factor because he is consciously present only after the new end has been formulated and accepted. The old self may enter only as an element over against the other personal interests involved. If he is the dominant factor it must be in defiance of the other selves whose interests are at stake. As the old self he is defined by his conflict with the others that assert themselves in his reflective analysis.

Solution is reached by the construction of a new world harmonizing the conflicting interests into which enters the new self.

The process is in its logic identical with the abandonment of the old theory with which the scientist has identified himself, his refusal to grant this old attitude any further weight than may be given to the other conflicting observations and hypotheses. Only when a successful hypothesis, which overcomes the conflicts, has been formulated and accepted, may the scientist again identify himself with this hypothesis as his own, and maintain it *contra mundum*. He may not state the scientific problem and solution in terms of his old personality. He may name his new hypothesis after himself and realize his enlarged scientific personality in its triumph.

The fundamental difference between the scientific and moral solution of a problem lies in the fact that the moral problem deals with concrete personal interests, in which the whole self is reconstructed in its relation to the other selves whose relations are essential to its personality.

The growth of the self arises out of a partial disintegration—the appearance of the different interests in the forum of reflection, the reconstruction of the social world, and the consequent appearance of the new self that answers to the new object.

A Behavioristic Account ∿ of the Significant Symbol ∿

The statement I wish to present rests upon the following assumptions, which I can do no more than state: I assume, provisionally, the hypothesis of the physical sciences, that physical objects and the physical universe may be analyzed into a complex of physical corpuscles. I assume that the objects of immediate experience exist in relationship to the biologic and social individuals whose environments they make up. This relationship involves on the one hand the selection through the sensitivities and reactions of the living forms of those elements that go to make up the object. On the other hand these objects affect the plants and animals whose natures are responsible for them as objects, e.g., food exists as an immediate experience in its relation to the individuals that eat it. There is no such thing as food apart from such individuals. The selection of the characters which go to make up food is a function of living individuals. The effect of this food upon the living individuals is what we call adaptation of the form to the environment or its opposite. Whatever may be said of a mechanical universe of ultimate physical particles, the lines that are drawn about objects in experience are drawn by the attitudes and conduct of individual living forms. Apart from such an experience involving both the form and its environment, such objects do not exist.

On the other hand these objects exist objectively, as they are in immediate experience. The relation of objects making up an environment to the plants and the animals in no sense renders these objects subjective. What are termed the natures of objects are in the objects, as are their so-called sensuous qualities, but these natures are not in the objects either as external or internal relations, they are of the very essence of the objects, and become relations only in the thought process. The so-called sensuous qualities exist also in the objects, but only in their relations to the sensitive organisms whose environments they form.

The causal effect of the living organisms on their environment in creating objects is as genuine as the effect of the environment upon the living organism. A digestive tract creates food as truly as the advance of a glacial cap wipes out some animals or selects others which can grow warm coats of hair. An animal's sensitiveness to a particular character in an object gives the object in its relation to the animal a peculiar nature. Where there is sensitiveness to two or more different characters of the object, answering to reactions that conflict and thus inhibit each other, the object is in so far analyzed. Thus the width of a stream would be isolated from the other characters of the stream through the inhibition of the animal's tendency to jump over it. In the immediate experience in which the animal organism and its environment are involved, these characters of the objects and the inhibited reactions that answer to them are there or exist, as characters, though as yet they have no significance nor are they located in minds or consciousnesses.

Among objects in the immediate experience of animals are the different parts of their own organisms, which have different characters from those of other objects—especially hedonic characters, and those of stresses and excitements—but characters not referred to selves until selves arise in experience. They are only accidentally private, *i.e.*, necessarily confined to the experience of single individuals. If—after the fashion of the Siamese Twins—two organisms were so joined that the same organ were connected with the central nervous system of each, each would have the same painful or pleasurable object in experience. A toothache or a pleased palate are objects for a single individual for reasons that are not essentially different from those which make the flame of a match scratched in a room in which there is only one individual an object only for that individual. It is not the exclusion of an object from the experience in which others are involved which renders it subjective; it is rendered subjective by being referred by an individual to his self, when selves have arisen in the development of conduct. Exclusive experiences are peculiarly favorable for such reference, but characteristics of objects for every one may be so referred in mental processes.

Among objects that exist only for separate individuals are so-called images. They are *there*, but are not necessarily *located* in space. They do enter into the structure of things, as notably on the printed page, or in the hardness of a distant object; and in hallucinations they may be spatially located. They are dependent for their existence upon conditions in the organism—especially those of the central nervous system—as are other objects in experience such as mountains and chairs. When referred to the self they become memory images, or those of a creative imagination, but they are not mental or spiritual stuff.

Conduct is the sum of the reactions of living beings to their environments, especially to the objects which their relation to the environment has "cut out of it," to use a Bergsonian phrase. Among these objects are certain which are of peculiar importance to which I wish to refer, viz., other living forms which belong to the same group. The attitudes and early indications of actions of these forms are peculiarly important stimuli, and to extend a Wundtian term may be called "gestures." These other living forms in the group to which the organism belongs may be called social objects and exist as such before selves come into existence. These gestures call out definite, and in all highly organized forms, partially predetermined reactions, such as those of sex, of parenthood, of hostility, and possibly others, such as the so-called herd instincts. In so far as these specialized reactions are present in the nature of individuals, they tend to arise whenever the appropriate stimulus, or gesture calls them out. If an individual uses such a gesture, and he is affected by it as another individual is affected by it, he responds or tends to respond to his own social stimulus, as another individual would respond. A notable instance of this is in the song, or vocal gesture of birds. The vocal gesture is of peculiar importance because it reacts upon the individual who makes it in the same fashion that it reacts upon another, but this is also true in a less degree of those of one's own gestures that he can see or feel.

The self arises in conduct, when the individual becomes a social object in experience to himself. This takes place when the individual assumes the attitude or uses the gesture which another individual would use and responds to it himself, or tends so to respond. It is a development that arises gradually in the life of the infant and presumably arose gradually in the life of the race. It arises in the life of the infant through what is unfortunately called imitation, and finds its expression in the normal play life of young children. In the process the child gradually becomes a social being in his own experience, and he acts toward himself in a manner analogous to that in which he acts toward others. Especially he talks to himself as he talks to others and in keeping up this conversation in the inner forum constitutes the field which is called that of mind. Then those objects and experiences which belong to his own body, those images which belong to his own past, become part of this self.

In the behavior of forms lower than man, we find one individual indicating objects to other forms, though without what we term signification. The hen that pecks at the angleworm is directly though without intention indicating it to the chicks. The animal in a herd that scents danger, in moving away indicates to the other members of the herd the direction of safety and puts them in the attitude of scenting the same danger. The hunting dog points to the hidden bird. The lost lamb that bleats, and the child that cries each points himself out to his mother. All of these gestures, to the intelligent observer, are significant symbols, but they are none of them significant to the forms that make them.

In what does this significance consist in terms of a behavioristic psychology? A summary answer would be that the gesture not only actually brings the stimulus-object into the range of the reactions of other forms, but that the nature of the object is also indicated; especially do we imply in the term significance that the individual who points out indicates the nature to *himself*. But it is not enough that he should indicate this meaning—whatever meaning is—as it exists for himself alone, but that he should indicate that meaning as it exists for the other to whom he is pointing it out. The widest use of the term implies that he indicates the meaning to any other individual to whom it might be pointed out in the same situation. In so far then as the individual takes the attitude of another toward himself, and in some sense arouses in himself the tendency to the action, which his conduct calls out in the other individual, he will have indicated to himself the meaning of the gesture. This implies a definition of meaning—that it is an indicated reaction which the object may call out. When we find that we have adjusted ourselves to a comprehensive set of reactions toward an object we feel that the meaning of the object is ours. But that the meaning may be ours, it is necessary that we should be able to regard ourselves as taking this attitude of adjustment to response. We must indicate to ourselves not only the object but also the readiness to respond in certain ways to the object, and this indication must be made in the attitude or rôle of the other individual to whom it is pointed out or to whom it may be pointed out. If this is not the case it has not that common property which is involved in significance. It is through the ability to be the other at the same time that he is himself that the symbol becomes significant. The common statement of this is that we have in mind, what we indicate to another that he shall do. In giving directions, we give the direction to ourselves at the same time that we give it to another. We assume also his attitude of response to our requests, as an individual to whom the direction has the same signification in his conduct that it has to ourselves.

But signification is not confined to the particular situation within which an indication is given. It acquires universal meaning. Even if the two are the only ones involved, the form in which it is given is universal—it would have the same meaning to any other who might find himself in the same position. How does this generalization arise? From the behavioristic standpoint it must take place through the individual generalizing himself in his attitude of the other. We are familiar enough with the undertaking, in social and moral instruction to children and to those who are not children. A child acquires the sense of property through taking what may be called the attitude of the generalized other. Those attitudes which all assume in given conditions and over against the same objects, become for him attitudes which every one assumes. In taking the rôle which is common to all, he finds himself speaking to himself and to others with the authority of the group. These attitudes become axiomatic. The generalization is simply the result of the identity of responses. Indeed it is only as he has in some sense amalgamated the attitudes of the different rôles in which he has addressed himself that he acquires the unity of personality. The "me" that he addresses is constantly varied. It answers to the changing play of impulse, but the group solidarity, especially in its uniform restrictions, gives him the unity of universality. This I take to be the sole source of the universal. It quickly passes the bounds of the specific group. It is the vox populi, vox dei, the "voice of men and of angels." Education and varied experience refine out of it what is provincial, and leave "what is true for all men at all times." From the first, its form is universal, for differences of the different attitudes of others wear their peculiarities away. In the play period, however, before the child has reached that of competitive games—in which he seeks to pit his own acquired self against others—in the play period this process is not fully carried out and the child is as varied as his varying moods; but in the game he sees himself in terms of the group or the gang and speaks with a passion for rules and standards. Its social advantage and even necessity makes this approach to himself imperative. He must see himself as the whole group sees him. This again has passed under the head of passive imitation. But it is not in uniform attitudes that universality appears as a recognized factor in either inner or outer behavior. It is found rightly in thought and thought is the conversation of this generalized other with the self.

The significant symbol is then the gesture, the sign, the word which is addressed to the self when it is addressed to another individual, and is addressed to another, in form to all other individuals, when it is addressed to the self.

Signification has, as we have seen, two references, one to the thing indicated, and the other to the response, to the instance and to the meaning or idea. It denotes and connotes. When the symbol is used for the one, it is a name. When it is used for the other, it is a concept. But it neither denotes nor connotes except, when in form at least, denotation and connotation are addressed both to a self and to others, when it is in a universe of discourse that is oriented with reference to a self. If the gesture simply indicates the object to another, it has no meaning to the individual who makes it, nor does the response which the other individual carries out become a meaning to him, unless he assumes the attitude of having his attention directed by an individual to whom it has a meaning. Then he takes his own response to be the meaning of the indication. Through this sympathetic placing of themselves in each other's rôles, and finding thus in their own experiences the responses of the others, what would otherwise be an unintelligent gesture, acquires just the value which is connoted by signification, both in its specific application and in its universality.

It should be added that in so far as thought—that inner conversation in which objects as stimuli are both separated from and related to their responses—is identified with consciousness, that is in so far as consciousness is identified with awareness, it is the result of this development of the self in experience. The other prevalent signification of consciousness is found simply in the presence of objects in experience. With the eyes shut we can say we are no longer conscious of visual objects. If the condition of the nervous system or certain tracts in it, cancels the relation of individual and his environment, he may be said to lose consciousness or some portion of it; *i.e.*, some objects or all of them pass out of experience for this individual. Of peculiar interest is the disappearance of a painful object, *e.g.*, an aching tooth under a local anesthetic. A general anesthetic shuts out all objects.

As above indicated analysis takes place through the conflict of responses which isolates separate features of the object and both separates them from and relates them to their responses, *i.e.*, their meanings. The response becomes a meaning, when it is indicated by a generalized attitude both to the self and to others. Mind, which is a process within which this analysis and its indications take place, lies in a field of conduct between a specific individual and the environment, in which the individual is able, through the generalized attitude he assumes, to make use of symbolic gestures, *i.e.*, terms, which are significant to all including himself.

While the conflict of reactions takes place within the individual, the analysis takes place in the object. Mind is then a field that is not confined to the individual much less is located in a brain. Significance belongs to things in their relations to individuals. It does not lie in mental processes which are enclosed within individuals.

⌒ The Philosophical Basis of Ethics ⌒

The evolutionary point of view has had more than one important result for philosophical thought. Not the least important among these has been the conception of the evolution of evolution. Not only can we trace in the history of thought the evolution of the conception of evolution, but we find ourselves with a consciousness which we conceive of as evolved; the contents and the forms of these contents can be looked upon as the products of development. Among these contents and forms are found the temporal and spatial qualities of things, of the world. The very time process as well as the space of the universe lies in experience which is itself presented as the result of an evolution that arises in and through spatial conditions, which is first and foremost a temporal process.

The peculiarity of this situation lies in the fact that the involution appears in the immediate findings of science. Our geological and biological sciences unhesitatingly present epochs antedating man in terms of man's consciousness, and biology and scientific psychology as unhesitatingly present that consciousness as an evolution within which all the distinctions must be explained by the same general laws as those which are appealed to to account for animal organs and functions. It is true that occasionally a scientist such as Poincaré recognizes that even the number system, as well as Euclidean space, is but a construction which has arisen and maintained itself because of its practical advantages, though we can draw no conclusions from these practical advantages to their metaphysical reality. If this position be generalized, there results the conception of an evolution within which the environment—that which our science has presented as a fixed datum in its physical nature—has been evolved as well as the form which had adapted itself to that environment; that the space within which evolution has taken place has arisen by the same laws; that the very time which makes an evolution presentable has arisen in like manner. Now, to a certain extent the conception of an evolution of environment as well as of the form has domesticated itself within our biological science. It has become evident that an environment can exist for a form only in so far as the environment answers to the susceptibilities of the organism; that the organism determines thus its own environment; that the effect of every adaptation is a new environment which must change with that which responds to it. The full recognition, however, that form and environment must be phases that answer to each other, character for character, appears in ethical theory.

In a certain sense this is found in the statement which genetic psychology makes of the development of the consciousness of the individual. Here there can be no evolution of the intelligence except in so far as the child's world answers to increased powers of conscious control. The world and the individual must keep pace with each other in the life history of the individual. But the child comes into a world which receives him as a child. The world of the adult, from the point of view of descriptive psychology, is an independent environment within which the child and his world evolve. Within the field of ethics, on the other hand, the moral individual and his world cannot consistently be presented as themselves lying inside another moral field. The growth of moral consciousness must be coterminous with that of the moral situation. The moral life lies in the interaction of these two; the situation rises up in accusation of the moral personality which is unequal to it, and the personality rises to the situation only by a process which reconstructs the situation as profoundly as it reconstructs the self. No man has found moral power within himself except in so far as he has found a meaning in his world that answered to the new-found power, or discovered a deeper ethical meaning in his environment that did not reveal new capacities for activities within himself. Moral evolution takes place then as does that of the child; the moral personality and its world must arise *pari passu*, but, unlike the psychologist's statement of the development of the child, it does not lie inside a larger determining environment.

I am not ignorant of evolutionary ethics, nor that every type of ethical theory in these days has felt itself bound to interpret the development of moral consciousness in terms of custom and institutions. Thus we seem to postulate not only a community moral consciousness, a moral world which determines the growth of the moral consciousness of the individual, but also we imply that this determining moral environment goes back into a past that antedates moral consciousness itself. From this point of view, morality, *i.e.*, control by community habit, has determined the development of individual moral consciousness as tyranically as the intellectual world has controlled the growth of intelligence in the members of society. But this paradox disappears when we recognize that this control by the community over its members provides indeed the material out of which reflective moral consciousness builds up its own situation, but cannot exist as a situation until the moral consciousness of the individual constructs it.

It is another statement of the same thing that moral consciousness is the most concrete consciousness—the most inclusive statement which can be given of immediate experience. There is no phase of activity, intellectual or physical, no type of inner experience, no presentation of outer reality, which does not find its place within the moral judgment. There is nothing which may not be a condition or an element of conduct, and moral consciousness reaches its climax in the estimation of every possible content of the individual and his situation. There is no other type of consciousness which must not abstract from other phases to assure its own existence. One cannot carry out an acute analysis and respond to the beauty of the object of analysis, one cannot swell with emotion and dispassionately observe. But we place every phase of our experience within the sweep of conscience; there is no one of these phases of consciousness which has not its legitimate function within the activity when viewed as moral. It is but a step further to claim that the abstractions of science and the expressions of the emotion and the direction of attention in perception and inference must find their functions, and hence their reason for existence, in the act; and that morality inheres in the act alone, but in none of these functions of the act (if I may be allowed two meanings of function in the same sentence).

It is, of course, possible to make this a metaphysical doctrine. If one finds reality in immediate experience and admits that the various intellectual, æsthetic, and perceptual processes exist only as parts and functions of an act which is the ultimate form of immediate experience, then the recognition of the ethical statement of this act as its fullest statement would found metaphysics upon ethics. The presentation of such a doctrine, however, would demand first of all a discussion of the meaning of the terms "immediate experience," of "reality," and the "cognitive state" that answers to it. I have no wish to enter this debatable field, that is loosely defined by the term pragmatism.

There are, however, certain implications of modern ethical doctrine which fall within the lines which I have indicated above; that are of interest quite apart from their relation to metaphysical and logical speculations. The implications to which I refer are those that flow from evolutionary doctrine on the one side and from the identification of purposive activity with moral activity, and the recognition that our intelligence is through and through purposive. The first implication that flows from this position is that the fundamental necessity of moral action is simply the necessity of action at all; or stated in other terms, that the motive does not arise from the relations of antecedently given ends of activities, but rather that the motive is the recognition of the end as it arises in consciousness. The other implication is that the moral interpretation of our experience must be found within the experience itself.

We are familiar with three ethical standpoints, that which finds in conscious control over action only the further development of conduct which has already unconsciously been determined by ends, that which finds conduct only where reflective thought is able to present a transcendental end, and that which recognizes conduct only where the individual and the environment—the situation—mutually determine each other. In the first case, moral necessity in conduct, for the conscious individual, is quite relative. It depends upon the degree of recognition which he reaches of the forces operating through him. Furthermore, the motive to act with reference to the end of the fullest life of the species is one which is primarily quite narrowly individualistic, and depends for a social interpretation upon the community of which the individual is a member. Moral necessity in conduct from this point of view is quite independent of the activity itself. So far from being the most fundamental reality it is a derivative by which, through what it is hard not to call a hocus pocus, the individual acts, for what is only indirectly his own—a distant end, through a social *dressur*. It is, of course, natural that this point of view should mediate the process of training by which men are to be led unwittingly to socially worthy action, rather than the immediate conduct of the individual who finds himself face to face with a moral problem. It is the standpoint of the publicist and the reformer of social institutions.

But if we admit that the evolutionary process consists in a mutual determination of the individual and his environment—not the determination of the individual by his environment, moral necessity in conduct is found in the very evolutionary situation. The possibility of intelligent action waits upon the determination of the conditions under which that action is to take place. The statement of these conditions becomes the end, when it is recognized that the statement is in terms of the activities that make up the personality of the individual. The content of the end is the mutuality of statement of personality, *i.e.*, the tendencies to activity, in terms of the personalities who make up the environment, *i.e.*, the conditions of the expression of the activities. It is because the man must recognize the public good in the exercise of his powers, and state the public good in terms of his own outgoing activities that his ends are moral. But it is not the public good which comes in from outside himself and lays a moral necessity upon him, nor is it a selfish propensity that drives him on to conduct.

It is inconceivable that such an outside end should have any but an extraneous position. It could never come into a personality except by the door of its own interest. The end could not be a social end. Nor could a purely individual propensity through the agency of community training become social. The moral necessity lies not in the end acting from without, nor in the push of inclination from within, but in the relation of the conditions of action to the impulses to action. The motive is neither a purely rational, external end, nor a private inclination, but the impulse presented in terms of its consequences over against the consequences of the other impulses. The impulse so conditioned, so interpreted, becomes a motive to conduct. The moral necessity is that all activity which appears as impulse and environment should enter into the situation, and there is nothing which ensures this completeness of expression except the full interrelationship of the self and the situation. That one fully recognized the conflict which the impulse involves in its consequences with the consequences of all the other social processes that go to make him up, is the moral dictum. From the reconstructions that this recognition involves the immediate statement of the end appears. To enforce this dictum is simply to live as fully and consciously and as determinedly as possible.

The moral necessity for education is not an ideal of intelligence that lies before us of the clear refulgence of the intellect. It is the necessity of knowledge to do what is trying to be done, the dependence of the uninformed impulse upon means, method, and interpretation. The necessity of uprightness in public affairs does not rest upon a transcendental ideal of perfection of the self, nor upon the attainment of the possible sum of human happiness, but upon the economy and effectiveness, and consistency demanded in the industrial, commercial, social, and æsthetic activities of those that make up the community. To push reform is to give expression to all these impulses and present them in their consequences over against those of all the other social impulses out of which an organism of personalities arises.

There is abroad a feeling of lack of moral force; we look before and after—to our ancestors, our posterity—for incentive to right conduct, when in fact there is no moral necessity which is not involved in the impulses to conduct themselves. To correct one abuse we must emphasize the interests it jeopardizes. There is no reservoir of moral power, except that which lies in the impulses behind these interests. To correct the sin of the individual is to awaken through the consequences of the sin the normal activities which are inhibited by the excess. It is this healthful, aggressive, moral attitude, which it seems to me is encouraged by the recognition that moral consciousness is the most concrete, the most inclusive of all. Here we must abstract from nothing, and here we cannot appeal from ourselves to a power without ourselves that makes for righteousness. In the fulness of immediate experience, with the consciousness that out of the struggle to act must arise all power to mediate action, lies salvation. In like manner evolution in moral conduct can appeal to no environment without to stamp itself upon the individual; nor to him to adapt himself to a fixed order of the universe, but environment as well as individual appears in immediate experience, the once coterminous with the other, and moral endeavor appears in the mutual determination of one by the other.

Nowhere is this point of view more needed than in the struggles which fill our industrial and commercial life. The individual is treated as if he were quite separable from his environment; and still more is the environment conceived as if it were quite independent of the individual. Both laborer and the society which employs him are exhorted to recognize their obligations to each other, while each continues to operate within its own narrow radius; and because the employer regards the labor union as a fixed external environment of his activity, and would have all the relations between laborer and employer determined by the method in which he bargains and does business, he becomes a narrow individualist; and because the laborer would determine these same relations by the methods which he has used in building up this union, he becomes a socialist. What will take that and other allied problems out of the vicious circles in which they are at present found, is the recognition that it is the incompleteness with which the different social interests are present that is responsible for the inadequacy of the moral judgments. If the community educated and housed its members properly, and protected machinery, food, market, and thoroughfares adequately, the problems at present vexing the industrial world would largely disappear. We resent the introduction of the standard of life into the question of the wages; and yet if the social activities involved in the conception of the standard of life were given full expression, the wage question would be nearly answered. Every such problem is the inevitable indication of what has been left undone, of impulses checked, or interest overlooked. We turn back to history and talk about the evolution of man as if his environment were not the projection of himself in the conditions of conduct, as if the fulfillment of the Law and the Prophets were not the realization of all that is in us. The sources of power lie in that which has been overlooked. Again and again we are surprised to find that the moral advance has not been along the straight line of the moral struggles in which a sin seemed to be faced by righteous effort, but by the appearance of a novel interest which has changed the whole nature of the problem. If we were willing to recognize that the environment which surrounds the moral self is but the statement of the conditions under which his different conflicting impulses may get their expression, we would perceive that the reorganization must come from a new point of view which comes to consciousness through the conflict. The environment must change *pari passu* with the consciousness. Moral advance consists not in adapting individual natures to the fixed realities of a moral universe, but in constantly reconstructing and recreating the world as the individuals evolve.

The second implication to which reference has been made, is that we must find the interpretation of moral consciousness within the act. The appeal to a moral order which transcends either metaphysically or temporally the moral situation; the besetting assumption of the moralist that a moral reconstruction can be made intelligible only by a perfect moral order from which we have departed, or toward which we are moving, have very grave practical consequences which it becomes us to consider. In the first place these assumptions rob our moral consciousness of the intellectual interest which belongs to them of right. If morality connotes merely conformity to a given order, our intellectual reaction is confined to the recognition of agreement and disagreement, beyond that the moral reaction can be only emotional and instinctive. There may be, indeed, intellectual processes involved in stating this moral order, but such statement is confined, in the nature of the case, to apologetic and speculative thought to thought which cannot be a part of the immediate moral consciousness.

A moral order to which we must conform can never be built up in thought in the presence of an exigency. There are only two types of reaction in a practical situation. One may respond to well-recognized cues by well-formed habits, or one may adapt and reconstruct his habits by new interpretation of the situation. In the first instance we have habitual conduct, in the second that type of reaction which has been most explicitly worked out by the natural sciences. Most of our action, of course, falls within the first category, and involves no moral struggle. The second type, on the other hand, is that in which practically all our moral issues arise. If a practical scientific problem arises, such as the engineering problems in constructing railroads or driving tunnels, we recognize that the intellectual process by which the problem is solved cannot be a mere reference to a perfect model of conduct already in existence. On the contrary, just because the engineer is face to face with a real problem he must find in the physical situation facts of which he is at present ignorant, and at the same time readjust his habits; in fact, it is the possible readjustment of the habit that directs his attention in investigating the situation, and, on the other hand, what is discovered serves to mediate the formation of the new habit. In a word, there is the typical play of attention back and forth between perception and response. In any such process the criterion which governs the whole and its two phases—three phases if we distinguish between perception of the new data and the formation of the hypothesis by which they are interpreted and mediated in the response—can never be external to the process. There exists as yet no plan of procedure which the engineer discovers or receives as a vision in the mount. The control is found in the relation of the different phases of the act which have been sketched above. It is the possibility of reaction to a stimulus that holds the reaction in the field of investigation and it is the continued investigation of the field of stimulus which keeps the reaction continuous and pertinent. The control is then that which was earlier referred to as the process of evolution in which individual and environment mutually determine each other. It is the criterion of action, which uses working hypotheses, but which cannot possibly be identified with an external ideal. This process, whether met in the field of mechanical invention, or the range of engineering, or that of scientific research, is recognized as the most absorbing, most interesting, most fascinating intellectually with which the mind of man can occupy itself, and this interest belongs legitimately to the solution of every moral problem, for the procedure is identical intellectually.

Yet we succeed in robbing our reflective moral consciousness of a great part of this interest. For there is and can be no interest in merely identifying certain types of conduct with those found in a given theory. For example, there is no intellectual interest involved in merely identifying the control exercised by a financier over an industry with the concept of property, and justifying him in doing what he will, within the limits of the law, with his own. There may be a very vigorous emotional reaction against the suggestion that he be interfered with in these vested rights; or, on the other hand, against an institution of property which permits such individualistic exploitation of social values, but there is no intellectual interest except that which is either apologetic or purely speculative. It does not come into the moral reaction to the situation. And yet the enormous content of interest which does attach to these moral questions is attested by the social sciences which have sprung up and expanded in every college and university.

It is interesting to compare the intellectual treatment which such problems receive at the hands of the scientific investigator and the pulpit. In the latter there is at present no apparatus for investigation. The pulpit is committed to a right and wrong which are unquestioned, and from its point of view unquestionable. Its function then is not the intellectual one of finding out what in the new situation is right, but in inspiring to a right conduct which is supposed to be so plain that he who runs may read. The result has been that in the great moral issues of recent industrial history, such as the child labor, woman's labor, protection of machinery, and a multitude more, the pulpit has been necessarily silent. It had not the means nor the technique for finding out what was the right thing to do. The science of hygiene threatens the universal issue of temperance, while we can look forward to the time when investigation may enable us to approach understandingly the prostitute and her trade, and change the social conditions which have made her possible instead of merely scourging an abstract sin.

The loss to the community from the elimination of the intellectual phase of moral conduct it would be difficult to over-estimate and this loss is unavoidable as long as the interpretation of conduct lies outside the immediate experience, as long as we must refer to a moral order without, to intellectually present the morality of conduct.

In conclusion may I refer to another loss which moral conduct dependent upon an external ideal involves. The interpretation of sin and wrong with reference to a moral order external to the conduct fails to identify the moral defect with the situation out of which it springs and by whose reconstruction it may be eliminated. An illustration will at once indicate, I think, what I have in mind. The responsibility for death and accident upon our railroads cannot be laid at the doors of the system and those that work it, if an abstract doctrine of property and contract is used to judge the conduct of railroad managers and directors. The imperative necessity of the situation is that responsibility should be tested by the consequences of an act; that the moral judgment should find its criterion in the mutual determination of the individual and the situation. As it is, men who would risk their own lives to save a drowning man, regard themselves as justified in slaughtering others by the thousand to save money. Abstract valuations take the place of concrete valuations, and as the abstract external valuations are always the precipitations of earlier conduct, they are pretty uniformly inadequate.

But not only does an external moral ideal rob immediate moral conduct of its most important values, but it robs human nature of the most profound solace which can come to those who suffer—the knowledge that the loss and suffering, with its subjective poignancy, has served to evaluate conduct, to determine what is and what is not worth while.

CHAPTER SEVEN

Alfred Schutz on Society and Intersubjectivity

～ Introduction ～

Alfred Schutz (1899–1959) was born in Vienna. After completing military service in World War I, he studied law at the University of Vienna and completed his doctoral studies. Thereafter, Schutz accepted a position as executive secretary of the Austrian Banker's Association and joined the bank of Reitler and Company, an association that lasted even after Schutz emigrated to the United States. In addition to enjoying a successful career in the banking industry, Schutz was seriously interested in philosophy and sociology. He took the opportunity to study with Edmund Husserl (1859–1938), the founder of the philosophical approach called phenomenology, who was teaching at the University of Freiberg in Germany.

Phenomenology takes the position that in order to grasp clearly what we perceive and think we must bracket out, or remove, extraneous conceptions. The idea is to acquire a better understanding of how we know what we know about the world and precisely what it is that we do know. Husserl's phenomenology was an innovative approach to accessing the functioning of subjectivity. Schutz was also interested in sociology, particularly Weber's theory of social action. As you will remember, "social action" refers to Weber's observation that individuals take account of one another in determining their own actions. Schutz was fascinated by the question of how individuals understand each other. As you will see, in dealing with this question of intersubjectivity, Schutz devised a phenomenological sociology based upon the work of Weber and Husserl, and in time he incorporated ideas from Thomas, Mead, and others.

Schutz did not stay in Vienna throughout his life. With the rise to power of Hitler in Germany and Germany's military aggression in other nations, Schutz moved first to Paris and then to New York. As a result of his involvement in assisting refugees to emigrate to the United States, Schutz became acquainted with the Graduate Faculty of Political and Social Sciences at the New School for Social Research in New York. Eventually, he became a full professor at the New School and established ties with many leading American intellectuals. Schutz was a cofounder of the International Phenomenological Society and was involved as an editor and contributor for the journal *Philosophy and Phenomenological Research* from its inception.

Unlike the other chapters in this anthology, this one is composed of short excerpts from six different writings. In the first selection, Schutz (1956: 57) observes that "the subjective meaning the group has for its members consists in their knowledge of a common situation, and with it of a common system of typifications and relevances." Individual experience is oriented by a common stock of knowledge (that is, the culture's belief system, including the culture's method of defining what is valid and true). This common stock of knowledge supplies members with interpretations of reality that become what we assume to be the case. For example, self-interest is assumed by many in our culture to be inherent. Hence, behaving in a way that strives to maximize self-interest, even at another's expense, while not always appreciated by others, is nevertheless considered justifiable. Why? The behavior is assumed to be valid (it is typified behavior) and is associated with other behaviors, ideas, objects (relevances), and such behaviors reinforce the common stock of knowledge. In essence, these are the ways in which individuals are socialized and oriented into their roles and into the feeling that their society makes sense.

One individual may occupy multiple roles, and these roles may involve conflicting relevances (i.e., have conflicting priorities concerning values). This will lead to role conflict. Individuals are free to adjust their group memberships or roles or values in order to reduce this personal sense of conflict. But in order to do that, they must recognize that the conflict of roles that they are experiencing is contingent upon their refusal to accept that which is taken for granted. The refusal to accept that which is taken for granted opens up the insight into different zones of relevance. With qualifications, Schutz describes four zones of relevance (four levels of conceptual understanding and behavioral manipulation), each having an increasingly abstract relation to one's sense of self and the world. The more one inquires into what one knows and how one knows it, the more one may be able to penetrate through the increasingly abstract cultural interpretations of that which is taken for granted. To continue our example, is it the case that human beings are self-interested by nature, or are human beings as likely to be other-interested as self-interested depending upon time (history) and place (culture)? This is not to suggest that penetrating the zones of relevance on this issue will provide a definitive answer. Rather, such inquiry may lead to a greater appreciation of the power of the taken for granted to formulate our assumptions (typifications) concerning reality.

Of course, in order to be understood by another (and feeling accepted is very important for maintaining a sense of well-being), one must use the relevances and typifications of one's group. A key element here is language: the exchange of sounds that are understood as words that have a common meaning. For example, gangs may share the common typification in society of "the successful life," though they may vary in what they define as being relevant for achieving it (that is, within a given subgroup, engaging in activities such as dealing drugs is the accepted means for achieving the society's definition of a successful life). The overlapping and distinct typifications and relevances will be reinforced or modified via language within given social circles, which will also overlap with, and be distinct from, the common typifications of society. As another example, let's say I'm in a clique that uses the third person to address oneself. When I say to a member of my group, "Nathan likes sociology," my friend will reply, because the grammar has meaning for him, because it is typical and relevant (has common meaning), "Joe thinks sociology is cool, too!" Now, if I were to approach a nongroup member in this way and say, "Nathan thinks sociology is cool," the other person would be likely to say, "Who is Nathan?" And even if they care about me, but don't recognize the means of self-reference, they may continue by saying, "Anyway, who cares what this Nathan likes." In this instance, the clique that exists within society shares the same language, but the typifications and relevances are different.

Continuing in our phenomenological examination of relating: Have you ever noticed that you can examine another person in a way that you cannot examine yourself? If you are truly witnessing and listening to another, you are catching them acting in the present. You are simultaneous with them in a way that you cannot be with yourself. Our tendency is to reflect on our thinking when we are engaged in self-examination. In this instance, our present consciousness refers to the past in order to assess itself. However, we observe others in the present. We can be more simultaneous with another than we can be with ourselves. "Being there" with another in a "face-to-face situation" establishes what Schutz calls the Thou-orientation (that is, grasping another as a living, conscious being), and if this orientation is reciprocal, Schutz maintains that a We-relationship is established. Within the We-relationship, the partners are intent upon each other rather than themselves. Hence, within the We-relationship, one is not really conscious of being in the We-relationship. We may examine it as we examine our self-relationship, a conscious present that moves into the past via reflection. Moreover, Schutz (1967: 169) notes that the We-relationship in the face-to-face situation is not a single act: "[r]ather . . . social interaction consists in a continuous series of Acts of meaning-establishment and meaning-interpretation." I can "approximate" your "intended meaning" and vice versa. In this way, the intersubjective world is constituted (that is, selves that have uniquely internalized a shared reality meet).

Of course, in the everyday world persons are not continuously engaged in the We-relationship with those around them. Schutz's notion of the reciprocity of perspectives is that in our everyday affairs (in our commonsense thinking of others in daily life—in what Schutz calls the natural attitude) we: (1) take it for granted that others differ from ourselves and (2) take it for granted, until proven otherwise, "that the differences in perspectives originating in my and his unique biographical situations are irrelevant for the purposes at hand" (1953: 8). In this way, selves who have uniquely internalized a common stock of knowledge nevertheless reinforce to each other the shared belief system. The reciprocity of perspectives reinforces an "Us." Schutz refers to the "Us" as contemporaries—those who we may encounter, but not in a We-relationship. Finally, as a reciprocal Thou-orientation establishes a We-relationship, "intentional Acts directed toward contemporaries," constitute a They-orientation which establishes an abstract relationship with contemporaries. Schutz cites as an example: "When I mail a letter, I assume that certain contemporaries of mine, namely postal employees, will read the address and speed the letter on its way. I am not thinking of these postal employees as individuals, I do not know them personally and never expect to" (1967: 184). One's range and depth of knowledge of others can increase, but as Schutz points out: "all such modifications will be within a very narrow range so long as the original situation and my interest in it remain fairly even" (1967: 204).

～ Society, Social Relations, and Intersubjectivity ～

I

The subjective meaning of the group, the meaning a group has for its members, has frequently been described in terms of a feeling among the members that they belong together, or that they share common interests. This is correct; but unfortunately, these concepts were only partially analyzed, namely, in terms of community and association (MacIver), Gemeinschaft and Gesellschaft (Toennies), primary and secondary groups (Cooley), and so on.

We do not intend to follow these lines of investigation, not because we doubt their importance but because we believe that precisely the feeling of "belonging together" and the "sharing of common interests" from which they start requires further analysis in terms of commonsense thinking. . . .

. . . [T]he subjective meaning the group has for its members consists in their knowledge of a common situation, and with it of a common system of typifications and relevances. This situation has its history in which the individual members' biographies participate; and the system of typification and relevances determining the situation forms a common relative natural conception of the world. Here the individual members . . . find their bearings without difficulty in the common surroundings, guided by a set of recipes of more or less institutionalized habits . . . that help them come to terms with beings and fellow men belonging to the same situation. The system of typifications and relevances shared with the other members of the group defines the social roles, positions, and statuses of each. This acceptance of a common system of relevances leads the members of the group to a homogenous self-typification.

Our description holds good for both a) existential groups with which I share a common social heritage, and b) so-called voluntary groups joined or formed by me. The difference, however, is that in the first case the individual member finds himself within a preconstituted system . . . not of his own making, but handed down to him as a social heritage. In the case of voluntary groups, however, this system is not experienced by the individual member as readymade; it has to be built up by the members and is therefore always involved in a process of dynamic evolution . . . .

. . . [A problem is, how] does the individual member of a group define his private situation within the framework of those common typifications and relevances in terms of which the group defines its situation?

. . . [Note that our] description . . . refers neither to the nature of the bond that holds the group together, nor to the extent, duration, or intimacy of the social contact. It is, therefore, equally applicable to a marriage or a business enterprise . . . . Each [group] . . ., of course, takes place within the general framework of the cultural setting of the larger group, and in accordance with the way of life . . . which is pregiven to the single actors as a scheme of orientation and interpretation of their actions. It is, however, up to the . . . partners to define, and continuously redefine, their individual (private) situation within this setting.

. . . Such a general framework is experienced by the individual members in terms of institutionalizations to be interiorized, and the individual has to define his personal unique situation by using the institutionalized pattern for the realization of his particular personal interests.

Here we have one aspect of the private definition of the individual's membership situation. A corollary to it is the particular attitude that the individual chooses to adopt toward the social role he has to fulfill with the group. One thing is the objective meaning of the social role and the role expectation as defined by the institutionalized pattern . . . ; another thing is the particular subjective way in which the [individual defines his situation within the role]. . . .

The most important element in the definition of the private situation is, however, the fact that the individual finds himself always a member of numerous social groups. As Simmel has shown, each individual stands at the intersection of several social circles, and their number will be the greater the more differentiated the individual's personality. This is so because that which makes a personality unique is precisely that which cannot be shared with others.

According to Simmel, the group is formed by a process in which *many* individuals unite *parts* of their personalities—specific impulses, interests, forces—while what each personality really is, remains outside this common area. Groups are characteristically different according to the members' total personalities and those parts of their personalities with which they participate in the group. Elsewhere, Simmel speaks of the consciousness of degradation and oppression felt by the individual in the descent of the whole ego to the lowlands of the social structure, an insight which will be of considerable consequence for our later investigations.

It must further be added that in the individual's definition of his private situation the various social roles originating in his multiple membership in numerous groups are experienced as a set of self-typifications which in turn are arranged in a particular private order of domains of relevances that is, of course, continuously in flux. It is possible that exactly those features of the individual's personality which are to him of the highest order of relevance are irrelevant from the point of view of any system of relevances taken for granted by the group of which he is a member. This may lead to conflicts within the personality, mainly originating in the endeavor to live up to the various and frequently inconsistent role expectations inhering in the individual's membership in various social groups. As we have seen, it is only with respect to voluntary, and not to existential group membership that the individual is free to determine of which group he wants to be a member, and of which social role therein he wants to be the incumbent. It is, however, at least one aspect of freedom of the individual that he may choose for himself with which part of his personality he wants to participate in group memberships; that he may define his situation within the role of which he is the incumbent; and that he may establish his own private order of relevances in which each of his memberships in various groups has its rank.

II

. . . What is taken for granted is, until invalidation, believed to be simply "given" and "given-as-it-appears-to-me"—that is, as I or others whom I trust have experienced and interpreted it. It is this zone of things taken for granted within which we have to find our bearings. All our possible questioning for the unknown arises only within such a world of supposedly preknown things, and presupposes its existence. Or, to use Dewey's terms, it is the indeterminate situation from which all possible inquiry starts with the goal of transforming it into a determinate one. Of course, what is taken for granted today may become questionable tomorrow, if we are induced by our own choice or otherwise to shift our interest and to make the accepted state of affairs a field of further inquiry.

In referring to a shift of our own interest we have touched upon the core of our problem. Before we can proceed in our analysis of the three types of knowledge under consideration, it is necessary to clarify the relationship between interest and the distribution of knowledge.

It is our interest at hand that motivates all our thinking, projecting, acting, and therewith establishes the problems to be solved by our thought and the goals to be attained by our actions. In other words, it is our interest that breaks asunder the unproblematic field of the preknown into various zones of various relevance with respect to such interest, each of them requiring a different degree of precision of knowledge.

For our purposes we may roughly distinguish four regions of decreasing relevance. First, there is that part of the world within our reach which can be immediately observed by us and also at least partially dominated by us—that is, changed and rearranged by our actions. It is that sector of the world within which our projects can be materialized and brought forth. This zone of primary relevance requires an optimum of clear and distinct understanding of its structure. In order to master a situation we have to possess the know-how—the technique and the skill—and also the precise understanding of why, when, and where to use them. Second, there are other fields not open to our domination but mediately connected with the zone of primary relevance because, for instance, they furnish ready-made tools to be used for attaining the projected goal or they establish the conditions upon which our planning itself or its execution depends. It is sufficient to be merely familiar with these zones of minor relevance, to be acquainted with the possibilities, the chances, and risks they may contain with reference to our chief interest. Third, there are other zones which, *for the time being*, have no such connection with the interests at hand. We shall call them relatively irrelevant, indicating thereby that we may continue to take them for granted as long as no changes occur within them which might influence the relevant sectors by novel and unexpected chances or risks. And, finally, there are the zones which we suggest calling absolutely irrelevant because no possible change occurring within them would—or so we believe—influence our objective in hand. For all practical purposes a mere blind belief in the That and the How of things within this zone of absolute irrelevancy is sufficient.

But this description is much too rough and requires several qualifications. First, we have spoken of an "interest at hand" which determines our system of relevances. There is, however, no such thing as an isolated interest at hand. The single interest at hand is just an element within a hierarchical system, or even a plurality of systems, of interests which in everyday life we call our plans—plans for work and thought, for the hour and for our life. To be sure, this system of interests is neither constant nor homogeneous. It is not constant because in changing from any Now to the succeeding Now the single interests obtain a different weight, a different predominance within the system. It is not homogeneous because even in the simultaneity of any Now we may have most disparate interests. The various social roles we assume simultaneously offer a good illustration. The interests I have in the same situation as a father, a citizen, a member of my church or of my profession, may not only be different but even incompatible with one another. I have, then, to decide which of these disparate interests I must choose in order to define the situation from which to start further inquiry. This choice will state the problem or set the goal in respect to which the world we are living in and our knowledge of it are distributed in zones of various relevance.

Second, the terms "zones" or "regions" of various relevance might suggest that there are closed realms of various relevance in our life-world and, correspondingly, of various provinces of our knowledge of it, each separated from the other by clean-cut border lines. The opposite is true. These various realms of relevances and precision are intermingled, showing the most manifold interpenetrations and enclaves, sending their fringes into neighbor provinces and thus creating twilight zones of sliding transitions. If we had to draw a map depicting such a distribution figuratively it would not resemble a political map showing the various countries with their well-established frontiers, but rather a topographical map representing the shape of a mountain range in the customary way by contour lines connecting points of equal altitude. Peaks and valleys, foothills and slopes, are spread over the map in infinitely diversified configurations. The system of relevances is much more similar to such a system of isohypses than to a system of coordinates originating in a center O and permitting measurement by an equidistant network.

Third, we have to define two types of systems of relevances which we propose to call the system of intrinsic, and the system of imposed, relevances. Again, these are merely constructive types which in daily life are nearly always intermingled with one another and are very rarely found in a pure state. Yet it is important to study them separately in their interaction. The intrinsic relevances are the outcome of our chosen interests, established by our spontaneous decision to solve a problem by our thinking, to attain a goal by our action, to bring forth a projected state of affairs. Surely we are free to choose what we are interested in, but this interest, once established, determines the system of relevances intrinsic to the chosen interest. We have to put up with the relevances thus set, to accept the situation determined by their internal structure, to comply with their requirements. And yet they remain, at least to a certain extent, within our control. Since the interest upon which the intrinsic relevances depend and in which they originate has been established by our spontaneous choice, we may at any time shift the focus of this interest and thereby modify the relevances intrinsic to it, obtaining thus an optimum of clarity by continued inquiry. This whole process will still show all the features of a spontaneous performance. The character of all these relevances as intrinsic relevances—that is, intrinsic to a chosen interest—will be preserved.

We are, however, not only centers of spontaneity, gearing into the world and creating changes within it, but also the mere passive recipients of events beyond our control which occur without our interference. Imposed upon us as relevant are situations and events which are not connected with interest chosen by us, which do not originate in acts of our discretion, and which we have to take just as they are, without any power to modify them by our spontaneous activities except by transforming the relevances thus imposed into intrinsic relevances. While that remains unachieved, we do not consider the imposed relevances as being connected with our spontaneously chosen goals. Because they are imposed upon us they remain unclarified and rather incomprehensible.

III

The factual world of our experience, as has been explained before, is experienced from the outset as a typical one. Objects are experienced as trees, animals, and the like, and more specifically as oaks, firs, maples, or rattlesnakes, sparrows, dogs. This table I am now perceiving is characterized as something recognized, as something foreknown and, nevertheless, novel. What is newly experienced is already known in the sense that it recalls similar or equal things formerly perceived. But what has been grasped once in its typicality carries with it a horizon of possible experience with corresponding references to familiarity, that is, a series of typical characteristics still not actually experienced but expected to be potentially experienced. If we see a dog, that is, if we recognize an object as being an animal and more precisely as a dog, we anticipate a certain behavior on the part of this dog, a typical (not individual) way of eating, of running, of playing, of jumping, and so on. Actually we do not see his teeth, but having experienced before what a dog's teeth typically look like, we may expect that the teeth of the dog before us will show the same typical features though with individual modifications. In other words, what has been experienced in the actual perception of one object is apperceptively transferred to any other similar object, perceived merely as to its type. Actual experience will or will not confirm our anticipation of the typical conformity of these other objects. If confirmed, the content of the anticipated type will be enlarged; at the same time, the type will be split up into subtypes. On the other hand, the concrete real object will prove to have its individual characteristics which, nevertheless, have a form of typicality. Now, and this seems to be of special importance, we *may* take the typically apperceived object as an example of a general type and allow ourselves to be led to the general concept of the type, but we do not *need* by any means to think of the concrete dog thematically as an exemplar of the general concept "dog." "In general," this dog here is a dog like any other dog and will show all the characteristics which the type "dog," according to our previous experience, implies; nevertheless, this known type carries along a horizon of still unknown typical characteristics pertaining not only to this or that individual dog but to dogs in general. Every empirical idea of the general has the character of an open concept to be rectified or corroborated by supervening experience.

IV

. . . [W]hat the sociologist calls "system," "role," "status," "role expectation," "situation," and "institutionalization," is experienced by the individual actor on the social scene in entirely different terms. To him all the factors denoted by these concepts are elements of a network of typifications—typifications of human individuals, of their course-of-action patterns, of their motives and goals, or of the sociocultural products which originated in their actions. These types were formed in the main by others, his predecessors or contemporaries, as appropriate tools for coming to terms with things and men, accepted as such by the group into which he was born. But there are also self-typifications: man typifies to a certain extent his own situation within the social world and the various relations he has to his fellow men and cultural objects.

The knowledge of these typifications and of their appropriate use is an inseparable element of the sociocultural heritage handed down to the child born into the group by his parents and his teachers and the parents of his parents and the teachers of his teachers; it is, thus, socially derived. The sum-total of these various typifications constitutes a frame of reference in terms of which not only the sociocultural, but also the physical world has to be interpreted, a frame of reference that, in spite of its inconsistencies and its inherent opaqueness, is nonetheless sufficiently integrated and transparent to be used for solving most of the practical problems at hand. . . .

V

... A system of relevances and typifications, as it exists at any historical moment, is itself a part of the social heritage and as such is handed down in the educational process to the members of the in-group. It has various important functions:

1. It determines which facts or events have to be treated as substantially— that is, typically—equal (homogeneous) for the purpose of solving in a typical manner typical problems that emerge or might emerge in situations typified as being equal (homogeneous).

2. It transforms unique individual actions of unique human beings into typical functions of typical social roles, originating in typical motives aimed at bringing about typical ends. The incumbent of such a social role is expected by the other members of the in-group to act in the typical way defined by this role. On the other hand, by living up to his role the incumbent typifies himself; that is, he resolves to act in the typical way defined by the social role he has assumed. He resolves to act in a way in which a businessman, soldier, judge, father, friend, gangleader, sportsman, buddy, regular fellow, good boy, American, taxpayer, etc., is supposed to act. Any role thus involves a self-typification on the part of the incumbent.

3. It functions as both a scheme of interpretation and as a scheme of orientation for each member of the in-group and constitutes therewith a universe of discourse among them. Whoever (I included) acts in the socially approved typical way is supposed to be motivated by the pertinent typical motives and to aim at bringing about the pertinent typical state of affairs. He has a reasonable chance, by such actions, of coming to terms with everyone who accepts the same system of relevances and takes the typifications originating therein for granted. On the one hand, I have—in order to understand another—to apply the system of typifications accepted by the group to which both of us belong. For example, if he uses the English language, I have to interpret his statements in terms of the code of the English dictionary and the English grammar. On the other hand, in order to make myself understandable to another, I have to avail myself of the same system of typifications as a scheme of orientation for my projected action. Of course, there is a mere chance, namely, a mere likelihood, that the scheme of typifications used by me as a scheme of orientation will coincide with that used by my fellow man as a scheme of interpretation; otherwise misunderstandings among people of goodwill would be impossible. But at least as a first approximation we take it for granted that we both mean what we say and say what we mean.

4. The chances of success of human interaction, that is, the establishment of a congruency between the typified scheme used by the actor as a scheme of orientation and by his fellow men as a scheme of interpretation, is enhanced if the scheme of typification is standardized, and the system of pertinent relevances institutionalized. The various means of social control (mores, morals, laws, rules, rituals) serve this purpose.

5. The socially approved system of typifications and relevances is the common field within which the private typifications and relevance structures of the individual members of the group originate. This is so, because the private situation of the individual as defined by him is always a situation within the group, his private interests are interests with reference to those of the group (whether by way of particularization or antagonism), his private problems are necessarily in a context with the group problems. Again, this private system of domains of relevance might be inconsistent in itself; it might also be incompatible with the socially approved one. For example, I may take entirely different attitudes toward the problems of rearmament of the United States in my social role as a father of a boy, as a taxpayer, as a member of my church, as a patriotic citizen, as a pacifist, and as a trained economist. Nevertheless, all these partially conflicting and intersecting systems of relevances, both those taken for granted by the group and my private ones, constitute particular domains of relevances; all objects, facts, and events are homogeneous in the sense that they are relevant to the same problem.

VI

. . . Now let us go back again to the naïve attitude of daily life in which we live in our acts directed towards their objects. Among those objects which we experience in the vivid present are other people's behavior and thoughts. In listening to a lecturer, for instance, we seem to participate immediately in the development of his stream of thought. But—and this point is obviously a decisive one—our attitude in doing so is quite different from that we adopt in turning to our own stream of thought by reflection. We catch the other's thought in its vivid presence and not *modo preterito*; that is, we catch it as a "Now" and not as a "Just now." The other's speech and our listening are experienced as a vivid simultaneity. Now he starts a new sentence, he attaches word to word; we do not know how the sentence will end, and before its end we are uncertain what it means. The next sentence joins the first, paragraph follows paragraph: now he has expressed a thought and passes to another, and the whole is a lecture among other lectures and so on. It depends on circumstances how far we want to follow the development of his thought. But as long as we do so we participate in the immediate present of the other's thought.

The fact that I can grasp the other's stream of thought, and this means the subjectivity of the alter ego in its vivid present, whereas I cannot grasp my own self but by way of reflection in its past, leads us to a definition of the alter ego: the alter ego is that subjective stream of thought which can be experienced in its vivid present. In order to bring it into view we do not have to stop fictitiously the other's stream of thought nor need we transform its "Nows" into "Just Nows." It is simultaneous with our own stream of consciousness, we share together the same vivid present—in one word: we grow old together. The alter ego therefore is that stream of consciousness whose activities I can seize in their present by my own simultaneous activities.

This experience of the other's stream of consciousness in vivid simultaneity I propose to call the *general thesis of the alter ego's existence*. It implies that this stream of thought which is not mine shows the same fundamental structure as my own consciousness. This means that the other is like me, capable of acting and thinking; that his stream of thoughts show the same through and through connectedness as mine; that analogous to my own life of consciousness his shows the same time-structure, together with the specific experiences of retentions, reflections, protentions, anticipations, connected therewith and its phenomena of memory and attention, of kernel and horizon of the thought, and all the modifications thereof. It means, furthermore, that the other can live, as I do, either in his acts and thoughts, directed towards their objects or turn to his own acting and thinking: that he can experience his own Self only *modo practerito*, but that he may look at my stream of consciousness in a vivid present; that, consequently, he has the genuine experience of growing old with me as I know that I do with him.

As a potentiality each of us may go back into his past conscious life as far as recollection goes, whereas our knowledge of the other remains limited to that span of his life and its manifestations observed by us. In this sense each of us knows more of himself than of the other. But in a specific sense the contrary is true. In so far as each of us can experience the other's thoughts and acts in the vivid present whereas either can grasp his own only as a past by way of reflection. I know more of the other and he knows more of me than either of us knows of his own stream of consciousness. This present, common to both of us, is the pure sphere of the "We." And if we accept this definition, we can agree with Scheler's tenet that the sphere of the "We" is pregiven to the sphere of the Self—although Scheler never had in mind the theory we have just outlined. We participate, namely, without an act of reflection in the vivid simultaneity of the "We," whereas the I appears only after the reflective turning. And our theory also converges (to be sure, on another level) with Scheler's statement that acts are not objectifiable and that the other's acts can be experienced only by co-performing them. For we cannot grasp our own acting in its actual present; we can seize only those past of our acts which have already gone by; but we experience the other's acts in their vivid performance.

VII

. . . [I]t will be understood that, simultaneous with *my* lived experience of you, there is *your* lived experience which belongs to you and is part of your stream of consciousness. Meanwhile, the specific nature of your experience is quite unknown to me, that is, I do not know the meaning-contexts you are using to classify those lived experience of yours, provided, indeed, you are even aware of the movements of your body.

However, I can know the meaning-context into which I classify my own lived experiences of you. We have already seen that this is not your intended meaning in the true sense of the term. What can be comprehended is always only an "approximate value" of the limiting concept "the other's intended meaning."

VIII

. . . In the natural attitude of common-sense thinking of daily life I take it for granted that intelligent fellowmen exist. This implies that the objects of the world are, as a matter of principle, accessible to their knowledge, namely, either known to them or knowable by them. This I know and take for granted beyond question. But I know also and take for granted that, strictly speaking, the "same" object must mean something different to me and to any of my fellowmen. This is so because

1. I, being "here," am at another distance from and experience other aspects as being typical of the objects than he, who is "there." For the same reason, certain objects are out of my reach (of my seeing, hearing, my manipulatory sphere, etc.) but within his and vice versa.

2. My and my fellowman's biographically determined situations, and therewith my and his purpose at hand and my and his system of relevances originating in such purposes, must needs differ, at least to a certain extent.

Common sense thinking overcomes the differences in individual perspectives resulting from these factors by two basic idealizations:

1. The idealization of the interchangeability of the standpoints: I take it for granted—and assume my fellowman does the same—that if I change places with him so that his "here" becomes mine, I would be at the same distance from things and see them in the same typicality as he actually does; moreover, the same things would be in my reach which are actually in his. (All this vice versa.)

2. The idealization of the congruency of the system of relevances: Until counter-evidence I take it for granted—and assume my fellowman does the same—that the differences in perspectives originating in my and his unique biographical situations are irrelevant for the purpose at hand of either of us and that he and I, that "We" assume that both of us have selected and interpreted the actually or potentially common objects and their features in an identical manner or at least an "empirically identical" manner, namely, sufficient for all practical purposes.

It is obvious that both idealizations, that of the interchangeability of the standpoints and that of the congruency of relevances—both together constituting the *general thesis of reciprocal perspectives*—are typifying constructs of objects of thought which supersede the thought objects of my and my fellowman's private experience. By the operation of these constructs of common-sense thinking it is assumed that the sector of the world taken for granted by me is also taken for granted by you, my individual fellowman, even more, that it is taken for granted by "Us," but this "We" does not merely include you and me but "everyone who belongs to us," namely everyone whose system of relevances is substantially (sufficiently) in conformity with yours and mine. Thus, the general thesis of reciprocal perspectives leads to the apprehension of objects and their aspects actually known by me and potentially known by you as everyone's knowledge. Such knowledge is conceived to be objective and anonymous, namely detached from and independent of my and my fellowman's definition of the situation, my and his unique biographical circumstances and the actual and potential purposes at hand therein involved.

The terms "objects" and "aspect of objects" have to be interpreted in the broadest possible sense as objects of knowledge taken for granted.

IX

I speak of another person as within reach of my direct experience when he shares with me a community of space and a community of time. He shares a community of space with me when he is present in person and I am aware of him as such, and, moreover, when I am aware of him as this person *himself*, this *particular* individual, and of his body as the field upon which play the symptoms of his inner consciousness. He shares a community of time with me when his experience is flowing side by side with mine, when I can at any moment look over and grasp his thoughts as they come into being, in other words, when we are growing older together. Persons thus in reach of each other's direct experience I speak of as being in the "face-to-face" situation. The face-to-face situation presupposes, then, an actual simultaneity with each other of two separate streams of consciousness. We have already made this point clear . . . when we were dealing with the general thesis of the alter ego. We are now adding to it the corollary of the spatial immediacy of the Other, in virtue of which his body is present to me as a field of expression for his subjective experiences.

This spatial and temporal immediacy is essential to the face-to-face situation. All acts of Other-orientation and of affecting-the-other, and therefore all orientations and relationships within the face-to-face situation, derive their own specific flavor and style from this immediacy.

Let us first look at the way in which the face-to-face situation is constituted from the point of view of a participant in that situation. In order to become aware of such a situation, the participant must become intentionally conscious of the person confronting him. He must assume a face-to-face Other-orientation toward the partner. We shall term this attitude "Thou-orientation," and shall now proceed to describe its main features.

First of all, the Thou-orientation is the pure mode in which I am aware of another human being as a person. I am already Thou-oriented from the moment that I recognize an entity which I directly experience as a fellow man (as a Thou), attributing life and consciousness to him. However, we must be quite clear that we are *not* here dealing with a conscious *judgment*. This is a predicative experience in which I become aware of a fellow human being *as a person*. The Thou-orientation can thus be defined as the intentionality of those Acts whereby the Ego grasps the existence of the other person in the mode of the original self. Every such external experience in the mode of the original self presupposes the actual presence of the other person and my perception of him as there.

. Now, we wish to emphasize that it is precisely the being there (*Dasein*) of the Other toward which the Thou-orientation is directed, not necessarily the Other's specific characteristics. The concept of the Thou-orientation does not imply awareness of what is going on in the Other's mind. In its "pure" form the Thou-orientation consists merely of being intentionally directed toward the pure being-there of another alive and conscious human being. To be sure, the "pure" Thou-orientation is a formal concept, an intellectual construct, or, in Husserl's terminology, an "ideal limit." In real life we never experience the "pure existence" of others; instead we meet real people with their own personal characteristics and traits. The Thou-orientation as it occurs in everyday life is therefore not the "pure" Thou-orientation but the latter *actualized* and *rendered determinate* to some degree or other.

Now the fact that I look upon you as a fellow man does not mean that I am also a fellow man for you, unless you are aware of me. And, of course, it is quite possible that you may not be paying any attention to me at all. The Thou-orientation can, therefore, be either one-sided or reciprocal. It is one-sided if only one of us notices the presence of the other. It is reciprocal if we are mutually aware of each other, that is, if each of us is Thou-oriented toward the other. In this way there is constituted out of the Thou-orientation the face-to-face relationship (or directly experienced social relationship). . . . The face-to-face relationship in which the partners are aware of each other and sympathetically participate in each other's lives for however short a time we shall call the "pure We-relationship." But the "pure We-relationship" is likewise only a limiting concept. The directly experienced social relationship of real life is the pure We-relationship concretized and actualized to a greater or lesser degree and filled with content.

Let us illustrate this with an example. Suppose that you and I are watching a bird in flight. The thought "bird-in-flight" is in each of our minds and is the means by which each of us interprets his own observations. Neither of us, however, could say whether our lived experiences on that occasion were identical. In fact, neither of us would even try to answer that question, since one's own subjective meaning can never be laid side by side with another's and compared.

Nevertheless, during the flight of the bird you and I have "grown older together"; our experiences have been simultaneous. Perhaps while I was following the bird's flight I noticed out of the corner of my eye that your head was moving in the same direction as mine. I could then say that the two of us, that *we*, had watched the bird's flight. What I have done in this case is to coordinate temporally a series of my own experiences with a series of yours. But in so doing I do not go beyond the assertion of a mere *general* correspondence between my perceived "bird in flight" and your experiences. I make no pretense to any knowledge of the content of your subjective experiences or of the particular way in which they were structured. It is enough for me to know that you are a fellow human being who was watching the same thing that I was. And if you have in a similar way coordinated my experiences with yours, then we can both say that *we* have seen a bird in flight.

The basic We-relationship is already given to me by the mere fact that I am born into the world of directly experienced social reality. From this basic relationship is derived the original validity of all my direct experiences of particular fellow men and also my knowledge that there is a larger world of my contemporaries whom I am not now experiencing directly. . . .

To explain how our experiences of the Thou are rooted in the We-relationship, let us take conversation as an example. Suppose you are speaking to me and I am understanding what you are saying. As we have already seen, there are two senses of this understanding. First of all I grasp the "objective meaning" of your words, the meaning which they would have had, had they been spoken by you or anyone else. But second, of course, there is the subjective meaning, namely, what is going on in your mind as you speak. In order to get to your subjective meaning, I must picture to myself your stream of consciousness as flowing side by side with my own. Within this picture I must interpret and construct your intentional Acts as you choose your words. To the extent that you and I can mutually experience this simultaneity, growing older together for a time, to the extent that we can live in it together, to *that* extent we can live in each other's subjective contexts of meaning. However, our ability to apprehend each other's subjective contexts of meaning should not be confused with the We-relationship itself. For I get to your subjective meaning in the first place only by starting out with your spoken words as given and then by asking how you came to use those words. But this question of mine would make no sense if I did not already assume an actual or at least potential We-relationship between us. For it is only within the We-relationship that I can concretely experience you at a particular moment of your life. To put the point in terms of a formula: I can live in your subjective meaning-contexts only to the extent that I directly experience you within an actualized content-filled We-relationship.

This is true for all stages of understanding another person in which attention to his subjective meaning is involved. For all my lived experiences of the other person (above all the directly apprehended other person), whether they manifest agreement or discrepancy, have their origin in the sphere of the We-relationship. Attention to the We-relationship in turn broadens the objective knowledge of other people which I have gained from the interpretation of my own experiences of them. It likewise broadens my objective knowledge of the particular person involved with me in this particular We-relationship. Thus the contents of the one undivided stream of the We are always enlarging and contracting. In this sense the We resembles my stream of consciousness in the flow of its duration. But this similarity is balanced by a difference. The We-relationship is spatial as well as temporal. It embraces the body of the other person as well as his consciousness.

And because I grasp what is going on in his mind only through the medium of his perceived bodily movements, this Act of grasping is for me a lived experience that transcends my own stream of consciousness. Nevertheless, it should be emphasized that, among all self-transcending experiences, the We-experience remains closest to the stream of consciousness itself.

Moreover, while I am living in the We-relationship, I am really living in *our* common stream of consciousness. And just as I must, in a sense, step outside my own stream of consciousness and "freeze" my subjective experiences if I am going to reflect on them, the same requirement holds for the We-relationship. When you and I are immediately involved with each other, every experience is colored by that involvement. To the extent that we are going to think about the experiences we have together, we must to that degree withdraw from each other. If we are to bring the We-relationship into the focus of our attention, we must stop focusing on each other. But that means stepping out of the face-to-face relationship, because only in the latter do we live *in* the We. And here we can apply at a higher level everything that we said about phenomenal time in our analysis of the solitary Ego. Attention to the lived experiences of the We-relationship likewise presupposes that these experiences are full blown and have already elapsed. And our retrospective grasp of the We-experiences can fall anywhere in the continuum from maximum clarity to complete confusion. And it can be characterized by all degrees of consciousness, just as self-awareness can. In particular, the greater my awareness of the We-relationship, the less is my involvement in it, and the less am I genuinely related to my partner. The more I reflect, the more my partner becomes transformed into a mere object of thought. . . .

If the *pure* We-relationship were merely a modification of social relationship in general, it could be identified equally with direct social orientation and with social interaction. But, strictly speaking, the pure We-relationship is given *prior* to either of these. The pure We-relationship is merely the reciprocal form of the pure Thou-orientation, that is, the pure awareness of the *presence* of another person. His presence, it should be emphasized, not his specific traits. The pure We-relationship involves our awareness of each other's presence and also the knowledge of each that the other is aware of him. But, if we are to have a social relationship, we must go beyond this. What is required is that the Other-orientation of each partner become colored by a specific knowledge of the specific manner in which he is being regarded by the other partner. This in turn is possible only within directly experienced social reality. Only here do our glances actually meet; only here can one actually note how the other is looking at him.

But one cannot become aware of this basic connection between the pure We-relationship and the face-to-face relationship while still a participant in the We-relationship. *One must step out of it and examine it.* The person who is still a participant in the We-relationship does not experience it in its pure form, namely, as an awareness *that* the other person is there. Instead, he simply lives within the We-relationship in the fullness of its concrete content. In other words, the pure We-relationship is a mere limiting concept which one uses in the attempt to get a theoretical grasp of the face-to-face situation. But there are no specific concrete experiences which correspond to it. For the concrete experiences which do occur within the We-relationship in real life grasp their object— the We—as something unique and unrepeatable. And they do this in *one* undivided intentional Act.

Concrete We-relationships exhibit many differences among themselves. The partner, for instance, may be experienced with different degrees of immediacy, different degrees of intensity, or different degrees of intimacy. Or he may be experienced from different points of view. He may appear within the center of attention or at its periphery.

These distinctions apply equally to orientation relationships and to social interactions, determining in each of them the directness with which the partners "know" each other. Compare, for instance, the knowledge two people have of each other in conversation with the knowledge they have of each other in sexual intercourse. What different degrees of intimacy occur here, what different levels of consciousness are involved! Not only do the partners experience the We more deeply in the one case than in the other, but each experiences himself more deeply and his partner more deeply. It is not only the *object*, therefore, that is experienced with greater or lesser directness; it is the *relationship* itself, the being turned toward the object, the relatedness.

These are only two *types* of relationship. But now consider the different ways in which they can actually take place! The conversation, for instance, can be animated or offhand, eager or casual, serious or light, superficial or quite personal.

The fact that we may experience others with such different degrees of directness is very important. It is, as a matter of fact, the key to understanding the transition from the direct experience of others to the indirect which is characteristic of the world of mere contemporaries. We shall be coming to this transition very shortly, but meanwhile let us continue our examination of direct social experience by describing the different types of face-to-face relationship.

First of all, let us remember that in the face-to-face situation I literally see my partner in front of me. As I watch his face and his gestures and listen to the tone of his voice, I become aware of much more than what he is deliberately trying to communicate to me. My observations keep pace with each moment of his stream of consciousness as it transpires. The result is that I am incomparably better attuned to him than I am to myself. I may indeed be more aware of my own past (to the extent that the latter can be captured in retrospect) than I am of my partner's. Yet I have never been face to face with myself as I am with him now; hence I have never caught myself in the act of actually living through an experience.

To this encounter with the other person I bring a whole stock of previously constituted knowledge. This includes both general knowledge of what another person is as such and any specific knowledge I may have of the person in question. It includes knowledge of other people's interpretive schemes, their habits, and their language. It includes knowledge of the taken-for-granted in-order-to and because-motives of others as such and of this person in particular. And when I am face to face with someone, my knowledge of him is increasing from moment to moment. My ideas of him undergo continuous revision as the concrete experience unfolds. For no direct social relationship is one isolated intentional Act. Rather it consists of a continuous series of such Acts. The orientation relationship, for instance, consists of a continuous series of intentional Acts of Other-orientation, while social interaction consists in a continuous series of Acts of meaning-establishment and meaning-interpretation. All these different encounters with my fellow man will be ordered in multiple meaning-contexts: they are encounters with a human being as such, with this particular human being, and with this particular human being at this particular moment of time. And these meaning-contexts of mine will be "subjective" to the extent that I am attending to your actual conscious experiences themselves and not merely to my own lived experiences of you. Furthermore, as I watch you, I shall see that you are oriented to me, that you are seeking the subjective meaning of my words, my actions, and what I have in mind insofar as you are concerned. And I will in turn take account of the fact that you are thus oriented to me, and this will influence both my intentions with respect to you and how I act toward you. This again you will see, I will see that you have seen it, and so on. This interlocking of glances, this thousand-faceted mirroring of each other, is one of the unique features of the face-to-face situation. We may say that it is a constitutive characteristic of this particular social relationship. However, we must remember that the pure We-relationship, which is the very form of every encounter with another person, is not itself grasped *reflectively* within the face-to-face situation. Instead of being observed, it is lived through. The many different mirror images of Self within Self are not therefore caught sight of one by one but are experienced as a continuum within a single experience. Within the unity of this experience I can be aware simultaneously of what is going on in my mind and in yours, *living through* the two series of experiences as one series—what we are experiencing together.

This fact is of special significance for the face-to-face situation. Within the face-to-face situation I can be a witness of your projects and also of their fulfillment or frustration as you proceed to action. Of course, once I know what you are planning to do, I may momentarily *suspend* the We-relationship in order to estimate *objectively* your chances of success. But it is only within the intimacy of the We-relationship itself that one can actually *live through* a course of action from its birth as a project to its ultimate outcome.

It is further essential to the face-to-face situation that you and I have the same environment. First of all I ascribe to you an environment corresponding to my own. Here, in the face-to-face situation, but only here, does this presupposition prove correct, to the extent that I can assume with more or less certainty within the directly experienced social realm that the table I see is identical (and identical in all its perspective variations) with the table you see, to the extent that I can assume this even if you are only my contemporary or my predecessor. Therefore, when I am in a face-to-face situation with you, I can *point to* something in our common environment, uttering the words "this table here" and, by means of the identification of lived experiences in the environmental object, I can assure the adequacy of my interpretive scheme to your expressive scheme. For practical social life it is of the greatest significance that I consider myself justified in equating my own interpretation of my lived experiences with your interpretation of yours on those occasions when we are experiencing one and the same object.

We have, then, the same undivided and common environment, which we may call "our environment." The world of the We is not private to either of us, but is our world, the one common intersubjective world which is right there in front of us. It is only from the face-to-face relationship, from the common lived experience of the world in the We, that the intersubjective world can be constituted. . . .

. . . [I]n the face-to-face situation, directness of experience is essential, regardless of whether our apprehension of the Other is central or peripheral and regardless of how adequate our grasp of him is. I am still "Thou-oriented" even to the man standing next to me in the subway. When we speak of "pure" Thou-orientation or "pure" We-relationship, we are ordinarily using these as limiting concepts referring to the simple givenness of the Other in abstraction from any specification of the degree of concreteness involved. But we can also use these terms for the lower limits of experience obtainable in the face-to-face relationship, in other words, for the most peripheral and fleeting kind of awareness of the other person.

We make the transition from direct to indirect social experience simply by following this spectrum of decreasing vividness. The first steps beyond the realm of immediacy are marked by a decrease in the number of perceptions I have of the other person and a narrowing of the perspectives within which I view him. At one moment I am exchanging smiles with my friend, shaking hands with him, and bidding him farewell. At the next moment he is walking away. Then from the far distance I hear a faint good-by, a moment later I see a vanishing figure give a last wave, and then he is gone. It is quite impossible to fix the exact instant at which my friend left the world of my direct experience and entered the shadowy realm of those who are merely my contemporaries. As another example, imagine a face-to-face conversation, followed by a telephone call, followed by an exchange of letters, and finally messages exchanged through a third party. Here too we have a gradual progression from the world of immediately experienced social reality to the world of contemporaries. In both examples the total number of the other person's reactions open to my observation is progressively diminished until it reaches a minimum point. It is clear, then, that the world of contemporaries is itself a variant function of the face-to-face situation. They may even be spoken of as two poles between which stretches a continuous series of experiences.

It would be the task of a detailed survey of the social world to study these transformations of direct social experience in terms of their specific meaning-content. The studies of "contact situations," especially those lying in the intermediate zone between direct and indirect social experience, and the studies of men's behavior toward and with respect to one another—in short, Wiese's whole "theory of relationships"—are now shown to be well founded and justified. They belong to the special theory of the social world. It was the great merit of Wiese, and recently also of Sander, to have seen these problems and to have made valuable contributions toward their solution.

Our purpose in this work, however, is not to set forth such a special theory of the social world. Nor is it our purpose even to formulate the basic principles of such a theory. But it is quite clear that before we describe the situation of being a contemporary, we must first discover how this is constituted out of the face-to-face situation.

In everyday life there seems to be no practical problem of where the one situation breaks off and the other begins. This is because we interpret both our own behavior and that of others within contexts of meaning that far transcend the immediate here and now. For this reason, the question whether a social relationship we participate in or observe is direct or indirect seems to be an academic one. But there is a yet deeper reason for our customary indifference to this question. Even after the face-to-face situation has receded into the past and is present only in memory, it still retains its essential characteristics, modified only by an aura of pastness. Normally we do not notice that our just-departed friend, with whom we have a moment ago been interacting, perhaps affectionately or perhaps in an annoyed way, now appears to us in a quite different perspective. Far from seeming obvious, it actually seems absurd that someone we are close to has somehow become "different" now that he is out of sight, except in the trite sense that our experiences of him bear the mark of pastness. However, we must still sharply distinguish between such memories of face-to-face situations, on the one hand, and an intentional Act directed toward a mere contemporary, on the other. The recollections we have of another bear all the marks of direct experience. When I have a recollection of you, for instance, I remember you as you were in the concrete We-relationship with me. I remember you as a unique person in a concrete situation, as one who interacted with me in the mode of "mutual mirroring" described above. I remember you as a person vividly present to me with a maximum of symptoms of inner life, as one whose experiences I witnessed in the actual process of formation. I remember you as one whom I was for a time coming to know better and better. I remember you as one whose conscious life flowed in one stream with my own. I remember you as one whose consciousness was continuously changing in content. However, now that you are out of my direct experience, you are no more than my contemporary, someone who merely inhabits the same planet that I do. I am no longer in contact with the living you, but with the you of yesterday. You, indeed, have not ceased to be a living self, but you have a "new self" now; and although I am contemporaneous with it, I am cut off from vital contact with it. Since the time we were last together, you have met with new experiences and have looked at them from new points of view. With each change of experience and outlook you have become a slightly different person. But somehow I fail to keep this in mind as I go about my daily round. I carry your image with me, and it remains the same. But then, perhaps, I hear that you have changed. I then begin to look upon you as a contemporary—not any contemporary, to be sure, but one whom I once knew intimately. . . .

. . . [W]e have been describing the intermediate zone between the face-to-face situation and the situation involving mere contemporaries. Let us continue our journey. As we approach the outlying world of contemporaries, our experience of others becomes more and more remote and anonymous. Entering the world of contemporaries itself, we pass through one region after another: (1) the region of those whom I once encountered face to face and could encounter again (for instance, my absent friend); then (2) comes the region of those once encountered by the person I am now talking to (for instance, your friend, whom you are promising to introduce to me); next (3) the region of those who are as yet *pure* contemporaries but whom I will soon meet (such as the colleague whose books I have read and whom I am now on my way to visit); then (4) those contemporaries of whose existence I know, not as concrete individuals, but as points in social space as defined by a certain function (for instance, the postal employee who will process my letter); then (5) those collective entities whose function and organization I know while not being able to name any of their members, such as the Canadian Parliament; then (6) collective entities which are by their very nature anonymous and of which I could never in principle have direct experience, such as "state" and "nation"; then (7) objective configurations of meaning which have been instituted in the world of my contemporaries and which live a kind of anonymous life of their own, such as the interstate commerce clause and the rules of French grammar; and finally (8) artifacts of any kind which bear witness to the subjective meaning-context of some unknown person. The farther out we get into the world of contemporaries, the more anonymous its inhabitants become, starting with the innermost region, where they can almost be seen, and ending with the region where they are by definition forever inaccessible to experience. . . .

. . . Let us call all such intentional Acts directed toward contemporaries cases of "They-orientation," in contrast to the "Thou-orientation" of the intentional Acts of direct social experience.

The term "They-orientation" serves to call attention to the peculiar way in which I apprehend the conscious experiences of my contemporaries. For I apprehend them as anonymous processes. Consider the contrast to the Thou-orientation. When I am Thou-oriented, I apprehend the other person's experiences within their setting in his stream of consciousness. I apprehend them as existing within a subjective context of meaning, as being the unique experiences of a particular person. All this is absent in the indirect social experience of the They-orientation. Here I am not aware of the ongoing flow of the Other's consciousness. My orientation is not toward the existence (*Dasein*) of a concrete individual Thou. It is not toward any subjective experiences now being constituted in all their uniqueness in another's mind nor toward the subjective configuration of meaning in which they are taking place. Rather, the object of my They-orientation is my own experience (*Erfahrung*) of social reality in general, of human beings and their conscious processes as such, in abstraction from any individual setting in which they may occur. My knowledge of my contemporaries is, therefore, inferential and discursive. It stands, by its essential nature, in an objective context of meaning and only in such. It has within it no intrinsic reference to persons nor to the subjective matrix within which the experiences in question were constituted. However, it is due to this very abstraction from subjective context of meaning that they exhibit the property which we have called their "again and again" character. They are treated as typical conscious experiences of "someone" and, as such, as basically homogeneous and repeatable. The unity of the contemporary is not constituted originally in his own stream of consciousness. (Indeed, whether the contemporary has any stream of consciousness at all is a difficult question and one which we shall deal with later.) Rather, the contemporary's unity is constituted in my own stream of consciousness, being built up out of a synthesis of my own interpretations of his experiences. This synthesis is a synthesis of recognition in which I monothetically bring within one view my own conscious experiences of someone else. Indeed, these experiences of mine may have been of more than one person. And they may have been of definite individuals or of anonymous "people." It is in this synthesis of recognition that the *personal ideal type* is constituted.

We must be quite clear as to what is happening here. The subjective meaning-context has been abandoned as a tool of interpretation. It has been replaced by a series of highly complex and systematically interrelated objective meaning-contexts. The result is that the contemporary is anonymized in direct proportion to the number and complexity of these meaning-contexts. Furthermore, the synthesis of recognition does not apprehend the unique person as he exists within his living present. Instead it pictures him as always the same and homogeneous, leaving out of account all the changes and rough edges that go along with individuality. Therefore, no matter how many people are subsumed under the ideal type, it corresponds to no one in particular. It is just this fact that justified Weber in calling it "ideal."

Let us give a few examples to clarify this point. When I mail a letter, I assume that certain contemporaries of mine, namely, postal employees, will read the address and speed the letter on its way. I am not thinking of these postal employees as individuals. I do not know them personally and never expect to. Again, as Max Weber pointed out, whenever I accept money I do so without any doubt that others, who remain quite anonymous, will accept it in turn from me. To use yet another Weberian example, if I behave in such a way as to avoid the sudden arrival of certain gentlemen with uniforms and badges, in other words, to the extent that I orient myself to the laws and to the apparatus which enforces them, here, too, I am relating myself socially to my contemporaries conceived under ideal types.

On occasions like these I am always expecting others to behave in a definite way, whether it be postal employees, someone I am paying, or the police. My social relationship to them consists in the fact that I interact with them, or perhaps merely that, in planning my actions, I keep them in mind. But they, on their part, never turn up as real people, merely as anonymous entities defined exhaustively by their functions. Only as bearers of these functions do they have any relevance for my social behavior. How they happen to feel as they cancel my letter, process my check, or examine my income-tax return—these are considerations that never even enter my mind. I just assume that there are "some people" who "do these things." Their behavior in the conduct of their duty is from my point of view defined purely through an objective context of meaning. In other words, when I am They-oriented, I have "types" for partners. . . .

The They-orientation is the pure form of understanding the contemporary in a predicative fashion, that is, in terms of his typical characteristics. Acts of They-orientation are, therefore, intentionally directed toward another person imagined as existing at the same time as oneself but conceived in terms of an ideal type. And just as in the cases of the Thou-orientation and the We-relationship, so also with the They-orientation can we speak of different *stages of concretization* and *actualization*.

In order to distinguish from one another the various stages of concretization of the We-relationship, we established as our criterion the degree of closeness to direct experience. We cannot use this criterion within the They-orientation. The reason is that the latter possesses by definition a high degree of remoteness from direct experience, and the other self which is its object possesses a correspondingly higher degree of anonymity.

It is precisely this degree of anonymity which we now offer as the criterion for distinguishing between the different levels of concretization and actualization that occur in the They-orientation. The more anonymous the personal ideal type applied in the They-orientation, the greater is the use made of objective meaning-contexts instead of subjective ones, and likewise, we shall find, the more are lower-level personal ideal types and objective meaning-contexts pregiven. (The latter have in turn been derived from other stages of concretization of the They-orientation.)

Let us get clear as to just what we mean by the anonymity of the ideal type in the world of contemporaries. The pure Thou-orientation consists of mere awareness of the existence of the other person, leaving aside all questions concerning the characteristics of that person. On the other hand, the pure They-orientation is based on the presupposition of such characteristics in the form of a type. Since these characteristics are genuinely typical, they can in principle be presupposed again and again. Of course, whenever I posit such typical characteristics, I assume that they now exist or did once exist. However, this does not mean that I am thinking of them as existing in a particular person in a particular time and place. The contemporary alter ego is therefore anonymous in the sense that its existence is only the individuation of a type, an individuation which is merely supposable or possible. Now since the very existence of my contemporary is always less than certain, any attempt on my part to reach out to him or influence him may fall short of its mark, and, of course, I am aware of this fact.

The concept which we have been analyzing is the concept of the anonymity of the partner in the world of contemporaries. It is crucial to the understanding of the nature of the indirect social relationship. . . .

As social relationships in the face-to-face situation are based on the pure Thou-orientation, so social relationships between contemporaries are based on the pure They-orientation. But the situation has now changed. In the face-to-face situation the partners look into each other and are mutually sensitive to each other's responses. This is not the case in relationships between contemporaries. Here each partner has to be content with the probability that the other, to whom he is oriented by means of an anonymous type, will respond with the same kind of orientation. And so an element of doubt enters into every such relationship.

When I board a train, for instance, I orient myself to the fact that the engineer in charge can be trusted to get me to my destination. My relationship to him is a They-relationship at this time, merely because my ideal type "railroad engineer" means by definition "one who gets passengers like myself to their destination." It is therefore characteristic of my social relationships with my contemporaries that the orientation by means of ideal types is mutual. Corresponding to my ideal type "engineer" there is the engineer's ideal type "passenger." Taking up mutual They-orientations, we think of each other as "one of them."

I am not therefore apprehended by my partner in the They-relationship as a real living person. From this it follows that I can expect from him only a typical understanding of my behavior.

A social relationship between contemporaries, therefore, consists in this: Each of the partners apprehends the other by means of an ideal type; each of the partners is aware of this mutual apprehension; and each expects that the other's interpretive scheme will be congruent with his own. The They-relationship here stands in sharp contrast to the face-to-face situation. In the face-to-face situation my partner and I are sensitively aware of the nuances of each other's subjective experiences. But in the They-relationship this is replaced by the assumption of a shared interpretive scheme. Now, even though I, on my side, make this assumption, I cannot verify it. I do, however, have more reason to expect an adequate response from my partner, the more standardized is the scheme which I impute to him. This is the case with schemes derived from law, state, tradition, and systems of order of all kinds. . . .

In the face-to-face situation the partners are constantly revising and enlarging their knowledge of each other. This is not true in the same sense of the They-relationship. Certainly it is true that my knowledge of the world of my contemporaries is constantly being enlarged and replenished through every new experience from whatever part of the social world the latter may come. Furthermore, my ideal-typical schemes will always be changing in accordance with every shift in my situation. But all such modifications will be within a very narrow range so long as the original situation and my interest in it remain fairly even.

CHAPTER EIGHT

~

Karl Mannheim on Self, Society, and the Sociology of Knowledge

~ **Introduction** ~

Karl Mannheim (1893–1947) was born in Budapest. After earning a degree in philosophy at the university there and witnessing the collapse of two postwar revolutionary regimes, Mannheim relocated to Germany. He taught in Heidelberg until he secured a position as professor of sociology at the University of Frankfurt in 1928. As a result of the Versailles Treaty, which ended World War I, Germany experienced extreme economic hardships that resulted in social and political unrest. It was in this climate that Mannheim wrote an influential series of essays collectively called *Ideology and Utopia*. Not long afterward, Mannheim lost his position at Frankfurt because of the National Socialist's policy of removing Jews from the academy. Mannheim was able to relocate to London and taught for a number of years as a lecturer at the London School of Economics. Eventually, he acquired a professorship at the University of London where he taught until his death.

According to Mannheim, members of a society tend to either participate in preserving the status quo (ideology) or seek social change (utopia). The choice of whether to preserve the status quo or seek change is contingent on a number of factors. Those who participate in preserving the status quo will tend to do so because (1) it is in their interest (in other words, they are benefiting from the status quo); (2) they see no other "realistic" options; or (3) they fear any other options.

Practically speaking, in regard to social interaction, those who are preserving the status quo will, perhaps unwittingly, reinforce a particular social order with specific roles pertaining to themselves and others; they will find a supportive network of interactions that will reinforce the legitimacy of their point of view. Conversely, those who pursue social change will tend to favor this option because (1)

168

it is in their interest (the status quo is not working for them); or (2) they see no other option than seeking some type, perhaps any type, of change. In regard to social interaction, those seeking change will, perhaps unwittingly, reinforce a particular worldview with specific roles pertaining to themselves and others; they will find a supportive network of interactions that will reinforce the legitimacy of their point of view. Mannheim points out that, regardless of where an individual comes down on the question of preserving the status quo or seeking social change, the probability is high that this is not an individually reasoned-through choice, but rather a product of political, economic, social, and historical circumstances. Ideology and utopia represent social-psychological worldviews, reinforced in social interaction, that maintain mindsets that do not necessarily reflect reality, but are ways of dealing with or coping with the conditions at hand.

Individuals are not necessarily passive receptacles of social conditioning, but they may become aware of the social trends that impinge upon their lives, and they can seek to make adjustments in social life via interaction. To this end it is crucial to understand the most subtle aspects of the cultural and historical factors shaping roles, norms, institutions, fads, and values pertaining to identity; as Schutz would say, one must come to see the taken for granted. Mannheim's sociological project, called the sociology of knowledge, asks us to engage in a radical process of self-examination. The consequences of such examination can lead us to evaluate the degree to which we may be participating in social trends (via interaction) that we say that we're against (for example, saying that we're against the exploitation of people, but supporting companies and governments that exploit people by purchasing their products).

You will remember Mead's discussion of the self as an "I" and a "me." Mead describes the "I" as the source of creative problem solving. In the process of interaction we may inhibit a response and consider alternative gestures, but what does the "I" consider at this moment? The "I" uses the tools available to craft a unique and creative response. Mannheim points out that during some periods in history, there are fewer competitive worldviews, and this makes it easier to preserve the status quo. During such times, the social order is maintained by an "intelligentsia" that monopolizes a society's worldview. Even countervailing ideas are subsumed under the umbrella of the dominating order. And even if a truly alternative conception should arise, it would not be taken seriously. This is so because, under these conditions, the prevailing view serves as the primary reference point when the selves comprising society are faced with ambiguous or complex situations.

It is important to recognize that during these periods, the range of individual creative thought, the tools available for the "I" to craft a unique response to problems, is relatively narrow. It follows, then, that thoughtful alternative considerations arise during historical periods when there are relatively significant inconsistencies in conceptions about the nature of the world; this was observed by the founders of sociology pertaining to the rise of sociology itself. According to Mannheim, the modern age has brought forth a situation where there is no prevailing worldview—

hence, the rise of the sociology of knowledge. And since the decline of the last period of the monopolization of thought in the West (Christendom), the trend has
been to seek "anchorage for objective existence in the knowing subject" (14).
Mannheim writes:

> Consequently, in place of the traditional, ecclesiastically guaranteed story of cre-
> ation, there emerged a conception of the formation of the world, the various parts
> of which are subject to intellectual control. . . . It was hoped that through insight
> into the origins of cognitive representation one could arrive at some notion of the
> role and significance of the subject for the act of knowing and of the truth-value of
> human knowledge in general. (15)

In today's social climate those who believe in the biblical account of creation, for
example, choose to believe in it, as opposed to their believing in creation because it is imposed on them as the only or prevailing worldview. For us, the biblical account of creation is creationism—one theory among other "isms." With
the modern age comes a dependence on the self to make sense of the world,
rather than a reified worldview impressing upon selves a "sensible" world. What
is also evident here is that social conditions give rise to the spread of individualism as a means of problem solving.

With the rising social interest in individualism coinciding with the prevalence of empiricism, beginning in the 1600s, the psyche was transformed into an
object of methodical, "mechanical" investigation. Despite this development,
however, there remains even to this day, "the question as to who I actually am,
what I actually am, or what it means to be a human being" (19). Hence, one can
live in a social climate that values individualism, where selves interact with the
assumption of a self that knows what it and the other is and yet not know the answers to the fundamental questions of self-awareness. A well-crafted scheme or
worldview can produce an understanding of self that integrates various elements
without revealing that it is a construction of the "definition of the situation."
Selves can interact with apparent self-interest without realizing that "the definition of the situation" is defining self-interest for them. Of course, some would argue that self-interest is nothing other than what is constituted by the situation.
But the point is that it is only later (as Mannheim says, "one discovers only afterwards") that selves may realize that their interests were not maximized by the
definition of the situation. Hence, whether the worldview is true or false, it
serves the "psychological-sociological function" of defining a situation for selves.
Mannheim notes in the reading:

> [T]he original difficulty, which was to have been solved through recourse to and
> concentration on the subject, was not thereby obviated. It it true that much that is
> new was discovered by the new empirical methods. They enabled us to gain insight
> into the psychic genesis of many cultural phenomena, but the answers which were
> brought forward deflected our attention from the fundamental question concerning
> the existence of mind in the order of reality. (23)

While the potential for greater individual expression exists by relocating the problem of meaning in the subject, such a transition also carries the potential of many individualized illusions, in particular, the atomization of worldviews that discounts the social origins of individual beliefs (i.e., being oblivious to the fact that economic status affects choice, which affects one's sense of individual emancipation). For example, many college students believe that they choose a subject to major in, that they are encouraged to do something that matches their strengths (note the subjectivist orientation here). However, if we were to examine what most students major in across the country, we would find a general pattern: most students seem to major in business, computer science, or psychology. If you were to ask these students why they had chosen these fields, they would probably reply, "Well, it seems interesting." Behind comments like this, however, would be social factors such as parental and peer pressure related to perceived economic opportunity based upon socioeconomic status. Individuals tend to make choices within predefined categories that they, themselves, do not have a hand in making. Key here is that the possibility for emancipation cannot be achieved until one is willing and able to examine the various ways in which one is determined, and situational factors affect whether or not this particular insight is realized.

According to Mannheim, the development of the political and social sciences opened up the possibility of examining the "collective unconscious" in a way that "mechanistic knowledge" could not. The political and social sciences opened up the possibility of conscious examination of situationally determined thinking. The realization of ideological and utopian complexes of thought opens up the possibility of grasping the elements that guide social interaction. During periods of social confusion due to the multiplicity of perspectives, the possibility of grasping more firmly the determinants of the collective unconscious are actually increased. Such periods of ferment, however, arising from seeking clarity, may exhaust themselves; people may not take full advantage of the insights gained and close themselves into "static, uniform" thinking. Closed-minded thinking tends to not be able to see the walls that enclose such thinking; the currently popular phrase "seeing outside the box" is an attempt to go beyond closed-minded thinking, but ironically, it tends to be focused within culturally determined specifications instead of serving individual creativity as an end in itself. Mannheim believes that, as a complicated creature, "men must learn to think anew, because man is a kind of creature who must continually readapt himself to his changing history" (107), a history people participate in making whether or not they are conscious of it. Mannheim says in the reading:

> For mastery of each historical situation, a certain structure of thought is required which will rise to the demands of the actual, real problems encountered, and is capable of integrating what is relevant in the various conflicting points of view. . . . A fearful and uncertain concealment of contradictions and gaps will no more lead us out of the crisis than the methods of the extreme right and left, who exploit it in propaganda for the glorification of the past or future. (105)

Ultimately, Mannheim advocates a position that asks citizens to confront how their thinking limits their ability to come to grips with the ever-present responsibility of forging the most inclusive ideal into the most practical real.

～ Ideology and Utopia ～

Strictly speaking it is incorrect to say that the single individual thinks. Rather it is more correct to insist that he participates in thinking further what other men have thought before him. He finds himself in an inherited situation with patterns of thought which are appropriate to this situation and attempts to elaborate further the inherited modes of response or to substitute others for them in order to deal more adequately with the new challenges which have arisen out of the shifts and changes in his situation. . . .

. . . Men living in groups do not merely coexist physically as discrete individuals. They do not confront the objects of the world from the abstract levels of a contemplating mind as such, nor do they do so exclusively as solitary beings. On the contrary they act with and against one another in diversely organized groups, and while doing so they think with and against one another. These persons, bound together into groups, strive in accordance with the character and position of the groups to which they belong to change the surrounding world of nature and society or attempt to maintain it in a given condition. It is the direction of this will to change or to maintain, of this collective activity, which produces the guiding thread for the emergence of their problems, their concepts, and their forms of thought. In accord with the particular context of collective activity in which they participate, men always tend to see the world which surrounds them differently. Just as pure logical analysis has severed individual thought from its group situation, so it also separated thought from action. It did this on the tacit assumption that those inherent connections which always exist in reality between thought on the one hand, and group and activity on the other, are either insignificant for "correct" thinking or can be detached from these foundations without any resultant difficulties. But the fact that one ignores something by no means puts an end to its existence. Nor can anyone who has not first given himself whole-heartedly to the exact observation of the wealth of forms in which men really think decide a priori whether this severance from the social situation and context of activity is always realizable. Nor indeed can it be determined offhand that such a complete dichotomy is fully desirable precisely in the interest of objective factual knowledge.

It may be that, in certain spheres of knowledge, it is the impulse to act which first makes the objects of the world accessible to the acting subject, and it may be further that it is this factor which determines the selection of those elements of reality which enter into thought. And it is not inconceivable that if this volitional factor were entirely excluded (in so far as such a thing is possible), the concrete content would completely disappear from the concepts, and the organizing principle which first makes possible an intelligent statement of the problem would be lost.

But this is not to say that in those domains where attachment to the group and orientation towards action seem to be an essential element in the situation, every possibility of intellectual, critical self-control is futile. Perhaps it is precisely when the hitherto concealed dependence of thought on group existence and its rootedness in action becomes visible that it really becomes possible for the first time, through becoming aware of them, to attain a new mode of control over previously uncontrolled factors in thought. . . .

. . . It would be a failure to recognize its relevance to our own plight if we did not see that it is a specific social situation which has impelled us to reflect about the social roots of our knowledge. It is one of the fundamental insights of the sociology of knowledge that the process by which collective-unconscious motives become conscious cannot operate in every epoch, but only in a quite specific situation. This situation is sociologically determinable. One can point out with relative precision the factors which are inevitably forcing more and more persons to reflect not merely about the things of the world, but about thinking itself and even here not so much about truth in itself, as about the alarming fact that the same world can appear differently to different observers.

It is clear that such problems can become general only in an age in which disagreement is more conspicuous than agreement. . . .

Was it not this process of social ascent which in the Athenian democracy called forth the first great surge of scepticism in the history of Occidental thought? Were not the Sophists of the Greek Enlightenment the expression of an attitude of doubt which arose essentially out of the fact that in their thinking about every object, two modes of explanation collided? On the one hand was the mythology which was the way of thinking of a dominant nobility already doomed to decline. On the other hand was the more analytical habit of thought of an urban artisan lower stratum, which was in the process of moving upwards. Inasmuch as these two forms of interpreting the world converged in the thought of the Sophists, and since for every moral decision there were available at least two standards, and for every cosmic and social happening at least two explanations, it is no wonder that they had a sceptical notion of the value of human thought. It is therefore pointless to censure them in schoolmaster fashion for having been sceptics in their epistemological efforts. They simply had the courage to express what every person who was really characteristic of the epoch felt, namely, that the previous unambiguity of norms and interpretations had been shattered, and that a satisfactory solution was to be found only in a thoroughgoing questioning and thinking through of the contradictions. This general uncertainty was by no means a symptom of a world doomed to general decay, but it was rather the beginning of a wholesome process which marked a crisis leading to recovery. . . .

In addition to those social factors which account for the early unity and subsequent multiplicity in the dominant forms of thought, another important factor should be mentioned. In every society there are social groups whose special task it is to provide an interpretation of the world for that society. We call these the "intelligentsia." The more static a society is, the more likely is it that this stratum will acquire a well-defined status or the position of a caste in that society. Thus the magicians, the Brahmins, the medieval clergy are to be regarded as intellectual strata, each of which in its society enjoyed a monopolistic control over the moulding of that society's world-view, and over either the reconstruction or the reconciliation of the differences in the naïvely formed world-views of the other strata. The sermon, the confession, the lesson, are, in this sense, means by which reconciliation of the different conceptions of the world takes place at less sophisticated levels of social development.

This intellectual stratum, organized as a caste and monopolizing the right to preach, teach, and interpret the world is conditioned by the force of two social factors. The more it makes itself the exponent of a thoroughly organized collectivity (e.g. the Church), the more its thinking tends towards "scholasticism." It must give a dogmatically binding force to modes of thought which formerly were valid only for a sect and thereby sanction the ontology and epistemology implicit in this mode of thought. The necessity of having to present a unified front to outsiders compels this transition. The same result may also be brought about by the possibility that the concentration of power within the social structure will be so pronounced that uniformity of thought and experience can be imposed upon the members of at least one's own caste with greater success than heretofore.

The second characteristic of this monopolistic type of thought is its relative remoteness from the open conflicts of everyday life; hence it is also "scholastic" in this sense, i.e. academic and lifeless. This type of thought does not arise primarily from the struggle with concrete problems of life nor from trial and error, nor from experiences in mastering nature and society, but rather much more from its own need for systematization, which always refers the facts which emerge in the religious as well as in other spheres of life back to given traditional and intellectually uncontrolled premises. The antagonisms which emerge in these discussions do not embody the conflict of various modes of experience so much as various positions of power within the same social structure, which have at the time identified themselves with the different possible interpretations of the dogmatized traditional "truth." The dogmatic content of the premises with which these divergent groups start and which this thought then seeks in different ways to justify turns out for the most part to be a matter of accident, if judged by the criteria of factual evidence. It is completely arbitrary in so far as it depends upon which sect happens to be successful, in accordance with historical-political destiny, in making its own intellectual and experiental traditions the traditions of the entire clerical caste of the church.

From a sociological point of view the decisive fact of modern times, in contrast with the situation during the Middle Ages, is that this monopoly of the ecclesiastical interpretation of the world which was held by the priestly caste is broken, and in the place of a closed and thoroughly organized stratum of intellectuals, a free intelligentsia has arisen. Its chief characteristic is that it is increasingly recruited from constantly varying social strata and life-situations, and that its mode of thought is no longer subject to regulation by a caste-like organization. Due to the absence of a social organization of their own, the intellectuals have allowed those ways of thinking and experiencing to get a hearing which ∪penly competed with one another in the larger world of the other strata. When one considers further that with the renunciation of the monopolistic privileges of a caste type of existence, free competition began to dominate the modes of intellectual production, one understands why, to the extent that they were in competition, the intellectuals adopted in an ever more pronounced fashion the most various modes of thought and experience available in society and played them off against one another. They did this inasmuch as they had to compete for the favour of a public which, unlike the public of the clergy, was no longer accessible to them without their own efforts. This competition for the favour of various public groups was accentuated because the distinctive modes of experiencing and thinking of each attained increasing public expression and validity.

In this process the intellectual's illusion that there is only one way of thinking disappears. The intellectual is now no longer, as formerly, a member of a caste or rank whose scholastic manner of thought represents for him thought as such. In this relatively simple process is to be sought the explanation for the fact that the fundamental questioning of thought in modern times does not begin until the collapse of the intellectual monopoly of the clergy. The almost unanimously accepted world-view which had been artificially maintained fell apart the moment the socially monopolistic position of its producers was destroyed. With the liberation of the intellectuals from the rigorous organization of the church, other ways of interpreting the world were increasingly recognized.

The disruption of the intellectual monopoly of the church brought about a sudden flowering of an unexampled intellectual richness. But at the same time we must attribute to the organizational disintegration of the unitary church the fact that the belief in the unity and eternal nature of thought, which had persisted since classical antiquity, was again shaken. The origins of the profound disquietude of the present day reach back to this period, even though in most recent times additional causes of a quite different nature have entered into the process. Out of this first upsurge of the profound disquietude of modern man there emerged those fundamentally new modes of thought and investigation, the epistemological, the psychological, and the sociological, without which to-day we could not even formulate our problem. . . .

All epistemological speculation is oriented within the polarity of object and subject. Either it starts with the world of objects, which in one way or another it dogmatically presupposes as familiar to all, and with this as a basis explains the position of the subject in this world-order, deriving therefrom his cognitive powers; or else it starts with the subject as the immediate and unquestioned datum and seeks to derive from him the possibility of valid knowledge. In periods in which the objective world-view remains more or less unshaken, and in epochs which succeed in presenting one unambiguously perceivable world-order, there exists the tendency to base the existence of the knowing human subject and his intellectual capacities on objective factors. Thus in the Middle Ages, which not only believed in an unambiguous world-order but which also thought that it knew the "existential value" to be attributed to every object in the hierarchy of things, there prevailed an explanation of the value of human capacities and thought which was based on the world of objects. But after the breakdown which we described, the conception of order in the world of objects which had been guaranteed by the dominance of the church became problematical, and there remained no alternative but to turn about and to take the opposite road, and with the subject as the point of departure, to determine the nature and the value of the human cognitive act, attempting thereby to find an anchorage for objective existence in the knowing subject.

Although precursors for this tendency are already to be found in medieval thought, it fully emerged for the first time in the rationalistic current of French and German philosophy from Descartes through Leibnitz to Kant on the one hand, and in the more psychologically oriented epistemology of Hobbes, Locke, Berkeley, and Hume on the other. This was above all else the meaning of Descartes' intellectual experiment, of the exemplary struggle in which he attempted to question all traditional theories in order, finally, to arrive at the no longer questionable *cogito ergo sum*. This was the only point from which he could again undertake anew to lay the foundations for a world-view.

All these attempts presuppose the more or less explicit consideration that the subject is more immediately accessible to us than the object which has become too ambiguous as a result of the many divergent interpretations to which it has been subjected. For this reason we must, wherever possible, empirically reconstruct the genesis of thought in the subject which is more accessible to our control. In the mere preference for the empirical observations and genetic criteria which gradually became supreme, the will to the destruction of the authoritarian principle was revealed in operation. It represents a centrifugal tendency in opposition to the church as the official interpreter of the universe. Only that has validity which I can control in my own perception, which is corroborated in my own experimental activity, or which I myself can produce or at least conceptually construct as producible.

Consequently, in place of the traditional, ecclesiastically guaranteed story of creation, there emerged a conception of the formation of the world, the various parts of which are subject to intellectual control. This conceptual model of the producibility of the world-view from the cognitive act led to the solution of the epistemological problem. It was hoped that through insight into the origins of cognitive representation one could arrive at some notion of the role and significance of the subject for the act of knowing and of the truth-value of human knowledge in general. . . .

The epistemological recourse to the subject rendered possible in this way the emergence of a psychology which became ever more precise, including a psychology of thought which, as we have indicated above, broke up into numerous fields of specialization. However, the more precise this empirical psychology became, the greater the appreciation of the scope of empirical observation, the more evident it became that the subject was by no means such a safe point of departure for the attainment of a new conception of the world as had previously been assumed. It is indeed true, in a certain sense, that inner experience is more immediately given than external experience, and that the inner connection between experiences can be more surely comprehended, if, among other things, one is able to have a sympathetic understanding of the motivations which produce certain actions. However, it was nonetheless clear that one could not entirely avoid the risks involved in an ontology. The psyche, too, with all its inwardly immediately perceivable "experiences" is a segment of reality. . . .

. . . In the meantime, however, as a result of this radical formalization, scientific psychic inward observation took on new forms. Fundamentally this psychic inward observation involved the same process which characterized the experiencing and thinking through of the objects of the external world. Such meaning-giving interpretations with qualitatively rich contents (as, for instance, sin, despair, loneliness, Christian love) were replaced by formalized entities such as the feeling of anxiety, the perception of inner conflict, the experiencing of isolation, and the "libido." These latter sought to apply interpretive schemes derived from mechanics to the inner experience of man. The aim here was not so much to comprehend as precisely as possible the inner contentual richness of experiences as they coexist in the individual and together operate towards the achievement of a meaningful goal; the attempt was rather to exclude all distinctive elements in experience from the content in order that, wherever possible, the conception of psychic events should approximate the simple scheme of mechanics (position, motion, cause, effect). The problem becomes not how a person understands himself in terms of his own ideals and norms and how, against the background of such norms, his deeds and renunciations are given their meaning, but rather how an external situation can, with an ascertainable degree of probability, mechanically call forth an inner reaction. The category of external causality was increasingly used. . . .

Although we may know a great deal about the conditions under which conflicts arise, we may still know nothing about the inner situation of living human beings, and how, when their values are shattered, they lose their bearings and strive again to find themselves. Just as the most exact theory of cause and function does not answer the question as to who I actually am, what I actually am, or what it means to be a human being, so there can never arise out of it that interpretation of one's self and the world demanded by even the simplest action based on some evaluative decision.

The mechanistic and functionalistic theory is highly valuable as a current in psychological research. It fails, however, when it is placed in the total context of life-experience. . . .

Thereby another aspect of the problem is revealed. Without evaluative conceptions, without the minimum of a meaningful goal, we can do nothing in either the sphere of the social or the sphere of the psychic. By this we mean that even when one takes a purely causal and functional point of view one discovers only afterwards what sense there was originally concealed in the ontology on which one proceeded. It guarded against the atomization of the experience into isolated observations, i.e. atomization from the standpoint of the activity. Expressed in terms of modern Gestalt theory, the meanings which our ontology gives us served to integrate the units of conduct and to enable us to see in a configurative context the individual observational elements which otherwise would tend to remain discreet.

Even if all the meaning conveyed by the magical-religious view of the world had been "false," it still served—when viewed from a purely functional standpoint—to make coherent the fragments of the reality of inner psychic as well as objective external experience, and to place them with reference to a certain complex of conduct. We see ever more clearly that from whatever source we get our meanings, whether they be true or false, they have a certain psychological-sociological function, namely to fix the attention of those men who wish to do something in common upon a certain "definition of the situation." A situation is constituted as such when it is defined in the same way for the members of the group. It may be true or false when one group calls another heretics, and as such struggles against them, but it is only through this definition that the struggle is a social situation. It may be true or false that a group struggles only to realize a fascist or a communist society, but it is only by means of this meaning-giving, evaluating definition that events produce a situation where activity and counteractivity are distinguishable, and the totality of events are articulated into a process. The juxtaposition *ex post facto* of elements voided of meaningful content does not bring home the unity of conduct. As a result of the extensive exclusion of meaningful elements from psychological theory, it becomes more and more evident that in psychology, too, psychic situations, to say nothing of inner life histories, cannot be perceived without meaningful context.

Furthermore, from a purely functionalist point of views, the derivation of our meanings, whether they be true or false, plays an indispensable role, namely, it socializes events for a group. We belong to a group not only because we are born into it, not merely because we profess to belong to it, nor finally because we give it our loyalty and allegiance, but primarily because we see the world and certain things in the world the way it does (i.e. in terms of the meanings of the group in question). In every concept, in every concrete meaning, there is contained a crystallization of the experiences of a certain group. . . .

Returning then to our discussion of the origins of modern psychology with the subject as the point of departure, it is now clear that the original difficulty, which was to have been solved through recourse to and concentration on the subject, was not thereby obviated. It is true that much that is new was discovered by the new empirical methods. They enabled us to gain insight into the psychic genesis of many cultural phenomena, but the answers which were brought forward deflected our attention from the fundamental question concerning the existence of mind in the order of reality. Especially was the unity of the mind as well as that of the person lost through the functionalization and mechanization of psychic phenomena. . . .

. . . [T]wo fundamentally different tendencies characterize modern psychology. Both became possible because the medieval world which gave a single set of meanings to men in the Western world was in the process of dissolution. The first of these is the tendency to look behind every meaning and to understand it in terms of its genesis in the subject (the genetic point of view). The second tendency consists in the attempt to construct a sort of mechanical science of the elements of psychic experience which have been formalized and emptied of meaning (psychic mechanics). It becomes evident here that the mechanistic thought-model is not, as was originally supposed, confined to the world of mechanical objects. The mechanistic thought-model represents primarily a kind of first approximation to objects in general. Here the aim is not the exact comprehension of qualitative peculiarities and unique constellations, but rather the determination of the most obvious regularities and principles of order obtaining between formalized simplified elements. We have traced out this last-mentioned method in detail and seen how the mechanistic method, in spite of the concrete achievements for which we are indebted to it, has, from the point of view of life-orientation and conduct, contributed very much to the general insecurity of modern man. . . .

The two methods of studying cultural phenomena dealt with above, the epistemological and the psychological, has in common an attempt to explain meaning from its genesis in the subject. What is important in this case is not so much whether they were thinking of the concrete individual or of a generalized mind as such, but that in both cases the individual mind was conceived as separate from the group. Thereby they unwittingly brought false assumptions into the fundamental problems of epistemology and psychology which the sociological approach has had to correct. What is most important about the latter is that it puts an end to the fiction of the detachment of the individual from the group, within the matrix of which the individual thinks and experiences.

The fiction of the isolated and self-sufficient individual underlies in various forms the individualistic epistemology and genetic psychology. Epistemology operated with this isolated and self-sufficient individual as if from the very first he possessed in essence all the capacities characteristic of human beings, including that of pure knowledge, and as if he produced his knowledge of the world from within himself alone, through mere juxtaposition with the external world. Similarly in the individualistic developmental psychology, the individual passes of necessity through certain stages of development in the course of which the external physical and social environment have no other function than to release these preformed capacities of the individual. Both of these theories grew out of the soil of an exaggerated theoretical individualism (such as was to be found in the period of the Renaissance and of individualistic liberalism) which could have been produced only in a social situation in which the original connection between individual and group had been lost sight of. Frequently in such social situations the observer loses sight of the role of society in the moulding of the individual to the extent that he derives most of the traits, which are evidently only possible as the result of a common life and the interaction between individuals, from the original nature of the individual or from the germ plasm. (We attack this fiction not from some ultimate philosophical point of view but because it simply draws incorrect data into the picture of the genesis of knowledge and experience.)

In actuality it is far from correct to assume that an individual of more or less fixed absolute capacities confronts the world and in striving for the truth constructs a world-view out of the data of his experience. Nor can we believe that he then compares his world-view with that of other individuals who have gained theirs in a similarly independent fashion, and in a sort of discussion the true world-view is brought to light and accepted by the others. In contrast to this, it is much more correct to say that knowledge is from the very beginning a co-operative process of group life, in which everyone unfolds his knowledge within the framework of a common fate, a common activity, and the overcoming of common difficulties (in which, however, each has a different share). Accordingly the products of the cognitive process are already, at least in part, differentiated because not every possible aspect of the world comes within the purview of the members of a group, but only those out of which difficulties and problems for the group arise. And even this common world (not shared by any outside groups in the same way) appears differently to the subordinate groups within the larger group. It appears differently because the subordinate groups and strata in a functionally differentiated society have a different experiential approach to the common contents of the objects of their world. In the intellectual mastery of life problems, each is allotted different segments with which each deals quite differently according to his different life-interests. The degree in which the individualistic conception of the problem of knowledge gives a false picture of collective knowing corresponds to what would occur if the technique, mode of work, and productivity of an internally highly specialized factory of 2,000 workers were thought of as if each of the 2,000 workers worked in a separate cubicle, performed the same operations for himself at the same time and turned out each individual product from beginning to end by himself. Actually, of course, the workers do not do the same thing in parallel fashion but rather, through a division of functions, they collectively bring the total product into existence. . . .

. . . [W]e become masters of ourselves only when the unconscious motivations which formerly existed behind our backs suddenly come into our field of vision and thereby become accessible to conscious control. Man attains objectivity and acquires a self with reference to his conception of his world not by giving up his will to action and holding his evaluations in abeyance but in confronting and examining himself. The criterion of such self-illumination is that not only the object but we ourselves fall squarely within our field of vision. We become visible to ourselves, not just vaguely as a knowing subject as such but in a certain role hitherto hidden from us, in a situation hitherto impenetrable to us, and with motivations of which we have not hitherto been aware. In such moments the inner connection between our role, our motivations, and our type and manner of experiencing the world suddenly dawns upon us. Hence the paradox underlying these experiences, namely the opportunity for relative emancipation from social determination, increases proportionately with insight into this determination. Those persons who talk most about human freedom are those who are actually most blindly subject to social determination, inasmuch as they do not in most cases suspect the profound degree to which their conduct is determined by their interests. In contrast with this, it should be noted that it is precisely those who insist on the unconscious influence of the social determinants in conduct, who strive to overcome these determinants as much as possible. They uncover unconscious motivations in order to make those forces which formerly ruled them more and more into objects of conscious rational decision.

This illustration of how the extension of our knowledge of the world is closely related to increasing personal self-knowledge and self-control of the knowing personality is neither accidental nor peripheral. The process of the self-extension of the individual represents a typical example of the unfolding of every kind of situationally determined knowledge. . . .

What we have hitherto hidden from ourselves and not integrated into our epistemology is that knowledge in the political and social sciences is, from a certain point on, different from formal mechanistic knowledge; it is different from that point where it transcends the mere enumeration of facts and correlations, and approximates the model of situationally determined knowledge to which we shall refer many times in the present work.

Once the interrelationship between social science and situationally bound thinking, as it is for instance found in political orientation, becomes evident, we have reason to investigate the positive potentialities as well as the limits and dangers of this type of thinking. . . .

. . . Our aim then is, first, to refine the analysis of meaning in the sphere of thought so thoroughly that grossly undifferentiated terms and concepts will be supplanted by increasingly exact and detailed characterizations of the various thought-styles; and, second, to perfect the technique of reconstructing social history to such an extent that, instead of scattered isolated facts, one will be able to perceive the social structure as a whole. . . .

To-day we have arrived at the point where we can see clearly that there are differences in modes of thought, not only in different historical periods but also in different cultures. Slowly it dawns upon us that not only does the content of thought change but also its categorical structure. Only very recently has it become possible to investigate the hypothesis that, in the past as well as in the present, the dominant modes of thought are supplanted by new categories when the social basis of the group, of which these thought-forms are characteristic, disintegrates or is transformed under the impact of social change.

Research in the sociology of knowledge promises to reach a stage of exactness if only because nowhere else in the realm of culture is the interdependence in the shifts of meaning and emphasis so clearly evident and precisely determinable as in thought itself. For thought is a particularly sensitive index of social and cultural change. The variation in the meaning of words and the multiple connotations of every concept reflect polarities of mutually antagonistic schemes of life implicit in these nuances of meaning.

Nowhere in the realm of social life, however, do we encounter such a clearly traceable interdependence and sensitivity to change and varying emphasis as in the meaning of words. The word and the meaning that attaches to it is truly a collective reality. The slightest nuance in the total system of thought reverberates in the individual word and the shades of meaning it carries. The word binds us to the whole of past history and, at the same time, mirrors the totality of the present. When, in communicating with others, we seek a common level of understanding the word can be used to iron out individual differences of meaning. But, when necessary, the word may become an instrument in emphasizing the differences in meaning and the unique experiences of each individual. It may then serve as a means for detecting the original and novel increments that arise in the course of the history of culture. . . .

. . . Interrelationships have now become evident, both in the present and in history, which formerly could never have been analysed so thoroughly. The recognition of this fact in all its ramifications gives to the modern investigator a tremendous advantage. He will no longer be inclined to raise the question as to which of the contending parties has the truth on its side, but rather he will direct his attention to discovering the approximate truth as it emerges in the course of historical development out of the complex social process. The modern investigator can answer, if he is accused of evading the problem of what is truth, that the indirect approach to truth through social history will in the end be more fruitful than a direct logical attack. Even though he does not discover "truth itself," he will discover the cultural setting and many hitherto unknown "circumstances" which are relevant to the discovery of truth. As a matter of fact, if we believe that we already have the truth, we will lose interest in obtaining those very insights which might lead us to an approximate understanding of the situation. . . .

At this point in history when all things which concern man and the structure and elements of history itself are suddenly revealed to us in a new light, it behooves us in our scientific thinking to become masters of the situation, for it is not inconceivable that sooner than we suspect, as has often been the case before in history, this vision may disappear, the opportunity may be lost, and the world will once again present a static, uniform, and inflexible countenance. . . .

Accordingly, from our point of view, an ethical attitude is invalid if it is oriented with reference to norms, with which action in a given historical setting, even with the best of intentions, cannot comply. It is invalid then when the unethical action of the individual can no longer be conceived as due to his own personal transgression, but must be attributed rather to the compulsion of an erroneously founded set of moral axioms. The moral interpretation of one's own action is invalid, when, through the force of traditional modes of thought and conceptions of life, it does not allow for the accommodation of action and thought to a new and changed situation and in the end actually obscures and prevents this adjustment and transformation of man. . . .

As examples of "false consciousness" taking the form of an incorrect interpretation of one's own self and one's role, we may cite those cases in which persons try to cover up their "real" relations to themselves and to the world, and falsify to themselves the elementary facts of human existence by deifying, romanticizing, or idealizing them, in short, by resorting to the device of escape from themselves and the world, and thereby conjuring up false interpretations of experience. We have a case of ideological distortion, therefore, when we try to resolve conflicts and anxieties by having recourse to absolutes, according to which it is no longer possible to live. This is the case when we create "myths," worship "greatness in itself," avow allegiance to "ideals," while in our actual conduct we are following other interests which we try to mask by simulating an unconscious righteousness. . . .

. . . As long as we see the objects in our experience from a particular standpoint only and as long as our conceptual devices suffice for dealing with a highly restricted sphere of life, we might never become aware of the need for inquiring into the total interrelationship of phenomena. . . .

Only when we are thoroughly aware of the limited scope of every point of view are we on the road to the sought-for comprehension of the whole. The crisis in thought is not a crisis affecting merely a single intellectual position, but a crisis of a whole world which has reached a certain stage in its intellectual development. To see more clearly the confusion into which our social and intellectual life has fallen represents an enrichment rather than a loss. That reason can penetrate more profoundly into its own structure is not a sign of intellectual bankruptcy. Nor is it to be regarded as intellectual incompetence on our part when an extraordinary broadening of perspective necessitates a thoroughgoing revision of our fundamental conceptions. . . .

Totality in the sense in which we conceive it is not an immediate and eternally valid vision of reality attributable only to a divine eye. It is not a self-contained and stable view. On the contrary, a total view implies both the assimilation and transcendence of the limitations of particular points of view. It represents the continuous process of the expansion of knowledge, and has as its goal not achievement of a super-temporally valid conclusion but the broadest possible extension of our horizon of vision.

To draw a simple illustration from everyday experience of the striving towards a total view, we may take the case of an individual in a given position of life who occupies himself with the concrete individual problems that he faces and then suddenly awakens to discover the fundamental conditions which determine his social and intellectual existence. In such a case, a person, who continually and exclusively occupies himself with his daily tasks, would not take a questioning attitude towards himself and his position, and yet such a person would, despite his self-assurance, be enslaved by a particularistic and partial point of view until he reached the crisis which brought disillusionment. Not until the moment, when he for the first time conceived of himself as being a part of a larger concrete situation, would the impulse awaken in him to see his own activities in the context of the whole. It is true that his perspective may still be as limited as his narrow range of experience allows; perhaps the extent to which he analysed his situation would not transcend the scope of the small town or the limited social circle in which he moves. Nevertheless to treat events and human beings as parts of situations similar to those situations in which he finds himself, is something quite different from merely reacting immediately to a stimulus or to a direct impression. Once the individual has grasped the method of orienting himself in the world, he is inevitably driven beyond the narrow horizon of his own town and learns to understand himself as part of a national, and later of a world, situation. In the same manner he will be able to understand the position of his own generation, his own immediate situation within the epoch in which he lives, and in turn this period as part of the total historical process.

PART THREE

MID-CENTURY CRITIQUES
AND REFINEMENTS

CHAPTER NINE

~

David Riesman on Social Character

~ Introduction ~

David Riesman (1909–) was born into a prominent family in Philadelphia, Pennsylvania. After earning his B.A. degree in biochemical sciences at Harvard in 1931, Riesman studied law, graduating from Harvard Law School in 1934. From 1937 to 1941 he taught at the University of Buffalo Law School. In 1946 Riesman accepted a position to teach undergraduate social science at the University of Chicago, and in 1958 he was appointed to an endowed chair in social science at Harvard.

Riesman's work received national attention in the early 1950s with the publication of his first book, *The Lonely Crowd*. The popularity of the book landed him on the cover of *Time* magazine in 1954. Written in collaboration with Nathan Glazer and Reuel Denney, the book struck a popular chord, examining issues of character and conformity. *The Lonely Crowd* suggests that social character had shifted three times—from being "tradition-directed" to being the "rugged individualist" or "inner-directed" type (an enduring American theme representing individual freedom) to being the more conformist-oriented or "other-directed" type. This shift was due to such factors as pressures exerted by the increasingly complex and pervasive mass media, the goal of success as defined by corporate structures, and the anxious desire to fill nonwork or leisure time with activities.

Riesman associates these changes with an S-shaped curve in the growth of the population. The bottom horizontal line represents stable population growth due to high birth and death rates. Character at this time is "tradition-directed," since little change provokes little examination of prevailing structures. The vertical line represents growth in population due to factors—such as innovations in technology

187

or practices pertaining to hygiene—that decrease infant mortality and increase life expectancy. Character at this time is "inner-directed," whereby the principles taught by one's parents provide the inner strength necessary to explore a world of ever-widening horizons. The top horizontal line represents a leveling-off of population growth due to a slowing birth rate. Character at this time is "other-directed," as individuals pursue goals consistent with their peers. While many (including Riesman) have come to question the relationship between population growth and character, the author's insights pertaining to character and conformity continue to produce valuable discussion.

The reading for this chapter contains a brief explanation of what is meant by the term social character, as well as a discussion of the changing, dynamic relationship between character and society, a brief comparison of the three "ideal types" of character and society, and a discussion of the implications of these types in reference to adjustment, anomie, and autonomy.

Riesman argues that adjusted individuals are those who have the prevailing character structure of their time and place (whether it is tradition-directed, inner-directed, or other-directed). Those who do not conform in characterological adjustment may be either anomic or autonomous. Anomic individuals are those who do not fit the prevailing character structure and have difficulty navigating through the norms of their time and place. The autonomous choose whether or not to follow the norms of the adjusted, and they pay less of an emotional price for deviating than the anomic. A key point that was (and may still be) missed by many reading the book is that being inner-directed is not synonymous with autonomy. While the inner-directed person may be less conformist in response to social pressures than the other-directed, the former is still driven by demands that are not freely chosen. The other-directed type has more of an opportunity to evaluate the general value of the principles inculcated early on by one's parents, since they are more open to the messages of others.

Riesman not only argues that one "can characterize an individual by the way in which one mode of adaptation predominates," but that one "can also characterize a society by examining the relative frequency with which the three modes of adaptation occur in it" (279). By examining character structure in society, one can examine the relative value of adjustment vs. maladjustment in achieving culturally honored goals as well as the relative degree of personal autonomy existent in a given time and place. For example, despite the material prosperity associated with other-directedness, Riesman nevertheless suggests that "anomics . . . constitute a sizable number" during this time. In response to living in an age of increased gadgetry and attention on leisure, many have become either apathetic or "overt outlaws."

Despite the "possibilities of being and becoming" that the present state of "abundance" suggests, Riesman does not observe people taking advantage of new possibilities related to autonomous development. There are several reasons for this. Propaganda has been transformed into seemingly harmless and legal advertising through innovations in technology, thereby obscuring clear thinking about autonomy. In a totalitarian state one is pressured into conforming to external standards; within a democratic state, one is likely to feel an inner compulsion to conform to an external standard in order to feel connected to something greater than oneself. Regardless of social environment, Riesman suggests that autonomy is also rooted to a state of mind. This state of mind is the ability to "choose oneself," regardless of the extent of external constraint and the ability to maintain this choosing of oneself without accumulating debilitating scars.

This description of autonomy brings to mind Nelson Mandela, who spent twenty-eight years in prison and emerged a seemingly whole, caring, and articulate senior citizen, rather than appearing bitter and closed-minded due to spending a significant part of his life behind bars for unjust reasons. Finally, Riesman points out that autonomy must always be understood against the backdrop of what is considered "adjusted" at the time. Riesman notes in the excerpt that "the autonomous at all times have been questioners. The autonomous among the inner-directed, however, were partially shaped by a milieu in which people took many psychological events for granted, while the autonomous among the other-directed live in a milieu in which people systematically question themselves in anticipation of the questions of others" (294). This statement underscores two key points: (1) personal autonomy or individualism is an ever-present but difficult aspect of social existence; and (2) the nature of individualism itself and the challenges involved in preserving personal autonomy vary due to time and place.

Riesman cites several examples of the difficulties of preserving personal autonomy within the present age. He notes in the reading, "young people today can find, in the wide variety of people and places of metropolitan life, a peer-group, conformity to which costs little in the way of search for principle" (296). As a second example, Riesman discusses the increasing casualness of sex and notes that this creates role conflicts, particularly for women. On the one hand, the liberated individual can freely choose the frequency with which to engage in sexual relations. On the other hand, social value systems tend to categorize or stereotype people, particularly women, for acting on such impulses. Moreover, such labeling has differential effects on men and women pursuing a professional life. Riesman notes that the way many women have chosen to deal with this conflict between wanting to feel autonomous but not wanting to be viewed as inappropriate is by simply following the more conventional path.

To summarize, Riesman observes that every society needs some level of conformity within its members in order to function effectively. How members have conformed over time has changed from tradition-directed to inner-directed to other-directed. Such modes of conformity dictate the norms within a given time and place. Hence, conformity to a given set of norms represents adjusted behavior. Deviations from such adjusted behavior may take the form of either anomie or autonomy. Each mode of conformity offers a unique set of challenges to those who aspire to autonomy. Riesman suggests that many fail, and these aspirants wind up joining the ranks of the anomic. Riesman suggests, however, that perhaps anomie is a better alternative to a type of adjustment that fails to reinterpret its culture resulting in the distortion of the self. Riesman's concluding comment in the book is noteworthy:

> [T]he enormous potentialities for diversity in nature's bounty and men's capacity to differentiate their experience can become valued by the individual himself, so that he will not be tempted and coerced into adjustment or, failing adjustment, into anomie. The idea that men are created free and equal is both true and misleading: men are created different; they lose their social freedom and their individual autonomy in seeking to become like each other. (349)

Riesman's solution to the social ills that he describes is greater and more widely spread autonomy.

~ Character and Society ~

This is a book about social character and about the differences in social character between men of different regions, eras, and groups. It considers the ways in which different social character types, once they are formed at the knee of society, are then deployed in the work, play, politics, and child-rearing activities of society. More particularly, it is about the way in which one kind of social character, which dominated America in the nineteenth century, is gradually being replaced by a social character of quite a different sort. Just why this happened; how it happened; what are its consequences in some major areas of life: this is the subject of this book.

But just what do we mean when we speak of "social character"? We do not speak of "personality," which in current social psychology is used to denote the total self, with its inherited temperaments and talents, its biological as well as psychological components, its evanescent as well as more or less permanent attributes. Nor even do we speak of "character" as such, which, in one of its contemporary uses, refers to only a part of personality—that part which is formed not by heredity but by experience (not that it is any simple matter to draw a line between the two): Character, in this sense, is the more or less permanent socially and historically conditioned organization of an individual's drives and satisfactions—the kind of "set" with which he approaches the world and people.

"Social character" is that part of "character" which is shared among significant social groups and which, as most contemporary social scientists define it, is the product of the experience of these groups. The notion of social character permits us to speak, as I do throughout this book, of the character of classes, groups, regions, and nations.

I do not plan to argue over the many ambiguities of the concept of social character—whether it may properly be ascribed to experience rather than to heredity; whether there is any empirical proof that it really exists; whether it is "more important" than the elements of character and personality that bind all people everywhere in the world together, or those other elements of character and personality that separate each individual from every other, even the closest. The assumption that a social character exists has always been a more or less invisible premise of ordinary parlance and is becoming today a more or less visible premise of the social sciences. It will consequently be familiar under one name or another to any of my readers who are acquainted with the writings of Erich Fromm, Abram Kardiner, Ruth Benedict, Margaret Mead, Geoffrey Gorer, Karen Horney, and many others who have written about social character in general, or the social character of different people and different times.

Most of these writers assume—as I do—that the years of childhood are of great importance in molding character. Most of them agree—as I do—that these early years cannot be seen in isolation from the structure of society, which affects the parents who raise the children, as well as the children directly. My collaborators and I base ourselves on this broad platform of agreement, and do not plan to discuss in what way these writers differ from each other and we from them.

What is the relation between social character and society? How is it that every society seems to get, more or less, the social character it "needs"? Erik H. Erikson writes, in a study of the social character of the Yurok Indians, that "systems of child training . . . represent unconscious attempts at creating out of human raw material that configuration of attitudes which is (or once was) the optimum under the tribe's particular natural conditions and economic-historic necessities."

From "economic-historic necessities" to "systems of child training" is a long jump. Much of the work of students of social character has been devoted to closing the gap and showing how the satisfaction of the largest "needs" of society is prepared, in some half-mysterious way, by its most intimate practices. Erich Fromm succinctly suggests the line along which this connection between society and character training may be sought: "In order that any society may function well, its members must acquire the kind of character which makes them *want* to act in the way they *have* to act as members of the society or of a special class within it. They have to *desire* what objectively is *necessary* for them to do. *Outer force* is replaced by *inner compulsion*, and by the particular kind of human energy which is channeled into character traits."

Thus, the link between character and society—certainly not the only one, but one of the most significant, and the one I choose to emphasize in this discussion—is to be found in the way in which society ensures some degree of conformity from the individuals who make it up. In each society, such a mode of ensuring conformity is built into the child, and then either encouraged or frustrated in later adult experience. (No society, it would appear, is quite prescient enough to ensure that the mode of conformity it has inculcated will satisfy those subject to it in every stage of life.) I shall use the term "mode of conformity" interchangeably with the term "social character"—though certainly conformity is not all of social character: "mode of creativity" is as much a part of it. However, while societies and individuals may live well enough—if rather boringly—without creativity, it is not likely that they can live without some mode of conformity—even be it one of rebellion.

My concern in this book is with two revolutions and their relation to the "mode of conformity" or "social character" of Western man since the Middle Ages. The first of these revolutions has in the last four hundred years cut us off pretty decisively from the family- and clan-oriented traditional ways of life in which mankind has existed throughout most of history; this revolution includes the Renaissance, the Reformation, the Counter-Reformation, the Industrial Revolution, and the political revolutions of the seventeenth, eighteenth, and nineteenth centuries. This revolution is, of course, still in process, but in the most advanced countries of the world, and particularly in America, it is giving way to another sort of revolution—a whole range of social developments associated with a shift from an age of production to an age of consumption. The first revolution we understand moderately well; it is, under various labels, in our texts and our terminology; this book has nothing new to contribute to its description, but perhaps does contribute something to its evaluation. The second revolution, which is just beginning, has interested many contemporary observers, including social scientists, philosophers, and journalists. Both description and evaluation are still highly controversial; indeed, many are still preoccupied with the first set of revolutions and have not invented the categories for discussing the second set. In this book I try to sharpen the contrast between, on the one hand, conditions and character in those social strata that are today most seriously affected by the second revolution, and, on the other hand, conditions and character in analogous strata during the earlier revolution; in this perspective, what is briefly said about the traditional and feudal societies which were overturned by the first revolution is in the nature of backdrop for these later shifts.

One of the categories I make use of is taken from demography, the science that deals with birth rates and death rates, with the absolute relative numbers of people in a society, and their distribution by age, sex, and other variables, for I tentatively seek to link certain social and characterological developments, as cause and effect, with certain population shifts in Western society since the Middle Ages.

It seems reasonably well established, despite the absence of reliable figures for earlier centuries, that during this period the curve of population growth in the Western countries has shown an S-shape of a particular type (as other countries are drawn more closely into the net of Western civilization, their populations also show a tendency to develop along the lines of this S-shaped curve). The bottom horizontal line of the S represents a situation where the total population does not increase or does so very slowly, for the number of births equals roughly the number of deaths, and both are very high. In societies of this type, a high proportion of the population is young, life expectancy is low, and the turnover of generations is extremely rapid. Such societies are said to be in the phase of "high growth potential"; for should something happen to decrease the very high death rate (greater production of food, new sanitary measures, new knowledge of the causes of disease, and so on), a "population explosion" would result and the population would increase very rapidly. This in effect is what happened in the West, starting with the seventeenth century. This spurt in population was most marked in Europe, and the countries settled by Europeans, in the nineteenth century. It is represented by the vertical bar of the S. Demographers call this the stage of "transitional growth," because the birth rate soon begins to follow the death rate in its decline. The rate of growth then slows down, and demographers begin to detect in the growing proportion of middle-aged and aged in the population the signs of a third stage, "incipient population decline." Societies in this stage are represented by the top horizontal bar of the S, again indicating, as in the first stage, that total population growth is small—but this time because births and deaths are low.

The S-curve is not a theory of population growth so much as an empirical description of what has happened in the West and in those parts of the world influenced by the West. After the S runs its course, what then? The developments of recent years in the United States and other Western countries do not seem to be susceptible to so simple and elegant a summing up. "Incipient population decline" has not become "population decline" itself, and the birth rate has shown an uncertain tendency to rise again, which most demographers think is temporary.

It would be very surprising if variations in the basic conditions of reproduction, livelihood, and survival chances, that is, in the supply of and demand for human beings, with all it implies in change of the spacing of people, the size of markets, the role of children, the society's feeling of vitality or senescence, and many other intangibles, failed to influence character. My thesis is, in fact, that each of these three different phases on the population curve appears to be occupied by a society that enforces conformity and molds social character in a definably different way.

The society of high growth potential develops in its typical members a social character whose conformity is insured by their tendency to follow tradition: these I shall term *tradition-directed* people and the society in which they live a *society dependent on tradition-direction*.

The society of transitional population growth develops in its typical members a social character whose conformity is insured by their tendency to acquire early in life an internalized set of goals. These I shall term *inner-directed* people and the society in which they live a *society dependent on inner-direction*.

Finally, the society of incipient population decline develops in its typical members a social character whose conformity is insured by their tendency to be sensitized to the expectations and preferences of others. These I shall term *other-directed* people and the society in which they live one *dependent on other-direction*.

Let me point out, however, before embarking on a description of these three "ideal types" of character and society, that I am not concerned here with making the detailed analysis that would be necessary before one could prove that a link exists between population phase and character type. Rather, the theory of the curve of population provides me with a kind of shorthand for referring to the myriad institutional elements that are also—though usually more heatedly—symbolized by such words as "industrialism," "folk society," "monopoly capitalism," "urbanization," "rationalization," and so on. Hence when I speak here of transitional growth or incipient decline of population in conjunction with shifts in character and conformity, these phrases should not be taken as magical and comprehensive explanations. . . .

. . . One way to see the structural differences between the three types is to see the differences in the emotional sanction or control in each type.

The tradition-directed person feels the impact of his culture as a unit, but it is nevertheless mediated through the specific, small number of individuals with whom he is in daily contact. These expect of him not so much that he be a certain type of person but that he behave in the approved way. Consequently the sanction for behavior tends to be the fear of being *shamed*.

The inner-directed person has early incorporated a psychic gyroscope which is set going by his parents and can receive signals later on from other authorities who resemble his parents. He goes through life less independent than he seems, obeying this internal piloting. Getting off course, whether in response to inner impulses or to the fluctuating voices of contemporaries, may lead to the feeling of *guilt*.

Since the direction to be taken in life has been learned in the privacy of the home from a small number of guides and since principles, rather than details of behavior, are internalized, the inner-directed person is capable of great stability. Especially so when it turns out that his fellows have gyroscopes too, spinning at the same speed and set in the same direction. But many inner-directed individuals can remain stable even when the reinforcement of social approval is not available—as in the upright life of the stock Englishman isolated in the tropics.

Contrasted with such a type as this, the other-directed person learns to respond to signals from a far wider circle than is constituted by his parents. The family is no longer a closely knit unit to which he belongs but merely part of a wider social environment to which he early becomes attentive. In these respects the other-directed person resembles the tradition-directed person: both live in a group milieu and lack the inner-directed person's capacity to go it alone. The nature of this group milieu, however, differs radically in the two cases. The other-directed person is cosmopolitan. For him the border between the familiar and the strange—a border clearly marked in the societies depending on tradition-direction—has broken down. As the family continuously absorbs the strange and so reshapes itself, so the strange becomes familiar. While the inner-directed person could be "at home abroad" by virtue of his relative insensitivity to others, the other-directed person is, in a sense, at home everywhere and nowhere, capable of a rapid if sometimes superficial intimacy with and response to everyone. . . .

. . . If the leaders have lost the power, why have the led not gained it? What is there about the other-directed man and his life situation which prevents the transfer? In terms of situation, it seems that the pattern of monopolistic competition of the veto groups resists individual attempts at power aggrandizement. In terms of character, the other-directed man simply does not seek power; perhaps, rather, he avoids and evades it. . . .

If the other-directed person does not seek power, then what does he seek? At the very least, he seeks adjustment. That is, he seeks to have the character he is supposed to have, and the inner experiences as well as outer appurtenances that are supposed to go with it. . . .

How, one may well ask, is it possible that a large group of influential people in a society should develop a character structure more constricted than the society's institutions require? One answer is to look at history and to see that earlier institutional inevitabilities tend to perpetuate themselves in ideology and character. . . . By the same token, disparities between social character and adult social role can be among the important leverages of social change. It is too simple to say that character structure lags behind social structure: as any element in society changes, all other elements must also change in form or function or both. But in a large society such as the American there is room for disparities, and hence for individuals to choose different modes of reconciliation. In the upper-income strata in America, many of the pressures which individuals feel spring from their shared interpretations of what is necessary to get along. As soon as one or two in a group emancipate themselves from these interpretations, without their work or their world coming to an end, others, too, may find the courage to do so. In that case, character will change in consonance with the altered interpretations of conditions.

In asking where the one or two innovators may come from, we must remember that social character is not all of character. The individual is capable of more than his society usually asks of him, though it is not at all easy to determine this, since potentialities may be hidden not only from others but from the individual himself.

Of course, social structures differ very much in the degree to which they evoke a social character that in the process of socialization fills up, crushes, or buries individuality. We may take, as extreme cases, the primitive societies of Dobu or Alor. People there seem to be so crushed from infancy on by institutionalized practices that, while they manage to do what their culture asks of them in the emotional tone which the culture fosters, they cannot do much more. The Rorschach tests taken of the Alorese, for instance, indicated that there is a good deal of characterological uniformity among individuals and that few reserves of depth or breadth exist beyond the cultural norm or what Kardiner calls the basic personality type. Such a society might die out as a result of its apathy and misery, especially when further disorganized by white contact, but it is hard to conceive of an internal rejuvenation led by the more autonomous members of the group. Caught between social character and rigid social institutions, the individual and his potentialities have little scope. Nevertheless, even in such a society there will be deviants; as Ruth Benedict has pointed out, we know of no cultures without them. However, before turning to see whether the extent of deviation may be related to population phase, it is necessary to understand more precisely what is meant by deviation.

The "adjusted" are those whom for the most part we have been describing. They are the typical tradition-directed, inner-directed, or other-directed people—those who respond in their character structure to the demands of their society or social class at its particular stage on the curve of population. Such people fit the culture as though they were made for it, as in fact they are. There is, characterologically speaking, an effortless quality about their adjustment, although as we have seen the mode of adjustment may itself impose heavy strains on the so-called "normal" people. That is, the adjusted are those who reflect their society, or their class within the society, with the least distortion.

In each society those who do not conform to the characterological pattern of the adjusted may be either anomic or autonomous. Anomic is English coinage from Durkheim's *anomique* (adjective of *anomie*) meaning ruleless, ungoverned. My use of anomic, however, covers a wider range than Durkheim's metaphor: it is virtually synonymous with maladjusted, a term I refrain from using because of its negative connotations; for there are some cultures where I would place a higher value on the maladjusted or anomic than on the adjusted. The "autonomous" are those who on the whole are capable of conforming to the behavioral norms of their society—a capacity the anomics usually lack—but are free to choose whether to conform or not.

In determining adjustment, the test is not whether an individual's overt behavior obeys social norms but whether his character structure does. A person who has the appropriate character for his time and place is "adjusted" even when he makes mistakes and does things which deviate sharply from what is expected of him—to be sure, the consequences of such mistakes may eventually produce maladjustment in character. (Much in the same way, a culture may be a going concern even if it behaves "irrationally" vis-à-vis its neighbors or material environment.) Conversely, just as nonconformity in behavior does not necessarily mean nonconformity in character structure, so utter conformity in behavior may be purchased by the individual at so high a price as to lead to character neurosis and anomie: the anomic person tends to sabotage either himself or his society, probably both. Thus, "adjustment," as the term is used here, means socio-psychological fit, not adequacy in any evaluative sense; to determine adequacy either of behavior or character we must study not only the individual but the gear box which, with various slips and reversals, ties behavior in with institutional forms. The person here defined as autonomous may or may not conform outwardly, but whatever his choice, he pays less of a price, and he *has* a choice: he can meet both the culture's definitions of adequacy and those which (to a still culturally determined degree) slightly transcend the norm for the adjusted.

These three universal types (the adjusted, the anomic, the autonomous), like our three historical types (tradition-directed, inner-directed, and other-directed) are, in Max Weber's sense, "ideal types," that is, constructions necessary for analytical work. Every human being will be one of these types to some degree; but no one could be completely characterized by any one of these terms. To put it in the extreme, even an insane person is not anomic in every sphere of life; nor could an autonomous person be completely autonomous, that is, not irrationally tied in some part of his character to the cultural requirements of his existence. Nevertheless, we can characterize an individual by the way in which one mode of adaptation predominates, and, when we study individuals, analysis by such a method provides certain helpful dimensions for descriptive and comparative purposes. We can also characterize a society by examining the relative frequency with which the three modes of adaptation occur in it, and the relative importance of the three types in the social structure.

About the anomics who arise as by-products, so to speak, of the attempt to create inner-direction and other-direction, a good deal has been suggested in the foregoing pages. Even a society depending on tradition-direction will have a certain number of anomics, those constitutionally and psychologically unable to conform or feel comfortable in the roles such a society assigns to its regularly recurring deviants. Some of these people can exploit the kinship system to keep going, but in a society of any size there will be some who are pushed out of that tight web. To these somewhat idiosyncratic and accidental outcrops of anomic character, more complex societies add the people who, once capable of adjustment, are thrust aside by the emergence of a new dominant type. Types brought up under a familial regime of tradition-direction may later find themselves misfits in a society by then dependent on inner-direction; likewise, the rise of other-direction may drive inner-directed as well as tradition-directed types into anomie. Reference has already been made to some of the possible political consequences of such anomic character types in America, how their political indifference can be mobilized by a crusade appealing to their inability to cope with the social demands of modern urban culture.

The anomics include not only those who, in their character, were trained to attend to signals that either are no longer given or no longer spell meaning or success. They also may be, as has just been said, those who are overadjusted, who listen too assiduously to the signals from within or without. Thus we have seen that in a society dependent on inner-direction there may be oversteered children and oversteered adults, people of too tight superego controls to permit themselves even the normal satisfactions and escapes of their fellows. Likewise, among those dependent on other-direction, some may be unable to shut off their radar even for a moment; their overconformity makes them a caricature of the adjusted pattern—a pattern that escapes them because they try too hard for it.

We have seen, for example, the effort of the other-directed person to achieve a political and personal style of tolerance, drained of emotion, temper, and moodiness. But, obviously, this can go so far that deadness of feeling comes to resemble a clinical symptom. The psychoanalyst Ralph Greenson, observing soldiers hospitalized for apathy in World War II, writes of them:

> The most striking characteristic of the apathetic patient is his visible lack of emotion and drive. At first glance he may seem to be depressed; closer scrutiny, however, reveals lack of affect. He appears slowed up in the psychic and motor responses; he shows an emptiness of expression and a mask-like facies . . . They behave very well in the ward, complying with all the rules and regulations. They rarely complain and make no demands . . . these patients had no urge to communicate their sufferings and no insight into their condition.

My own belief is that the ambulatory patients in the ward of modern culture show many analogous symptoms of too much compliance and too little insight, though of course their symptoms are not as sudden and severe. Their lack of emotion and emptiness of expression are as characteristic of many contemporary anomics as hysteria or outlawry was characteristic of anomics in the societies depending on earlier forms of direction.

Taken all together, the anomics—ranging from overt outlaws to "catatonic" types who lack even the spark for living, let alone for rebellion—constitute a sizable number in America. Quite a little is known about them in terms of personality type, social class, "preference" in illness, and so on. In fact, social science and psychiatry have until recently been preoccupied with understanding the anomic and suggesting therapies, just as medicine has been concerned with fighting the external agents that make people sick rather than with understanding the internal mysteries that keep them well. Indeed, it is usually not too difficult to explain why someone is anomic, since the tragedies and warpings of life, like germs, are omnipresent, and any personal disaster can be traced back to its "cause."

We obviously know much less about those whom I call autonomous. Many will even deny that there are such people, people capable of transcending their culture at any time or in any respect. Those who become autonomous in our own society, for instance, seem to arise in a family background and class or regional setting that have had quite different consequences for others. In fact, autonomous, adjusted, and anomic types can be brothers and sisters within the same family, associates on the same job, residents in the same housing project or suburb. When someone fails to become autonomous, we can very often see what blockages have stood in his way, but when someone succeeds in the same overt setting in which others have failed, I myself have no ready explanation of this, and am sometimes tempted to fall back on constitutional or genetic factors—what people of an earlier era called the divine spark. Certainly, if one observes week-old infants in a hospital crèche, one is struck with the varieties in responsiveness and aliveness before there has been much chance for culture to take hold. But, since this is a book about culture and character, I must leave such speculations to others.

It seems reasonable to assume that a decisive step in the road toward autonomy is connected with the social shifts I have linked to the curve of population. To put this in the negative, it is difficult, almost impossible, in a society of high population growth potential, for a person to become aware of the possibility that he might change, that there are many roles open to him, roles other people have taken in history or in his milieu. As the philosopher G. H. Mead saw, this taking the role of the other leads to becoming aware of actual differences and potential similarities between the other and the self. That is why culture contact alone does not lead people to change when their interpretations of the contact spring out of a tradition-directed mode of life. High population growth potential, tradition-direction, and the inability of the individual to change roles—to think of himself as an individual capable of such change—these, as we saw, go together.

For centuries the peasant farmers of Lebanon suffered from invasions by Arab horsemen. After each invasion the peasants began all over again to cultivate the soil, though they might do so only to pay tribute to the next marauder. The process went on until eventually the fertile valleys became virtual deserts, in which neither peasants nor nomads could hope for much. The peasants obviously never dreamed they could become horsemen; the marauders obviously never dreamed that they too might become cultivators of the soil. This epic has the quality not of human history but of animal life. The herbivores are unable to stop eating grass though they eat only to be devoured by the carnivores. And the carnivores cannot eat grass when they have thinned out the herbivores. In these societies dependent on tradition-direction there is scarcely a notion that one might change character or role.

If Arabs could imagine becoming cultivators, and vice versa, it would not necessarily follow that the symbiotic ecology of the two main groups would change. These tradition-directed types might still go on doing what they realized they need not do. Nevertheless, once people become aware, with the rise of inner-direction, that they as individuals with a private destiny are not tied to any given ecological pattern, something radically new happens in personal and social history. Then people can envisage adapting themselves not only within the narrow confines of the animal kingdom but within the wide range of alternative possibilities illustrated— but no more than illustrated—by human experience to date. Perhaps this is the most important meaning of the ever renewed discovery of the oneness of mankind as a species: that all human experience becomes relevant.

The Arab who can see himself as a peasant, even though he would be, for reasons of temperament or other factors, unable to make so radical a shift, has already gained a new perspective on the relation: Arab-peasant. He may conceive of structuring it in some other way, by manipulation rather than by force, for instance. But if he did that, he would change, and so would the peasant: their relations could never again have the old animal-like simplicity.

The more advanced the technology, on the whole, the more possible it is for a considerable number of human beings to imagine being somebody else. In the first place, the technology spurs the division of labor, which, in turn, creates a greater variety of life experiences and human types. In the second place, the improvement in technology permits sufficient leisure to contemplate change—a kind of capital reserve in men's self-adaptation to nature—not on the part of a ruling few but on the part of many. In the third place, the combination of technology and leisure helps to acquaint people with other historical solutions—to provide them, that is, not only with more goods and more experiences but also with an increased variety of personal and social models.

How powerful such an influence can be the Renaissance indicates. Then, a richer picture of the past made it possible to live toward a more open future. Italians, newly rich and self-conscious, tried to imitate Greeks; and northern peoples, such as the Elizabethan English, tried to imitate Italians. The inner-directed character type emerged as the dominant type from the new possibilities created at this period; he built both those possibilities and the limits he put on them into his character. From the masses of the tradition-directed there arose many mobile ones who decided that they could be "horsemen" and no longer had to be "cultivators"; and the new technology and new lands beyond the sea gave them the necessary physical and intellectual store for the shift, while at the same time making it possible for the cultivators to support more noncultivators. Ever since, in the countries of transitional population growth, men have robbed the earth of its fruits and the farmer of his progeny in order to build the industrial civilization (and the lowered birth rate) of today. In this process the farmer's progeny had to learn how to become something other than cultivators.

Today again, in the countries of incipient population decline, men stand on the threshold of new possibilities of being and becoming—though history provides a less ready, perhaps only a misleading, guide. They no longer need limit their choices by gyroscopic adaptation but can respond to a far wider range of signals than any that could possibly be internalized in childhood. However, with the still further advance of technology and the change of frontiers from production to consumption, the new possibilities do not present themselves in the same dramatic form of passing from one class to another, of joining one or another side—the exploiting or the exploited—in the factory and at the barricades. In fact, those, namely the Communists, who try to structure matters according to these older images of power, have become perhaps the most reactionary and most menacing force in world politics.

In a society of abundance that has reached the population phase of incipient decline, the class struggle alters as the middle class expands until it may number more than half of the whole population in occupational terms, with an even larger proportion, measured in terms of income, leisure, and values. The new possibilities opening up for the individual are possibilities not so much for entering a new class but rather for changing life style and changing character within the middle class.

Under these conditions autonomy will not be related to class. In the era dependent on inner-direction, when character was largely formed for work and at work, it made a great deal of difference whether one owned means of production or not. Today, however, the psychological advantages of ownership are very much reduced in importance; character is increasingly formed for leisure and during leisure—and both leisure and means of consumption are widely distributed. Thus, adjusted, autonomous, and anomic outcomes are often the result of very impalpable variations in the way people are treated by and react to their education, their consumer training, and, generally, their encounters with people— all within the broad status band of the middle class.

To be sure, there may be correlations, as yet unnoticed, between autonomy and occupation. Work is far from having lost its relevance for character even today. And occupational status affects leisure status. Those who are potentially autonomous may select some occupations in preference to others; beyond that, the day-by-day work experiences of members of different occupational groups will shape character. On the whole, however, it seems likely that the differences that will divide societies in the phase of incipient population decline will no longer be those between back-breaking work on the one hand and *rentier* status on the other, between misery and luxury, between long life and short life—those differences that dominated the thinking of men as varied as Charles Kingsley, Bellamy, Marx, and Veblen during the era of transitional population growth. Most people in America today—the "overprivileged" two thirds, let us say, as against the underprivileged third—can afford to attend to, and allow their characters to be shaped by, situational differences of a subtler nature than those arising from bare economic necessity and their relations to the means of production.

The autonomous person, living like everyone else in a given cultural setting, employs the reserves of his character and station to move away from the adjusted mean of the same setting. Thus, we cannot properly speak of an "autonomous other-directed man" (nor of an "anomic other-directed man") but only of an autonomous man emerging from an era or group depending on other-direction (or of an anomic man who has become anomic through his conflict with other-directed or inner-directed patterns or some combination of them). For autonomy, like anomie, is a deviation from the adjusted patterns, though a deviation controlled in its range and meaning by the existence of those patterns.

The autonomous person in a society depending on inner-direction, like the adjusted person of the same society, possessed clear-cut, internalized goals and was disciplined for stern encounters with a changing world. But whereas the adjusted person was driven toward his goals by a gyroscope over whose speed and direction he had hardly a modicum of control and of the existence of which he was sometimes unaware, his autonomous contemporary was capable of choosing his goals and modulating his pace. The goals, and the drive toward them, were rational, nonauthoritarian and noncompulsive for the autonomous; for the adjusted, they were merely given.

Obviously, however, as long as tight despotic or theocratic controls of conduct existed, it was difficult to "choose oneself" either in work or play. For, while it is possible to be autonomous no matter how tight the supervision of behavior as long as thought is free—and thought as such is not invaded effectively until modern totalitarianism—in practice most men need the opportunity for some freedom of behavior if they are to develop and confirm their autonomy of character. Sartre, I believe, is mistaken in his notion that men—other than a few heroic individuals—can "choose themselves" under conditions of extreme despotism.

The autonomous are not to be equated with the heroes. Heroism may or may not bespeak autonomy; the definition of the autonomous refers to those who are in their character capable of freedom, whether or not they are able to, or care to, take the risks of overt deviation. The case of Galileo illustrates both points. In order to accomplish his work, Galileo needed *some* freedom, such as the freedom to exchange astronomical tests and instruments, to write down results, and so on. Yet he chose a nonheroic course. In the Soviet Union and its satellites today he could not make this choice, since the choice between martyrdom or secrecy is not available under the grisly regime of the NKVD.

The four centuries since the Renaissance have seen the rise and fall of many periods when theocratic, royal, or other authoritative controls were not as tight as in Soviet Russia today; periods also when economic life for many was raised above mere subsistence, thus providing opportunities for autonomy. And there were loopholes for autonomy even in the earlier despotic periods, since the despots were inefficient, corrupt, and limited in their aims. Modern totalitarianism is also more inefficient and corrupt than it is often given credit for being, but its aims are unlimited and for this reason it must wage total war on autonomy— with what ultimate effectiveness we do not yet know. For the autonomous person's acceptance of social and political authority is always conditional: he can cooperate with others in action while maintaining the right of private judgment. There can be no recognition whatever of such a right under totalitarianism—one reason why in the Soviet Union artistic works and scientific theories are so relentlessly scrutinized for "deviationism," lest they conceal the seeds even of unconscious privacy and independence of perception.

Fortunately for us, the enemies of autonomy in the modern democracies are less total and relentless. However, as Erich Fromm has insisted in *Escape from Freedom*, the diffuse and anonymous authority of the modern democracies is less favorable to autonomy than one might assume. One reason, perhaps the chief reason, is that the other-directed person is trained to respond not so much to overt authority as to subtle but nonetheless constricting interpersonal expectations. Indeed, autonomy in an era depending on inner-direction looks easier to achieve than autonomy today. Autonomy in an inner-directed mode is, however, no longer feasible for most people. To understand why this is so requires a glance at the powerful bulwarks or defenses for autonomy that an era dependent on inner-direction provided and that are no longer so powerful today. These include, in the Protestant lands, certain attitudes toward conscience, and everywhere, the bulwarks of work, property, class, and occupation as well as the comforting possibilities of escape to the frontier.

In the first place, a Protestant or secular-Protestant society of adjusted inner-directed types expects people to conform, not by looking to others but by obedience to their internal gyroscopes or consciences. This affords privacy, for while society may punish people more or less for what they *do*, it lacks the interest and psychological capacity to find out what they *are*. People are like the yachts in a Bermuda race, attentive not to each other but to the goal in view and the favoring winds.

In the second place, there was always available a line of defense in the existence of frontiers of settlement and the right of asylum. The power to move around the globe in the days before passports placed limits on the tyrants' reach and gave reality to the concept of inalienable rights. Roger Williams lighting out for himself; Voltaire shuttling back and forth over Europe; Karl Marx finding refuge in the British Museum; Carl Schurz fleeing to America—these are scenes from an almost vanished past.

In the third place, the autonomous in the era dependent on inner-direction had available to them the defense provided by work itself, in a period when the adjusted people also were mainly work-oriented. Though it was hard to admit that one found joy in one's work in the puritan countries, it was permissible to regard it as an end in itself, as well as a means to other ends. The "hardness of the material" attracted the autonomous, indeed—again, like their less autonomous fellows—often hardened them to all other considerations. The following passage from Claude Bernard's *Experimental Medicine*, first published in 1865, expresses this outlook:

> After all this, should we let ourselves be moved by the sensitive cries of people of fashion or by the objections of men unfamiliar with scientific ideas? All feelings deserve respect, and I shall be very careful never to offend anyone's. I easily explain them to myself, and that is why they cannot stop me. . . . A physiologist is not a man of fashion, he is a man of science, absorbed by the scientific idea which he pursues; he no longer hears the cry of animals, he no longer sees the blood that flows, he sees only his idea and perceives only organisms concealing problems which he intends to solve. Similarly, no surgeon is stopped by the most moving cries and sobs, because he seeks only his idea and the purpose of his operation. . . . After what has gone before we shall deem all discussion of vivisection futile or absurd. It is impossible for men, judging facts by such different ideas, ever to agree; and as it is impossible to satisfy everybody, a man of science should attend only to the opinion of men of science who understand him, and should derive rules of conduct only from his own conscience.

Such a man as Claude Bernard looked to his scientific colleagues, not for approval of himself as a person but for the validation of his objective work. He had less need for people, for warm interpersonal response, than the autonomous man who arises among the groups dependent on other-direction.

In the fourth place, property and class were substantial defenses for those who strove for autonomy. They protected not only the crazy millionaire's conspicuous consumption but the irreverence of the secluded Bentham and the integrated double life of that fine horseman and industrialist of Manchester, Friedrich Engels. People were protected, too, not only by their work and their property but by their position, be it elevated or humble. If people could manage to fulfill their occupational role, what they did in their off hours was more or less up to them.

Charles Lamb as a petty official could write in his spare time. Hawthorne, and many other nineteenth-century American writers, held posts that did not require them to give much of themselves—certainly not the self-exploitation on and off the job asked of far better paid writers who hold hack jobs today. The hierarchical chain of occupations, once one achieved a position in it, held people in place with some degree of security, while permitting sufficient tether for the autonomous. Within certain given limits of property and place, one could move without arousing shocked antagonism, traumatic either in terms of one's feelings or one's worldly fate.

Many of these same defenses, however, operated far more frequently as barriers to autonomy than as defenses for it. A society organized in terms of class, private property, and occupation resisted autonomy with all the weapons of family, wealth, religion, and political power: the complaints and protests of political and religious reformers, artists, and artisans against this type of largely bourgeois social organization, now vanishing, were true and just enough. But we must never forget that these barriers could frequently be organized as defenses of the individual; once their flanks were turned by energy and talent, they provided the freedom in which autonomy as well as *rentier* complacency could flourish.

In biographies and memoirs of the last several hundred years, we can reconstruct, as it were, the way in which individuals begin their struggle for autonomy within the despotic walls of the patriarchal family. The family operated, much more than the state, as the "executive committee" of the inner-directed bourgeois class, training the social character both of future members of that class and of future servants to it. Print, however, as we have seen, might succor a child in his lonely battle with parents, teachers, and other adult authorities—though a book might also disorient him and increase the pressure on him. But with good luck a book, like a sympathetic teacher or relative, might break the solid front of authority in the home.

Not until adolescence were other children likely to be of much help, though then, especially when adolescent youth groups later took institutional form, they might assist the break from home. Adolescence, in fact, was usually the period of crisis for the boy or girl who sought autonomy. While even the adjusted had to make the passage from home, they moved thence into a social system that still held them fast, finding such authoritative parent surrogates as were necessary to calibrate their already internalized parental signals. However, the would-be autonomous youth, in breaking with parents, were breaking with authority as such, internalized as well as external. One can trace this process in all its poignancy in the development of John Stuart Mill, who got out from under his father only when well along in life, or of Franz Kafka, who never did.

Once out in the world, the person struggling for autonomy faced directly the barriers of property—if he was without it; of hierarchy—if he sought to climb or oppose it; of religion—if he contravened its controls on expression. In strongly Protestant communities in particular, one's discreet overt behavior could not assure to oneself the freedom of Erasmus or Galileo had made use of. The result was that between the oversteered and the understeered there was little room for autonomy. The struggle to turn these obstacles into defenses was often too tough, and the individual was scarred for life, as were Marx, Balzac, Nietzsche, Melville, E. A. Robinson, and many other great men of the era dependent on inner-direction. Still others, however—John Dewey, wiry Vermonter, was a magnificent example and so, in a very different way, is Bertrand Russell—more favored by fortune, could live lives of personal and intellectual collision and adventure with little inner conflict.

Lawyers and lawmakers have a technique called "incorporation by reference"; by means of it they can refer in one statute or document to another without full quotation. In the same way I would like to incorporate by reference here the writings of Mill which deal with individuality: the *Autobiography*, the essays *On Liberty* and *On Social Freedom*, and *The Subjection of Women*. These writings represent an extraordinary foreshadowing of the problems of the autonomous individual when, with the decline of the older barriers to freedom, the newer and far more subtle barriers of public opinion in a democracy arise. Indeed, in reading modern writers, such as Sartre, Simone de Beauvoir, Erich Fromm, José Ortega y Gasset, and Bertrand Russell, who deal with similar themes, one is struck by the degree to which, underneath differences in idiom, their philosophic outlook resembles Mill's in many important respects.

Mill wrote: "In this age the mere example of nonconformity, the mere refusal to bend the knee to custom, is itself a service." But his interest was more in the individual than in the service. He observed two tendencies that have grown much more powerful since he wrote. He saw, as many others did, that people no longer took their cues "from dignitaries in Church or State, from ostensible leaders, or from books" but rather from each other—from the peer-group and its mass-media organs, as we would say. He saw, as few others did, that this occurred not only in public matters but also in private ones, in the pursuit of pleasure and in the development of a whole style of life. All that has changed, perhaps, since he and Tocqueville wrote, is that the actions they saw as based on the fear of what people might say—on conscious opportunism, that is—are today the more automatic outcome of a character structure governed, not only from the first but throughout life, by signals from outside. In consequence, a major difference between the problems of Mill's day and ours is that someone who today refuses "to bend the knee to custom" is tempted to ask himself: "Is this what I really want? Perhaps I only want it because . . ."

This comparison may overstate historical changes; the autonomous at all times have been questioners. The autonomous among the inner-directed, however, were partially shaped by a milieu in which people took many psychological events for granted, while the autonomous among the other-directed live in a milieu in which people systematically question themselves in anticipation of the questions of others. More important, in the upper socio-economic levels in the western democracies today—these being the levels, except for the very highest, most strongly permeated by other-direction—the coercions upon those seeking autonomy are not the visible and palpable barriers of family and authority that typically restricted people in the past.

This is one reason why it is difficult, as an empirical matter, to decide who is autonomous when we are looking at the seemingly easy and permissive life of a social class in which there are no "problems" left, except for persons striving for autonomy. These latter, in turn, are incapable of defining the "enemy" with the relative ease of the autonomous person facing an inner-directed environment. Is the inside-dopester an enemy, with his sympathetic tolerance, but veiled disinterest, and his inability to understand savage emotions? Are they enemies, those friends who stand by, not to block but to be amused, to understand and pardon everything? An autonomous person of today must work constantly to detach himself from shadowy entanglements with this top level of other-direction—so difficult to break with because its demands appear so reasonable, even trivial.

One reason for this is that the autonomous person of today is the beneficiary of the greater sensitivity brought into our society, at great personal cost, by his autonomous predecessors of the era of inner-direction. The latter, in rejecting the Philistine norm, were frequently very much preoccupied with taste, with what they liked; in their sensuous openness to experience, their awareness of personal nuance, many of the Romantic poets and other artists of the nineteenth century were strikingly "modern." What they put into their poems and other works, in refinement and subjectivity, is part of their legacy to the emotional vocabularies of our own day. These precursors, moreover, had no doubt as to who their enemies were: they were the adjusted middle-class people who aggressively knew what they wanted, and demanded conformity to it—people for whom life was not something to be tasted but something to be hacked away at. Such people of course still exist in great numbers but, in the better educated strata of the larger cities, they are on the defensive; and opposition to them is no longer enough to make a person stand out as autonomous.

Autonomy, I think, must always to some degree be relative to the prevailing modes of conformity in a given society; it is never an all-or-nothing affair, but the result of a sometimes dramatic, sometimes imperceptible struggle with those modes. Modern industrial society has driven great numbers of people into anomie, and produced a wan conformity in others, but the very developments which have done this have also opened up hitherto undreamed-of possibilities for autonomy. As we come to understand our society better, and the alternatives it holds available to us, I think we shall be able to create many more alternatives, hence still more room for autonomy.

It is easier to believe this than to prove or even illustrate it. Let me instead point to a number of areas in which people today try to achieve autonomy—and to the enormous difficulties they meet.

Bohemia. As has just been indicated, among the groups dependent on inner-direction the deviant individual can escape, geographically or spiritually, to Bohemia; and still remain an "individual." Today, whole groups are matter-of-factly Bohemian; but the individuals who compose them are not necessarily free. On the contrary, they are often zealously tuned in to the signals of a group that finds the meaning of life, quite unproblematically, in an illusion of attacking an allegedly dominant and punishing majority of Babbitts and Kwakiutl chiefs. That is, under the aegis of the veto groups, young people today can find, in the wide variety of people and places of metropolitan life, a peer-group, conformity to which costs little in the way of search for principle.

The nonconformist today may find himself in the position unanticipated by Mill, of an eccentric who must, like a movie star, accept the roles in which he is cast, lest he disappoint the delighted expectations of his friends. The very fact that his efforts at autonomy are taken as cues by the "others" must make him conscious of the possibility that the effort toward autonomy might degenerate into other-directed play-acting.

Sex. What is here the autonomous path? Resistance to the seemingly casual demand of the "sophisticated" peer-group that one's achievements be taken casually, or acceptance of this "advanced" attitude? What models is one to take? One's forefathers, who were surrounded by chaste and modest women? Or the contemporary Kinsey athletes who boast of "freedom" and "experience"? And, as women become more knowing consumers, the question of whether or when to "assume the initiative" becomes a matter for anxious speculation. Perhaps even more difficult roles are forced upon women. Also pioneers of the sex frontier, they must foster aggressiveness and simulate modesty. They have less chance to escape the frontier even temporarily through their work, for, if they have a profession, both men and women are apt to think that their skill detracts from their sexual life or that their sexual life detracts from their skill. Many middle-class women appear to have turned back, in a futile effort to recapture the older and seemingly more secure patterns.

Tolerance. Tolerance is no problem when there is a wide gap between the tolerant and the tolerated. The mere expression of good will, and perhaps a contribution now and then, is all that is demanded. But when the slaves become freed men, and the proletarians self-respecting workers, tolerance in this earlier sense must be replaced by a more subtle and appropriate attitude. Again, the would-be autonomous individual is hard put to it to approximate this.

One frequently observes that, in emancipated circles, everything is forgiven Negroes who have behaved badly, because they are Negroes and have been put upon. This sails dangerously close to prejudice in reverse. Moral issues are befogged on both sides of the race line, since neither whites nor Negroes are expected to react as individuals striving for autonomy but only as members of the tolerating or the tolerated race. Plainly, to sort out what is valid today in the mood of tolerance from what is suspect requires a high level of self-consciousness.

This heightened self-consciousness, above all else, constitutes the insignia of the autonomous in an era dependent on other-direction. For, as the inner-directed man is more self-conscious than his tradition-directed predecessor and as the other-directed man is more self-conscious still, the autonomous man growing up under conditions that encourage self-consciousness can disentangle himself from the adjusted others only by a further move toward even greater self-consciousness. His autonomy depends not upon the ease with which he may deny or disguise his emotions but, on the contrary, upon the success of his effort to recognize and respect his own feelings, his own potentialities, his own limitations. This is not a quantitative matter, but in part an awareness of the problem of self-consciousness itself, an achievement of a higher order of abstraction.

As we know all too well, such an achievement is a difficult thing; many of those who attain it cannot manage to mold it into the structure of an autonomous life but succumb to anomie. Yet perhaps the anomie of such processes is preferable to the less self-conscious, though socially supported, anxiety of the adjusted who refuse to distort or reinterpret their culture and end by distorting themselves.

CHAPTER TEN

Erving Goffman on the Presentation of Self

∿ Introduction ∿

Erving Goffman (1922–1982) grew up in Dauphin, near Winnipeg, Canada, the son of Jewish immigrants from Ukraine. While he initially attended the University of Manitoba and studied chemistry, his experiences working at the National Film Board of Ottawa (where he met influential sociologist Dennis Wrong) prompted a change in his academic direction. Goffman transferred to the University of Toronto and earned a B.A. degree in sociology in 1945. He then pursued a graduate degree in sociology at the University of Chicago. As part of his doctoral research, Goffman collected ethnographic data on the island of Unst (one of Shetland Isles in Scotland). Goffman observed the face-to-face interactions of the islanders without their knowledge. After defending his dissertation in 1953, he worked as a research associate for Edward Shils at the University of Chicago. These experiences culminated in Goffman's influential book *The Presentation of Self in Everyday Life*. As you will read, this work provides a detailed, descriptive analysis of the component parts of interaction. Goffman employs a dramaturgical approach to the study of interaction, meaning that his analyses describe interaction as theater—the elements that comprise interaction are viewed as a performance between actor and audience.

From Chicago, Goffman moved to Washington, D.C., where he worked at a mental hospital in order to conduct fieldwork about its institutional practices; this research formed the basis of his next book, *Asylums*. Thereafter, Goffman acquired a position at the University of California at Berkeley where he continued to publish influential works, such as *Stigma*. Goffman was well on his way to altering permanently the vocabulary used to describe interaction and institutions. Toward the latter part of his career, his research focused on the analysis of everyday talk. This research culminated in the production of his final book, *Forms of Talk*. In 1982, before he was able to deliver his presidential address to the American Sociological Association, Goffman died of cancer.

The primary selection for this chapter is *The Presentation of Self in Everyday Life*. Goffman (xi) states in the preface of the book: "The perspective employed in this report is that of the theatrical performance; the principles derived are dramaturgical ones. I shall consider the way in which the individual in ordinary work situations presents himself and his activity to others, the ways in which he guides and controls the impression they form of him, and the kind of things he may and may not do while sustaining his performance before them." Goffman uses his experiences from the Shetland Isles as examples to support the arguments he makes in this book.

Goffman (15) defines interaction "as the reciprocal influence of individuals upon one another's actions." *Performances* are conducted by participants in order to influence interaction. When participants follow through on a preestablished pattern of action in a situation, their performances are referred to as playing a "part" or "routine." A performance entails a *front*, which is the individual's conscious or unconscious presentation of self to observers. The front functions to define the situation for onlookers. A front includes several parts: setting (physical layout, props, the scene of a performance), personal front (clothing, size and looks, facial and body gestures) and social front. Goffman points out that, despite how unique the performance is, observers will tend to look for familiar categories with which to make sense of it—easing the work of observers and making the performer's task easier in conveying a message. Advertisers take advantage of such routines—get an actor with white hair, put a lab coat on him, have him talk about a medication, and observers tend to place the performer in the role of a medical doctor. Such stage production goes on everyday, for example, when we say of the president who is appearing on television, "He just seems presidential!" or when we comment to a classmate during a lecture in class, "There's something I like about this teacher, and, you know, that's a really nice cardigan he's wearing."

It is typical for a performance to highlight the accepted values of a society; in this way, performances reinforce the society's sanctioned value system. Goffman illustrates this point in terms of social class: in an affluent society such as the United States, many people value wealth and the style and symbols that come with it. We may engage in particular performances tied to maintaining the front of affluence. Goffman notes also that such performances typically idealize a certain version of self as it underplays incompatible elements. We may present different versions of ourselves or present different social selves depending upon the audience. The maintenance of a front pleases the audience and the self in that situation, but at the same time it creates a collection of personal secrets or situationally disclosed selves. Goffman suggests that in order to be understood by the audience, we will minimize behaviors inconsistent with the intended performance. Socialization teaches us the cues necessary to present specific fronts for specific performances, and the audience will assist the performer by disregarding faux pas when possible. In effect, our performances become the "masks" we desire to wear. Goffman (36) states, "The world, in truth, is a wedding." This statement is reminiscent of Thomas's insight: "If men define situations as real, they are real in their consequences." Goffman relates this insight to that of the theater, in that socialization involves the learning of scripts, fronts, performances, and we participate in the play not only because of sanctions, but because this play is our baseline in defining reality. The idea of a presentation of self and reality is made clear in Goffman's discussion of the front and back regions of a performance. He states:

> [W]hen one's activity occurs in the presence of other persons, some aspects of the activity are expressively accentuated and other aspects, which might discredit the fostered impression, are suppressed. It is clear that accentuated facts make their appearance in what I have called a front region; it should be just as clear that there may be another region—a "back region" or "backstage"—where the suppressed facts make an appearance. (111–112)

He adds,

> The line dividing front and back regions is illustrated everywhere in our society. As suggested, the bathroom and bedroom, in all but lower-class homes, are places from which the downstairs audience can be excluded. Bodies that are cleansed, clothed, and made up in these rooms can be presented to friends in others. (123)

Goffman notes that front and back regions also pertain to roles and material factors. One is just as unlikely to see dish washers serving as hosts or hostesses at a fine restaurant as one is unlikely to see dirty coffee mugs piled up in a physician's waiting room. Socialization (and in general, social life) involves the learning of basic scripts, fronts, and performances as defined by the social grouping for the situation. And in our need to make sense of situations, we will read whatever cues are available in order to respond appropriately. Interaction reinforces a standard definition of a situation.

Such activity may appear to be a moral enterprise: behavior motivated by a sense of mutual obligation. But instead, according to Goffman (251), such activity is a performance that merely reflects the "amoral issue of engineering a convincing impression."

While Goffman uses terminology appropriate to the illusions realized in theatrical performances, he is well aware that such terminology has its limitations when applied to describing the consequences of social interaction in the real world. The nagging question for the reader is whether citizens in their day-to-day interactions are aware of the limitations of such theatrical techniques in creating the practical affairs that forge social existence.

∼ The Presentation of Self ∼

. . . [W]hen an individual appears before others he will have many motives for trying to control the impression they receive of the situation. This report is concerned with some of the common techniques that persons employ to sustain such impressions and with some of the common contingencies associated with the employment of these techniques. The specific content of any activity presented by the individual participant, or the role it plays in the interdependent activities of an on-going social system, will not be at issue; I shall be concerned only with the participant's dramaturgical problems of presenting the activity before others. The issues dealt with by stagecraft and stage management are sometimes trivial but they are quite general; they seem to occur everywhere in social life, providing a clear-cut dimension for formal sociological analysis.

It will be convenient to end this introduction with some definitions that are implied in what has gone before and required for what is to follow. For the purpose of this report, interaction (that is, face-to-face interaction) may be roughly defined as the reciprocal influence of individuals upon one another's actions when in one another's immediate physical presence. An interaction may be defined as all the interaction which occurs throughout any one occasion when a given set of individuals are in one another's continuous presence; the term "an encounter" would do as well. A "performance" may be defined as all the activity of a given participant on a given occasion which serves to influence in any way any of the other participants. Taking a particular participant and his performance as a basic point of reference, we may refer to those who contribute the other performances as the audience, observers, or co-participants. The pre-established pattern of action which is unfolded during a performance and which may be presented or played through on other occasions may be called a "part" or "routine." These situational terms can easily be related to conventional structural ones. When an individual or performer plays the same part to the same audience on different occasions, a social relationship is likely to arise. Defining social role as the enactment of rights and duties attached to a given status, we can say that a social role will involve one or more parts and that each of these different parts may be presented by the performer on a series of occasions to the same kinds of audience or to an audience of the same persons. . . .

. . . I have been using the term "performance" to refer to all the activity of an individual which occurs during a period marked by his continuous presence before a particular set of observers and which has some influence on the observers. It will be convenient to label as "front" that part of the individual's performance which regularly functions in a general and fixed fashion to define the situation for those who observe the performance. Front, then, is the expressive equipment of a standard kind intentionally or unwittingly employed by the individual during his performance. For preliminary purposes, it will be convenient to distinguish and label what seem to be the standard parts of front.

First, there is the "setting," involving furniture, décor, physical layout, and other background items which supply the scenery and stage props for the spate of human action played out before, within, or upon it. A setting tends to stay put, geographically speaking, so that those who would use a particular setting as part of their performance cannot begin their act until they have brought themselves to the appropriate place and must terminate their performance when they leave it. It is only in exceptional circumstances that the setting follows along with the performers; we see this in the funeral cortège, the civic parade, and the dream-like processions that kings and queens are made of. In the main, these exceptions seem to offer some kind of extra protection for performers who are, or who have momentarily become, highly sacred. . . .

If we take the term "setting" to refer to the scenic parts of expressive equip-ment, one may take the term "personal front" to refer to the other items of ex-pressive equipment, the items that we most intimately identify with the per-former himself and that we naturally expect will follow the performer wherever he goes. As part of personal front we may include: insignia of office or rank; clothing; sex, age, and racial characteristics; size and looks; posture; speech patterns; facial expressions; bodily gestures; and the like. Some of these vehicles for conveying signs, such as racial characteristics, are relatively fixed and over a span of time do not vary for the individual from one situation to another. On the other hand, some of these sign vehicles are relatively mo-bile or transitory, such as facial expression, and can vary during a performance from one moment to the next.

It is sometimes convenient to divide the stimuli which make up personal front into "appearance" and "manner," according to the function performed by the information that these stimuli convey. "Appearance" may be taken to refer to those stimuli which function at the time to tell us of the performer's social statuses. These stimuli also tell us of the individual's temporary ritual state, that is, whether he is engaging in formal social activity, work, or infor-mal recreation, whether or not he is celebrating a new phase in the season cy-cle or in his life-cycle. "Manner" may be taken to refer to those stimuli which function at the time to warn us of the interaction role the performer will ex-pect to play in the oncoming situation. Thus a haughty, aggressive manner may give the impression that the performer expects to be the one who will ini-tiate the verbal interaction and direct its course. A meek, apologetic manner may give the impression that the performer expects to follow the lead of oth-ers, or at least that he can be led to do so.

We often expect, of course, a confirming consistency between appearance and manner; we expect that the differences in social statuses among the interactants will be expressed in some way by congruent differences in the indications that are made of an expected interaction role. This type of coherence of front may be illustrated by the following description of the procession of a mandarin through a Chinese city:

> Coming closely behind . . . the luxurious chair of the mandarin, carried by eight bearers, fills the vacant space in the street. He is mayor of the town, and for all

practical purposes the supreme power in it. He is an ideal-looking official, for he is large and massive in appearance, whilst he has that stern and uncompromising look that is supposed to be necessary in any magistrate who would hope to keep his subjects in order. He has a stern and forbidding aspect, as though he were on his way to the execution ground to have some criminal decapitated. This is the kind of air that the mandarins put on when they appear in public. In the course of many years' experience, I have never once seen any of them, from the highest to the lowest, with a smile on his face or a look of sympathy for the people whilst he was being carried officially through the streets.

But, of course, appearance and manner may tend to contradict each other, as when a performer who appears to be of higher estate than his audience acts in a manner that is unexpectedly equalitarian, or intimate, or apologetic, or when a performer dressed in the garments of a high position presents himself to an individual of even higher status.

In addition to the expected consistency between appearance and manner, we expect, of course, some coherence among setting, appearance, and manner. Such coherence represents an ideal type that provides us with a means of stimulating our attention to and interest in exceptions. In this the student is assisted by the journalist, for exceptions to expected consistency among setting, appearance, and manner provide the piquancy and glamor of many careers and the salable appeal of many magazine articles. For example, a *New Yorker* profile on Roger Stevens (the real estate agent who engineered the sale of the Empire State Building) comments on the startling fact that Stevens has a small house, a meager office, and no letterhead stationery.

In order to explore more fully the relations among the several parts of social front, it will be convenient to consider here a significant characteristic of the information conveyed by front, namely, its abstractness and generality.

However specialized and unique a routine is, its social front, with certain exceptions, will tend to claim facts that can be equally claimed and asserted of other, somewhat different routines. For example, many service occupations offer their clients a performance that is illuminated with dramatic expressions of cleanliness, modernity, competence, and integrity. While in fact these abstract standards have a different significance in different occupational performances, the observer is encouraged to stress the abstract similarities. For the observer this is a wonderful, though sometimes disastrous, convenience. Instead of having to maintain a different pattern of expectation and responsive treatment for each slightly different performer and performance, he can place the situation in a broad category around which it is easy for him to mobilize his past experience and stereo-typical thinking. Observers then need only be familiar with a small and hence manageable vocabulary of fronts, and know how to respond to them, in order to orient themselves in a wide variety of situations. Thus in London the current tendency for chimney sweeps and perfume clerks to wear white lab coats tends to provide the client with an understanding that the delicate tasks performed by these persons will be performed in what has become a standardized, clinical, confidential manner.

There are grounds for believing that the tendency for a large number of different acts to be presented from behind a small number of fronts is a natural development in social organization. Radcliffe-Brown has suggested this in his claim that a "descriptive" kinship system which gives each person a unique place may work for very small communities, but, as the number of persons becomes large, clan segmentation becomes necessary as a means of providing a less complicated system of identifications and treatments. We see this tendency illustrated in factories, barracks, and other large social establishments. Those who organize these establishments find it impossible to provide a special cafeteria, special modes of payment, special vacation rights, and special sanitary facilities for every line and staff status category in the organization, and at the same time they feel that persons of dissimilar status ought not to be indiscriminately thrown together or classified together. As a compromise, the full range of diversity is cut at a few crucial points, and all those within a given bracket are allowed or obliged to maintain the same social front in certain situations.

In addition to the fact that different routines may employ the same front, it is to be noted that a given social front tends to become institutionalized in terms of the abstract stereotyped expectations to which it gives rise, and tends to take on a meaning and stability apart from the specific tasks which happen at the time to be performed in its name. The front becomes a "collective representation" and a fact in its own right.

When an actor takes on an established social role, usually he finds that a particular front has already been established for it. Whether his acquisition of the role was primarily motivated by a desire to perform the given task or by a desire to maintain the corresponding front, the actor will find that he must do both.

Further, if the individual takes on a task that is not only new to him but also unestablished in the society, or if he attempts to change the light in which his task is viewed, he is likely to find that there are already several well-established fronts among which he must choose. Thus, when a task is given a new front we seldom find that the front it is given is itself new.

Since fronts tend to be selected, not created, we may expect trouble to arise when those who perform a given task are forced to select a suitable front for themselves from among several quite dissimilar ones. Thus, in military organizations, tasks are always developing which (it is felt) require too much authority and skill to be carried out behind the front maintained by one grade of personnel and too little authority and skill to be carried out behind the front maintained by the next grade in the hierarchy. Since there are relatively large jumps between grades, the task will come to "carry too much rank" or to carry too little.

An interesting illustration of the dilemma of selecting an appropriate front from several not quite fitting ones may be found today in American medical organizations with respect to the task of administering anesthesia. In some hospitals anesthesia is still administered by nurses behind the front that nurses are allowed to have in hospitals regardless of the tasks they perform—a front involving ceremonial subordination to doctors and a relatively low rate of pay. In order to establish anesthesiology as a specialty for graduate medical doctors, interested practitioners have had to advocate strongly the idea that administering anesthesia is a sufficiently complex and vital task to justify giving to those who perform it the ceremonial and financial reward given to doctors. The difference between the front maintained by a nurse and the front maintained by a doctor is great; many things that are acceptable for nurses are *infra dignitatem* for doctors. Some medical people have felt that a nurse "under-ranked" for the task of administering anesthesia and that doctors "over-ranked"; were there an established status midway between nurse and doctor, an easier solution to the problem could perhaps be found. Similarly, had the Canadian Army had a rank halfway between lieutenant and captain, two and a half pips instead of two or three, then Dental Corps captains, many of them of a low ethnic origin, could have been given a rank that would perhaps have been more suitable in the eyes of the Army than the captaincies they were actually given.

I do not mean here to stress the point of view of a formal organization or a society; the individual, as someone who possesses a limited range of sign-equipment, must also make unhappy choices. Thus, in the crofting community studied by the writer, hosts often marked the visit of a friend by offering him a shot of hard liquor, a glass of wine, some home-made brew, or a cup of tea. The higher the rank or temporary ceremonial status of the visitor, the more likely he was to receive an offering near the liquor end of the continuum. Now one problem associated with this range of sign-equipment was that some crofters could not afford to keep a bottle of hard liquor, so that wine tended to be the most indulgent gesture they could employ. But perhaps a more common difficulty was the fact that certain visitors, given their permanent and temporary status at the time, outranked one potable and under-ranked the next one in line. There was often a danger that the visitor would feel just a little affronted or, on the other hand, that the host's costly and limited sign-equipment would be misused. In our middle classes a similar situation arises when a hostess has to decide whether or not to use the good silver, or which would be the more appropriate to wear, her best afternoon dress or her plainest evening gown.

I have suggested that social front can be divided into traditional parts, such as setting, appearance, and manner, and that (since different routines may be presented from behind the same front) we may not find a perfect fit between the specific character of a performance and the general socialized guise in which it appears to us. These two facts, taken together, lead one to appreciate that items in the social front of a particular routine are not only found in the social fronts of a whole range of routines but also that the whole range of routines in which one item of sign-equipment is found will differ from the range of routines in which another item in the same social front will be found. Thus, a lawyer may talk to a client in a social setting that he employs only for this purpose (or for a study), but the suitable clothes he wears on such occasions he will also employ, with equal suitability, at dinner with colleagues and at the theater with his wife. Similarly, the prints that hang on his wall and the carpet on his floor may be found in domestic social establishments. Of course, in highly ceremonial occasions, setting, manner, and appearance may all be unique and specific, used only for performances of a single type of routine, but such exclusive use of sign-equipment is the exception rather than the rule. . . .

If we alter our frame of reference for a moment and turn from a particular performance to the individuals who present it, we can consider an interesting fact about the round of different routines which any group or class of individuals helps to perform. When a group or class is examined, one finds that the members of it tend to invest their egos primarily in certain routines, giving less stress to the other ones which they perform. Thus a professional man may be willing to take a very modest role in the street, in a shop, or in his home, but, in the social sphere which encompasses his display of professional competency, he will be much concerned to make an effective showing. In mobilizing his behavior to make a showing, he will be concerned not so much with the full round of the different routines he performs but only with the one from which his occupational reputation derives. It is upon this issue that some writers have chosen to distinguish groups with aristocratic habits (whatever their social status) from those of middle-class character. The aristocratic habit, it has been said, is one that mobilizes all the minor activities of life which fall outside the serious specialities of other classes and injects into these activities an expression of character, power, and high rank.

> By what important accomplishments is the young nobleman instructed to support the dignity of his rank, and to render himself worthy of that superiority over his fellow-citizens, to which the virtue of his ancestors had raised them: Is it by knowledge, by industry, by patience, by self-denial, or by virtue of any kind? As all his words, as all his motions are attended to, he learns a habitual regard to every circumstance of ordinary behavior, and studies to perform all those small duties with the most exact propriety. As he is conscious of how much he is observed, and how much mankind are disposed to favor all his inclinations, he acts, upon the most indifferent occasions, with that freedom and elevation which the thought of this naturally inspires. His air, his manner, his deportment, all mark that elegant, and graceful sense of his own superiority, which those who are born to inferior stations can hardly ever arrive at. These are the arts by which he proposes to make mankind more easily submit to his authority, and to govern their inclinations according to his own pleasure: and in this he is seldom disappointed. These arts, supported by rank and pre-eminence, are, upon ordinary occasions, sufficient to govern the world. . . .

. . . [W]hen the individual presents himself before others, his performance will tend to incorporate and exemplify the officially accredited values of the society, more so, in fact, than does his behavior as a whole.

To the degree that a performance highlights the common official values of the society in which it occurs, we may look upon it, in the manner of Durkheim and Radcliffe-Brown, as a ceremony—as an expressive rejuvenation and reaffirmation of the moral values of the community. Furthermore, in so far as the expressive bias of performances comes to be accepted as reality, then that which is accepted at the moment as reality will have some of the characteristics of a celebration. To stay in one's room away from the place where the party is given, or away from where the practitioner attends his client, is to stay away from where reality is being performed. The world, in truth, is a wedding.

One of the richest sources of data on the presentation of idealized performances is the literature on social mobility. In most societies there seems to be a major or general system of stratification, and in most stratified societies there is an idealization of the higher strata and some aspiration on the part of those in low places to move to higher ones. (One must be careful to appreciate that this involves not merely a desire for a prestigeful place but also a desire for a place close to the sacred center of the common values of the society.) Commonly we find that upward mobility involves the presentation of proper performances and that efforts to move upward and efforts to keep from moving downward are expressed in terms of sacrifices made for the maintenance of front. Once the proper sign-equipment has been obtained and familiarity gained in the management of it, then this equipment can be used to embellish and illumine one's daily performances with a favorable social style.

Perhaps the most important piece of sign-equipment associated with social class consists of the status symbols through which material wealth is expressed. American society is similar to others in this regard but seems to have been singled out as an extreme example of wealth-oriented class structure—perhaps because in America the license to employ symbols of wealth and financial capacity to do so are so widely distributed. . . .

If an individual is to give expression to ideal standards during his performance, then he will have to forgo or conceal action which is inconsistent with these standards. When this inappropriate conduct is itself satisfying in some way, as is often the case, then one commonly finds it indulged in secretly; in this way the performer is able to forgo his cake and eat it too. For example, in American society we find that eight-year-old children claim lack of interest in the television programs that are directed to five- and six-year-olds, but sometimes surreptitiously watch them. We also find that middle-class housewives sometimes employ—in a secret and surreptitious way—cheap substitutes for coffee, ice cream, or butter; in this way they can save money, or effort, or time, and still maintain an impression that the food they serve is of high quality. The same women may leave *The Saturday Evening Post* on their living room end table but keep a copy of *True Romance* ("It's something the cleaning woman must have left around") concealed in their bedroom. . . .

I have suggested that a performer tends to conceal or underplay those activities, facts, and motives which are incompatible with an idealized version of himself and his products. In addition, a performer often engenders in his audience the belief that he is related *to them* in a more ideal way than is always the case. . . .

[I]ndividuals often foster the impression that the routine they are presently performing is their only routine or at least their most essential one. As previously suggested, the audience, in their turn, often assume that the character projected before them is all there is to the individual who acts out the projection for them. As suggested in the well-known quotation from William James:

> . . . we may practically say that he has as many different social selves as there are distinct *groups* of persons about whose opinion he cares. He generally shows a different side of himself to each of these different groups. Many a youth who is demure enough before his parents and teachers, swears and swaggers like a pirate among his "tough" young friends. We do not show ourselves to our children as to our club companions, to our customers as to the laborers we employ, to our own masters and employers as to our intimate friends. . . .

It has been suggested that the performer can rely upon his audience to accept minor cues as a sign of something important about his performance. This convenient fact has an inconvenient implication. By virtue of the same sign-accepting tendency, the audience may misunderstand the meaning that a cue was designed to convey, or may read an embarrassing meaning into gestures or events that were accidental, inadvertent, or incidental and not meant by the performer to carry any meaning whatsoever.

In response to these communication contingencies, performers commonly attempt to exert a kind of synecdochic responsibility, making sure that as many as possible of the minor events in the performance, however instrumentally inconsequential these events may be, will occur in such a way as to convey either no impression or an impression that is compatible and consistent with the over-all definition of the situation that is being fostered. When the audience is known to be secretly skeptical of the reality that is being impressed upon them, we have been ready to appreciate their tendency to pounce on trifling flaws as a sign that the whole show is false; but as students of social life we have been less ready to appreciate that even sympathetic audiences can be momentarily disturbed, shocked, and weakened in their faith by the discovery of a picayune discrepancy in the impressions presented to them. . . .

. . . [W]e tend to blind ourselves to the fact that everyday secular performances in our own Anglo-American society must often pass a strict test of aptness, fitness, propriety, and decorum. Perhaps this blindness is partly due to the fact that as performers we are often more conscious of the standards which we might have applied to our activity but have not than of the standards we unthinkingly apply. In any case, as students we must be ready to examine the dissonance created by a misspelled word, or by a slip that is not quite concealed by a skirt; and we must be ready to appreciate why a near-sighted plumber, to protect the impression of rough strength that is *de rigueur* in his profession, feels it necessary to sweep his spectacles into his pocket when the housewife's approach changes his work into a performance, or why a television repairman is advised by his public relations counsels that the screws he fails to put back into the set should be kept alongside his own so that the unreplaced parts will not give an improper impression. In other words, we must be prepared to see that the impression of reality fostered by a performance is a delicate, fragile thing that can be shattered by very minor mishaps.

The expressive coherence that is required in performances points out a crucial discrepancy between our all-too-human selves and our socialized selves. As human beings we are presumably creatures of variable impulse with moods and energies that change from one moment to the next. As characters put on for an audience, however, we must not be subject to ups and downs. As Durkheim suggested, we do not allow our higher social activity "to follow in the trail of our bodily states, as our sensations and our general bodily consciousness do." A certain bureaucratization of the spirit is expected so that we can be relied upon to give a perfectly homogeneous performance at every appointed time. As Santayana suggests, the socialization process not only transfigures, it fixes:

> But whether the visage we assume be a joyful or a sad one, in adopting and emphasizing it we define our sovereign temper. Henceforth, so long as we continue under the spell of this self-knowledge, we do not merely live but act; we compose and play our chosen character, we wear the buskin of deliberation, we defend and idealize our passions, we encourage ourselves eloquently to be what we are, devoted or scornful or careless or austere; we soliloquize (before an imaginary audience) and we wrap ourselves gracefully in the mantle of our inalienable part. So draped, we solicit applause and expect to die amid a universal hush. We profess to live up to the fine sentiments we have uttered, as we try to believe in the religion we profess. The greater our difficulties the greater our zeal. Under our published principles and plighted language we must assiduously hide all the inequalities of our moods and conduct, and this without hypocrisy, since our deliberate character is more truly ourself than is the flux of our involuntary dreams. The portrait we paint in this way and exhibit as our true person may well be in the grand manner, with column and curtain and distant landscape and finger pointing to the terrestrial globe or to the Yorick-skull of philosophy; but if this style is native to us and our art is vital, the more it transmutes its model the deeper and truer art it will be. The severe bust of an archaic sculpture, scarcely humanizing the block, will express a spirit far more justly than the man's dull morning looks or casual grimaces. Everyone who is sure of his mind, or proud of his office, or anxious about his duty assumes a tragic mask. He deputes it to be himself and transfers to it almost all his vanity. While still alive and subject, like all existing things, to the undermining flux of his own substance, he has crystallized his soul into an idea, and more in pride than in sorrow he has offered up his life on the altar of the Muses. Self-knowledge, like any art or science, renders its subject-matter in a new medium, the medium of ideas, in which it loses its old dimensions and its old place. Our animal habits are transmuted by conscience into loyalties and duties, and we become "persons" or masks.

Through social discipline, then, a mask of manner can be held in place from within. But, as Simone de Beauvoir suggests, we are helped in keeping this pose by clamps that are tightened directly on the body, some hidden, some showing:

> Even if each woman dresses in conformity with her status, a game is still being played: artifice, like art, belongs to the realm of the imaginary. It is not only that girdle, brassiere, hair-dye, make-up disguise body and face; but that the least so-

phisticated of women, once she is "dressed," does not present *herself* to observation; she is, like the picture or the statue, or the actor on the stage, an agent through whom is suggested someone not there—that is, the character she represents, but is not. It is this identification with something unreal, fixed, perfect as the hero of a novel, as a portrait or a bust, that gratifies her; she strives to identify herself with this figure and thus to seem to herself to be stabilized, justified in her splendor. . . .

In our own Anglo-American culture there seems to be two common-sense models according to which we formulate our conceptions of behavior: the real, sincere, or honest performance; and the false one that thorough fabricators assemble for us, whether meant to be taken unseriously, as in the work of stage actors, or seriously, as in the work of confidence men. We tend to see real performances as something not purposely put together at all, being an unintentional product of the individual's unselfconscious response to the facts in his situation. And contrived performances we tend to see as something painstakingly pasted together, one false item on another, since there is no reality to which the items of behavior could be a direct response. It will be necessary to see now that these dichotomous conceptions are by way of being the ideology of honest performers, providing strength to the show they put on, but a poor analysis of it.

First, let it be said that there are many individuals who sincerely believe that the definition of the situation they habitually project is the real reality. In this report I do not mean to question their proportion in the population but rather the structural relation of their sincerity to the performances they offer. If a performance is to come off, the witnesses by and large must be able to believe that the performers are sincere. This is the structural place of sincerity in the drama of events. Performers may be sincere—or be insincere but sincerely convinced of their own sincerity—but this kind of affection for one's part is not necessary for its convincing performance. There are not many French cooks who are really Russian spies, and perhaps there are not many women who play the part of wife to one man and mistress to another; but these duplicities do occur, often being sustained successfully for long periods of time. This suggests that while persons usually are what they appear to be, such appearances could still have been managed. There is, then, a statistical relation between appearances and reality, not an intrinsic or necessary one. In fact, given the unanticipated threats that play upon a performance, and given the need (later to be discussed) to maintain solidarity with one's fellow performers and some distance from the witnesses, we find that a rigid incapacity to depart from one's inward view of reality may at times endanger one's performance. Some performances are carried off successfully with complete dishonesty, others with complete honesty; but for performances in general neither of these extremes is essential and neither, perhaps, is dramaturgically advisable.

The implication here is that an honest, sincere, serious performance is less firmly connected with the solid world than one might first assume. And this implication will be strengthened if we look again at the distance usually placed between quite honest performances and quite contrived ones. In this connection take, for example, the remarkable phenomenon of stage acting. It does take deep skill, long training, and psychological capacity to become a good stage actor. But this fact should not blind us to another one: that almost anyone can quickly learn a script well enough to give a charitable audience some sense of realness in what is being contrived before them. And it seems this is so because ordinary social intercourse is itself put together as a scene is put together, by the exchange of dramatically inflated actions, counteractions, and terminating replies. Scripts even in the hands of unpracticed players can come to life because life itself is a dramatically enacted thing. All the world is not, of course, a stage, but the crucial ways in which it isn't are not easy to specify.

The recent use of "psychodrama" as a therapeutic technique illustrates a further point in this regard. In these psychiatrically staged scenes patients not only act out parts with some effectiveness, but employ no script in doing so. Their own past is available to them in a form which allows them to stage a recapitulation of it. Apparently a part once played honestly and in earnest leaves the performer in a position to contrive a showing of it later. Further, the parts that significant others played to him in the past also seem to be available, allowing him to switch from being the person that he was to being the persons that others were for him. This capacity to switch enacted roles when obliged to do so could have been predicted; everyone apparently can do it. For in learning to perform our parts in real life we guide our own productions by not too consciously maintaining an incipient familiarity with the routine of those to whom we will address ourselves. And when we come to be able properly to manage a real routine we are able to do this in part because of "anticipatory socialization," having already been schooled in the reality that is just coming to be real for us.

When the individual does move into a new position in society and obtains a new part to perform, he is not likely to be told in full detail how to conduct himself, nor will the facts of his new situation press sufficiently on him from the start to determine his conduct without his further giving thought to it. Ordinarily he will be given only a few cues, hints, and stage directions, and it will be assumed that he already has in his repertoire a large number of bits and pieces of performances that will be required in the new setting. The individual will already have a fair idea of what modesty, deference, or righteous indignation looks like, and can make a pass at playing these bits when necessary. He may even be able to play out the part of a hypnotic subject or commit a "compulsive" crime on the basis of models for these activities that he is already familiar with.

A theatrical performance or a staged confidence game requires a thorough scripting of the spoken content of the routine; but the vast part involving "expression given off" is often determined by meager stage directions. It is expected that the performer of illusions will already know a good deal about how to manage his voice, his face, and his body, although he—as well as any person who directs him—may find it difficult indeed to provide a detailed verbal statement of this kind of knowledge. And in this, of course, we approach the situation of the straightforward man in the street. Socialization may not so much involve a learning of the many specific details of a single concrete part—often there could not be enough time or energy for this. What does seem to be required of the individual is that he learn enough pieces of expression to be able to "fill in" and manage, more or less, any part that he is likely to be given. The legitimate performances of everyday life are not "acted" or "put on" in the sense that the performer knows in advance just what he is going to do, and does this solely because of the effect it is likely to have. The expressions it is felt he is giving off will be especially "inaccessible" to him. But as in the case of less legitimate performers, the incapacity of the ordinary individual to formulate in advance the movements of his eyes and body does not mean that he will not express himself through these devices in a way that is dramatized and pre-formed in his repertoire of actions. In short, we all act better than we know how.

When we watch a television wrestler gouge, foul, and snarl at his opponent we are quite ready to see that, in spite of the dust, he is, and knows he is, merely playing at being the "heavy," and that in another match he may be given the other role, that of clean-cut wrestler, and perform this with equal verve and proficiency. We seem less ready to see, however, that while such details as the number and character of the falls may be fixed beforehand, the details of the expressions and movements used do not come from a script but from command of an idiom, a command that is exercised from moment to moment with little calculation or forethought.

In reading of persons in the West Indies who become the "horse" or the one possessed of a voodoo spirit, it is enlightening to learn that the person possessed will be able to provide a correct portrayal of the god that has entered him because of "the knowledge and memories accumulated in a life spent visiting congregations of the cult"; that the person possessed will be in just the right social relation to those who are watching; that possession occurs at just the right moment in the ceremonial undertakings, the possessed one carrying out his ritual obligations to the point of participating in a kind of skit with persons possessed at the time with other spirits. But in learning this, it is important to see that this contextual structuring of the horse's role still allows participants in the cult to believe that possession is a real thing and that persons are possessed at random by gods whom they cannot select.

And when we observe a young American middle-class girl playing dumb for the benefit of her boy friend, we are ready to point to items of guile and contrivance in her behavior. But like herself and her boy friend, we accept as an unperformed fact that this performer *is* a young American middle-class girl. But surely here we neglect the greater part of the performance. It is commonplace to say that different social groupings express in different ways such attributes as age, sex, territory, and class status, and that in each case these bare attributes are elaborated by means of a distinctive complex cultural configuration of proper ways of conducting oneself. To *be* a given kind of person, then, is not merely to possess the required attributes, but also to sustain the standards of conduct and appearance that one's social grouping attaches thereto. The unthinking ease with which performers consistently carry off such standard-maintaining routines does not deny that a performance has occurred, merely that the participants have been aware of it.

A status, a position, a social place is not a material thing, to be possessed and then displayed; it is a pattern of appropriate conduct, coherent, embellished, and well articulated. Performed with ease or clumsiness, awareness or not, guile or good faith, it is none the less something that must be enacted and portrayed, something that must be realized. Sartre, here, provides a good illustration:

> Let us consider this waiter in the café. His movement is quick and forward, a little too precise, a little too rapid. He comes toward the patrons with a step a little too quick. He bends forward a little too eagerly; his voice, his eyes express an interest a little too solicitous for the order of the customer. Finally there he returns, trying to imitate in his walk the inflexible stiffness of some kind of automaton while carrying his tray with the recklessness of a tightrope-walker by putting it in a perpetually unstable, perpetually broken equilibrium which he perpetually re-establishes by a light movement of the arm and hand. All his behavior seems to us a game. He applies himself to chaining his movements as if they were mechanisms, the one regulating the other; his gestures and even his voice seem to be mechanisms; he gives himself the quickness and pitiless rapidity of things. He is playing, he is amusing himself. But what is he playing? We need not watch long before we can explain it: he is playing at being a waiter in a café. There is nothing there to surprise us. The game is a kind of marking out and investigation. The child plays with his body in order to explore it, to take inventory of it; the waiter in the café plays with his condition in order to *realize* it. This obligation is not different from that which is imposed on all tradesmen. Their condition is wholly one of ceremony. The public demands of them that they realize it as a ceremony; there is the dance of the grocer, of the tailor, of the auctioneer, by which they endeavor to persuade their clientele that they are nothing but a grocer, an auctioneer, a tailor. A grocer who dreams is offensive to the buyer, because such a grocer is not wholly a grocer. Society demands that he limit himself to his function as a grocer, just as the soldier at attention makes himself into a soldier-thing with a direct regard which does not see at all, which is not longer meant to see, since it is the rule and not the interest of the moment which determines the point he must fix his eyes on (the sight "fixed at ten paces"). There are indeed many precautions to imprison a man in what he is, as if we lived in perpetual fear that he might escape from it, that he might break away and suddenly elude his condition. . . .

. . . [W]hen one's activity occurs in the presence of other persons, some aspects of the activity are expressively accentuated and other aspects, which might discredit the fostered impression, are suppressed. It is clear that accentuated facts make their appearance in what I have called a front region; it should be just as clear that there may be another region—a "back region" or "backstage"—where the suppressed facts make an appearance.

A back region or backstage may be defined as a place, relative to a given performance, where the impression fostered by the performance is knowingly contradicted as a matter of course. . . .

One of the most interesting times to observe impression management is the moment when a performer leaves the back region and enters the place where the audience is to be found, or when he returns therefrom, for at these moments one can detect a wonderful putting on and taking off of character. Orwell, speaking of waiters, and speaking from the backstage point of view of dishwashers, provides us with an example:

> It is an instructive sight to see a waiter going into a hotel dining-room. As he passes the door a sudden change comes over him. The set of his shoulders alters; all the dirt and hurry and irritation have dropped off in an instant. He glides over the carpet, with a solemn priest-like air. I remember our assistant *maître d'hôtel*, a fiery Italian, pausing at the dining-room door to address his apprentice who had broken a bottle of wine. Shaking his fist above his head he yelled (luckily the door was more or less soundproof).
>
> *"Tu me fais*—Do you call yourself a waiter, you young bastard? You a waiter! You're not fit to scrub floors in the brothel your mother came from. *Maquereau!"*
>
> Words failing him, he turned to the door; and as he opened it he delivered a final insult in the same manner as Squire Western in *Tom Jones*.
>
> Then he entered the dining-room and sailed across it dish in hand, graceful as a swan. Ten seconds later he was bowing reverently to a customer. And you could not help thinking, as you saw him bow and smile, with that benign smile of the trained waiter, that the customer was put to shame by having such an aristocrat to serve him. . . .

The decorations and permanent fixtures in a place where a particular performance is usually given, as well as the performers and performance usually found there, tend to fix a kind of spell over it; even when the customary performance is not being given in it, the place tends to retain some of its front region character. Thus a cathedral and a schoolroom retain something of their tone even when only repairmen are present, and while these men may not behave reverently while doing their work, their irreverence tends to be of a structured kind, specifically oriented to what in some sense they ought to be feeling but are not. . . .

However, while there is a tendency for a region to become identified as the front region or back region of a performance with which it is regularly associated, still there are many regions which function at one time and in one sense as a front region and at another time and in another sense as a back region. Thus the private office of an executive is certainly the front region where his status in the organization is intensively expressed by means of the quality of his office furnishings. And yet it is here that he can take his jacket off, loosen his tie, keep a bottle of liquor handy, and act in a chummy and even boisterous way with fellow executives of his own rank. . . .

Two kinds of bounded regions have been considered: front regions where a particular performance is or may be in progress, and back regions where action occurs that is related to the performance but inconsistent with the appearance fostered by the performance. It would seem reasonable to add a third region, a residual one, namely, all places other than the two already identified. Such a region could be called "the outside." The notion of an outside region that is neither front nor back with respect to a particular performance conforms to our common-sense notion of social establishments, for when we look at most buildings we find within them rooms that are regularly or temporarily used as back regions and front regions, and we find that the outer walls of the building cut both types of rooms off from the outside world. Those individuals who are on the outside of the establishment we may call "outsiders."

While the notion of outside is obvious, unless handled with care it can mislead and confuse us, for when we shift our consideration from the front or back region to the outside we tend also to shift our point of reference from one performance to another. Given a particular ongoing performance as a point of reference, those who are outside will be persons for whom the performers actually or potentially put on a show, but a show (as we shall see) different from, or all too similar to, the one in progress. When outsiders unexpectedly enter the front or the back region of a particular performance-in-progress, the consequence of their inopportune presence can often best be studied not in terms of its effects upon the performance-in-progress but rather in terms of its effects upon a different performance, namely, the one which the performers or the audience would ordinarily present before the outsiders at a time and place when the outsiders would be the anticipated audience. . . .

. . . [I]t should be understood that access to the back and front regions of a performance is controlled not only by the performers but by others. Individuals voluntarily stay away from regions into which they have not been invited. (This kind of tact in regard to place is analagous to "discretion" . . . .) And when outsiders find they are about to enter such a region, they often give those already present some warning, in the form of a message, or a knock, or a cough, so that the intrusion can be put off if necessary or the setting hurriedly put in order and proper expressions fixed on the faces of those present. . . .

. . . In this report the expressive component of social life has been treated as a source of impressions given to or taken by others. Impression, in turn, has been treated as a source of information about unapparent facts and as a means by which the recipients can guide their response to the informant without having to wait for the full consequences of the informant's actions to be felt. Expression, then, has been treated in terms of the communicative role it plays during social interaction and not, for example, in terms of consummatory or tension-release function it might have for the expresser.

Underlying all social interaction there seems to be a fundamental dialectic. When one individual enters the presence of others, he will want to discover the facts of the situation. Were he to possess this information, he could know, and make allowances for, what will come to happen and he could give the others present as much of their due as is consistent with his enlightened self-interest. To uncover fully the factual nature of the situation, it would be necessary for the individual to know all the relevant social data about the others. It would also be necessary for the individual to know the actual outcome or end product of the activity of the others during the interaction, as well as their innermost feelings concerning him. Full information of this order is rarely available; in its absence, the individual tends to employ substitutes—cues, tests, hints, expressive gestures, status symbols, etc.—as predictive devices. In short, since the reality that the individual is concerned with is unperceivable at the moment, appearances must be relied upon in its stead. And, paradoxically, the more the individual is concerned with the reality that is not available to perception, the more must he concentrate his attention on appearances.

The individual tends to treat the others present on the basis of the impression they give now about the past and the future. It is here that communicative acts are translated into moral ones. The impressions that the others give tend to be treated as claims and promises they have implicitly made, and claims and promises tend to have a moral character. In his mind the individual says: "I am using these impressions of you as a way of checking up on you and your activity, and you ought not to lead me astray." The peculiar thing about this is that the individual tends to take this stand even though he expects the others to be unconscious of many of their expressive behaviors and even though he may expect to exploit the others on the basis of the information he gleans about them. Since the sources of impression used by the observing individual involve a multitude of standards pertaining to politeness and decorum, pertaining both to social intercourse and task-performance, we can appreciate afresh how daily life is enmeshed in moral lines of discrimination.

Let us shift now to the point of view of the others. If they are to be gentlemanly, and play the individual's game, they will give little conscious heed to the fact that impressions are being formed about them but rather act without guile or contrivance, enabling the individual to receive valid impressions about them and their efforts. And if they happen to give thought to the fact that they are being observed, they will not allow this to influence them unduly, content in the belief that the individual will obtain a correct impression and give them their due because of it. Should they be concerned with influencing the treatment that the individual gives them, and this is properly to be expected, then a gentlemanly means will be available to them. They need only guide their action in the present so that its future consequences will be the kind that would lead a just individual to treat them now in a way they want to be treated; once this is done, they have only to rely on the perceptiveness and justness of the individual who observes them.

Sometimes those who are observed do, of course, employ these proper means of influencing the way in which the observer treats them. But there is another way, a shorter and more efficient way, in which the observed can influence the observer. Instead of allowing an impression of their activity to arise as an incidental by-product of their activity, they can reorient their frame of reference and devote their efforts to the creation of desired impressions. Instead of attempting to achieve certain ends by acceptable means, they can attempt to achieve the impression that they are achieving certain ends by acceptable means. It is always possible to manipulate the impression the observer uses as a substitute for reality because a sign for the presence of a thing, not being that thing, can be employed in the absence of it. The observer's need to rely on representations of things itself creates the possibility of misrepresentation.

There are many sets of persons who feel they could not stay in business, whatever their business, if they limited themselves to the gentlemanly means of influencing the individual who observes them. At some point or other in the round of their activity they feel it is necessary to band together and directly manipulate the impression that they give. The observed become a performing team and the observers become the audience. Actions which appear to be done on objects become gestures addressed to the audience. The round of activity becomes dramatized.

We come now to the basic dialectic. In their capacity as performers, individuals will be concerned with maintaining the impression that they are living up to the many standards by which they and their products are judged. Because these standards are so numerous and so pervasive, the individuals who are performers dwell more than we might think in a moral world. But, *qua* performers, individuals are concerned not with the moral issue of realizing these standards, but with the amoral issue of engineering a convincing impression that these standards are being realized. Our activity, then, is largely concerned with moral matters, but as performers we do not have a moral concern with them. As performers we are merchants of morality. Our day is given over to intimate contact with the goods we display and our minds are filled with intimate understandings of them; but it may well be that the more attention we give to these goods, then the more distant we feel from them and from those who are believing enough to buy them. To use a different imagery, the very obligation and profitability of appearing always in a steady moral light, of being a socialized character, forces one to be the sort of person who is practiced in the ways of the stage. . . .

And now a final comment. In developing the conceptual framework employed in this report, some language of the stage was used. I spoke of performers and audiences; of routines and parts; of performances coming off or falling flat; of cues, stage settings and backstage; of dramaturgical needs, dramaturgical skills, and dramaturgical strategies. Now it should be admitted that this attempt to press a mere analogy so far was in part a rhetoric and a maneuver.

The claim that all the world's a stage is sufficiently commonplace for readers to be familiar with its limitations and tolerant of its presentation, knowing that at any time they will easily be able to demonstrate to themselves that it is not to be taken too seriously. An action staged in a theater is a relatively contrived illusion and an admitted one; unlike ordinary life, nothing real or actual can happen to the performed characters—although at another level of course something real and actual can happen to the reputation of performers *qua* professionals whose everyday job is to put on theatrical performances.

And so here the language and mask of the stage will be dropped. Scaffolds, after all, are to build other things with, and should be erected with an eye to taking them down. This report is not concerned with aspects of theater that creep into everyday life. It is concerned with the structure of social encounters—the structure of those entities in social life that come into being whenever persons enter one another's immediate physical presence. The key factor in this structure is the maintenance of a single definition of the situation, this definition having to be expressed, and this expression sustained in the face of a multitude of potential disruptions.

A character staged in a theater is not in some ways real, nor does it have the same kind of real consequences as does the thoroughly contrived character performed by a confidence man; but the *successful* staging of either of these types of false figures involves use of *real* techniques—the same techniques by which everyday persons sustain their real social situations. Those who conduct face to face interaction on a theater's stage must meet the key requirement of real situations; they must expressively sustain a definition of the situation: but this they do in circumstances that have facilitated their developing an apt terminology for the interactional tasks that all of us share.

~

CHAPTER ELEVEN

Peter Berger and Thomas Luckmann on the Social Construction of Self and Society

~ Introduction ~

Peter Berger (1929–), sociologist and lay Lutheran theologian, was born in Vienna, Austria. He came to the United States when he was seventeen and earned a B.A. degree from Wagner College in New York City and his master's and doctoral degrees at the New School for Social Research in Manhattan. He later did postgraduate work at Yale University and at the Lutheran Theological Seminary in Philadelphia. Early in his career Berger was an assistant professor at the University of North Carolina at Greensboro. He then accepted a position to teach sociology at the Hartford Seminary Foundation in Connecticut. He has taught at the New School for Social Research, Brooklyn College, Rutgers University, Boston College, and since 1981, has been on the faculty at Boston University.

In the early 1960s Berger wrote three books: *The Noise of Solemn Assemblies* (1961), *A Precarious Vision* (1961), and *Invitation to Sociology: A Humanist Perspective* (1963). He coauthored with Thomas Luckmann *The Social Construction of Reality* (1966) and wrote *The Sacred Canopy* (1967) and *A Rumor of Angels* (1969). A trip to Mexico (and subsequent trips to India) fueled his interest in Third World poverty as well as in comparative religion. He coauthored, with Brigitte Berger (his wife) and Hansfried Kellner (his brother-in-law), *The Homeless Mind* (1973) and was the author of *Pyramids of Sacrifice* (1974) and *The Heretical Imperative* (1979), among many other publications. In recent years Berger coauthored another book with Luckmann, *Modernity, Pluralism and the Crisis of Meaning* (1995), and has written *Redeeming Laughter: The Comic Dimensions of Human Experience* (1997). Throughout his prolific career, Berger has contributed significantly to the sociology of knowledge, the sociology of religion, and our understanding of the relationship between self and society, and his works have fueled valuable debates for both those on the political Right and on the political Left.

Thomas Luckmann (1927–) was born in Jesenice, Slovenia. He attended the University of Vienna, the University of Innsbruck, and received his master's and doctoral degrees from the New School for Social Research. He taught at Hobart College in Geneva, New York, the New School for Social Research, and the University of Frankfurt, and has been a professor of sociology at the University of Constance in Germany since 1970. A Fellow of the Center for Advanced Studies in the Behavioral Sciences at Stanford University, Luckmann has been a frequent lecturer in both Europe and the United States. In addition to coauthoring with Peter Berger *The Social Construction of Reality* and with Alfred Schutz *The Structures of the Life World*, he has produced many works including the edited volumes *Phenomenology and Sociology* and *The Structures of the Life-World II*.

The Social Construction of Reality synthesizes important elements from the sociology of knowledge, phenomenology, and social interaction. The authors argue that an important distinction between human beings and most other animals is that the latter are born with relatively more developed and specialized instinctual reactions to environmental conditions that allow them to survive. Conversely, human beings require more time to develop after birth but gradually display great plasticity, or adaptability, in relation to environmental conditions. Because of this plasticity, human beings are able to manipulate environmental conditions and create a human world (or human reality) out of a natural order. Since human beings develop more slowly after birth and early development occurs within a humanly created social order, Berger and Luckmann conclude that what is distinctive about humankind is our ability to produce ourselves. While we are subject to some biological tendencies, our plasticity and our world-openness create the conditions necessary to develop and teach to our young those aspects that are distinctively human, such as culture and complex language. Our open nature, along with socialization, has made us human. It is important to point out that a social order is not the product of natural forces (since humankind is an instinctually unspecialized organism), but rather, that a social order develops as a product of human activity. Human beings create a social order and reinforce it in their young, generation after generation, by imparting their understanding of human culture as it currently exists.

Human activities become subject to habitualization over time. While on the one hand, this results in activities engaged in without much consideration, on the other, such freedom from constant decision making concerning the day-to-day enables contemplation and innovation. Even so, the build-up of reciprocal typifications (or habitualized behaviors in interaction) results in institutionalization, which comes to control behavior because it sets up "predefined patterns of conduct." Stated otherwise, the repetition of coordinated behaviors in social interaction generates roles that may result in the social institutions that come to define individual behavior. We are born into a social order established by the externalization of human activity. The social order has an objective quality. Human activity acts back upon its producers in the sense of transforming human activity, via the internalization of socializing processes, into an objectively felt sense of what constitutes reality. For example, as an American Christian may believe that Christ is the son of God, a Buddhist may believe that meditation on emptiness reveals the material world to be illusion, including the idea of a man as God. Both positions may have their merit, but via socialization, we tend to internalize the world as it has been taught to us by others as *the* world. This worldview is reinforced by conversations with others who believe as we do, and this process creates the feeling that this order of things is objectively valid (despite periodic challenges to the contrary). However the objective order is defined, it is maintained as objectively real and is reinforced via socialization by the acceptance of the taken-for-granted roles that we play in the institutions that comprise society. Roles constitute the bridge between subjective attitudes and individual behavior on the one hand, and the maintenance of a particular social order and its definition of reality on the other.

It was noted above that habitualization opens up the possibility for contemplation and innovation. However, it would seem that habitualization and institutionalization lead to more instances of structuring behavior than to opportunities for contemplation and innovation. Certainly, the faster the pace of society, the less time there is for contemplation, and the pace itself may feel like continuous innovation when it may, instead, simply be change, as innovation and change are not synonymous. This points to an important feature of objectification. The creators of social order may become dominated by their own creations. A good example of this is money. Human beings create it, but it structures (and perhaps even dominates) everyday decision making for millions of people—a human creation acting as a force over its creator. This phenomenon is called reification.

Despite the fact that the structures of social existence are created by interaction, they feel objectively real. Moreover, we tend to want to think of these structures as objectively real because they provide a sense of order in our lives. The products of institutionalization may feel like great weights bearing down on us at times, but they also provide our lives with a sense of coherence. For example, we may wonder why we are here. We don't really know. But there are plenty of scientific, political, and religious theories and rituals (comprising a symbolic universe) that can make us feel better about the whole question.

As the reading by Berger and Luckmann unfolds, the authors deal more and more specifically with socialization and describe it in terms that are reminiscent of Cooley and Mead. As was indicated above, we internalize a world in childhood that is predefined. We internalize this world via our most important socializing agents, our parents. They constitute the first significant others in our lives. We uncritically internalize the worldview that *they* have internalized (which, in turn, we tend to pass along as we socialize our own children). This is not where socialization stops, however. As we grow older and go off to school and interact with peers and have additional authority figures in our lives (such as teachers), another phase of socialization begins—secondary socialization. At this point primary socialization undergoes some modifications as we internalize aspects of these secondary influences via communication in interaction. As this process unfolds, we become socialized into the institutionalized patterns of behavior (for example, what success means or what constitutes beauty) and acquire the attitudes (the reality-maintenance mechanisms) of the generalized other. It is important to stress that socialization is a never-ending process, as interactions modify preexisting patterns; hence, there are never-ending modifications in language (such as slang), fads, fashion, modifications in attitudes concerning what is deemed "socially appropriate behavior," and inventions. Note that such modifications rarely touch the symbolic universe of what constitutes reality.

While socialization provides the social structures necessary to give our lives coherence, socialization is never total and complete. In fact, individualism is more likely in a social milieu where socialization is relatively unsuccessful and thereby allows for more frequent opportunities of personal contemplation. In a social milieu where individualism becomes a value, individualism itself becomes a part of the process of socialization. Thus, in a social climate that values individualism, even those who are more successfully socialized will prize the value of individualism.

Implicit in this discussion is Berger and Luckmann's observation that as society forms identity, "the interplay of organism, individual consciousness, and social structure reacts upon the given social structure, maintaining it, modifying it, or even reshaping it" (173). The categories that define our psychology are rooted in a social history and culture whereby the culture itself is modified by changing patterns in social interaction and accounts of self. For example, the Freudian categories of id, ego, and super ego, which are so prominent today in how we refer to our sense of self, have foundations that precede Freud and would have little value if these conceptualizations were radically inconsistent with other preexisting institutionalized patterns. Moreover, the popularization of this scheme in describing personal psychology has affected other aspects of culture. For example, there is little question that the notion of id and ego are more valuable mechanisms of personal motivation in an economically competitive environment than a psychology that would emphasize no-self. The vast market for self-help books and self-improvement videos would likely collapse without the culturally reinforced value of an ambitious self. Categories that define individualism and personal psychology are not separate from the history and culture that the self finds itself in; it is true that selves can modify that very culture, but the process requires activity outside of the habitualizations of the taken-for-granted.

⌒ Society as Objective Reality ⌒

Man occupies a peculiar position in the animal kingdom. Unlike the other higher mammals, he has no species-specific environment, no environment firmly structured by his own instinctual organization. There is no man-world in the sense that one may speak of a dog-world or a horse-world. Despite an area of individual learning and accumulation, the individual dog or the individual horse has a largely fixed relationship to its environment, which it shares with all other members of its respective species. One obvious implication of this is that dogs and horses, as compared with man, are much more restricted to a specific geographical distribution. The specificity of these animals' environment, however, is much more than a geographical delimitation. It refers to the biologically fixed character of their relationship to the environment, even if geographical variation is introduced. In this sense, all non-human animals, as species and as individuals, live in closed worlds whose structures are predetermined by the biological equipment of the several animal species.

By contrast, man's relationship to his environment is characterized by world-openness. Not only has man succeeded in establishing himself over the greater part of the earth's surface, his relationship to the surrounding environment is everywhere very imperfectly structured by his own biological constitution. The latter, to be sure, permits man to engage in different activities. But the fact that he continued to live a nomadic existence in one place and turned to agriculture in another cannot be explained in terms of biological processes. This does not mean, of course, that there are no biologically determined limitations to man's relations with his environment; his species-specific sensory and motor equipment imposes obvious limitations on his range of possibilities. The peculiarity of man's biological constitution lies rather in its instinctual component.

Man's instinctual organization may be described as underdeveloped, compared with that of the other higher mammals. Man does have drives, of course. But these drives are highly unspecialized and undirected. This means that the human organism is capable of applying its constitutionally given equipment to a very wide and, in addition, constantly variable and varying range of activities. This peculiarity of the human organism is grounded in its ontogenetic development. Indeed, if one looks at the matter in terms of organismic development, it is possible to say that the fetal period in the human being extends through about the first year after birth. Important organismic developments, which in the animal are completed in the mother's body, take place in the human infant after its separation from the womb. At this time, however, the human infant is not only *in* the outside world, but interrelating with it in a number of complex ways.

The human organism is thus still developing biologically while already standing in a relationship to its environment. In other words, the process of becoming man takes place in an interrelationship with an environment. This statement gains significance if one reflects that this environment is both a natural and a human one. That is, the developing human being not only interrelates with a particular natural environment, but with a specific cultural and social order, which is mediated to him by the significant others who have charge of him. Not only is the survival of the human infant dependent upon certain social arrangements, the direction of his organismic development is socially determined. From the moment of birth, man's organismic develop-ment, and indeed a large part of his biological being as such, are subjected to continuing socially determined interference.

Despite the obvious physiological limits to the range of possible and different ways of becoming man in this double environmental interrelationship the human organism manifests an immense plasticity in its response to the environmental forces at work on it. This is particularly clear when one observes the flexibility of man's biological constitution as it is subjected to a variety of socio-cultural deter-minations. It is an ethnological commonplace that the ways of becoming and be-ing human are as numerous as man's cultures. Humanness is socio-culturally vari-able. In other words, there is no human nature in the sense of a biologically fixed substratum determining the variability of socio-cultural formations. There is only human nature in the sense of anthropological constants (for example, world-openness and plasticity of instinctual structure) that delimit and permit man's so-cio-cultural formations. But the specific shape into which this humanness is molded is determined by those socio-cultural formations and is relative to their numerous variations. While it is possible to say that man has a nature, it is more significant to say that man constructs his own nature, or more simply, that man produces himself. . . .

. . . [T]hat man produces himself in no way implies some sort of Promethean vision of the solitary individual. Man's self-production is always, and of necessity, a social enterprise. Men *together* produce a human environment, with the total-ity of its socio-cultural and psychological formations. None of these formations may be understood as products of man's biological constitution, which, as indi-cated, provides only the outer limits for human productive activity. Just as it is impossible for man to develop as man in isolation, so it is impossible for man in isolation to produce a human environment. Solitary human being is being on the animal level (which, of course, man shares with other animals). As soon as one observes phenomena that are specifically human, one enters the realm of the so-cial. Man's specific humanity and his sociality are inextricably intertwined. *Homo sapiens* is always, and in the same measure, *homo socius*.

The human organism lacks the necessary biological means to provide stabil-ity for human conduct. Human existence, if it were thrown back on its organis-mic resources by themselves, would be existence in some sort of chaos. Such chaos is, however, empirically unavailable, even though one may theoretically conceive of it. Empirically, human existence takes place in a context of order, di-rection, stability. The question then arises: From what does the empirically ex-isting stability of human order derive? An answer may be given on two levels. One may first point to the obvious fact that a given social order precedes any in-dividual organismic development. That is, world-openness, while intrinsic to man's biological make-up, is always pre-empted by social order. One may say that the biologically intrinsic world-openness of human existence is always, and in-deed must be, transformed by social order into a relative world-closedness. While this reclosure can never approximate the closedness of animal existence, if only because of its humanly produced and thus "artificial" character, it is nevertheless capable, most of the time, of providing direction and stability for the greater part of human conduct. The question may then be pushed to another level. One may ask in what manner social order itself arises.

The most general answer to this question is that social order is a human product, or, more precisely, an ongoing human production. It is produced by man in the course of his ongoing externalization. Social order is not biologically given or derived from any biological *data* in its empirical manifestations. Social order, needless to add, is also not given in man's natural environment, though particular features of this may be factors in determining certain features of a social order (for example, its economic or technological arrangements). Social order is not part of the "nature of things," and it cannot be derived from the "laws of nature." Social order exists *only* as a product of human activity. No other ontological status may be ascribed to it without hopelessly obfuscating its empirical manifestations. Both in its genesis (social order is the result of past human activity) and its existence in any instant of time (social order exists only and insofar as human activity continues to produce it) it is a human product. . . .

All human activity is subject to habitualization. Any action that is repeated frequently becomes cast into a pattern, which can then be reproduced with an economy of effort and which, *ipso facto*, is apprehended by its performer *as* that pattern. Habitualization further implies that the action in question may be performed again in the future in the same manner and with the same economical effort. This is true of non-social as well as of social activity. Even the solitary individual on the proverbial desert island habitualizes his activity. When he wakes up in the morning and resumes his attempts to construct a canoe out of matchsticks, he may mumble to himself, "There I go again," as he starts on step one of an operating procedure consisting of, say, ten steps. In other words, even solitary man has at least the company of his operating procedures.

Habitualized actions, of course, retain their meaningful character for the individual although the meanings involved become embedded as routines in this general stock of knowledge, taken for granted by him and at hand for his projects into the future. Habitualization carries with it the important psychological gain that choices are narrowed. While in theory there may be a hundred ways to go about the project of building a canoe out of matchsticks, habitualization narrows these down to one. This frees the individual from the burden of "all those decisions," providing a psychological relief that has its basis in man's undirected instinctual structure. Habitualization provides the direction and the specialization of activity that is lacking in man's biological equipment, thus relieving the accumulation of tensions that result from undirected drives. And by providing a stable background in which human activity may proceed with a minimum of decision-making most of the time, it frees energy for such decisions as may be necessary on certain occasions. In other words, the background of habitualized activity opens up a foreground for deliberation and innovation.

In terms of the meanings bestowed by man upon his activity, habitualization makes it unnecessary for each situation to be defined anew, step by step. A large variety of situations may be subsumed under its predefinitions. The activity to be undertaken in these situations can then be anticipated. Even alternatives of conduct can be assigned standard weights.

These processes of habitualization precede any institutionalization, indeed can be made to apply to a hypothetical solitary individual detached from any social interaction. The fact that even such a solitary individual, assuming that he has been formed as a self (as we would have to assume in the case of our matchstick-canoe builder), will habitualize his activity in accordance with biographical experience of a world of social institutions preceding his solitude need not concern us at the moment. Empirically, the more important part of the habitualization of human activity is coextensive with the latter's institutionalization. The question then becomes how do institutions arise.

Institutionalization occurs whenever there is a reciprocal typification of habitualized actions by types of actors. Put differently, any such typification is an institution. What must be stressed is the reciprocity of institutional typifications and the typicality of not only the actions but also the actors in institutions. The typifications of habitualized actions that constitute institutions are always shared ones. They are *available* to all the members of the particular social group in question, and the institution itself typifies individual actors as well as individual actions. The institution posits that actions of type X will be performed by actors of type X. For example, the institution of the law posits that heads shall be chopped off in specific ways under specific circumstances, and that specific types of individuals shall do the chopping (executioners, say, or members of an impure caste, or virgins under a certain age, or those who have been designated by an oracle).

Institutions further imply historicity and control. Reciprocal typifications of actions are built up in the course of a shared history. They cannot be created instantaneously. Institutions always have a history, of which they are the products. It is impossible to understand an institution adequately without an understanding of the historical process in which it was produced. Institutions also, by the very fact of their existence, control human conduct by setting up predefined patterns of conduct. . . .

An institutional world, then, is experienced as an objective reality. It has a history that antedates the individual's birth and is not accessible to his biographical recollection. It was there before he was born, and it will be there after his death. This history itself, as the tradition of the existing institutions, has the character of objectivity. The individual's biography is apprehended as an episode located within the objective history of the society. The institutions, as historical and objective facticities, confront the individual as undeniable facts. The institutions are *there*, external to him, persistent in their reality, whether he likes it or not. He cannot wish them away. They resist his attempts to change or evade them. They have coercive power over him, both in themselves, by the sheer force of their facticity, and through the control mechanisms that are usually attached to the most important of them. The objective reality of institutions is not diminished if the individual does not understand their purpose or their mode of operation. He may experience large sectors of the social world as incomprehensible, perhaps oppressive in their opaqueness, but real nonetheless. Since institutions exist as external reality, the individual cannot understand them by introspection. He must "go out" and learn about them, just as he must to learn about nature. This remains true even though the social world, as a humanly produced reality, is potentially understandable in a way not possible in the case of the natural world.

It is important to keep in mind that the objectivity of the institutional world, however massive it may appear to the individual, is a humanly produced, constructed objectivity. The process by which the externalized products of human activity attain the character of objectivity is objectivation. The institutional world is objectivated human activity, and so is every single institution. In other words, despite the objectivity that marks the social world in human experience, it does not thereby acquire an ontological status apart from the human activity that produced it. The paradox that man is capable of producing a world that he then experiences as something other than a human product will concern us later on. At the moment, it is important to emphasize that the relationship between man, the producer, and the social world, his product, is and remains a dialectical one. That is, man (not, of course, in isolation but in his collectivities) and his social world interact with each other. The product acts back upon the producer. Externalization and objectivation are moments in a continuing dialectical process. The third moment in this process, which is internalization (by which the objectivated social world is retrojected into consciousness in the course of socialization), will occupy us in considerable detail later on. It is already possible, however, to see the fundamental relationship of these three dialectical moments in social reality. Each of them corresponds to an essential characterization of the social world. *Society is a human product. Society is an objective reality. Man is a social product.* It may also already be evident than an analysis of the social world that leaves out any one of these three moments will be distortive. . . .

. . . Institutions are embodied in individual experience by means of roles. The roles, objectified linguistically, are an essential ingredient of the objectively available world of any society. By playing roles, the individual participates in a social world. By internalizing these roles, the same world becomes subjectively real to him. . . .

The roles *represent* the institutional order. This representation takes place on two levels. First, performance of the role represents itself. For instance, to engage in judging is to represent the role of judge. The judging individual is not acting "on his own," but *qua* judge. Second, the role represents an entire institutional nexus of conduct. The role of judge stands in relationship to other roles, the totality of which comprises the institution of law. The judge acts as the representative of this institution. Only through such representation in performed roles can the institution manifest itself in actual experience. The institution, with its assemblage of "programmed" actions, is like the unwritten libretto of a drama.

The realization of the drama depends upon the reiterated performance of its pre-scribed roles by living actors. The actors embody the roles and actualize the drama by representing it on the given stage. Neither drama nor institution exist empirically apart from this recurrent realization. To say, then, that roles represent institutions is to say that roles make it possible for institutions to exist, ever again, as a real presence in the experience of living individuals. . . .

. . . Looked at from the perspective of the institutional order, the roles appear as institutional representations and mediations of the institutionally objecti-vated aggregates of knowledge. Looked at from the perspective of the several roles, each role carries with it a socially defined appendage of knowledge. Both perspectives, of course, point to the same global phenomenon, which is the es-sential dialectic of society. The first perspective can be summed up in the propo-sition that society exists only as individuals are conscious of it, the second in the proposition that individual consciousness is socially determined. Narrowing this to the matter of roles, we can say that, on the one hand, the institutional order is real only insofar as it is *realized* in performed roles and that, on the other hand, roles are representative of an institutional order that defines their character (in-cluding their appendages of knowledge) and from which they derive their objec-tive sense.

The analysis of roles is of particular importance to the sociology of knowledge because it reveals the mediations between the macroscopic universes of meaning objectivated in a society and the ways by which these universes are subjectively real to individuals. Thus it is possible, for example, to analyze the macroscopic social roots of a religious world view in certain collectivities (classes, say, or eth-nic groups, or intellectual coteries), and also to analyze the manner in which this world view is manifested in the consciousness of an individual. The two analyses can be brought together only if one inquires into the ways in which the individ-ual, in his total social activity, relates to the collectivity in question. Such an in-quiry will, of necessity, be an exercise in role analysis. . . .

A final question of great theoretical interest arising from the historical vari-ability of institutionalization has to do with the manner in which the institu-tional order is objectified: To what extent is an institutional order, or any part of it, apprehended as a non-human facticity? This is the question of the reification of social reality.

Reification is the apprehension of human phenomena as if they were things, that is, in non-human or possibly suprahuman terms. Another way of saying this is that reification is the apprehension of the products of human activity *as if* they were something else than human products—such as facts of nature, results of cos-mic laws, or manifestations of divine will. Reification implies that man is capable of forgetting his own authorship of the human world, and further, that the di-alectic between man, the producer, and his products is lost to consciousness. The reified world is, by definition, a dehumanized world. It is experienced by man as a strange facticity, an *opus alienum* over which he has no control rather than as the *opus proprium* of his own productive activity.

It will be clear from our previous discussion of objectivation that, as soon as an objective social world is established, the possibility of reification is never far away. The objectivity of the social world means that it confronts man as something outside of himself. The decisive question is whether he still retains the awareness that, however objectivated, the social world was made by men—and, therefore, can be remade by them. In other words, reification can be described as an extreme step in the process of objectivation, whereby the objectivated world loses its comprehensibility as a human enterprise and becomes fixated as a non-human, non-humanizable, inert facticity. Typically, the real relationship between man and his world is reversed in consciousness. Man, the producer of a world, is apprehended as its product, and human activity as an epiphenomenon of non-human processes. Human meanings are no longer understood as world-producing but as being, in their turn, products of the "nature of things." It must be emphasized that reification is a modality of consciousness, more precisely, a modality of man's objectification of the human world. Even while apprehending the world in reified terms, man continues to produce it. That is, man is capable paradoxically of producing a reality that denies him. . . .

The symbolic universe is conceived of as the matrix of *all* socially objectivated and subjectively real meanings; the entire historic society and the entire biography of the individual are seen as events taking place *within* this universe. What is particularly important, the marginal situations of the life of the individual (marginal, that is, in not being included in the reality of everyday existence in society) are also encompassed by the symbolic universe. Such situations are experienced in dreams and fantasies as provinces of meaning detached from everyday life, and endowed with a peculiar reality of their own. Within the symbolic universe these detached realms of reality are integrated within a meaningful totality that "explains," perhaps also justifies them (for instance, dreams may be "explained" by a psychological theory, both "explained" *and* justified by a theory of metempsychosis, and either theory will be grounded in a much more comprehensive universe—a "scientific" one, say, as against a "metaphysical" one). The symbolic universe is, of course, constructed by means of social objectivations. Yet its meaning-bestowing capacity far exceeds the domain of social life, so that the individual may "locate" himself within it even in his most solitary experiences. . . .

The symbolic universe also makes possible the ordering of the different phases of biography. In primitive societies the rites of passage represent this nomic function in pristine form. The periodization of biography is symbolized at each stage with reference to the totality of human meanings. To be a child, to be an adolescent, to be an adult, and so forth—each of these biographical phases is legitimated as a mode of being in the symbolic universe (most often, as a particular mode of relating to the world of the gods). We need not belabor the obvious point that such symbolization is conducive to feelings of security and belonging. It would be a mistake, however, to think here only of primitive societies. A modern psychological theory of personality development can fulfill the same function. In both cases, the individual passing from one biographical phase to another can view himself as repeating a sequence that is given in the "nature of things," or in his own "nature." That is, he can reassure himself that he is living "correctly." The "correctness" of his life program is thus legitimated on the highest level of generality. As the individual looks back upon his past life, his biography is intelligible to him in these terms. As he projects himself into the future, he may conceive of his biography as unfolding within a universe whose ultimate co-ordinates are known. . . .

A strategic legitimating function of symbolic universes for individual biography is the "location" of death. The experience of the death of others and, subsequently, the anticipation of one's own death posit the marginal situation par excellence for the individual. Needless to elaborate, death also posits the most terrifying threat to the taken-for-granted realities of everyday life. The integration of death within the paramount reality of social existence is, therefore, of the greatest importance for any institutional order. This legitimation of death is, consequently, one of the most important fruits of symbolic universes. Whether it is done with or without recourse to mythological, religious or metaphysical interpretations of reality is not the essential question here. The modern atheist, for instance, who bestows meaning upon death in terms of a *Weltanschauung* of progressive evolution or of revolutionary history also does so by integrating death within a reality-spanning symbolic universe. All legitimations of death must carry out the same essential task—they must enable the individual to go on living in society after the death of significant others and to anticipate his own death with, at the very least, terror sufficiently mitigated so as not to paralyze the continued performance of the routines of everyday life. It may readily be seen that such ligitimation is difficult to achieve short of integrating the phenomenon of death within a symbolic universe. Such legitimation, then, provides the individual with a recipe for a "correct death." Optimally, this recipe will retain its plausibility when his own death is imminent and will allow him, indeed, to "die correctly."

It is in the legitimation of death that the transcending potency of symbolic universes manifests itself most clearly, and the fundamental terror-assuaging character of the ultimate legitimations of the paramount reality of everyday life is revealed. The primacy of the social objectivations of everyday life can retain its subjective plausibility only if it is constantly protected against terror. On the level of meaning, the institutional order represents a shield against terror. . . .

The origins of a symbolic universe have their roots in the constitution of man. If man in society is a world-constructor, this is made possible by his constitutionally given world-openness, which already implies the conflict between order and chaos. Human existence is, *ab initio*, an ongoing externalization. As man externalizes himself, he constructs the world *into* which he externalizes himself. In the process of externalization, he projects his own meanings into reality. Symbolic universes, which proclaim that *all* reality is humanly meaningful and call upon the *entire* cosmos to signify the validity of human existence, constitute the farthest reaches of this projection. . . .

～ Society as Subjective Reality ～

Since society exists as both objective and subjective reality, any adequate theoretical understanding of it must comprehend both these aspects. As we have already argued, these aspects receive their proper recognition if society is understood in terms of an ongoing dialectical process composed of the three moments
of externalization, objectivation, and internalization. As far as the societal phenomenon is concerned, these moments are *not* to be thought of as occurring in
a temporal sequence. Rather society and each part of it are simultaneously characterized by these three moments, so that any analysis in terms of only one or
two of them falls short. The same is true of the individual member of society,
who simultaneously externalizes his own being into the social world and internalizes it as an objective reality. In other words, to be in society is to participate
in its dialectic.

The individual, however, is not born a member of society. He is born with
a predisposition toward sociality, and he becomes a member of society. In the
life of every individual, therefore, there *is* a temporal sequence, in the course
of which he is inducted into participation in the societal dialectic. The beginning point of this process is internalization: the immediate apprehension
or interpretation of an objective event as expressing meaning, that is, as a
manifestation of another's subjective processes which thereby becomes subjectively meaningful to myself. This does not mean that I understand the
other adequately. I may indeed misunderstand him: he is laughing in a fit of
hysteria, but I understand his laughter as expressing mirth. But his subjectivity is nevertheless objectively available to me and becomes meaningful to me,
whether or not there is congruence between his and my subjective processes.
Full congruence between the two subjective meanings, and reciprocal knowledge of that congruence, presupposes signification. . . . However, internalization in the general sense used here underlies both signification and its own
more complex forms. More precisely, internalization in this general sense is
the basis, first, for an understanding of one's fellowmen and, second, for the
apprehension of the world as a meaningful and social reality.

This apprehension does not result from autonomous creations of meaning by
isolated individuals, but begins with the individual "taking over" the world in
which others already live. To be sure, the "taking over" is in itself, in a sense, an
original process for every human organism, and the world, once "taken over,"
may be creatively modified or (less likely) even re-created. In any case, in the
complex form of internalization, I not only "understand" the other's momentary
subjective processes, I "understand" the world in which he lives, and that world
becomes my own. This presupposes that he and I share time in a more than
ephemeral way and a comprehensive perspective, which links sequences of situations together intersubjectively. We now not only understand each other's definitions of shared situations, we define them reciprocally. A nexus of motivations
is established between us and extends into the future. Most importantly, there is

now an ongoing mutual identification between us. We not only live in the same world; we participate in each other's being.

Only when he has achieved this degree of internalization is an individual a member of society. The ontogenetic process by which this is brought about is socialization, which may thus be defined as the comprehensive and consistent induction of an individual into the objective world of a society or a sector of it. Primary socialization is the first socialization an individual undergoes in childhood, through which he becomes a member of society. Secondary socialization is any subsequent process that inducts an already socialized individual into new sectors of the objective world of his society. We may leave aside here the special question of the acquisition of knowledge about the objective world of societies other than the one of which we first became a member, and the process of internalizing such a world as reality—a process that exhibits, at least superficially, certain similarities with both primary and secondary socialization, yet is structurally identical with neither.

It is at once evident that primary socialization is usually the most important one for an individual, and that the basic structure of all secondary socialization has to resemble that of primary socialization. Every individual is born into an objective social structure within which he encounters the significant others who are in charge of his socialization. These significant others are imposed upon him. Their definitions of his situation are posited for him as objective reality. He is thus born into not only an objective social structure but also an objective social world. The significant others who mediate this world to him modify it in the course of mediating it. They select aspects of it in accordance with their own location in the social structure, and also by virtue of their individual, biographically rooted idiosyncrasies. The social world is "filtered" to the individual through this double selectivity. Thus the lower-class child not only absorbs a lower-class perspective on the social world, he absorbs it in the idiosyncratic coloration given it by his parents (or whatever other individuals are in charge of his primary socialization). The same lower-class perspective may induce a mood of contentment, resignation, bitter resentment, or seething rebelliousness. Consequently, the lower-class child will not only come to inhabit a world greatly different from that of an upper-class child, but may do so in a manner quite different from the lower-class child next door.

It should hardly be necessary to add that primary socialization involves more than purely cognitive learning. It takes place under circumstances that are highly charged emotionally. . . . Indeed, there is good reason to believe that without such emotional attachment to the significant others the learning process would be difficult if not impossible. The child identifies with the significant others in a variety of emotional ways. Whatever they may be, internalization occurs only as identification occurs. The child takes on the significant others' roles and attitudes, that is, internalizes them and makes them his own. And by this identification with significant others the child becomes capable of identifying himself, of acquiring a subjectively coherent and plausible identity. In other words, the self is a reflected entity, reflecting the attitudes first taken by significant others toward it; the individual becomes what he is addressed as by his significant others. This is not a one-sided, mechanistic process. It entails a dialectic between identification by others and self-identification, between objectively assigned and subjectively appropriated identity. The dialectic, which is present each moment the individual *identifies with* his significant others, is, as it were, the particularization in individual life of the general dialectic of society. . . .

. . . The child does not internalize the world of his significant others as one of many possible worlds. He internalizes it as *the* world, the only existent and only conceivable world, the world *tout court*. It is for this reason that the world internalized in primary socialization is so much more firmly entrenched in consciousness than worlds internalized in secondary socializations. However much the original sense of inevitability may be weakened in subsequent disenchantments, the recollection of a never-to-be-repeated certainty—the certainty of the first dawn of reality—still adheres to the first world of childhood. . . .

It is possible to conceive of a society in which no further socialization takes place after primary socialization. Such a society would, of course, be one with a very simple stock of knowledge. All knowledge would be generally relevant, with different individuals varying only in their perspectives on it. This conception is useful in positing a limiting case, but there is no society known to us that does not have *some* division of labor and, concomitantly, *some* social distribution of knowledge; and as soon as this is the case, secondary socialization becomes necessary.

Secondary socialization is the internalization of institutional or institution-based "subworlds." Its extent and character are therefore determined by the complexity of the division of labor and the concomitant social distribution of knowledge. . . .

The reality accent of knowledge internalized in primary socialization is given quasi-automatically. In secondary socialization it must be reinforced by specific pedagogic techniques, "brought home" to the individual. The phrase is suggestive. The original reality of childhood is "home." It posits itself as such, inevitably and, as it were, "naturally." By comparison with it, all later realities are "artificial." Thus the school teacher tries to "bring home" the contents he is imparting by making them vivid (that is, making them seem as alive as the "home world" of the child), relevant (that is, linking them to the relevance structures already present in the "home world") and interesting (that is, inducing the attentiveness of the child to detach itself from its "natural" objects to these more "artificial" ones). These maneuvers are necessary because an internalized reality is already there, persistently "in the way" of new internalizations. The degree and precise character of these pedagogic techniques will vary with the motivations the individual has for the acquisition of new knowledge.

The more these techniques make subjectively plausible a continuity between the original and the new elements of knowledge, the more readily they acquire the accent of reality. One learns a second language by building on the taken-for-granted reality of one's "mother tongue." For a long time, one continually retranslates into the original language whatever elements of the new language one is acquiring. Only in this way can the new language begin to have any reality. As this reality comes to be established in its own right, it slowly becomes possible to forego retranslation. One becomes capable of "thinking in" the new language. . . .

The most important vehicle of reality-maintenance is conversation. One may view the individual's everyday life in terms of the working away of a conversational apparatus that ongoingly maintains, modifies and reconstructs his subjective reality. Conversation means mainly, of course, that people speak with one another. This does not deny the rich aura of non-verbal communication that surrounds speech. Nevertheless speech retains a privileged position in the total conversational apparatus. It is important to stress, however, that the greater part of reality-maintenance in conversation is implicit, not explicit. Most conversation does not in so many words define the nature of the world. Rather, it takes place against the background of a world that is silently taken for granted. Thus an exchange such as, "Well, it's time for me to get to the station," and "Fine, darling, have a good day at the office" implies an entire world *within which* these apparently simple propositions make sense. By virtue of this implication the exchange confirms the subjective reality of this world.

If this is understood, one will readily see that the great part, if not all, of everyday conversation maintains subjective reality. Indeed, its massivity is achieved by the accumulation and consistency of casual conversation—conversation that can *afford to be casual* precisely because it refers to the routines of a taken-for-granted world. The loss of casualness signals a break in the routines and, at least potentially, a threat to the taken-for-granted reality. Thus one may imagine the effect on casualness of an exchange like this: "Well, it's time for me to get to the station," "Fine, darling, don't forget to take along your gun."

At the same time that the conversational apparatus ongoingly maintains reality, it ongoingly modifies it. Items are dropped and added, weakening some sectors of what is still being taken for granted and reinforcing others. . . .

Subjective reality is thus always dependent upon specific plausibility structures, that is, the specific social base and social processes required for its maintenance. One can maintain one's self-identification as a man of importance only in a milieu that confirms this identity. . . .

Socialization always takes place in the context of a specific social structure. Not only its contents but also its measure of "success" have social-structural conditions and social-structural consequences. In other words, the micro-sociological or social-psychological analysis of phenomena of internalization must always have as its background a macro-sociological understanding of their structural aspects.

On the level of theoretical analysis attempted here we cannot enter into a detailed discussion of the different empirical relationships between the contents of socialization and social-structural configurations. Some general observations may, however, be made on the social-structural aspects of the "success" of socialization. By "successful socialization" we mean the establishment of a high degree of symmetry between objective and subjective reality (as well as identity, of course). Conversely, "unsuccessful socialization" is to be understood in terms of asymmetry between objective and subjective reality. As we have seen, totally successful socialization is anthropologically impossible. Totally unsuccessful socialization is, at the very least, extremely rare, limited to cases of individuals with whom even minimal socialization fails because of extreme organic pathology. Our analysis must, therefore, be concerned with gradations on a continuum. . . .

The possibility of "individualism" (that is, of individual choice between discrepant realities and identities) is directly linked to the possibility of unsuccessful socialization. We have argued that unsuccessful socialization opens up the question of "Who am I?" In the social-structural context in which unsuccessful socialization becomes so recognized, the same question arises for the *successfully* socialized individual by virtue of his reflection about the unsuccessfully socialized. . . .

Identity, is, of course, a key element of subjective reality, and like all subjective reality, stands in a dialectical relationship with society. . . .

. . . [P]sychological status is relative to the social definitions of reality in general and is itself socially defined.

The emergence of psychologies introduces a further dialectical relationship between identity and society—the relationship between psychological theory and those elements of subjective reality it purports to define and explain. The level of such theorizing may, of course, vary greatly, as in the case of all theoretical legitimations. What has been said previously about the origins and phases of ligitimating theories applies here with equal validity, but with one not unimportant difference. Psychologies pertain to a dimension of reality that is of the greatest and most continuous subjective relevance for all individuals. Therefore the dialectic between theory and reality affects the individual in a palpably direct and intensive manner.

When psychological theories attain a high degree of intellectual complexity they are likely to be administered by personnel specially trained in this body of knowledge. Whatever the social organization of these specialists may be, psychological theories re-enter everyday life by providing the interpretative schemes for disposing of problematic cases. Problems arising out of the dialectic between either subjective identity and social identity-assignments, or identity and its biological substratum . . . , can be classified according to theoretical categories—which is, of course, the presupposition for any therapy. The psychological theories then serve to legitimate the identity-maintenance and identity-repair procedures established in the society, providing the theoretical linkage between identity and world, as these are both socially defined and subjectively appropriated.

Psychological theories may be empirically adequate or inadequate, by which we do *not* mean their adequacy in terms of the procedural canons of empirical science, but rather, as interpretative schemes applicable by the expert or the layman to empirical phenomena in everyday life. For example, a psychological theory positing demoniacal possession is unlikely to be adequate in interpreting the identity problems of middle-class, Jewish intellectuals in New York City. These people simply do not have an identity capable of producing phenomena that could be so interpreted. The demons, if such there are, seem to avoid them. On the other hand, psychoanalysis is unlikely to be adequate for the interpretation of identity problems in rural Haiti, while some sort of Voudun psychology might supply interpretative schemes with a high degree of empirical accuracy. The two psychologies demonstrate their empirical adequacy by their applicability in therapy, but neither thereby demonstrates the ontological status of its categories. Neither the Voudun gods nor libidinal energy may exist outside the world defined in the respective social contexts. But in these contexts they do exist by virtue of social definition and are internalized as realities in the course of socialization. Rural Haitians *are* possessed and New York intellectuals *are* neurotic. Possession and neurosis are thus constituents of both objective and subjective reality *in these contexts*. This reality is empirically available in everyday life. The respective psychological theories are empirically adequate in precisely the same sense. The problem of whether or how psychological theories could be developed to transcend this socio-historical relativity need not concern us here.

Insofar as psychological theories are adequate in this sense, they are capable of empirical verification. Again, what is at issue is not verification in the scientific sense, but testing in the experience of everyday social life. For example, it may be proposed that individuals born on certain days of the month are likely to be possessed, or that individuals with domineering mothers are likely to be neurotic. Such propositions are empirically verifiable to the extent that they belong to adequate theories, in the afore-mentioned sense. Such verification may be undertaken by participants as well as by outside observers of the social situations in question. A Haitian ethnologist can empirically discover New York neurosis, just as an American ethnologist can empirically discover Voudun possession. The presupposition for such discoveries is simply that the outside observer is willing to employ the conceptual machinery of the indigenous psychology for the inquiry at hand. Whether he is also willing to accord that psychology a more general epistemological validity is irrelevant to the immediate empirical investigation.

Another way of saying that psychological theories are adequate is to say that they reflect the psychological reality they purport to explain. But if this were the whole story, the relationship between theory and reality here would not be a dialectical one. A genuine dialectic is involved because of the *realizing* potency of psychological theories. Insofar as psychological theories are elements of the social definition of reality, their reality-generating capacity is a characteristic they share with other legitimating theories; however, their realizing potency is particularly great because it is actualized by emotionally charged processes of identity-formation. If a psychology becomes socially established (that is, becomes generally recognized as an adequate interpretation of objective reality), it tends to realize itself forcefully in the phenomena it purports to interpret. Its internalization is accelerated by the fact that it pertains to internal reality, so that the individual realizes it in the very act of internalizing it. Again, since a psychology by definition pertains to identity, its internalization is likely to be accompanied by identification, hence is *ipso facto* likely to be identity-forming. In this close nexus between internalization and identification, psychological theories differ considerably from other types of theory. Not surprisingly, since problems of unsuccessful socialization are most conducive to this kind of theorizing, psychological theories are more apt to have socializing effects. This is not the same thing as saying that psychologies are self-verifying. As we have indicated, verification comes by confronting psychological theories and psychological reality as empirically available. Psychologies produce a reality, which in turn serves as the basis for their verification. In other words, we are dealing here with dialectics, not tautology.

The rural Haitian who internalizes Voudun psychology will become possessed as soon as he discovers certain well-defined signs. Similarly, the New York intellectual who internalizes Freudian psychology will become neurotic as soon as he diagnoses certain well-known symptoms. Indeed, it is possible that, given a certain biographical context, signs or symptoms will be produced by the individual himself. The Haitian will, in that case, produce not symptoms of neurosis but signs of possession, while the New Yorker will construct his neurosis in conformity with the recognized symptomatology. This has nothing to do with "mass hysteria," much less with malingering, but with the imprint of societal identity types upon the individual subjective reality of ordinary people with commonsense. The degree of identification will vary with the conditions of internalization, as previously discussed, depending, for instance, on whether it takes place in primary or secondary socialization. The social establishment of a psychology, which also entails the accordance of certain social roles to the personnel administering the theory and its therapeutic application, will naturally depend upon a variety of socio-historical circumstances. But the more socially established it becomes, the more abundant will be the phenomena it serves to interpret.

If we posit the possibility that certain psychologies come to be adequate in the course of a realizing process, we imply the question of why as-yet-inadequate theories (as they would have to be in the earlier stages of this process) arise in the first place. Put more simply, why should one psychology replace another in history? The general answer is that such change occurs when identity appears as a problem, for whatever reasons. The problem may arise out of the dialectic of psychological reality and social structure. Radical changes in the social structure (such as, for instance, the changes brought about by the Industrial Revolution) may result in concomitant changes in the psychological reality. In that case, new psychological theories may arise because the old ones no longer adequately explain the empirical phenomena at hand. Theorizing about identity will then seek to take cognizance of the transformations of identity that have actually occurred, and will be itself transformed in the process. . . .

Man is biologically predestined to construct and to inhabit a world with others. This world becomes for him the dominant and definitive reality. Its limits are set by nature, but once constructed, this world acts back upon nature. In the dialectic between nature and the socially constructed world the human organism itself is transformed. In this same dialectic man produces reality and thereby produces himself. . . .

~

CHAPTER TWELVE

Herbert Blumer on Symbolic Interactionism

~ Introduction ~

Herbert Blumer (1900–1987) was born in St. Louis, Missouri. He received his B.A. and M.A. degrees from the University of Missouri and studied under George Herbert Mead while earning his Ph.D. in 1928 at the University of Chicago. While working on his doctoral degree (and for a few years thereafter), he played professional football for the Chicago Cardinals, where he competed against such football legends as Red Grange and Jim Thorpe. Blumer taught at the University of Chicago from 1928 to 1951 and then at the University of California at Berkeley from 1952 until his retirement in 1967.

At the University of Chicago, Blumer took over Mead's social psychology course when Mead became ill. Several years later Blumer coined the term "symbolic interactionism" to describe a growing body of scholarship that approached the study of social behavior from the point of view of social interaction; in the process, he demonstrated the sociological relevance of Mead's philosophical approach. Blumer not only introduced Mead's ideas to a wider audience, but he advanced qualitative methodologies as the appropriate means of investigating social interaction in the empirical world (see his classic book, *Symbolic Interactionism: Perspective and Method*). Blumer's demonstration of the value of this approach initially brought criticism because sociology then emphasized quantitative methods and structural-functional theories. Years later some controversy arose as to whether he had misrepresented Mead's theories. In response, Blumer defended and continued to develop his interpretation of Mead.

Blumer's contributions to social theory, methodology, and social psychology have been immense. In 1983, he was recognized by the American Sociological Association, receiving the organization's award for a career of distinguished scholarship. Like his mentor Mead, Blumer was keenly aware of the macrosocial relevance of his work in social interaction and wrote on such diverse topics as racial prejudice and the social effects of industrialization.

The reading for this chapter presents Blumer's interpretation of Mead and the relevance of Mead's philosophy for sociology. Blumer achieves these goals by defining and elaborating on some of Mead's key concepts, such as self, action, and interaction. While we are used to thinking of the self as an entity situated in the body and separate from other selves (due to cultural and historical factors that have been touched on in previous and forthcoming chapters in this book), Blumer emphasizes that the self may be more accurately understood as a process rather than as a situated structure. The self is constituted by the ability of the mind to read and reflect upon itself (reflexivity), which leads to the recognition of oneself as a distinct object acting in the world. The phenomenon of reflexivity is stimulated by activity in the world, particularly activity with other reflexive selves. The self is a product of a natural event (the reflexivity of the mind) and a social event (the interaction of increasingly reflexive, problem-solving selves). The self is not merely a passive recipient of internalized norms; due to interaction and reflexivity, the self is an active agent participating in the world by taking account of itself, others, and objects. Hence, there is value in a qualitative methodological approach that views the self as a process and does not predefine the subject but rather permits the researcher to take account of the subject's agency and linkage in a group.

Because the self is not merely a passive conduit of drives or norms, action is the product of indications taken into account by the self. What the self takes into account and how he or she takes account of objects in constructing a course of action, however, may not be optimal. Nevertheless, human action is not determined, but rather, self-directed.

Action is, of course, a significant factor in social interaction. Social interaction may be nonsymbolic, where actors respond directly, spontaneously, to each other. Symbolic interaction refers to situations where actors interpret, derive meaning, and act on the basis of taking the other's actions into account. Where psychologists tend to view interaction as the meeting of distinct selves who may or may not establish rapport, and where sociologists tend to view interaction as a product of the social forces impinging upon the actors, symbolic interaction stresses the dynamic process of selves taking account of each other and themselves and thereby affecting and being affected by the interaction itself. Since active agents form and are formed by their interaction, symbolic interactionism goes beyond the notion that a single principle, such as social conflict or common sentiments or the tension between id and ego operating in individual minds trying to relate, guides the direction of interaction. As a result, symbolic interactionism is in a better position to take account of the full range of interactions taking place in a social milieu.

Blumer uses the term "joint action" to explain the linkages that form the basis of relations between two actors to interactions that form the linkages constituting organizations, institutions, and society itself. A marriage ceremony involves distinct actors engaging in joint actions in order to pull off a mutually recognizable social event. Every marriage ceremony may be distinct due to social custom and individual idiosyncrasies; nevertheless, the joint actions of the participants will form a social phenomenon recognizable as a particular event. It will be a social event that does not look like a funeral or a football game but rather one that conveys some notion of what the disparate parties understand as a wedding. Joint actions define "appropriate" social behaviors in their making; joint actions orient actors to each other. This then orients the product of their actions. Joint actions have a "career." This means, in part, that joint actions orient the actors in particular ways given the circumstances; everyone "knows" how to act at a wedding even if the details of the wedding vary enormously—the key is for actors to recognize the joint action as "wedding." However, because joint actions have a career, they are subject to change. Because interaction is a process involving active agents, the parties may abandon or transform the joint action. The main point is that an organization, an institution, indeed, an entire society, is composed of joint actions or the "articulation of the acts of the participants." For example, if most individuals constituting a society claim that they value honor over prestige and profit but engage in activities that reinforce joint actions of prestige and profit at the cost of joint actions reinforcing honor, the product of this will be a society that not only says one thing and acts on another, but also demonstrates in its actions, inside and outside of its borders, that it values prestige and profit over honor. This value orientation will be maintained until the career of the joint action changes due to changes in the accounts taken by the parties involved.

In *Symbolic Interactionism*, Blumer (1969, 2) states that symbolic interactionism may be understood in terms of three basic premises: (1) "human beings act toward things on the basis of the meanings that the things have for them"; (2) "the meaning of such things . . . arises out of the social interaction that one has with one's fellows"; and, (3) "these meanings are handled in, and modified through, an interpretative process used by the person in dealing with the things he encounters." In terms of methodology, Blumer (1969, 47) states: "Symbolic interactionism is a down-to-earth approach to the scientific study of human group life and human conduct. It lodges its problems in this natural world, conducts its studies in it, and derives its interpretations from such naturalistic studies." Blumer's work highlights "process" in the nature of social relations and the value of exploratory and analytical procedures for the study of the "empirical social world."

⌣ Sociological Implications of the ⌣ Thought of George Herbert Mead

My purpose is to depict the nature of human society when seen from the point of view of George Herbert Mead. While Mead gave human society a position of paramount importance in his scheme of thought he did little to outline its character.

His central concern was with cardinal problems of philosophy. The development of his ideas of human society was largely limited to handling these problems. His treatment took the form of showing that human group life was the essential condition for the emergence of consciousness, the mind, a world of objects, human beings as organisms possessing selves, and human conduct in the form of constructed acts. He reversed the traditional assumption underlying philosophical, psychological, and sociological thought to the effect that human beings possess minds and consciousness as original "givens," that they live in worlds of pre-existing and self-constituted objects, that their behavior consists of responses to such objects, and that group life consists of the association of such reacting human organisms. In making his brilliant contributions along this line he did not map out a theoretical scheme of human society. However, such a scheme is implicit in his work. It has to be constructed by tracing the implications of the central matters which he analyzed. This is what I propose to do. The central matters I shall consider are (1) the self, (2) the act, (3) social interaction, (4) objects, and (5) joint action.

The Self

Mead's picture of the human being as an actor differs radically from the conception of man that dominates current psychological and social science. He saw the human being as an organism having a self. The possession of a self converts the human being into a special kind of actor, transforms his relation to the world, and gives his action a unique character. In asserting that the human being has a self, Mead simply meant that the human being is an object to himself. The human being may perceive himself, have conceptions of himself, communicate with himself, and act toward himself. As these types of behavior imply, the human being may become the object of his own action. This gives him the means of interacting with himself—addressing himself, responding to the address, and addressing himself anew. Such self-interaction takes the form of making indications to himself and meeting these indications by making further indications. The human being can designate things to himself—his wants, his pains, his goals, objects around him, the presence of others, their actions, their expected actions, or whatnot. Through further interaction with himself, he may judge, analyze, and evaluate the things he has designated to himself. And by continuing to interact with himself he may plan and organize his action with regard to what he has designated and evaluated. In short, the possession of a self provides the human being with a mechanism of self-interaction with which to meet the world—a mechanism that is used in forming and guiding his conduct.

I wish to stress that Mead saw the self as a process and not as a structure. Here Mead clearly parts company with the great bulk of students who seek to bring a self into the human being by identifying it with some kind of organization or structure. All of us are familiar with this practice because it is all around us in the literature. Thus, we see scholars who identify the self with the "ego," or who regard the self as an organized body of needs or motives, or who think of it as an organization of attitudes, or who treat it as a structure of internalized norms and values. Such schemes which seek to lodge the self in a structure make no sense since they miss the reflexive process which alone can yield and constitute a self. For any posited structure to be a self, it would have to act upon and respond to itself—otherwise, it is merely an organization awaiting activation and release without exercising any effect on itself or on its operation. This marks the crucial weakness or inadequacy of the many schemes such as referred to above, which misguidingly associate the self with some kind of psychological or personality structure. For example, the ego, as such, is not a self; it would be a self only by becoming reflexive, that is to say, acting toward or on itself. And the same thing is true of any other posited psychological structure. Yet, such reflexive action changes both the status and the character of the structure and elevates the process of self-interaction to the position of major importance.

We can see this in the case of the reflexive process that Mead has isolated in the human being. As mentioned, this reflexive process takes the form of the person making indications to himself, that is to say, noting things and determining their significance for his line of action. To indicate something is to stand over against it and to put oneself in the position of acting toward it instead of automatically responding to it. In the face of something which one indicates, one can withhold action toward it, inspect it, judge it, ascertain its meaning, determine its possibilities, and direct one's action with regard to it. With the mechanism of self-interaction the human being ceases to be a responding organism whose behavior is a product of what plays upon him from the outside, the inside, or both. Instead, he acts toward his world, interpreting what confronts him and organizing his action on the basis of the interpretation. To illustrate: a pain one identifies and interprets is very different from a mere organic feeling and lays the basis for doing something about it instead of merely responding organically to it; to note and interpret the activity of another person is very different from having a response released by that activity; to be aware that one is hungry is very different from merely being hungry; to perceive one's "ego" puts one in the position of doing something with regard to it instead of merely giving expression to the ego. As these illustrations show, the process of self-interaction puts the human being over against his world instead of merely in it, requires him to meet and handle his world through a defining process instead of merely responding to it, and forces him to construct his action instead of merely releasing it. This is the kind of acting organism that Mead sees man to be as a result of having a self.

The Act
Human action acquires a radically different character as a result of being formed through a process of self-interaction. Action is built up in coping with the world instead of merely being released from a pre-existing psychological structure by factors playing on that structure. By making indications to himself and by interpreting what he indicates, the human being has to forge or piece together a line of action. In order to act the individual has to identify what he wants, establish an objective or goal, map out a prospective line of behavior, note and interpret

the actions of others, size up his situation, check himself at this or that point, figure out what to do at other points, and frequently spur himself on in the face of dragging dispositions or discouraging settings. The fact that the human act is self-directed or built up means in no sense that the actor necessarily exercises excellence in its construction. Indeed, he may do a very poor job in constructing his act. He may fail to note things of which he should be aware, he may misinterpret things that he notes, he may exercise poor judgment, he may be faulty in mapping out prospective lines of conduct, and he may be half-hearted in contending with recalcitrant dispositions. Such deficiencies in the construction of his acts do not belie the fact that his acts are still constructed by him out of what he takes into account. What he takes into account are the things that he indicates to himself. They cover such matters as his wants, his feelings, his goals, the actions of others, the expectations and demands of others, the rules of his group, his situation, his conceptions of himself, his recollections, and his images of prospective lines of conduct. He is not in the mere recipient position of responding to such matters; he stands over against them and has to handle them. He has to organize or cut out his lines of conduct on the basis of how he does handle them.

This way of viewing human action is directly opposite to that which dominates psychological and social sciences. In these sciences human action is seen as a product of factors that play upon or through the human actor. Depending on the preference of the scholar, such determining factors may be physiological stimulations, organic drives, needs, feelings, unconscious motives, conscious motives, sentiments, ideas, attitudes, norms, values, role requirements, status demands, cultural prescriptions, institutional pressures, or social-system requirements. Regardless of which factors are chosen, either singly or in combination, action is regarded as their product and hence is explained in their terms. The formula is simple: Given factors play on the human being to produce given types of behavior. The formula is frequently amplified so as to read: Under specified conditions, given factors playing on a given organization of the human being will produce a given type of behavior. The formula, in either its simple or amplified form, represents the way in which human action is seen in theory and research. Under the formula the human being becomes a mere medium or forum for the operation of the factors that produce the behavior. Mead's scheme is fundamentally different from this formula. In place of being a mere medium for operation of determining factors that play upon him, the human being is seen as an active organism in his own right, facing, dealing with, and acting toward the objects he indicates. Action is seen as conduct which is constructed by the actor instead of response elicited from some kind of preformed organization in him. We can say that the traditional formula of human action fails to recognize that the human being is a self. Mead's scheme, in contrast, is based on this recognition.

Social Interaction
I can give here only a very brief sketch of Mead's highly illuminating analysis of social interaction. He identified two forms or levels—non-symbolic interaction

and symbolic interaction. In non-symbolic interaction human beings respond directly to one another's gestures or actions; in symbolic interaction they interpret each other's gestures and act on the basis of the meaning yielded by the interpretation. An unwitting response to the tone of another's voice illustrates non-symbolic interaction. Interpreting the shaking of a fist as signifying that a person is preparing to attack illustrates symbolic interaction. Mead's concern was predominatly with symbolic interaction. Symbolic interaction involves *interpretation*, or ascertaining the meaning of the actions or remarks of the other person, and *definition*, or conveying indications to another person as to how he is to act. Human association consists of a process of such interpretation and definition. Through this process the participants fit their own acts to the ongoing acts of one another and guide others in doing so.

Several important matters need to be noted in the case of symbolic interaction. First, it is a formative process in its own right. The prevailing practice of psychology and sociology is to treat social interaction as a neutral medium, as a mere forum for the operation of outside factors. Thus psychologists are led to account for the behavior of people in interaction by resorting to elements of the psychological equipment of the participants—such elements as motives, feelings, attitudes, or personality organization. Sociologists do the same sort of thing by resorting to societal factors, such as cultural prescriptions, values, social roles, or structural pressures. Both miss the central point that human interaction is a positive shaping process in its own right. The participants in it have to build up their respective lines of conduct by constant interpretation of each other's ongoing lines of action. As participants take account of each other's ongoing acts, they have to arrest, reorganize, or adjust their own intentions, wishes, feelings, and attitudes; similarly, they have to judge the fitness of norms, values, and group prescriptions for the situation being formed by the acts of others. Factors of psychological equipment and social organization are not substitutes for the interpretative process; they are admissible only in terms of how they are handled in the interpretative process. Symbolic interaction has to be seen and studied in its own right.

Symbolic interaction is noteworthy in a second way. Because of it human group life takes on the character of an ongoing process—a continuing matter of fitting developing lines of conduct to one another. The fitting together of the lines of conduct is done through the dual process of definition and interpretation. This dual process operates both to sustain established patterns of joint conduct and to open them to transformation. Established patterns of group life exist and persist only through the continued use of the same schemes of interpretation; and such schemes of interpretation are maintained only through their continued confirmation by the defining acts of others. It is highly important to recognize that the established patterns of group life just do not carry on by themselves but are dependent for their continuity on recurrent affirmative definition. Let the interpretations that sustain them be undermined or disrupted by changed definitions from others and the patterns can quickly collapse. This dependency of interpretations on the defining acts of others also explains why symbolic interaction conduces so markedly to the transformation of the forms of joint activity that make up group life. In the flow of group life there are innumerable points at which the participants are redefining each other's acts. Such redefinition is very common in adversary relations, it is frequent in group discussion, and it is essentially intrinsic to dealing with problems. (And I may remark here that no human group is free of problems.) Redefinition imparts a formative character to human interaction, giving rise at this or that point to new objects, new conceptions, new relations, and new types of behavior. In short, the reliance on symbolic interaction makes human group life a developing process instead of a mere issue or product of psychological or social structure.

There is a third aspect of symbolic interaction which is important to note. In making the process of interpretation and definition of one another's acts central in human interaction, symbolic interaction is able to cover the full range of the generic forms of human association. It embraces equally well such relationships as cooperation, conflict, domination, exploitation, consensus, disagreement, closely knit identification, and indifferent concern for one another. The participants in each of such relations have the same common task of constructing their acts by interpreting and defining the acts of each other. The significance of this simple observation becomes evident in contrasting symbolic interaction with the various schemes of human interaction that are to be found in the literature. Almost always such schemes construct a general model of human interaction or society on the basis of a particular type of human relationship. An outstanding contemporary instance is Talcott Parsons' scheme which presumes and asserts that the primordial and generic form of human interaction is the "complementarity of expectations." Other schemes depict the basic and generic model of human interaction as being "conflict," others assert it to be "identity through common sentiments," and still others that it is agreement in the form of "consensus." Such schemes are parochial. Their great danger lies in imposing on the breadth of human interaction an image derived from the study of only one form of interaction. Thus, in different hands, human society is said to be fundamentally a sharing of common values; or, conversely, a struggle for power; or, still differently, the exercise of consensus; and so on. The simple point implicit in Mead's analysis of symbolic interaction is that human beings, in interpreting and defining one another's acts, can and do meet each other in the full range of human relations. Proposed schemes of human society should respect this simple point.

Objects

The concept of object is another fundamental pillar in Mead's scheme of analysis. Human beings live in a world or environment of objects, and their activities are formed around objects. This bland statement becomes very significant when it is realized that for Mead objects are human constructs and not self-existing entities with intrinsic natures. Their nature is dependent on the orientation and action of people toward them. Let me spell this out. For Mead, an object is anything that can be designated or referred to. It may be physical as a chair or imaginary as a ghost, natural as a cloud in the sky or manmade as an automobile, material as the Empire State Building or abstract as the concept of liberty, animate as an elephant or inanimate as a vein of coal, inclusive of a class of people as politicians or restricted to a specific person as President de Gaulle, definite as a multiplication table or vague as a philosophical doctrine. In short, objects consist of whatever people indicate or refer to.

There are several important points in this analysis of objects. First, the nature of an object is constituted by the meaning it has for the person or persons for whom it is an object. Second, this meaning is not intrinsic to the object but arises from how the person is initially prepared to act toward it. Readiness to use a chair as something in which to sit gives it the meaning of a chair; to one with no experience with the use of chairs the object would appear with a different meaning, such as a strange weapon. It follows that objects vary in their meaning. A tree is not the same object to a lumberman, a botanist, or a poet; a star is a different object to a modern astronomer than it was to a sheepherder of antiquity; communism is a different object to a Soviet patriot than it is to a Wall Street broker. Third, objects—all objects—are social products in that they are formed and transformed by the defining process that takes place in social interaction. The meaning of the objects—chairs, trees, stars, prostitutes, saints, communism, public education, or whatnot—is formed from the ways in which others refer to such objects or act toward them. Fourth, people are prepared or set to act toward objects on the basis of the meaning of the objects for them. In a genuine sense the organization of a human being consists of his objects, that is, his tendencies to act on the basis of their meanings. Fifth, just because an object is something that is designated, one can organize one's actions toward it instead of responding immediately to it; one can inspect the object, think about it, work out a plan of action toward it, or decide whether or not to act toward it. In standing over against the object in both a logical and psychological sense, one is freed from coercive response to it. In this profound sense an object is different from a stimulus as ordinarily conceived.

This analysis of objects puts human group life into a new and interesting perspective. Human beings are seen as living in a world of meaningful objects—not in an environment of stimuli or self-constituted entities. This world is socially produced in that the meanings are fabricated through the process of social interaction. Thus, different groups come to develop different worlds—and these worlds change as the objects that compose them change in meaning. Since people are set to act in terms of the meanings of their objects, the world of objects of a group represents in a genuine sense its action organization. To identify and understand the life of a group it is necessary to identify its world of objects; this identification has to be in terms of the meanings objects have for the members of the group. Finally, people are not locked to their objects; they may check action toward objects and indeed work out new lines of conduct toward them. This condition introduces into human group life an indigenous source of transformation.

Joint Action

I use the term "joint action" in place of Mead's term "social act." It refers to the larger collective form of action that is constituted by the fitting together of the lines of behavior of the separate participants. Illustrations of joint action are a trading transaction, a family dinner, a marriage ceremony, a shopping expedition, a game, a convivial party, a debate, a court trial, or a war. We note in each instance an identifiable and distinctive form of joint action, comprised by an articulation of the acts of the participants. Joint actions range from a simple collaboration of two individuals to a complex alignment of the acts of huge organizations or institutions. Everywhere we look in a human society we see people engaging in forms of joint action. Indeed, the totality of such instances—in all of their multitudinous variety, their variable connections, and their complex networks—constitutes the life of a society. It is easy to understand from these remarks why Mead saw joint action, or the social act, as the distinguishing characteristic of society. For him, the social act was the fundamental unit of society. Its analysis, accordingly, lays bare the generic nature of society.

To begin with, a joint action cannot be resolved into a common or same type of behavior on the part of the participants. Each participant necessarily occupies a different position, acts from that position, and engages in a separate and distinctive act. It is the fitting together of these acts and not their commonality that constitutes joint action. How do these separate acts come to fit together in the case of human society? Their alignment does not occur through sheer mechanical juggling, as in the shaking of walnuts in a jar or through unwitting adaptation, as in an ecological arrangement in a plant community. Instead, the participants fit their acts together, first, by identifying the social act in which they are about to engage and, second, by interpreting and defining each other's acts in forming the joint act. By identifying the social act or joint action the participant is able to orient himself; he has a key to interpreting the acts of others and a guide for directing his action with regard to them. Thus, to act appropriately, the participant has to identify a marriage ceremony as a marriage ceremony, a holdup as a holdup, a debate as a debate, a war as a war, and so forth. But, even though this identification be made, the participants in the joint action that is being formed still find it necessary to interpret and define one another's ongoing acts. They have to ascertain what the others are doing and plan to do and make indications to one another of what to do.

This brief analysis of joint action enables us to note several matters of distinct importance. It calls attention, first, to the fact that the essence of society lies in an ongoing process of action—not in a posited structure of relations. Without action, any structure of relations between people is meaningless. To be understood, a society must be seen and grasped in terms of the action that comprises it. Next, such action has to be seen and treated, not by tracing the separate lines of action of the participants—whether the participants be single individuals, collectivities, or organizations—but in terms of the joint action into which the separate lines of action fit and merge. Few students of human society have fully grasped this point or its implications. Third, just because it is built up over time by the fitting together of acts, each joint action must be seen as having a career or a history. In having a career, its course and fate are contingent on what happens during its formation. Fourth, this career is generally orderly, fixed and repetitive by virtue of a common identification or definition of the joint action that is made by its participants. The common definition supplies each participant with decisive guidance in directing his own act so as to fit into the acts of the others. Such common definitions serve, above everything else, to account for the regularity, stability, and repetitiveness of joint action in vast areas of group life; they are the source of the established and regulated social behavior that is envisioned in the concept of culture. Fifth, however, the career of joint actions also must be seen as open to many possibilities of uncertainty. Let me specify the more important of these possibilities. One, joint actions have to be initiated—and they may not be. Two, once started a joint action may be interrupted, abandoned, or transformed. Three, the participants may not make a common definition of the joint action into which they are thrown and hence may orient their acts on different premises. Four, a common definition of a joint action may still allow wide differences in the direction of the separate lines of action and hence in the course taken by the joint action; a war is a good example. Five, new situations may arise calling for hitherto unexisting types of joint action, leading to confused exploratory efforts to work out a fitting together of acts. And, six, even in the context of a commonly defined joint action, participants may be led to rely on other considerations in interpreting and defining each other's lines of action. Time does not allow me to spell out and illustrate the importance of these possibilities. To mention them should be sufficient, however, to show that uncertainty, contingency, and transformation are part and parcel of the process of joint action. To assume that the diversified joint actions which comprise a human society are set to follow fixed and established channels is a sheer gratuitous assumption.

From the foregoing discussion of the self, the act, social interaction, objects, and joint action we can sketch a picture of human society. The picture is composed in terms of action. A society is seen as people meeting the varieties of situations that are thrust on them by their conditions of life. These situations are met by working out joint actions in which participants have to align their acts to one another. Each participant does so by interpreting the acts of others and, in turn, by making indications to others as to how they should act. By virtue of this process of interpretation and definition joint actions are built up; they have careers. Usually, the course of a joint action is outlined in advance by the fact that the participants make a common identification of it; this makes for regularity, stability, and repetitiveness in the joint action. However, there are many joint actions that encounter obstructions, that have no pre-established pathways, and that have to be constructed along new lines. Mead saw human society in this way—as a diversified social process in which people were engaged in forming joint actions to deal with situations confronting them.

This picture of society stands in significant contrast to the dominant views of society in the social and psychological sciences—even to those that pretend to view society as action. To point out the major differences in the contrast is the best way of specifying the sociological implications of Mead's scheme of thought.

The chief difference is that the dominant views in sociology and psychology fail, alike, to see human beings as organisms having selves. Instead, they regard human beings as merely responding organisms and, accordingly, treat action as mere response to factors playing on human beings. This is exemplified in the efforts to account for human behavior by such factors as motives, ego demands, attitudes, role requirements, values, status expectations, and structural stresses. In such approaches the human being becomes a mere medium through which such initiating factors operate to produce given actions. From Mead's point of view such a conception grossly misrepresents the nature of human beings and human action. Mead's scheme interposes a process of self-interaction between initiating factors and the action that may follow in their wake. By virtue of self-interaction the human being becomes an acting organism coping with situations in place of being an organism merely responding to the play of factors. And his action becomes something he constructs and directs to meet the situations in place of an unrolling of reactions evoked from him. In introducing the self, Mead's position focuses on how human beings handle and fashion their world, not on disparate responses to imputed factors.

If human beings are, indeed, organisms with selves, and if their action is, indeed, an outcome of a process of self-interaction, schemes that purport to study and explain social action should respect and accommodate these features. To do so, current schemes in sociology and psychology would have to undergo radical revision. They would have to shift from a preoccupation with initiating factor and terminal result to a preoccupation with a process of formation. They would have to view action as something constructed by the actor instead of something evoked from him. They would have to depict the milieu of action in terms of how the milieu appears to the actor in place of how it appears to the outside student. They would have to incorporate the interpretive process which at present they scarcely deign to touch. They would have to recognize that any given act has a career in which it is constructed but in which it may be interrupted, held in abeyance, abandoned, or recast.

On the methodological or research side the study of action would have to be made from the position of the actor. Since action is forged by the actor out of what he perceives, interprets, and judges, one would have to see the operating situation as the actor sees it, perceive objects as the actor perceives them, ascertain their meaning in terms of the meaning they have for the actor, and follow the actor's line of conduct as the actor organizes it—in short, one would have to take the role of the actor and see his world from his standpoint. This methodological approach stands in contrast to the so-called objective approach so dominant today, namely, that of viewing the actor and his action from the perspective of an outside, detached observer. The "objective" approach holds the danger of the observer substituting his view of the field of action for the view held by the actor. It is unnecessary to add that the actor acts toward his world on the basis of how he sees it and not on the basis of how that world appears to the outside observer.

In continuing the discussion of this matter, I wish to consider especially what we might term the structural conception of human society. This conception views society as established organization, familiar to us in the use of such terms as social structure, social system, status position, social role, social stratification, institutional structure, cultural pattern, social codes, social norms, and social values. The conception presumes that a human society is structured with regard to (a) the social positions occupied by the people in it and with regard to (b) the patterns of behavior in which they engage. It is presumed further that this interlinked structure of social positions and behavior patterns is the over-all determinant of social action; this is evidenced, of course, in the practice of explaining conduct by such structural concepts as role requirements, status demands, strata differences, cultural prescriptions, values, and norms. Social action falls into two general categories: conformity, marked by adherence to the structure, and deviance, marked by departure from it. Because of the central and determinative position into which it is elevated, structure becomes necessarily the encompassing object of sociological study and analysis—epitomized by the well-nigh universal assertion that a human group or society is a "social system." It is perhaps unnecessary to observe that the conception of human society as structure or organization is ingrained in the very marrow of contemporary sociology.

Mead's scheme definitely challenges this conception. It sees human society not as an established structure but as people meeting their conditions of life; it sees social action not as an emanation of societal structure but as a formation made by human actors; it sees this formation of action not as societal factors coming to expression through the medium of human organisms but as constructions made by actors out of what they take into account; it sees group life not as a release or expression of established structure but as a process of building up joint actions; it sees social actions as having variable careers and not as confined to the alternatives of conformity to or deviation from the dictates of established structure; it sees the so-called interaction between parts of a society not as a direct exercising of influence by one part on another but as mediated throughout by interpretations made by people; accordingly, it sees society not as a system, whether in the form of a static, moving or whatever kind of equilibrium, but as a vast number of occurring joint actions, many closely linked, many not linked at all, many prefigured and repetitious, others being carved out in new directions, and all being pursued to serve the purposes of the participants and not the requirements of a system. I have said enough, I think, to point out the drastic differences between the Meadian conception of society and the widespread sociological conceptions of it as structure.

The differences do not mean, incidentally, that Mead's view rejects the existence of structure in human society. Such a position would be ridiculous. There are such matters as social roles, status positions, rank orders, bureaucratic organizations, relations between institutions, differential authority arrangements, social codes, norms, values, and the like. And they are very important. But their importance does not lie in an alleged determination of action nor in an alleged existence as parts of a self-operating societal system. Instead, they are important only as they enter into the process of interpretation and definition out of which joint actions are formed. The manner and extent to which they enter may vary greatly from situation to situation, depending on what people take into account and how they assess what they take account of. Let me give one brief illustration. It is ridiculous, for instance, to assert, as a number of eminent sociologists have done, that social interaction is an interaction between social roles. Social interaction is obviously an interaction between *people* and not between roles; the needs of the participants are to interpret and handle what confronts them—such as a topic of conversation or a problem—and not to give expression to their roles. It is only in highly ritualistic relations that the direction and content of conduct can be explained by roles. Usually, the direction and content are fashioned out of what people in interaction have to deal with. That roles affect in varying degrees phases of the direction and content of action is true but is a matter of determination in given cases. This is a far cry from asserting action to be a product of roles. The observation I have made in this brief discussion of social roles applies with equal validity to all other structural matters.

Another significant implication of Mead's scheme of thought refers to the question of what holds a human society together. As we know, this question is converted by sociologists into a problem of unity, stability, and orderliness. And, as we know further, the typical answer given by sociologists is that unity, stability, and orderliness come from a sharing in common of certain basic matters, such as codes, sentiments, and, above all, values. Thus, the disposition is to regard common values as the glue that holds a society together, as the controlling regulator that brings and keeps the activities in a society in orderly relationship, and as the force that preserves stability in a society. Conversely, it is held that conflict between values or the disintegration of values creates disunity, disorder, and instability. This conception of human society becomes subject to great modification if we think of society as consisting of the fitting together of acts to form joint action. Such alignment may take place for any number of reasons, depending on the situations calling for joint action, and need not involve, or spring from, the sharing of common values. The participants may fit their acts to one another in orderly joint actions on the basis of compromise, out of duress, because they may use one another in achieving their respective ends, because it is the sensible thing to do, or out of sheer necessity. This is particularly likely to be true in our modern complex societies with their great diversity in composition, in lines of interest, and in their respective worlds of concern. In very large measure, society becomes the formation of workable relations. To seek to encompass, analyze, and understand the life of a society on the assumption that the existence of a society necessarily depends on the sharing of values can lead to strained treatment, gross misrepresentation, and faulty lines of interpretation. I believe that the Meadian perspective, in posing the question of how people are led to align their acts in different situations in place of presuming that this necessarily requires and stems from a sharing of common values, is a more salutary and realistic approach.

There are many other significant sociological implications in Mead's scheme of thought which, under the limit of space, I can do no more than mention. Socialization shifts its character from being an effective internalization of norms and values to a cultivated capacity to take the roles of others effectively. Social control becomes fundamentally and necessarily a matter of self-control. Social change becomes a continuous indigenous process in human group life instead of an episodic result of extraneous factors playing on established structure. Human group life is seen as always incomplete and undergoing development instead of jumping from one completed state to another. Social disorganization is seen not as a breakdown of existing structure but as an inability to mobilize action effectively in the face of a given situation. Social action, since it has a career, is recognized as having a historical dimension which has to be taken into account in order to be adequately understood.

In closing I wish to say that my presentation has necessarily skipped much in Mead's scheme that is of great significance. Further, I have not sought to demonstrate the validity of his analyses. However, I have tried to suggest the freshness, the fecundity, and the revolutionary implications of his point of view.

CHAPTER THIRTEEN

Harold Garfinkel
on Ethnomethodology

～ Introduction ～

Harold Garfinkel (1917–) was born in Newark, New Jersey. He received his B.A. degree from University College, Newark (a part of Rutgers), his M.A. from the University of North Carolina, and, after serving in the military during World War II, a Ph.D. from Harvard University. At Harvard, Garfinkel studied under Talcott Parsons, the chair of the newly formed Department of Social Relations. At the same time he was introduced to the phenomenological sociology of Alfred Schutz. Even though Garfinkel's dissertation, "The Perception of the Other: A Study of Social Order," was written under the supervision of Parsons, it effectively challenged the structural-functionalist school of thought that Parsons represented. Specifically, while Parsons's work stressed the social structural factors that impinge upon individuals and their interactions, Garfinkel placed greater emphasis on the experience of individuals in interaction. Hence, Parsons and Garfinkel approached Weber's theory of social action from opposing points of view—the former treating social action from without (that is, individual acts and interaction are a product of the internalization of social norms) and the latter treating social action from within (that is, interaction is the product of interpretative decision making by actors). Schutz's theoretical formulations on such topics as intersubjectivity assisted Garfinkel in developing a unique approach to the study of interaction.

In 1954 Garfinkel accepted a position at the University of California, Los Angeles (UCLA), where he was to remain until his retirement in 1987. It was in 1967 that he published his most influential work, *Studies in Ethnomethodology*, a collection of studies that would introduce a new branch in sociology. Literally meaning "people's methods," ethnomethodology refers to the study of communication in everyday interactions and, in particular, how actors construct a sensible social world via communication. Communication includes language, which is seen as a tool to clarify social interactions. Communication also involves indexicality—the ability of actors to fill in the background assumptions that go with every interaction.

Because *Studies in Ethnomethodology* does not provide much in the way of orienting newcomers to its unique approach, the reading for this chapter will be from John Heritage's 1984 publication, *Garfinkel and Ethnomethodology*. Heritage received his Ph.D. in 1977 from the University of Leeds. A professor of sociology at the University of California, Los Angeles, he has published numerous articles and several books on conversation analysis.

Disrupting patterns of interaction was one of the methods used by Garfinkel to demonstrate how individuals interpret, construct, and derive meaning from interactions. When we engage in conversation with someone else, we make the assumption that if the other person also speaks our language, that the person will basically understand the point that we are making. We assume what Schutz called "the general thesis of reciprocal perspectives"; in other words, while we may recognize that biographical differences exist, we assume that such differences are irrelevant in carrying out a verbal exchange. Garfinkel demonstrates this point when a subject is talking to an experimenter about having a flat tire and the latter responds, "What do you mean, you had a flat tire?" In response, the subject is taken aback by the experimenter's failure to understand the initiating comment. Garfinkel points out that this phenomenon pervades all social interaction: we assume that the other person will basically understand what we are talking about, and if we find that he or she doesn't, we will wonder (interpret to ourselves), what is wrong with this person and sanction the unexpected response. The initiating party will allow for such a breach if he or she interprets that breach as a movement to another topic of interaction. Such experiments demonstrate that subjects work to maintain reasonableness even in the face of breaches to socially defined expectations.

Making sense of the world around us is also facilitated by what Garfinkel calls "the documentary method of interpretation." We do not merely see an object in front of us, we see successive images of an object that constitute a unity. The successive images constitute a pattern in cognition that is matched with what is previously known about the pattern constituting the object. The fitting-together of such images in cognition, or the strength of a previously acquired pattern to override subsequent contradictory experiences, allows us to make sense of the objects and events that occupy every moment of our everyday experiences. There is rarely, if ever, a time when the documentary method is not in operation; such a situation would be experienced as cognizing nothing. A key point here is that we carry underlying, "partially formulated, recipe-like" notions in cognition as a means to make sense of objects (including other people) and events. We use these underlying patterns as a means of cognitively constructing a world of social interaction that we each believe we share. Hence, breaches to this underlying pattern are disturbing to us, they disrupt a worldview that makes sense to us, and we will either work to fit disruptions into the underlying pattern, adjust our underlying pattern, or sanction those who interfere with what we understand to be true and real—"Hey, what is wrong with you?" Such individual sense-making operations in interaction constitute a moral order.

When we are acknowledged by a greeting from someone, the norm is to acknowledge the greeter with some type of reply. In one sense, this scenario reflects the internalization of norms. However, more is going on here. The scenario would not be very meaningful if reflexivity (constituting the self) did not take into account the norm. The fact is that selves always have a choice in following, breaching, or redefining the underlying pattern. Reflexivity in this example demonstrates the actors' role in perpetuating a norm. Selves do not merely internalize norms and use them as guidelines for behavior; selves continually choose, via the documentary method, the norms they agree to follow. If we decide not to acknowledge the greeter with a reply, we are choosing to participate in the creation of a different scenario. (Note that, regardless of our response, the scenario is meaningful.) In the process of choosing our response to the greeter, it is not uncommon for us to anticipate the reaction of a breach from the norm (for example, by not responding, the greeter will think that we're unfriendly or not a nice person or are experiencing some personal difficulties that might result in the asking of personal questions). Thus, our response does not entail merely following a norm, or simply behaving in response to the pressures of a norm in the situation; rather, our response is one of choosing a reaction that gets a desired effect. Norms do not necessarily have a "constraining" effect upon selves in interaction, but they may provide a "grid" upon which selves, who are accountable to each other, choose courses of action. Individuals unavoidably participate in the maintenance or reformulation of their circumstances.

Disrupting patterns of interaction was not the only method used by Garfinkel to demonstrate how group members participate in constructing social order. A second method was the study of the social organization of talk, or "conversation analysis." Consider how we typically recognize the appropriate use of a term, such as "box," when it can have multiple meanings. The term comes to have a specific meaning because of the context within which it is used. This points out two important aspects of language: (1) because of the plasticity of language, new words are not necessary to describe every nuance of human experience; this would produce a lexicon that could overwhelm its users; and (2) despite its plasticity or generality, language applications can be very specific. The flexibility of language allows users to contextualize different meanings from a relatively small number of words. Moreover, group members tend to hold each other accountable for establishing a context for the appropriate interpretation of words. In this way, language is used by actors, once again, to maintain or reformulate their circumstances.

Garfinkel's case study of Agnes (a pseudonym) demonstrates a number of important points made above. In 1958, at the age of nineteen, Agnes was referred to the UCLA Department of Psychiatry. Agnes was born a boy but wanted a sex-change operation. In order to demonstrate that she was a good candidate for the operation, Agnes had to present herself continuously in a feminine light. As a result, she became perceptively aware of the sexually charged ways in which social actors take account of each other and maintain an institutionalized division of gender-based behaviors and attitudes. Because of their pervasiveness, these practices are accepted by social actors as natural behavior. The case of Agnes demonstrates that presumed attitudes and behaviors closely tied to identity are not merely ascribed and internalized manifestations but may be the achievement of social actors who are conscious of the social practices that maintain a particular cultural orientation. The desire to be female was a breach that provided the reflexivity that could benefit Agnes in choosing gender-appropriate talk and manners. Garfinkel's research, and the case of Agnes in particular, reveals how group members actively participate in the seemingly "constraining power of normative conventions."

⌒ Ethnomethodology ⌒

. . . Parsons treats the organization of action as maintained largely through the operation of externally and internally constraining 'moral' rules, while taking little or no interest in the properties of the actors' common-sense judgements. Schutz, on the contrary, is preoccupied with these latter properties, but takes little interest in the 'moral' force with which common-sense judgements are invested.

It thus fell to Garfinkel to effect an integration of the 'moral' with the 'cognitive.' This he accomplished through a series of ingenious experiments and with brilliant interpretations of their results. His conclusions are intellectually compelling and they permit us to remove the scare quotation marks from the term 'moral'; for they are consistent with the mundane actors' treatment of one another's actions as the chosen products of knowledgeable agents. It is this view of action treated as the product of accountable moral choice which, in turn, Garfinkel places at the centre of his analysis of social organization. . . .

. . . [W]e will find that his work can be usefully viewed as the product of the consistent pursuit of a single question: how do social actors come to know, and know in common, what they are doing and the circumstances in which they are doing it? . . .

. . . The substance of his approach was the famous series of 'breaching experiments.'

The simplest of these experiments were conducted with the game of ticktacktoe—a game similar to (British) 'noughts and crosses.' Here the experimenters (E) were instructed to ask the subjects (S) to make the first move. After this, the E erased the S's mark, moved it to another cell and made his own mark while avoiding making any indication that what he was doing was unusual. In 253 experimental trials, 95 per cent of subjects reacted to this action in some way and over 75 per cent of subjects objected to it or demanded some kind of explanation for it. Those subjects who simply assumed that some new game was in progress (for example by copying the experimenter's move), or who assumed that the experimenter was playing a practical joke, or trying out a new method of play, and who therefore abandoned 'ticktacktoe' as an interpretative framework for understanding these events showed little disturbance. By contrast, those who continued to assume that a game of ticktacktoe was still in progress and tried to make sense of the anomalous events in terms of this assumption showed most disturbance. These findings held firm independently of the S's age, the degree of acquaintance between S and E, and the fact that Ss and Es were of the same or different sex.

The 'ticktacktoe' experiment yielded two significant conclusions. First, behaviours which were at variance with the basic rules of the game 'immediately motivated attempts to normalize the discrepancy, i.e. to treat the observed behaviour as an instance of a legally possible event.' Second, senselessness and disturbance was increased if the subject attempted to normalize the discrepancy while retaining an unaltered view of the 'rules of the game.'

Despite these interesting conclusions, Garfinkel was wary of attempting to extrapolate these results to 'real life' situations, and for a number of reasons. Games, he suggested, have a peculiar time structure such that, throughout a game's events, the participants know what it will take for the game to be complete. Again, success or failure is accomplished *within* the events of a game and is not subject to later developments (or re-evaluations) *outside* the parameters of the game itself. Games are fully 'public' in that their events are defined in terms of consensually understood 'basic rules.' Moreover, they are defined 'over against' everyday life, such that to 'leave' or 'finish' the game is to 'return to' the world of everyday life. Perhaps most importantly, the basic rules of a game, e.g. chess, are independent of the 'state of the game' or the strategies operated by the players. They are not altered by, or over, the actual course of play. There is practically perfect correspondence between the basic rules as normative descriptions of game conduct and actually occurring game conduct. (And, although the 'basic rules' do not cover every aspect of the player's comportment— think here of the famous chess game in the film *The Thomas Crowne Affair* or the notorious Fischer–Spassky championship—they do define game constitutive events.) Finally, the basic rules define rational, realistic and understandable game activities.

It is this role of the basic rules in the constitution of game relevant events which made the 'ticktacktoe' breaches comparatively easy to engineer. But equally, since this role—together with the other characteristics of games—is not replicated in the world of daily life, further experiments which were more difficult to devise would have to be developed.

In the best known of the latter, students were instructed to 'engage an acquaintance or friend in an ordinary conversation and, without indicating that what the experimenter was saying was in any way out of the ordinary, to insist that the person clarify the sense of his commonplace remarks.' Some of the reported results are reproduced below:

Case 1: The subject was telling the experimenter, a member of the subject's car pool, about having had a flat tire while going to work the previous day.

> S: I had a flat tire.
> E: What do you mean, you had a flat tire?
> She appeared momentarily stunned. Then she answered in a hostile way: 'What do you mean? What do you mean? A flat tire is a flat tire. That is what I mean. Nothing special. What a crazy question!'

Case 3: On Friday night my husband and I were watching television. My husband remarked that he was tired. I asked, 'How are you tired? Physically, mentally, or just bored?'

> S: I don't know, I guess physically, mainly.
> E: You mean that your muscles ache, or your bones?
> S: I guess so. Don't be so technical.
> (After more watching)
> S: All these old movies have the same kind of old iron bedstead in them.
> E: What do you mean? Do you mean all old movies, or some of them, or just the ones you have seen?
> S: What's the matter with you? You know what I mean.
> E: I wish you would be more specific.
> S: You know what I mean! Drop dead!

Case 6: The victim waved his hand cheerily.

> S: How are you?
> E: How am I in regard to what? My health, my finance, my school work, my peace of mind, my . . .
> S: (Red in the face and suddenly out of control.) Look! I was just trying to be polite. Frankly, I don't give a damn how you are.

In these cases, Garfinkel proposes, the student experimenters had successfully breached one of the idealizations making up Schutz's 'general thesis of reciprocal perspectives,' namely the idealization of the congruency of relevances. According to this idealization, it will be recalled, the actors assume that differences arising from their unique biographical circumstances are irrelevant for the purposes at hand of each and that they have 'selected and interpreted the actually or potentially common objects and their features in an identical manner or at least an "empirically identical" manner, i.e. one sufficient for all practical purposes.' In each of the above cases, the subjects had expected that the experimenters would, by drawing upon background knowledge of 'what everybody knows,' supply a sense to their remarks that was 'empirically identical' with the sense intended by the Ss. The S thus assumed, in each case, that both parties knew 'what he is talking about without any requirement of a check-out.' In each case, the S took for granted that E would supply whatever unstated understandings would be required in order to make recognizable sense of his talk. This requirement, as we shall see, pervades all interaction. As Garfinkel extensively demonstrated in his 'conversation clarification experiment,' in any two-party conversation, 'much that is being talked about is not mentioned, although each expects that the adequate sense of the matter being talked about is settled.'

It is noticeable that the Es' breaches of this requirement resulted in interactional breakdowns which were extraordinarily rapid and complete and, as such, surprising in their extent even to Garfinkel himself. Moreover it is noticeable that, in most cases, the Es' breaches were very rapidly and powerfully sanctioned. Thus in cases 1 and 6 above, the Ss assumed postures of 'righteous hostility' after only a single breaching move from the E and, in the second part of case 3, after two such moves. In all the other cases reported, the Ss made strenuous efforts to restore the situation of reciprocity and ended up either proposing or demanding explanations for the E's conduct. In each case, the S treated the intelligible character of his own talk as something to which he was morally entitled and, correspondingly, treated the breaching move as illegitimate, deserving of sanction and requiring explanation. The experiment thus indicated that maintaining the 'reciprocity of perspectives' (as one of the presuppositions of the attitude of daily life) is not merely a cognitive task, but one which each actor 'trusts' that the other will accomplish as a matter of moral necessity. As Garfinkel subsequently put it, summarizing the observations of his 1963 paper, 'the term "trust" is used there to refer to a person's compliance with the expectancies of the attitude of daily life as a morality.' With just this evidence behind us, such compliance already appears to be the object of spectacular moral constraints.

In only one instance reported by Garfinkel were the above consequences of breaching incompletely realized. This instance was reported as case 8 in Garfinkel. In it, the subject of the experiment was successful in transforming the sense of the 'breaching moves' by interpreting them as a part of a different order of possibilities—a game or a childish joke. Moreover the subject in this case was successful in eliciting a sequence of activities from the E which were consistent with, and confirmatory of, his election of this new order of possibilities. . . .

. . . One of the most commonly cited terms in Garfinkel's conceptual armoury is 'the documentary method of interpretation.' Garfinkel derived the term from Mannheim who proposed that the documentary method involves the search for 'an identical homologous pattern underlying a vast variety of totally different realizations of meaning.' As Garfinkel elaborated it, 'the method consists of treating an actual appearance as "the document of," as "pointing to," as "standing on behalf of" a presupposed underlying pattern.'

Although Garfinkel took the term itself from Mannheim, the basic idea had previously received very considerable theoretical explication at the hands of phenomenologists from Husserl onwards. The phenomenologists had, indeed, developed an analysis of perceptual and cognitive activity which treated all acts of consciousness as involving a 'documentary' process. For example, the brief discussion of the phenomenological treatment of the perception of a chair in the previous chapter—in which it was indicated that as we walk towards 'a chair,' successive presented appearances are referred to the intended object 'this chair'—was in effect a reference to the workings of the 'documentary method.' Although Garfinkel's discussion of the latter has sometimes been interpreted as a recommendation of it as a special sociological technique, it is clear that this interpretation is incorrect. As the above example implies and as we shall subsequently see, Garfinkel endorses the phenomenological treatment of acts of cognition and proposes the documentary method as an invariant and unavoidable feature of all acts of mundane perception and cognition.

Our chair example forms a convenient starting point for discussion of the documentary method because it illustrates two important aspects of its use. The first aspect is easily disclosed by stressing that it is *successive* presentations of 'the chair' which are referred to the intended object 'this chair.' Any intended object, the phenomenologist argues, is constituted as a unity from a succession of appearances which wax and wane in the course of 'inner time' or '*durée*.' Time is thus a constitutive feature of objects. Although the point is most obvious when we are considering a succession of appearances of an object as we move in relation to it, it is just as valid for the perception of an object from a static position. In fact, the similarity of successive presented appearances of an object is one of the means by which we can gauge whether our position is static or not. Thus the existence of an object for an observer is, as it were, permeated with temporal specifications. Time is an integral feature of the organization of a mundane 'world' of objects. The role of time as an integral feature of the constitution of objects and events will become particularly significant in the treatment of action and Garfinkel is generally critical of Parson's failure to acknowledge its significance in the interpretation of action.

The second aspect of the documentary method in use which must be stressed is that its use is pervasive. To revert to our chair once again, it will be obvious that there is no absolute or privileged 'position-in-general' from which the chair can be viewed or in terms of which perspectival appearances can be abandoned in favour of immediate access to the 'chair itself.' The chair exists as a self-same object *only* insofar as successive perspectival appearances are referred to the intended object 'this chair.' There is, as Garfinkel sometimes puts it, no 'time out' or escape from the documentary process into an all-encompassing viewpoint. Or to put it another way, 'time out' from the documentary process merely results in 'noise'—a state of confusion in which nothing is cognized.

Just as the above points hold for the perception of a physical object such as a chair, so too they hold for social objects. Social objects such as 'a cheerful person' or 'a woman walking to the shops' are the products of complicated judgements in which an 'underlying pattern' is built up from a temporally qualified succession of appearances. It is important to note that the process may operate completely unconsciously as when, after the fashion of Weber's 'observational understanding,' we simply 'see' a man running for a train or, alternatively, aspects of the process may be brought to consciousness, for example, when we struggle to 'make out' what somebody is doing or 'form hypotheses' about it. . . .

In his studies of the documentary method at work, Garfinkel developed a demonstration which was designed to exaggerate the process and, as he put it, 'catch the work of "fact production" in flight.' The demonstration consisted of a 'student counselling experiment' in which undergraduates were invited to partici-pate in research exploring 'alternative means to psychotherapy "as a way of giving persons advice about their personal problems."' In each case, the subject was asked to describe the background of his problem and to ask the 'counsellor' at least ten questions about it. Each question was to be designed so as to permit a 'yes' or 'no' answer. The subject and experimenter-counsellor were situated in adjoining rooms and connected by intercom. The subject was required to tape record his reflections on each answer after disconnecting the intercom 'so that the counsellor will not hear your remarks.' Unknown to the subject, the experimenter-counsellor prede-termined his sequence of 'yes' and 'no' answers with a table of random numbers. At the completion of the questions and answers, the subject was asked to summa-rize his impressions of the exchange as a whole. . . .

. . . Garfinkel notes that the subjects perceived the experimenter's 'answers' to have been motivated by their questions and were able to see 'what the adviser had in mind' in producing his answers. The answers were treated as 'advice' whose substance was found by interpreting what the adviser said against the background established by the question or series of questions. Garfinkel further found that the subjects' conceptions of 'the underlying problem' which was be-ing dealt with were extended, elaborated and reshaped responsively to the 'an-swers': 'The sense of the problem was progressively accomodated to each present answer, while the answer motivated fresh aspects of the underlying problem.' Moreover this elaboration and accomodation of the problem was done 'so as to maintain the "course of advice."' In this process, incomplete or incongruous or unsatisfactory answers were handled by waiting to see whether they would be clarified by subsequent answers, by imputing special reasons or intents to the 'ad-viser,' by deciding that the 'adviser' had 'learned more' about the problem, or changed his mind or was unfamiliar with its intricacies. Through these and other means, Garfinkel concludes, the subjects so managed their interpretations as to view the 'advice' they had been given as coherent, as compatible with 'given conditions' as represented by the normatively valued social structures perceived by the subject, and as the trustworthy product of properly motivated advisers. This management, moreover, was not principled in the sense of rule-governed or subject to well-defined decision procedures. Rather the management was re-sponsive to whatever exigencies emerged and was accomplished so as to deal with each exigency by whatever means were available to maintain whatever overall sense could be salvaged from the interchange-in-progress.

The findings from the 'student counselling experiment' indicate that the sub-jects' pursuit of a consistent underlying pattern in the 'advice' they were receiv-ing involved a scarcely conscious recourse to a vast and unpredictable range of considerations which, at best, had the status of partially formulated, recipe-like knowledge. These considerations were consulted in an apparently haphazard manner, being taken up, discounted and dropped 'as the situation demanded.' As in a whirlpool, the documentary 'vortex' retained a degree of focus and clarity

while the materials contributing to its maintenance rotated around it with varying degrees of ellipse.

These features might reasonably be regarded as artefacts of the highly unusual
experimental situation in which the subjects were placed, which, it will be recalled, was a deliberately contrived one. Although plausible, this interpretation
of the results is incorrect, for these same features were demonstrated in a complementary study directed at an apparently much simpler task—the clarification
of understandings implicit in ordinary conversation.

In this study, students were asked to report the substance of an actual mundane conversation and then to describe what the conversationalists understood
they were talking about. . . .

The exercise revealed that the participants in 'ordinary conversation' engage
in the same practices that the subjects in the 'counselling experiment'
engaged in. Characteristically, utterances were not treated 'literally' or at 'face
value' but were understood by reference to unspoken assumptions and presuppositions that each party attributed to the other. Each utterance was understood by
being treated as a member of a developing sequence and, as such, as having 'retrospective' and 'prospective' significances. Each party permitted some present
sense of an utterance to be altered by what was subsequently said with the result
that 'many expressions had the property of being progressively realized and realizable through the further course of the conversation.' . . .

. . . '[C]ommon understandings' achieved by the parties to conversations
can only be achieved by the parties doing whatever is necessary at the time to
'fill-in' a background of 'seen but unnoticed' interpretation for whatever is
said as it is said. An announced failure to accomplish this task . . . threatens
the very possibility of mutual understanding and, with it, the existence of a
shared world. . . .

. . . [T]he 'underlying pattern' was assumed from the outset to be the basis on
which the appearances should be interpreted. At every possible point, the participants seemed to be willing to give the 'underlying pattern' the benefit of the
doubt. . . .

. . . Consider, to begin with, a situation in which a social actor is walking
down the corridor of an office building, interactively disengaged from any others
on the scene. From the moment this actor is greeted by another, his or her circumstances are radically reconstituted from a situation of mutual disengagement
between the parties to one in which some, at least minimal, engagement is proposed by the other. At this initial and elementary level, the first greeter's action
has reflexively reconstituted the scene. Moreover, this first greeting transforms
the scene for both parties—for the greeter (who moves from a circumstance of
disengagement to one of engagement which he or she proposes, via the norm,
will be reciprocated) and for the recipient of the greeting (who must now deal
with this reconstituted circumstance).

In this context, and with the use of the norm for greetings, our recipient is
now faced with a situation of 'choice.' If the recipient returns the greeting, he or

she thereby reciprocates the proposal of interactional engagement made by the first greeter and, in so doing, ratifies it. In this case, the sense of the scene has undergone a further transformation from one in which interactional engagement was merely proposed unilaterally to one in which it is a bilaterally acknowledged fact. It is essential here to keep in mind that the scene does not remain unaltered by the second greeting. Rather it is developed and elaborated in a particular direction—the direction of mutual interactional engagement which was proposed by the first speaker.

Alternatively, of course, the recipient may not return the greeting. In this case, such a recipient will 'observably-reportably' develop the substance of the scene in a different direction—counteracting what was proposed by the greeter. Once again, it is essential to note that, although a circumstance of mutual disengagement may well ensue from such an action, it will not be the 'same' circumstance of mutual disengagement as existed prior to the first greeting. Rather, as in the case of the 'breaching' experiments, the re-reconstituted scene may well be accountably attended to by the participants (and reported to others) as an 'intended,' 'produced' or 'motivated' outcome and, probably, as a product of good or bad reasons.

A number of important points about the nature of conduct and its normative organization can be made from this elementary example. First, it should by now be obvious that regardless of whether the recipient consciously 'chose' to respond in a particular way, he or she was nonetheless placed in a 'situation of choice.' This is so by virtue of the fact that actions reflexively and accountably redetermine the features of the scenes in which they occur. Thus regardless of what our recipient does—of whether the greeting is returned or not—the scene will be reconstituted. The unfolding scene, in other words, cannot 'mark time' or 'stall' for a while; it will unavoidably be transformed.

Second, it can be noticed that the norm 'return a greeting' may be used as an interpretative base for the scene, regardless of which among the alternatives of action the recipient in fact accomplishes. Thus the parties to the scene not only maintain and develop the 'perceivedly normal' course of the scene by perceiving, judging and acting in accordance with the dictates of the norm, they also use this same norm to notice, interpret and sanction departures from its dictates. The norm is thus *doubly constitutive* of the circumstances it organizes. It provides both for the intelligibility and accountability of 'continuing and developing the scene as normal' and for the visibility of other, alternative courses of action. It follows, therefore, that whatever the outcome of the 'choice,' the availability of the norm will provide a means by which the conduct and its circumstances can be rendered sensible, describable and accountable.

Finally, it may be noted that, once the norm 'return a greeting' has made an actor's 'choice' visible, there is available a great mass of interpretative devices in terms of which a 'non-standard' choice may itself become elaboratively interpreted. Thus: recipient did not hear or was preoccupied; recipient did not know the greeter, or failed to recognize him, or thought the greeter was initiating a sexual 'pass'; recipient deliberately 'snubbed' the greeter as a social inferior, or sought to renew a quarrel, or to declare a state of enmity by visibly 'refusing' to return the greeting, and so on. And these interpretative resources are themselves accountably implemented by reference to the particulars of the actions, persons, places and circumstances of their occurrence.

Emerging out of this discussion is a point which is absolutely central both to Garfinkel's work and the subsequent traditions of research which he has stimulated. This concerns the role of norms, or maxims of conduct, in the organization of ordinary actions. A characteristic assumption within the theory of action, Parsons's included, is that the role of norms is essentially one of guiding, regulating, determining or causing the conduct which may occur in *circumstances which are treated as if they are already pre-established or pre-defined.* As already noted, within the terms of such assumptions, the theory treats the actors as cognitively equipped to recognize situations in common and, once the situation is commonly recognized, the application of common norms enables the actors to produce joint actions. Moreover the theory, we can now notice, treats the actors' circumstances as essentially unchanged by their courses of action. Hence the role of time as an essential component in the unfolding succession of 'here-and-now' reconstitutions of the actors' circumstances is ignored. Instead time is treated within the theory as, to use Garfinkel's expression, a 'fat moment.'

Garfinkel's perspective, emerging as it does out of a preoccupation with the nature of 'common understandings,' reverses this tradition of theorizing. Within his viewpoint, the common norms, rather than regulating conduct in pre-defined scenes of action, *are instead reflexively constitutive of the activities and unfolding circumstances to which they are applied.* The argument, described in the previous chapter, concerning the role of the expectancies of the attitude of daily life in the constitution of 'perceivedly normal' courses of conduct is here simply particularized to specific, 'concrete' norms of conduct. Thus what the activities are, with all the subsequent interpretative elaboration of motive and circumstance, is only visible and available in the first place through the reflexive application of norms and maxims of conduct to temporally extended sequences of actions. Norms and maxims of conduct are, then, materials through which, via the documentary method of interpretation, the reflexive determination of the 'whatness' of conduct is possible. In this perspective, once again, the cognitive and the moral are deeply intertwined. . . .

Introduced into the theory of action, the relevance of reflexive phenomena can no longer be confined to the essentially academic concerns of the armchair theorizer or observer. Instead, as we have seen, they directly enter as 'seen but unnoticed,' but nevertheless constitutive, features of what the actions consist of and hence into the concerns and calculations of ordinary actors pursuing their daily affairs. For it is precisely through the reflexive accountability of action that ordinary actors find themselves in a world of practical actions having the property that *whatever* they do will be intelligible and accountable as a sustaining of, or a development or violation, etc. of, some order of activity. This order of activity is, as Garfinkel puts it, 'incarnate' in the specific, concrete, contexted and sequential details of actors' actions. It is via the reflexive properties of actions that the participants—regardless of their degree of 'insight' into the matter—find themselves in a world whose characteristics they are visibly and describably engaged in producing and reproducing. It is through these same properties that the actors' actions, to adapt Merleau-Ponty's phrase, are condemned to be meaningful. . . .

. . . [L]et us re-examine our greetings example once more while holding on to the 'double constitution' property of norms. Viewed from the perspective of the one who performed the initial greeting (which he or she expects, via the norm, to be returned), a return greeting not only meets the standard expectation, it also confirms that some standard relationship (e.g. of acquaintance) continues to hold good between the parties as, indeed, the first speaker had expected it would.

On the other hand, returning to the second alternative action (no return greeting), we have already noted that a mass of considerations might be brought to bear in interpreting an 'observable and reportable' deviation. Our initial greeter may conclude that the recipient did not hear and, accordingly, repeat the greeting; or, noticing the anxious expression on the recipient's face, he or she may enquire into the recipient's circumstances. Alternatively, the greeter may silently attribute the unreturned greeting to the recipient's preoccupation, or to an argument the previous day, or to the recipient's rank or rudeness. Whatever the conclusion, there is a sharp contrast between the 'life-as-usual' nature of the greeting-and-its-return which is not given a second thought, and the occasions where the recipient does not return the greeting, which are commonly the objects of 'post-mortem' thought and discussion.

This contrast instructs us that the 'perceived normality' of ordinary conduct is, in fact, normatively provided for even though this provision is 'seen but unnoticed' and often becomes visible only in the breach. For, to explain the normal action, we merely cite the norm: 'I said "Hello" to return the greeting.' To explain breaches of the norm, we cite accounts which are overwhelmingly treated as excuses or justifications for the breach: 'I didn't hear him,' 'I had a terrible hangover,' 'I don't speak to people who insult me.' And, given this bifurcation in the types of accounts which are given for conformity to and deviation from the norm, we can begin to see some basis for the participants' belief that breaches of norms are commonly more revealing about the attitudes, motives and circumstances of other people than is conformity.

Turning now to view the greeting situation from the perspective of the recipient of the first greeting, we have already suggested that although the recipient may not be fully aware of it at the time, he or she is, in effect, presented with a choice. The choice is between: (1) returning the greeting and sustaining a 'life-as-usual' stance which, among other things, confirms that the relationship between greeter and recipient holds as the greeter proposes it; or (2) not returning the greeting and creating the circumstances in which the initial greeter may accountably infer that 'normal circumstances' do not obtain and that 'something is up' which needs looking into.

Where, for whatever reasons, actors wish to avoid the second of these consequences, they will engage in the 'perceivedly normal'/normatively provided for conduct. Given these considerations, it will be apparent that three basic conditions are required to get greetings regularly returned: (1) social participants are aware of the norm; (2) they are, on occasion, capable of reflexive anticipation of the interpretative consequences of breaches of the norm; and (3) they attribute (1) and (2) to each other. Where these three conditions hold, a social world will exist in which the participants hold one another accountable as the producers of 'chosen' courses of action which, particularly in the breach, will be held to reflect significant real dispositions, opinions, characters, commitments and beliefs.

Generalizing the theorem, we can suggest that the 'internalization of norms' is (1) not a necessary source of constraint in engendering normatively appropriate conduct, nor (2) an essential bulwark against the unloosed anarchy of interests. With respect to the production of normatively appropriate conduct, all that is required is that the actors have, and attribute to one another, a reflexive awareness of the normative accountability of their actions. For actors who, under these conditions, calculate the consequences of their actions in reflexively transforming the circumstances and relationships in which they find themselves, will routinely find that their interests are well served by normatively appropriate conduct. With respect to the anarchy of interests, the choice is not between normatively organized co-operative conduct and the disorganized pursuit of interests. Rather, normative accountability is the 'grid' by reference to which *whatever* is done will become visible and assessable. . . .

. . . [A]ny detailed investigation of the organization of social action will rapidly arrive at the conclusion that, as Garfinkel proposes, social action cannot be analysed as 'governed' or 'determined' by rules in any straightforward sense. This is so for two basic reasons. First, even where indisputable rules of conduct can be formulated, their relevance to action will be found to be surrounded by a mass of unstated conditions which are, in various ways, tacitly oriented to by social participants. Thus even in the simplest cases, such as our greetings example, an analysis of social action simply in terms of the rule will grossly understate the complexity of the scene of activity as it is available to the participants' reasoning procedures.

Second, many classes of actions are not analysable by reference to clear-cut rules which either delimit them as a class or, still less, could be held to constrain or determine their empirical occurrence. Rather these actions are produced and recognized by reference to reasoning procedures which draw upon complex, tacit and inductively based arrays of 'considerations' and 'awarenesses.' . . . References to underlying rule systems may well have some part to play in this understanding, though it is by no means obvious that this part will necessarily be a large one. Moreover, however large this part turns out to be, the final analysis will not involve an appeal to rules as consciously inculcated or consciously oriented to phenomena. Nor will the analytic appeal to rules involve the proposal that the latter are, in any sense, determinate or determinative causes of action. . . .

. . . [U]nderstanding language is not to be regarded as a matter of 'cracking a code' which contains a set of pre-established descriptive terms combined, by the rules of grammar, to yield sentence meanings which express propositions about the world. Understanding language is not, in the first instance, a matter of understanding sentences but of understanding *actions*—utterances—which are constructively interpreted in relation to their contexts. This involves viewing an utterance against a background of *who* said it, *where* and *when*, *what* was being accomplished by saying it and in the light of what possible *considerations* and in virtue of what *motives* it was said. An utterance is thus the starting point for a complicated process of interpretative inference rather than something which can be treated as self-subsistently intelligible.

It will be apparent that Garfinkel's approach to the phenomena of mundane description is consistent with his overall focus on the accountable nature of social action. As we have seen, he views social action as designed with reference to how it will be recognized and described. Descriptions are no different. They are not to be regarded as disembodied commentaries on states of affairs. Rather, in the ways in which they (1) make reference to states of affairs and (2) occur in particular interactional and situational contexts, they will unavoidably be understood as actions which are chosen and consequential. Like other actions, descriptions are 'indexical' and are to be understood by reference to where and when etc. they occur. Like other actions, too, descriptions are 'reflexive' in maintaining or altering the sense of the activities and unfolding circumstances in which they occur. . . .

In sum, Garfinkel's interest is in descriptive accounts and accountings as data which are to be examined to see how they organize, and are organized by, the empirical circumstances in which they occur. Far from being treated as external to social activity, accounts are to be treated as subject to the same range of circumstantial and interpretative contingencies as the actions and circumstances they describe. In this context, Garfinkel begins his discussion of accounts by noting that their 'fit' to the circumstances they describe is 'loose' and subject to adjustment by *ad hoc* devices; that accounts, like actions, are understood by reference to a mass of unstated assumptions and that the sense of an account is heavily dependent on the context of its production. . . .

. . . Any sustained observation of mundane description will very quickly yield the conclusion that it is impossible to characterize the relationship between descriptors and described in terms of clear-cut correspondences. Consider the following:

> The human visual system can discriminate some 7,500,000 different colours, but the most colour names reported in any language are 4,000 English names of which only 8 are used very commonly. No two plants—no two leaves, in fact—are iden-

tical, nor is any plant quite the same on successive days; however all cultures possess plant classification systems by which, at one or another levels of abstraction, billions of discrete, discriminable plants are rendered equivalent.

This immense order of difference between what we are capable of discriminating and what we are able to communicate about with the use of language is strongly supportive of Schutz's proposal that language is inherently *typifying*, a kind of 'treasure house of ready-made pre-constituted types and characteristics all socially derived and carrying along an open horizon of unexplored content.' Thus, although every state of affairs may be unique, this fact is not reflected in our vocabulary. If it were, the result would necessarily be the continual invention of new terms. It is easy to see the uselessness of such a strategy. A lexicon which was continually expanded to accommodate each new circumstance would be unlearnable and unusable since, once the situation for which each term was formulated had passed, the term itself would lapse from use. Descriptors exist as formulations of commonalities across states of affairs, otherwise they would not 'describe.' Through their use, discriminable items—shades of colour, objects and events—are bundled together and treated as equivalent despite their individual differences from one another. Language is the medium through which these common-sense equivalence classes are constituted and communicated. It embodies a continual compromise between generality and specificity. There is thus an inherently approximate relationship between a descriptor and the range of states of affairs it may be used to describe.

In turn, this suggests that the boundaries of the applicability of a term will be indeterminate, negotiable and subject to change. . . .

. . . Cavell invites us to consider the use of the term 'feed' in such expressions as 'feed the kitty,' 'feed the lion,' 'feed the swans,' 'feed the meter,' 'feed in the film,' 'feed the machine,' 'feed his pride' and 'feed wire.' Plainly the commonalities across this range of expressions are not great, yet somehow resemblances are drawn out from expression to expression such that all are intelligible and none appears as a misuse of the term. . . .

. . . [G]iven the approximate quality of descriptive terms, the uttering of a description, rather than pinpointing a definite property, must instead establish a focus for active 'contextualizing' work by the hearer which is aimed at interpreting what is meant.

The essentials of this work involve the documentary method of interpretation in which the description and its context elaborate each other. Thus the description evokes a context to be searched and, in turn, the results of this search elaborate the specific sense of the description. . . .

. . . [O]rdinary descriptions are never produced in the abstract. They occur in contexts which elaborate and particularize their sense. For example, the descriptor 'red,' predicated of a London bus coming down the street, has its sense reflexively elaborated and refined by the particular colour of the referent object present to the vision of speaker and hearer. The sense for 'red' that is proposed by the speaker and achieved by the hearer will therefore be particular and locally situated. The term, elaborated by its circumstance of use, will be *sufficient*—to pick out the bus, or identify an aspect of it, or indicate the colour the speaker plans to paint his front door. And because this is the case, and the 'redness of red' is not the issue, there is no anxiety about the 'abstract indeterminacy' of the term. Neither the speaker nor the hearer notices or cares that, after all, the hearer's sweater could also be called 'red' and it is not the same colour. The term, understood in relation to its referent context, is adequate-for-all-practical-purposes.

It is, then, the practical and situated use of descriptions which permits their clarification and refinement to the point that they can be supplied with a sense that is adequate to their inferred task. In the same way, a description of a man as 'jealous' may be elaborated with a story of what he did when he thought he saw his wife with another man. Or again if, in a pencil and paper test situation, I am asked to 'name some typical birds,' I may very likely mention robins and sparrows. But neither is at all likely to come to mind when I am greeted at the door with: 'I've just put the bird in the oven.' In each case, although the descriptors 'red,' 'jealous' and 'bird'—considered in the abstract—seem to locate fields of possibilities rather than nominating objects or their properties with precision, some aspect of the contexts in which they occur will, as Garfinkel puts it, 'unavoidably elaborate' their sense. It will be obvious that this process of contextualization in which descriptor and context mutually elaborate one another contributes immense refinement and definition to an apparently crude and undifferentiated descriptive system. . . .

In sum, speakers produce descriptive expressions with a view to having hearers make whatever range of contextual determinations as are required in order to find the sense of the description. This may involve invoking, *inter alia*, various aspects of the physical context—both referenced and unreferenced—in which the utterance occurs, conventions about the use of descriptive resources, the conversational or wider social context in which the utterance occurs, its institutional background, together with a range of assumptions about competent speaking, the goals of speaking and the nature of speakers. Here, then, we re-encounter the network of 'background assumptions' . . . which speakers trust one another to implement and in terms of which they hold one another accountable as competent users of natural language. . . .

We are now in a position to add a further 'layer' to the analysis of action—the layer of social institutions. For although we have deliberately ignored the fact until now, it will be obvious that, in maintaining, elaborating or transforming their circumstances by their actions, the actors are also simultaneously reproducing, developing or modifying the institutional realities which envelop those actions. . . .

. . . 'Agnes' is the pseudonym of a patient who was referred to the Department of Psychiatry at the University of California at Los Angeles (UCLA) in 1958. She was born a boy with normal appearing male genitals, certified and named appropriately and, until the age of 17, was generally recognized to be a boy. Nonetheless, by the time she presented herself at UCLA at the age of 19,

> Agnes's appearance was convincingly female. She was tall, slim, with a very female shape. Her measurements were 38-25-38. She had long, fine dark-blond hair, a young face with pretty features, a peaches-and-cream complexion, no facial hair, subtly plucked eyebrows, and no make-up except for lipstick . . . Her usual manner of dress did not distinguish her from a typical girl of her age or class. There was nothing garish or exhibitionistic in her attire, nor was there any hint of poor taste or that she was ill at ease in her clothing . . . Her manner was appropriately feminine with a slight awkwardness that is typical of middle adolescence.

Agnes's purpose in presenting herself at UCLA was to obtain a sex-change operation and, prior to this, she was examined by a number of specialists. The latter were interested in a range of her characteristics, including her unique endocrinological configuration, her psychological make-up, her gender identity, the causes of her desire to be made anatomically female and her psychiatric management. Garfinkel, however, used her case as an occasion to focus on the ways in which sexual identity is produced and managed as a 'seen but unnoticed,' but nonetheless institutionalized, feature of ordinary social interactions and institutional workings. He conducted the investigation with the use of tape-recorded conversations with Agnes in which the latter discussed her biography and prospects, triumphs and disasters and the hopes and fears associated with her self-imposed task of 'passing' for a woman. The result of this investigation was a profound analysis of gender considered as a produced institutional fact.

This last observation requires some additional comment. In studies of gender, it has been traditional to treat the conventional categories 'male' and 'female' as starting points from which to portray the different outlooks, life chances and activities of the sexes in relation to social structure. Despite their various differences, this analytic standpoint unites writings as divergent as Parsons's classic essays on sex roles and the family, Engels's (1968) *The Origin of the Family, Private Property and the State* and more recent feminist writings. In these studies, sexual status is treated as a 'social fact' in a fully Durkheimian sense as an 'external and constraining' phenomenon. Garfinkel, by contrast, wanted to treat sexual status as a produced and reproduced fact. It is the constitution and reproduction of the ordinary facts of gender which is the object of inquiry. The reproduced differentiation of culturally specific 'males' and 'females' is thus the terminus of his investigation rather than its starting point. This differentiation is an overwhelming fact of social structure. Its reproduction, he proposes, is the outcome of a mass of indiscernible, yet familiar, socially organized practices. It was these latter which, in 1958, Garfinkel sought to disclose with the assistance of Agnes—a person whose determination to achieve 'femininity' and whose insight into its component features greatly helped Garfinkel to distance himself from the familiar phenomena of gender and to come to view them as 'anthropologically strange.'

In reading Garfinkel's account of Agnes, it is useful to bear in mind that she was, in effect, presented with two separate, but overlapping, problems in managing her claims to be female. First, she had the problem of dealing with those who took her at 'face value' and knew nothing of her potentially discrediting male genitalia and previously masculine biography. With these persons—the majority of her associates—Agnes was preoccupied with generating and living within a female identity which was above suspicion. Second, Agnes was compelled to deal with a range of persons—her parents and relatives, the medical and psychiatric staff at UCLA and, ultimately, her boyfriend Bill—who knew about these incongruous aspects of her anatomy and biography. With this second group of persons, Agnes's task became one of insisting that, despite the incongruities, she was 'essentially' and 'all along and in the first place' a female. This task, as we shall see, was necessitated as part of her long-term campaign to secure the sex-change operation as a moral right. . . .

As part of her task of maintaining herself as a bona fide female, Agnes—like other 'intersexed' persons—had become a sensitive ethnographer of gender. Continually anxious about the successful management of her self-presentation as a woman, she had indeed become acutely aware of the ways in which sexual status can have implications for the conduct of ordinary social activities. The range and scope of these implications are so great and so easily overlooked that it is worth beginning with an initial list of some of their aspects.

There are, first of all, the self-evident problems of achieving convincingly female dress, make-up, grooming and accoutrements as an initial precondition of being taken for female. To judge from Garfinkel's description, Agnes had largely overcome these problems before she presented herself at UCLA for the first time. Then there are the problems of managing appropriately feminine comportment—the behavioural manifestations of femininity: 'sitting like a woman,' 'walking like a woman,' 'talking like a woman' and so on. These behaviours are minutely accountable. For example, Agnes recollected that her brother had complained about her carrying her books to school like a girl and had 'demonstrated to her and insisted that she carry them like a boy.' While, once again, Agnes had clearly mastered fundamental aspects of female behavioural comportment by the time she arrived at UCLA, the tasks of 'talking like a woman' continued to prove troublesome. For, it turned out, to talk like a woman required a reservoir of biographical experiences and 'knowhow'—all of which had to have been experienced and appreciated in detail from the point of view of a girl. This reservoir of detailed experiences was necessary, first, to produce appropriately feminine talk and, secondly and more generally, to serve as an accumulating series of precedents with which to manage current situations. In this context, Agnes repeatedly complained of her lack of an appropriate biography. After the change to living as a female, but before her operation, Agnes began to exchange 'gossip, and analyses of men, parties, and dating post-mortems' with roommates and wider circles of girlfriends. Here,

Garfinkel comments, 'two years of arduous female activities furnished for her a fascinating input of new experiences' which she used as resources to construct and reconstruct her own biography. In what follows, we will briefly consider some aspects of Agnes's management of her sexual identity with those who did not know her secrets and with those who did. . . .

In dealing with those who knew nothing of her 'male' anatomy and biography, Agnes's central preoccupation was to avoid the disclosure of her secrets.

> In instance after instance the situation to be managed can be described in general as one in which the attainment of commonplace goals and attendant satisfactions involved with it a risk of exposure . . . Her characteristic situation in passing was one in which she had to be prepared to choose, and frequently chose, between securing the feminine identity and accomplishing *ordinary* goals . . . Security was to be protected first. The common satisfactions were to be obtained only if the prior conditions of the secured identity could be satisfied. Risks in this direction entailed the sacrifice of the other satisfactions.

The nature and overriding extent of Agnes's sacrifices of ordinary satisfactions can be glossed by noting that, although she could drive, Agnes did not own a car because she feared the exposure of her secret while unconscious from an accident.

In order to protect her identity, Agnes engaged in extensive pre-planning and rehearsal of ordinary activities so as to minimize the risk of enforced exposure. In 'open' or 'unplannable' situations she adopted a range of procedures, which Garfinkel refers to as acting as a 'secret apprentice' and 'anticipatory following,' through which she remained inconspicuous while acquiring important feminine 'knowhow.' In all situations, Agnes was concerned not only with managing to present herself as an accountable (i.e. 'observable-reportable') female, but also with the accountability of her management strategies themselves.

Thus, in pre-planning a medical examination for a job, Agnes determined in advance that under no circumstances would she permit the examination to proceed lower than her abdomen. At the same time, she formulated the reasonable grounds ('modesty') in terms of which her refusal, if necessary, would be made accountable. These same grounds provided the basis for a 'no nudity' rule which Agnes and a girlfriend adopted in their shared apartment. Or again, in visiting the beach,

> She would go along with the crowd, reciprocating their enthusiasm for bathing, if or until it was clear that a bathroom or the bedroom of a private home would be available in which to change to her bathing suit. Public baths and automobiles were to be avoided. If the necessary facilities were not available excuses were easy to make. As she pointed out, one is permitted not to be 'in the mood' to go bathing, though to like very much to sit on the beach.

Here then, as in the other cases, there was a concern to make contingent on-the-spot decisions necessary for securing the female identity together with a concern for the secondary accountability of the management devices themselves.

A similar duality is evident in less structured contexts. In the context of gossip exchanges, post-mortems on social events or commentaries on the behaviour of other women, Agnes tended to play a passive role permitting the talk to instruct her as to proper conduct. Here, as Garfinkel comments, 'not only did she adopt the pose of passive acceptance of instructions, but she learned as well the value of passive acceptance as a desirable feminine character trait.' Or again,

> Another common set of occasions arose when she engaged in friendly conversation without having biographical or group affiliation data to swap off with her conversational partner. As Agnes said, "Can you imagine all the blank years I have to fill in? Sixteen or seventeen years of my life that I have to make up for. I have to be careful of the things that I say, just natural things that could slip out . . . I just never say anything at all about my past that in any way would make a person ask what my past life was like. I say general things. I don't say anything that could be misconstrued.' Agnes said that with men she was able to pass as an interesting conversationalist by encouraging her male partners to talk about themselves. Women partners, she said, explained the general and indefinite character of her biographical remarks, which she delivered with a friendly manner, by a combination of her niceness and modesty. 'They probably figure that I just don't like to talk about myself.'

In these remarks, once again, we find the 'dual accountability' constraints to which Agnes oriented. They surface too in other aspects of her 'secret apprenticeship.' For example, in permitting her boyfriend's mother to teach her to cook Dutch national dishes, Agnes simultaneously learned how to cook, *tout court*. This learning, secretly accomplished, was done under the accountable auspices of 'learning to cook Dutch-style.'

In reviewing Agnes's practices for passing with the ignorant, Garfinkel emphasizes the exceptional precision and detail of her observation of the particulars of ordinary social arrangements. He points to the fact that she was compelled to protect her identity across ranges of contingencies which could not be known in advance and 'in situations known with the most faltering knowledge, having marked uncertainties about the rules of practice.' In an eloquent description of Agnes's predicament, Garfinkel summarizes it as follows:

> In the conduct of her everyday affairs she had to choose among alternative courses of action even though the goal that she was trying to achieve was most frequently not clear to her prior to her having to take the actions whereby some goal might in the end have been realized. Nor had she any assurances of what the consequences of the choice might be prior to or apart from her having to deal with them. Nor were there clear rules that she could consult to decide the wisdom of the choice before the choice had to be exercised. For Agnes, stable routines of everyday life were 'disengageable' attainments assured by unremitting, momentary, situated courses of improvisation. Throughout these was the inhabiting presence of talk, so that how-

ever the action turned out, poorly or well, she would have been required to 'explain' herself, to have furnished 'good reasons' for having acted as she did.

The nature of Agnes's task in managing, constructing and reconstructing her social identity is thus perhaps well caught by the famous Neurath-Quine metaphor of being compelled to build the boat while already being out on the ocean. It was, unavoidably, a bootstrapping operation.

Above all, Garfinkel emphasizes, Agnes encountered scarcely any situations which could be treated as 'time out' from the work of passing. Always 'on parade,' Agnes was compelled at all times to secure her female identity 'by the acquisition and use of skills and capacities, the efficacious display of female appearances and performances and the mobilization of appropriate feelings and purposes.' In this context,

> the work and socially structured occasions of sexual passing were obstinately unyielding to (her) attempts to routinize the grounds of daily activities. This obstinacy points to the omnirelevance of sexual statuses to affairs of daily life as an invariant but unnoticed background in the texture of relevances that comprise the changing actual scenes of everyday life.

These problems and relevancies extended to the tasks of passing with those who, in part at least, knew of her secrets and it is to these latter that we now turn.

As we have seen, Agnes's purpose in coming to UCLA was to secure a sex-change operation. This operation was the central preoccupation of her life and, as time progressed, it also became critical for the continuation of the relationship with her boyfriend which she treated as a major emblem of her femininity. In order to obtain this operation, Agnes had to undergo a wide variety of tests—anatomical, physiological, psychological and psychiatric—the results of which would form the basis on which the decision to operate or not would be made. In this context, Agnes's task became one of insisting that she had a right to the operation regardless of the results of the technical tests by doctors and others. She treated this right as a *moral* right and advanced it on the basis of what she urged as the *natural facts* of her femininity. Her task then, in a nutshell, was to insist that she was 'all along and in the first place' a *natural* female despite the incongruous anatomical, physiological, psychological and biological facts which might be amassed against the claim, and, on this basis, to urge the surgeons to remedy her condition in the direction 'intended by nature.'

It is clear, especially with the advantage of hindsight, that the task of presenting herself to those who knew her secrets as a 'natural-female-despite-the-incongruities' presented Agnes with management problems every bit as serious as those she encountered in presenting herself as a normal female to those who did not know them.

In her dealings with the specialists, Agnes systematically emphasized all aspects of her appearance, behaviour, motivation, biography and anatomy which could be held to be bona fide 'female' in character. Simultaneously, she downgraded every aspect which could be treated as evidence of her masculinity. Thus, in addition to her very feminine physical appearance described above, Agnes presented herself as 'ultra-female' both in her descriptions of her conduct and motivation in real world situations and in her actual conversations with the medical and psychiatric specialists who, indeed, 'came to refer to her presentation of the 120 per cent female.' Throughout

> Agnes was the coy, sexually innocent, fun-loving, passive, receptive, 'young thing.' ... As a kind of dialectical counterpart to the 120 per cent female Agnes portrayed her boyfriend as a 120 percent male who, she said, when we first started to talk, and repeated through eight stressful weeks following the operation when post-operative complications had subsided and the recalcitrant vagina was finally turning out to be the thing the physicians had promised, 'wouldn't have been interested in me at all if I was abnormal.'

Closely aligned with this self-presentation was Agnes's account of her biography in which all 'evidences of a male upbringing were rigorously suppressed':

> The child Agnes of Agnes's accounts did not like to play rough games like baseball; her *'biggest'* problem was having to play boys' games; Agnes was more or less considered a sissy; Agnes was always the littlest one; Agnes played with dolls and cooked mud patty cakes for her brother; Agnes helped her mother with the household duties. Agnes doesn't remember what kinds of gifts she received from her father when she was a child.

Similarly, evidences of male sexual feelings were never avowed:

> The penis of Agnes's accounts had never been erect; she was never curious about it; it was never scrutinized by her or by others; it never entered into games with other children; it never moved 'voluntarily'; it was never a source of pleasurable feelings.

Related to this suppression of Agnes's male biography and her non-acknowledgement of male sexual feelings was her attitude to her present anatomical state. Here Agnes downgraded her incongruous anatomical features with a *moral* idiom while upgrading those anatomical features which supported her claims to be female in a *naturalistic* way. Thus Agnes's penis 'had always been an accidental appendage stuck on by a cruel trick of fate.' While,

> with genitals ruled out as essential signs of her femininity, and needing essential and natural signs of female sexuality, she counted instead the life-long desire to be female and her prominent breasts. ... Before all she counted her breasts as essential insignia. On several occasions in our conversations she expressed the relief and joy she felt when she noticed at the age of twelve that her breasts were starting to develop.

In this way, Agnes presented both her physical development and her female psychological make-up as corresponding elements of a natural feminine development. This insistence on a naturalistic orientation to her female insignia would cost her dear after the operation was finally performed:

Thus, after the operation she was a female with a 'man-made' vagina. In her anxious words, 'Nothing that is made by man can ever be as good as something that nature makes.' She and her boyfriend were agreed on this. In fact, her boyfriend who, in her accounts of him, prided himself as a harsh realist, insisted on this and taught it to her to her dismayed agreement.

It is significant, in this context, that Agnes made her final disclosures concerning the origins of her condition only after a further five years of successful life as a woman and after a leading urologist had told her 'unequivocally that her genitalia were quite beyond suspicion.'

Agnes's successful 'feminization' of her biography was not without its lacunae. Reviewing the data obtained by all the researchers on her case, it was found that, despite their best efforts, no data were available about

(1) the possibility of an exogenous source of hormones; (2) the nature and extent of collaboration that occurred between Agnes and her mother and other persons; (3) any usable evidence let alone any detailed findings dealing with her male feelings and her male biography; (4) what her penis had been used for besides urination; (5) how she sexually satisfied herself and others and most particularly her boyfriend both before and after the disclosure; (6) the nature of any homosexual feelings, fears, thoughts and activities; (7) her feelings about herself as a 'phony female.'

In presenting herself as a natural female, Agnes was concerned to avoid saying or doing anything which might permit others to include her within a category of persons—homosexuals or transvestites—who could be held to be essentially masculine. She had no interest in meeting 'other trans-sexuals' on the grounds of having nothing in common. She insisted that she had always 'steered clear of boys that acted like sissies' and 'just as normals frequently will be at a loss to understand "why a person would do that," i.e. engage in homosexual activities or dress as a member of the opposite sex, so did Agnes display the same lack of "understanding" for such behaviour.' Here, then, Agnes sought to avoid any contamination of her essential femininity which might arise from an interest in, or understanding of, or having something in common with persons whose essential identities could be held to be other than female. Her concern, once again, was to portray herself as an exclusively normal, natural female who was such 'without residue.' So scrupulous was this concern that she would not even permit verbal formulations of her desires and achievements in such terms as 'living or being treated *as a female.*' In these contexts she would insist 'not as a female, naturally.'

Finally, it will be recalled that Agnes treated her own desire to live as a female as itself evidence of her natural sexual status. In this context, she portrayed these desires as fundamental, axiomatic and inexplicable and avoided any psychological or other form of explanation of them that would relativize their status. Instead, she appealed to their life-long biographical continuity as evidence for their naturalness. Thus,

In common with normals, she treated her femininity as independent of the conditions of its occurrence and invariant to the vicissitudes of desires, agreements, random or wilful election, accident, considerations of advantage, available resources
and opportunities . . . It remained the self-same thing in essence under all imagi-
nable transformations of actual appearances, time, and circumstances. It withstood
all exigencies.

This achievement of the objectivity, transcendence and naturalness of her femininity was critical for the advancement of Agnes's moral claim to the body which
she felt she should have had all along. The nature of her claim, in turn, was sensitive to the character of sexual status as a 'natural-moral' institution, which we
will now discuss.

. . . [O]ne of Garfinkel's theoretical preoccupations is with the 'double-
edged' character of the accountable objects, events and activities which are
treated as existent within a society or collectivity. When he proposes that 'a
society's members encounter and know the moral order as perceivedly normal
courses of action' or, reversing the formulation, that the real-world features of
a society are treated by its members as 'objective, institutionalized facts, i.e.
moral facts,' he announces an interest in the fact that the ordinary members
of a society treat its undoubted, objective features as both 'normal' and
'moral.' Social facts are treated both as 'factual,' 'natural' and 'regular' and as
phenomena which the member is morally required to attend to, take into account and respect.

This interpenetration of the 'factual' and 'moral' aspects of social activities,
Garfinkel proposes, is a core feature of the ways in which society members orient
towards the world of everyday life:

They refer to this world as the 'natural facts of life' which, for members, are through
and through moral facts of life. For members not only are matters so about familiar
scenes, but they are so because it is morally right or wrong that they are so.

In sum, the everyday world as an institutionalized and institutionally provided-
for domain of accountably real objects, events and activities is, from the society
member's point of view, a 'natural-moral' world.

Sexual status is not excluded from this characterization. On the contrary, it
vividly illustrates Garfinkel's analysis of the mutual interpenetration of the 'natural' with the 'moral.' As Garfinkel pointedly puts it, if one examines sexual status from the point of view of those who can take their own normally sexed status for granted, then 'perceived environments of sexed persons are populated
with natural males, natural females, and persons who stand in moral contrast
with them, i.e. incompetent, criminal, sick and sinful.' The evidence from
Garfinkel's study of Agnes profoundly illustrates this phenomenon. It indicates
that everyone—the 'man on the street,' Agnes's relatives, the physicians on the
case and Agnes herself—treated sexual status as a matter of 'objective, institu-

tionalized facts, i.e. moral facts.' Let us briefly review each of their attitudes in turn.

Garfinkel begins by noting that the ordinary member of society finds it odd to claim that decisions about sexuality can be problematic.

> The normal finds it strange and difficult to lend credence to 'scientific' distributions of *both* male and female characteristics among persons, or a procedure for deciding sexuality which adds up lists of male and female characteristics and takes the excess as the criterion of the member's sex.

The normal, Garfinkel continues, finds these assertions strange because he (or she) cannot treat normal sexuality as a matter of technical niceties or of purely theoretical interest. Ordinary people are interested in normal sexual status as the legitimate grounds for initiating morally sanctionable and morally appropriate (i.e. accountable) courses of action. In this context, normal sexual status is treated as decided by reference to the 'sexual insignia' witnessed from birth onwards and 'decided by *nature.*' These insignia subsequently form the accountable grounds for differentiated courses of treatment to their bearers. Decisions about sexual status cannot, if social life is to proceed smoothly, and need not await authoritative zoological or psychiatric determination.

The fact that this 'natural' distribution of sexual status is, simultaneously, a 'moral' distribution is revealed by ordinary reactions to persons who perceivedly deviate from the distribution. These reactions commonly take the form of moral retribution. The reactions of Agnes's family to her various changes illustrate this phenomenon and its vicissitudes. After her initial assumption of female status, Agnes reported, her cousin's attitude changed from one which was favourable to Agnes to one of strong disapproval. Other family members displayed 'open hostility' and 'consternation and severe disapproval.' Thus, although philosophers have extensively criticized the 'naturalistic fallacy' (that is, reasoning from what is the case to what ought to be the case), Agnes's family members repeatedly employed this device to assert the grounds (Agnes's upbringing as a boy) on which she should mend her ways.

However, if the employment of the 'naturalistic fallacy' worked against Agnes before the operation, it worked in her favour afterwards when family members exhibited 'relieved acceptance and treatment of her as a "real female after all."' In this context, Garfinkel comments:

> [A]lthough the vagina was man-made it *was* a case of the real thing since it was what she was now seen to have been entitled to all along. Both the aunt and the mother were strongly impressed by the fact that the operation had been done at all 'in this country.' That the physicians at the UCLA Medical Centre by their actions reconstructed and validated Agnes's claim to her status as a natural female needs, of course, to be stressed.

Turning now to the physicians, it is again clear that, in making the decision to operate or not, they also sought a determination of Agnes's sexual status and thus similarly employed an 'is-to-ought' line of reasoning to support their decision. This use of what Agnes 'naturally was' as grounds to support the line of treatment decided upon is vividly displayed in Stoller's account of Agnes's case. In that part of his account reproduced by Garfinkel, Stoller goes to considerable lengths to show the grounds on which he had determined that Agnes did not desire the operation as a matter of wilful election and, in particular, that her condition was not the product of ingesting female hormones (estrogens). He concludes the discussion by accounting for the decision to operate as follows: 'Not being considered a transsexual, her genitalia were surgically transformed so that she now had the penis and testes removed and an artificial vagina constructed from the skin of the penis.' The critical phrase in this passage is the first: 'not being considered a transsexual.' It expresses the belief of Stoller and his colleagues that Agnes was 'fundamentally' female and did not simply desire to be female as a matter of deliberate choice. The phrase indicates that, despite the technical expertise of Stoller and his colleagues, the fundamental grounds in terms of which he presented their decision to an audience of medical professionals were the same 'natural-moral' grounds which were invoked as the basis of their treatments of Agnes by all of her 'significant others.'

Thus in her dealings with her entire world of associates—family, friends, boyfriend, medical specialists, psychiatrists and Garfinkel himself—Agnes was presented with one consuming and overriding problem: the presentation of herself as someone who was naturally, all along and in the first place a bona fide female. The task had to be carried forward across every possible exigency, across every possible or actual state of knowledge possessed individually or severally by these others. And it had to be managed as a condition, not only of acquiring the 'sexual insignia' which would place her beyond suspicion with those who would meet her in the future, but also as a condition of convincing those who, fully knowing her past, could nonetheless be persuaded that she was, finally, what she had claimed to be all along. To meet these tasks, Agnes had only one asset: her skills as a 'practical methodologist' acquired as a student of normal sexuality:

> Her studies armed her with knowledge of how the organized features of ordinary settings are used by members as procedures for making appearances-of-sexuality-as-usual decidable as a matter of course. The scrutiny that she paid to appearances; her concerns for adequate motivation, relevance, evidence and demonstration; her sensitivity to devices of talk; her skill in detecting and managing 'tests' were attained as part of her mastery of trivial but necessary social tasks, to secure ordinary rights to live. Agnes was self-consciously equipped to teach normals how normals make sexuality happen in commonplace settings as an obvious, familiar, recognizable, natural, and serious matter of fact. Her specialty consisted of treating the 'natural facts of life' of socially recognized, socially managed sexuality as a managed production so as to be making these facts of life true, relevant, demonstrable, testable, countable, and available to inventory, cursory representation, anecdote,

enumeration, or professional psychological assessment; in short, so as unavoidably in concert with others to be making these facts of life visible and reportable—accountable—for all practical purposes.

To summarize: Agnes subscribed to the 'natural-moral' order of sexual status within which normal sexual status is treated as a 'natural fact' while aberrations from the norm are treated as morally accountable. She subscribed to the objective reality of normal sexual status, despite her knowledge of its intricate management in daily life, both as a condition of maintaining her own identity and as a condition of achieving her desired objective—the operation. In this regard, as Garfinkel remarks, Agnes was no revolutionary. Rather, in deploying her considerable methodological talents, Agnes sought in every way to conform with (and thus reproduce) the 'natural-moral' institutional order in which she so dearly wished to participate—as a normal, natural female. . . .

The variety of Agnes's management strategies and procedures, the resistance of ordinary social occasions to her attempts to routinize her daily life as a female and the fact that almost every occasion could somehow take on the features of a "character and fitness" test' suggest that, in almost any occasion of social life, institutionalized features of sexual status are being produced and reproduced by 'normally sexed' males and females. Agnes's case further suggests that, while institutionalized sexuality is being produced and reproduced in this way as a supremely natural 'matter of fact,' its reproduction is simultaneously supported by a massive 'repair machinery' of moral accountability which is brought to bear in cases of discrepancy or deviance. To make these—potentially relativizing—observations on the socially organized character of accountable sexuality is not to deny its objectivity or facticity. On the contrary, it is to begin to gain some appreciation of what its objectivity and facticity consist of. As Garfinkel summarizes it:

> Agnes's methodological practices are our sources of authority for the finding, and recommended study policy, that normally sexed persons are cultural events in societies whose character as visible orders of practical activities consist of members' recognition and production practices. We learned from Agnes, who treated sexed persons as cultural events that members make happen, that members' practices alone produce the observable-tellable normal sexuality of persons, and do so only, entirely, exclusively in actual, singular, particular occasions through actual witnessed displays of common talk and conduct. . . . The inordinate stresses in Agnes's life were part and parcel of the concerted practices with normals, whereby the 'normal, natural female' as a moral thing to be and a moral way to feel and act was made to be happening, in demonstrable evidence, for all practical purposes.

This reference to the stresses which Agnes experienced, however, raises a core problem in Agnes's management of 'normality.' While normals can routinize their management and detection of displays of 'normally sexed' conduct so that the latter become a 'seen but unnoticed' background to the texture of commonplace events, Agnes's secrets were such that she could not lose sight of what, for normals, is so massively invisible:

> For Agnes, in contrast to normals, the commonplace recognition of normal sexuality as a 'case of the real thing' consisted of a serious, situated, and prevailing accomplishment . . . Her anguish and triumphs resided in the observability, which was particular to her and uncommunicable, of the steps whereby the society hides from its members its activities of organization and thus leads them to see its features as determinate and independent objects. For Agnes the observably normally sexed person *consisted* of inexorable, organizationally located work that provided the way that such objects arise.

In this context, Garfinkel remarks that Agnes found psychological and sociological theories of the 'judgemental dope' variety flattering. For these approaches 'theorized out of recognition' her excruciating perception of the work of managing sexual status. They thus 'naturalized' (in the way that ordinary society members 'naturalize') the sexual status which she longed to treat as just that—*natural*. Within these theories, sexual status is unproblematically treated as ascribed and internalized. Whereas what Agnes knew without doubt was that this 'ascribed' status is through and through *achieved* as the product of unnoticed, yet unremitting, work.

Reflecting for a moment on the Agnes study, it is surprising to realize the extent to which gender differentiation consists of a filigree of small-scale, socially organized behaviours which are unceasingly iterated. Together these—individually insignificant—behaviours interlock to constitute the great public institution of gender as a morally-organized-as-natural fact of life. This institution is comparatively resistant to change. To adapt Wittgenstein's famous analogy, the social construction of gender from a mass of individual social practices resembles the spinning of a thread in which fibre is spun on fibre. And, as Wittgenstein points out, 'the strength of the thread does not reside in the fact that some one fibre runs through its whole length, but in the overlapping of many fibres.' But if gender manifests itself as a density of minutiae, the latter are nonetheless stabilized both individually and collectively by the apparatus of moral accountability which we have repeatedly seen in action. In this context it is perhaps ironic that Freud could not trust the facts of culture sufficiently to base his account of the differentiation between the sexes on cultural mechanisms. For Freud, gender differentiation is ultimately based on a single slender thread: the psychological responses of males and females to the facts of anatomy. For Garfinkel, by contrast, the institution of gender appears as a densely woven fabric of morally accountable cultural practices which are throughout both accountable, and accountably treated, as natural. . . .

. . . Garfinkel bridges the gap between cognition and action by stressing that action is through and through a *temporal* affair which is *reflexively accountable*. Each actor inhabits a setting of action which is unfolding on a moment-by-moment basis in and as a temporal succession of actions. Each 'next' action, in occurring in temporal juxtaposition to the sequence of actions comprising a setting, constitutes both an 'incarnate' commentary on and an intervention in the setting in which it occurs. Actions-as-constitutive-of-their-settings and settings-as-constitutive-of-their-actions are two halves of a simultaneous equation which the actors are continually solving through a mass of *methodic* procedures. It is through these methods, brought to bear on a temporal succession of actions, that actors are continually able to establish the 'state of play' between them, to grasp the nature of the circumstances in which they are currently placed and, not least, to assess the moral character, dispositions and identities of those with whom they are dealing.

In short, it is through the application of methods of practical reasoning to a temporal succession of activities that all aspects of social action are rendered accountable. . . .

. . . Compliance with the normative requirements of a setting may thus be most realistically treated not as the unreflecting product of the prior internalization of norms, but as contingent upon a reflexive awareness of how alternative courses of action will be analysed and interpreted. This treatment has the important consequence that the constraining power of normative conventions can be construed as, at most, a 'tendency to bind' rather than as a matter of the normative determination of action. Additionally, this constraining power can be treated as variously and varyingly infused with considerations of self-presentation and self-interest.

THE LAST QUARTER CENTURY

PART FOUR

THE LAST QUARTER CENTURY

~

CHAPTER FOURTEEN

Arlie Russell Hochschild
on the Management of Emotion

~ Introduction ~

Arlie Russell Hochschild (1940–) was born in Boston, Massachusetts, received her B. A. degree at Swarthmore College in 1962, and completed her Ph.D. at the University of California, Berkeley, in 1969. After teaching at the University of California, Santa Cruz, Hochschild returned to Berkeley. She is presently professor of sociology at Berkeley and co-director of the Center for Working Families there. Her publications include *The Unexpected Community* (1978); *The Managed Heart* (1983), excerpts from which will be the reading for this chapter; *The Second Shift* (1989); and *The Time Bind* (1997).

In 1983 *The Managed Heart* won the Charles Cooley Award, was one of the notable books of the year in the social sciences selected by *New York Times Book Review*, and received a C. Wright Mills Award, Honorary Mention. *The Managed Heart* offers an insightful discussion of the commercialization of personal feelings in interaction.

Hochschild observes that feelings are not merely expressions of one's inner experience. The manifestation of feelings and our self-reading of what we feel often coincide with social circumstances. In fact, we tend to manage our feelings as they become manifest, and in the process we contribute to the type of emotional experience we have. Hochschild states as examples, "The party guest summons up a gaiety owed to the host, the mourner summons up a proper sadness for a funeral. Each offers up feeling as a momentary contribution to the collective good." An emotion is an internal response to a stimulus, and our reading or interpreting of this internal response shapes the expression of it. As we become aware of our feelings, we work to manage them, and in the process, "we contribute to the creation of [emotion]" (18).

The expression of emotion is typically managed according to "feeling rules." These rules guide the expression and intensity of emotional display. For example, when someone tells a joke that is not particularly funny at a social gathering, the participants are still likely to laugh, but they will not laugh uproariously; they will not overdo it. If people were to laugh and laugh at such a joke, then they would be "overpaying" in their emotion management. Conversely, if they were to remain stone-faced in such a situation, then they would be "underpaying" in their emotion management. The balancing act of emotional exchange plays an important role in guiding social interaction.

Hochschild uses the term "transmutation" to express the increasing practices of socially engineering emotional expression and manipulating feeling rules for such utilitarian purposes as maximizing financial gain. Hochschild explains in the selection you will read, "By the grand phrase 'transmutation of an emotional system' I mean to convey what it is that we do privately, often unconsciously, to feelings that nowadays often fall under the sway of large organizations, social engineering, and the profit motive" (19). In everyday interactions we manage feelings in order to express an appropriate response or in order to try to get from another a desired response. Hochschild inquires what the consequences are for participants and on a culture of intentionally manipulating feeling rules for a particular effect. This inquiry is important because, as Hochschild points out, "managing feeling is an art fundamental to civilized living" (21). Managing feeling permits the flow of social interaction to continue; however, when feeling becomes an instrument or skill that is required eight hours a day in order to do one's job—what she calls emotion work—the result may be, for example, a sense of numbness in response to one's own and others' expressions of feeling, or the disengagement of one's sense of self from the world, particularly the commercial world, and a strong desire to protect and fortify this disengaged self as an inner "real self."

In everyday relations of relatively equal status, people will "overpay" or "underpay" in order to maintain some level of equitable emotional reciprocity. However, when interacting parties are of unequal status, the party with less status is expected to engage in more emotion work. Moreover, in those occupying lower-status positions, commercial or institutional priorities may foster the necessity of not merely displaying a particular emotion, but suggesting techniques that change how persons actually feel (what Hochschild refers to as deep acting) in order to make a display seem more spontaneous. Hochschild points out that emotion work is required more often in vocations involving interactions with people as opposed to working with things, and that more women than men engage in such work. A key point here is that persons in lower-status positions who engage in emotion work are viewed socially as persons naturally skilled at handling emotional exchanges. Also, an important feature separating lower- and higher-status positions is the socially perceived lack of the necessity for those in higher status positions to engage in emotion work. In terms of gender and occupation, Hochschild observes:

> The deferential behavior of servants and women—the encouraging smiles, the attentive listening, the appreciative laughter, the comments of affirmation, admiration, or concern—comes to seem normal, even built into personality rather than inherent in the kinds of exchange that lower-status people commonly enter into. Yet the absence of smiling, of appreciative laughter, of statements of admiration or concern are thought attractive when understood as an expression of machismo. (84–85)

The transmutation of emotion is demonstrated empirically by Hochschild's research into the policies and practices of Delta Airlines. Hochschild states that she chose to study Delta for the following reasons: it emphasizes service more than other airlines; its in-flight training program is highly regarded in the industry; its service is highly ranked; and at the time of the study, Delta flight attendants had no union, and so company demands could be higher than worker demands. The rationale here is that by focusing on a nonunion company with a highly regarded training program where the work emphasizes service, one can more readily examine the training and management of feeling. In Hochschild's observations, besides the emotions that flight attendants have to suppress in response to customers' flirtations and propositioning (brought about, in part, from company marketing), flight attendants are asked by the company to imagine the airplane cabin as their home and to think of the passengers as guests in their "living room." In this way, according to Hochschild, "[t]he company brilliantly extends and uses its workers' basic human empathy, all the while maintaining that it is not interfering in their 'personal lives'" (106). In reading this material, two important social ironies arise: (1) as the value of individual expression increases, workers actually find the routinization of work extending more into their sense of self; and, (2) work is typically referred to as the "real world," yet work seems to increasingly emphasize fantasy for both customers and workers. It seems as though as the worker's "real self" retreats into a protected inner domain, the world of work (which that real self depends upon for a livelihood) becomes subject to, with participation from workers, subtler forms of manipulation or fantasy. As Hochschild points out, some workers not only maintain an inner "real self," but acquire a sense of distinct selves for given situations. Hence, one may have a "real self" and a "work self." As a means of coming to terms with working conditions, the whole self becomes divided as different selves. This division may bring forth cynicism and issues of self-esteem, but if such issues do arise, they are viewed by workers as issues needing *personal* rather than social adjustments.

As noted above, lower-status persons engage in more emotion work than those in higher-status positions. Those occupying lower-status positions have less power, and according to Hochschld, those occupying such positions will seek "secondary gains" from emotion work as a form of compensation. Hochschild argues, "Within the traditional female subculture, subordination at close quarters is understood, especially in adolescence, as a 'fact of life.' Women accommodate, then, but not passively. They actively adapt feeling to a need or a purpose at hand, and they do it so that it *seems* to express a passive state of agreement" (167). Such emotion work is interpreted by those in higher-status positions as natural, and therefore, they do not see it as labor. A particularly good example of this sort of exchange is Hochschild's observation in our reading: "The world turns to women for mothering, and this fact silently attaches itself to many a job description" (170). The emotion work of mothering tends to be interpreted as the natural gift of interpersonal nurturing. And since it is not work, it is not a skill that may be cultivated and rewarded in any other way than emotional acknowledgement by those occupying higher-status positions. Those who engage in such emotion work may then strive to protect "certain limited domains" in order to achieve a sense of overall equality, and nurturing itself goes unnoticed as an essential aspect of all forms of interpersonal exchange, including the interpersonal exchanges involved in getting work done. As long as this emotion work is not perceived as work, those who engage in it will be perceived as natural nurturers, and such labeling will undermine the possibility of redefining what constitutes power in society. As a result, the same job will be different for a woman than for a man. Since women are considered to be natural nurturers, they will be the ones whom customers seek for emotional support as well as for dumping on emotionally. Not only is such emotion work expected less from male workers, but because of the inequities associated with status position, meaningful labor, and gender, male workers are viewed by customers with greater authority even in situations where men and women have equal status. Hochschild demonstrates how such status differences are reinforced in social interactions:

> [B]oth male and female workers adapted to this fictional redistribution of authority. Both, in different ways, made it more real. Male flight attendants tended to react to passengers *as if they had more authority* than they really did. This made them less tolerant of abuse and firmer in handling it. They conveyed the message that *as authorities* they expected compliance. . . . Female flight attendants, on the other hand, assuming that passengers would honor their authority less, used more tactful and deferential means of handling abuse. . . . And they were less successful in preventing the escalation of abuse. (178)

Hochschild suggests that the way to eliminate these inequities is to eliminate the connection between gender and status. However, in a world where "success" is defined largely in economic terms and where the way to achieve such success is by any means necessary (including the exploitation of states or traits that define personal identity), inequities may not disappear but rather become submerged into subtler forms of expression and exchange. Despite contemporary insights based upon an accumulated body of literature showing the social ills associated with reinforcing inequities in social systems, Hochschild's research stands as a good reason for persons to consider *once again* the type of social relations they reinforce and perpetuate in social interaction.

⌒ The Managed Heart ⌒

Private Life

We feel. But what is a feeling? I would define feeling, like emotion, as a sense, like the sense of hearing or sight. In a general way, we experience it when bodily sensations are joined with what we see or imagine. Like the sense of hearing, emotion communicates information. It has, as Freud said of anxiety, a "signal function." From feeling we discover our own viewpoint on the world.

We often say that we *try* to feel. But how can we do this? Feelings, I suggest, are not stored "inside" us, and they are not independent of acts of management. Both the act of "getting in touch with" feeling and the act of "trying to" feel may become part of the process that makes the thing we get in touch with, or the thing we manage, *into* a feeling or emotion. In managing feeling, we contribute to the creation of it.

If this is so, what we think of as intrinsic to feeling or emotion may have always been shaped to social form and put to civic use. Consider what happens when young men roused to anger go willingly to war, or when followers rally enthusiastically around their king, or mullah, or football team. Private social life may always have called for the management of feeling. The party guest summons up a gaiety owed to the host, the mourner summons up a proper sadness for a funeral. Each offers up feeling as a momentary contribution to the collective good. In the absence of an English-language name for feelings-as-contribution-to-the-group (which the more group-centered Hopi culture called *arofa*), I shall offer the concept of a gift exchange. Muted anger, conjured gratitude, and suppressed envy are offerings back and forth from parent to child, wife to husband, friend to friend, and lover to lover. I shall try to illustrate the intricate designs of these offerings, to point out their shapes, and to study how they are made and exchanged.

What gives social pattern to our acts of emotion management? I believe that when we try to feel, we apply latent feeling rules. . . . We say, "I shouldn't feel so angry at what she did," or "given our agreement, I have no right to feel jealous." Acts of emotion management are not simply private acts; they are used in exchanges under the guidance of feeling rules. Feeling rules are standards used in emotional conversation to determine what is rightly owed and owing in the currency of feeling. Through them, we tell what is "due" in each relation, each role. We pay tribute to each other in the currency of the managing act. In interaction we pay, overpay, underpay, play with paying, acknowledge our dues, pretend to pay, or acknowledge what is emotionally due another person. In these ways . . . we make our try at sincere civility.

Because the distribution of power and authority is unequal in some of the relations of private life, the managing acts can also be unequal. The myriad momentary acts of management compose part of what we summarize in the terms *relation* and *role*. Like the tiny dots of a Seurat painting, the microacts of emotion management compose, through repetition and change over time, a movement of form. Some forms express inequality, others equality.

Now what happens when the managing of emotion comes to be sold as labor? What happens when feeling rules, like rules of behavioral display, are established not through private negotiation but by company manuals? What happens when social exchanges are not, as they are in private life, subject to change or termination but ritually sealed and almost inescapable?

What happens when the emotional display that one person owes another reflects a certain inherent inequality? The airline passenger may choose not to smile, but the flight attendant is obliged not only to smile but to try to work up some warmth behind it. What happens, in other words, when there is a *transmutation* of the private ways we use feeling?

One sometimes needs a grand word to point out a coherent pattern between occurrences that would otherwise seem totally unconnected. My word is "transmutation." When I speak of the transmutation of an emotional system, I mean to point out a link between a private act, such as attempting to enjoy a party, and a public act, such as summoning up good feeling for a customer. I mean to expose the relation between the private act of trying to dampen liking for a person—which overcommitted lovers sometimes attempt—and the public act of a bill collector who suppresses empathy for a debtor. By the grand phrase "transmutation of an emotional system" I mean to convey what it is that we do privately, often unconsciously, to feelings that nowadays often fall under the sway of large organizations, social engineering, and the profit motive.

Trying to feel what one wants, expects, or thinks one ought to feel is probably no newer than emotion itself. Conforming to or deviating from feeling rules is also hardly new. In organized society, rules have probably never been applied only to observable behavior. "Crimes of the heart" have long been recognized because proscriptions have long guarded the "preactions" of the heart; the Bible says not to covet your neighbor's wife, not simply to avoid acting on that feeling. What is new in our time is an increasingly prevalent *instrumental stance* toward our native capacity to play, wittingly and actively, upon a range of feelings for a private purpose and the way in which that stance is engineered and administered by large organizations.

This transmutation of the private use of feeling affects the two sexes and the various social classes in distinctly different ways. . . . As a matter of tradition, emotion management has been better understood and more often used by women as one of the offerings they trade for economic support. Especially among dependent women of the middle and upper classes, women have the job (or think they ought to) of creating the emotional tone of social encounters: expressing joy at the Christmas presents others open, creating the sense of surprise at birthdays, or displaying alarm at the mouse in the kitchen. Gender is not the only determinant of skill in such managed expression and in the emotion work needed to do it well. But men who do this work well have slightly less in common with other men than women who do it well have with other women. When the "womanly" art of living up to *private* emotional conventions goes public, it attaches itself to a different profit-and-loss statement.

Similarly, emotional labor affects the various social classes differently. If it is women, members of the less advantaged gender, who specialize in emotional labor, it is the middle and upper reaches of the class system that seem to call most for it. And parents who do emotional labor on the job will convey the importance of emotion management to their children and will prepare them to learn the skills they will probably need for the jobs they will probably get.

In general, lower-class and working-class people tend to work more with things, and middle-class and upper-class people tend to work more with people. More working women than men deal with people as a job. Thus, there are both gender patterns and class patterns to the civic and commercial use of human feeling. That is the social point.

But there is a personal point, too. There is a cost to emotion work: it affects the degree to which we listen to feeling and sometimes our very capacity to feel. Managing feeling is an art fundamental to civilized living, and I assume that in broad terms the cost is usually worth the fundamental benefit. Freud, in *Civilization and Its Discontents*, argued analogously about the sexual instinct: enjoyable as that instinct is, we are wise in the long run to give up some gratification of it. But when the transmutation of the private use of feeling is successfully accomplished—when we succeed in lending our feelings to the organizational engineers of worker-customer relations—we may pay a cost in how we hear our feelings and a cost in what, for better or worse, they tell us about ourselves. When a speed-up of the human assembly line makes "genuine" personal service harder to deliver, the worker may withdraw emotional labor and offer instead a thin crust of display. Then the cost shifts: the penalty becomes a sense of being phony or insincere. In short, when the transmutation works, the worker risks losing the signal function of feeling. When it does not work, the risk is losing the signal function of display. . . .

One day at Delta's Stewardess Training Center an instructor scanned the twenty-five faces readied for her annual Self-Awareness Class set up by the company in tandem with a refresher course in emergency procedures required by the Federal Aviation Administration. She began: "This is a class on thought processes, actions, and feelings. I believe in it. I have to believe in it, or I couldn't get up here in front of you and be enthusiastic." What she meant was this: "Being a sincere person, I couldn't say one thing to you and believe in another. Take the fact of my sincerity and enthusiasm as testimony to the value of the techniques of emotion management that I'm going to talk about."

Yet, as it became clear, it was precisely by such techniques of emotion management that sincerity itself was achieved. And so, through this hall of mirrors, students were introduced to a topic scarcely mentioned in Initial Training but central to Recurrent Training: stress and one of its main causes—anger at obnoxious passengers.

"What happens," the instructor asked the class, in the manner of a Southern Baptist minister inviting a response from the congregation, "when you become angry?" Answers: Your body becomes tense. Your heart races. You breathe more quickly and get less oxygen. Your adrenalin gets higher.

"What do you do when you get angry?" Answers: Cuss. Want to hit a passenger. Yell in a bucket. Cry. Eat. Smoke a cigarette. Talk to myself. Since all but the last two responses carry a risk of offending passengers and thus losing sales, the discussion was directed to ways that an obnoxious person could be reconceived in an honest but useful way. The passenger demanding constant attention could be conceived as a "victim of fear of flying." A drunk could be reconceived as "just like a child." It was explained why a worker angered by a passenger would do better to avoid seeking sympathy from co-workers.

"How," the instructor asked the class, "do you alleviate anger at an irate?" (An "irate," a noun born of experience, is an angry person.) Answering her own question, she went on:

> I pretend something traumatic has happened in their lives. Once I had an irate that was complaining about me, cursing at me, threatening to get my name and report me to the company. I later found out his son had just died. Now when I meet an irate I think of that man. If you think about the *other* person and why they're so upset, you've taken attention off of yourself and your own frustration. And you won't feel so angry.

If anger erupts despite these preventive tactics, then deep breathing, talking to yourself, reminding yourself that "you don't have to go home with him" were offered as ways to manage emotion. Using these, the worker becomes less prone to cuss, hit, cry, or smoke.

The instructor did not focus on what might have *caused* the worker's anger. When this did come up, the book was opened to the mildest of examples (such as a passenger saying, "Come here, girl!"). Rather, the focus was kept on the worker's response and on ways to prevent an angry response through "anger-desensitization.". . .

Relevant to both trainer and student is the proposition that emotion, like seeing and hearing, is a way of knowing about the world. It is a way of testing reality. As Freud pointed out in *Inhibitions, Symptoms, and Anxiety* (1926), anxiety has a signal function. It signals danger from inside, as when we fear an overload of rage, or from outside, as when an insult threatens to humiliate us beyond easy endurance.

Actually, every emotion has a signal function. Not every emotion signals danger. But every emotion does signal the "me" I put into seeing "you." It signals the often unconscious perspective we apply when we go about seeing. Feeling signals that inner perspective. Thus, to suggest helpful techniques for changing feeling—in the service of avoiding stress on the worker and making life pleasanter for the passenger—is to intervene in the signal function of feeling. . . .

The word *objective*, according to the *Random House Dictionary*, means "free from personal feelings." Yet ironically, we need feeling in order to reflect on the external or "objective" world. Taking feelings into account as clues and then correcting for them may be our best shot at objectivity. Like hearing or seeing, feeling provides a useful set of clues in figuring out what is real. A show of feeling by someone else is interesting to us precisely because it may reflect a buried perspective and may offer a clue as to how that person may act. . . .

. . . In jobs that require dealing with the public, employers are wise to want workers to be sincere, to go well beyond the smile that's "just painted on." Gregg Snazelle, who directed all the commercials for Toyota's fall 1980 campaign, teaches his advertising students in the first class "to always be honest." Behind the most effective display is the feeling that fits it, and that feeling can be managed.

As workers, the more seriously social engineering affects our behavior and our feelings, the more intensely we must address a new ambiguity about who is directing them (is this me or the company talking?). As customers, the greater our awareness of social engineering, the more effort we put into distinguishing between gestures of real personal feeling and gestures of company policy. We have a practical knowledge of the commercial takeover of the signal function of feeling. In a routine way, we make up for it; at either end, as worker or customer, we try to correct for the social engineering of feeling. We mentally subtract feeling with commercial purpose to it from the total pattern of display that we sense to be sincerely felt. In interpreting a smile, we try to take out what social engineering put in, pocketing only what seems meant just for us. We say, "It's her job to be friendly," or "They have to believe in their product like that in order to sell it."

In the end, it seems, we make up an idea of our "real self," an inner jewel that remains our unique possession no matter whose billboard is on our back or whose smile is on our face. We push this "real self" further inside, making it more inaccessible. Subtracting credibility from the parts of our emotional machinery that are in commercial hands, we turn to what is left to find out who we "really are." And around the surface of our human character, where once we were naked, we don a cloak to protect us against the commercial elements. . . .

We all do a certain amount of acting. But we may act in two ways. In the first way, we try to change how we outwardly appear. As it is for the people observed by Erving Goffman, the action is in the body language, the put-on sneer, the posed shrug, the controlled sigh. This is surface acting. The other way is deep acting. Here, display is a natural result of working on feeling; the actor does not try to *seem* happy or sad but rather expresses spontaneously, as the Russian director Constantin Stanislavski urged, a real feeling that has been self-induced. . . .

In our daily lives, offstage as it were, we also develop feeling for the parts we play; and along with the workaday props of the kitchen table or office restroom mirror we also use deep acting, emotion memory, and the sense of "as if this were true" in the course of trying to feel what we sense we ought to feel or want to feel. Usually we give this little thought, and we don't name the momentary acts involved. Only when our feeling does not fit the situation, and when we sense this as a problem, do we turn our attention to the inward, imagined mirror, and ask whether we are or should be acting.

Consider, for example, the reaction of this young man to the unexpected news that a close friend had suffered a mental breakdown:

I was shocked, yet for some reason I didn't think my emotions accurately reflected the bad news. My roommate appeared much more shaken than I did. *I thought that I should be more upset by the news than I was.* Thinking about this conflict I realized that one reason for my emotional state might have been the spatial distance separating me from my friend, who was in the hospital hundreds of miles away. I then tried to focus on his state . . . and began to picture my friend as I thought he then existed.

Sensing himself to be less affected than he should be, he tried to visualize his friend—perhaps in gray pajamas, being led by impassive attendants to the electric-shock room. After bringing such a vivid picture to mind, he might have gone on to recall smaller private breakdowns in his own life and thereby evoked feelings of sorrow and empathy. Without at all thinking of this as acting, in complete privacy, without audience or stage, the young man can pay, in the currency of deep acting, his emotional respects to a friend.

Sometimes we try to stir up a feeling we wish we had, and at other times we try to block or weaken a feeling we wish we did not have. Consider this young woman's report of her attempt to keep feelings of love in check.

Last summer I was going with a guy often, and I began to feel very strongly about him. I knew, though, that he had broken up with a girl a year ago because she had gotten too serious about him, so I was afraid to show any emotion. I also was afraid of being hurt, so I attempted to change my feelings. *I talked myself into not caring about him* . . . but I must admit it didn't work for long. To sustain this feeling I had to *invent bad things about him and concentrate on them* or continue to tell myself he didn't care. It was a hardening of emotions, I'd say. It took a lot of work and was unpleasant because I had to concentrate on anything I could find that was irritating about him.

In this struggle she hit upon some techniques of deep acting. "To invent bad things about him and concentrate on them" is to make up a world she could honestly respond to. She could tell herself, "If he is self-absorbed, then he is unlovable, and *if* he is unlovable, which at the moment I believe, then I don't love him.". . .

In the theater, the illusion that the actor creates is recognized beforehand as an illusion by actor and audience alike. But in real life we more often participate in the illusion. We take it into ourselves, where it struggles against the sense we ordinarily make of things. In life, illusions are subtle, changeable, and hard to define with certainty, and they matter far more to our sanity.

The other side of the matter is to live with a dropped illusion and yet want to sustain it. Once an illusion is clearly defined as an illusion, it becomes a lie. The work of sustaining it then becomes redefined as lying to oneself so that one becomes self-stigmatized as a liar. This dilemma was described by a desperate wife and mother of two:

I am desperately trying to change my feelings of being trapped [in marriage] into feelings of wanting to remain with my husband voluntarily. Sometimes I think I'm succeeding—sometimes I know I haven't. *It means I have to lie to myself and know I am lying.* It means I don't like myself very much. It also makes me wonder whether or not I'm a bit of a masochist. I feel responsible for the children's future and for my husband's, and there's the old self-sacrificer syndrome. I know what I'm doing. I just don't know how long I can hold out. . . .

. . . In everyday life there is also illusion, but how to define it is chronically unclear; the matter needs constant attention, continual questioning and testing. In acting, the illusion starts out as an illusion. In everyday life, that definition is always a possibility and never quite a certainty. On stage, the illusion leaves as it came, with the curtain. Off stage, the curtains close, too, but not at our bidding, not when we expect, and often to our dismay. On stage, illusion is a virtue. But in real life, the lie to oneself is a sign of human weakness, of bad faith. . . .

The professional actress has a modest say over how the stage is assembled, the props selected, and the other characters positioned, as well as a say over her own presence in the play. This is also true in private life. In both cases the person is the *locus* of the acting process.

But something more operates when institutions are involved, for within institutions various elements of acting are taken away from the individual and replaced by institutional mechanisms. The locus of acting, of emotion management, moves up to the level of the institution. Many people and objects, arranged according to institutional rule and custom, together accomplish the act. Companies, prisons, schools, churches—institutions of virtually any sort—assume some of the functions of a director and alter the relation of actor to director. Officials in institutions believe they have done things right when they have established illusions that foster the desired feelings in workers, when they have placed parameters around a worker's emotion memories, a worker's use of the *as if*. It is not that workers are allowed to see and think as they like and required only to show feeling (surface acting) in institutionally approved ways. The matter would be simpler and less alarming if it stopped there. But it doesn't. Some institutions have become very sophisticated in the techniques of deep acting; they suggest how to imagine and thus how to feel. . . .

All of us try to feel, and pretend to feel, but we seldom do so alone. Most often we do it when we exchange gestures or signs of feeling with others. . . .

. . . [D]isplay and emotion work are not matters of chance. They come into play, back and forth. They come to mean payment or nonpayment of latent dues. "Inappropriate emotion" may be construed as a nonpayment or mispayment of what is due, and indication that we are not seeing things in the right light. The Bar Mitzvah not enjoyed, the Christmas that raises anger, the party that proves boring, the funeral that seems meaningless, the sexual contact that feels lonely, times when a mother is not loved or a friend not missed—all these are moments without their appropriate feeling, moments of unmade bows from the heart.

There are many things people do for each other to maintain reciprocity. . . .
The exchange between people of equal status in a stable relationship is normally even. . . .

However, when one person has higher status than another, it becomes acceptable to both parties for the bottom dog to contribute more. Indeed, to have higher status is to have a stronger claim to rewards, including emotional rewards. It is also to have greater access to the means of enforcing claims. The deferential behavior of servants and women—the encouraging smiles, the attentive listening, the appreciative laughter, the comments of affirmation, admiration, or concern—comes to seem normal, even built into personality rather than inherent in the kinds of exchange that low-status people commonly enter into. Yet the absence of smiling, of appreciative laughter, of statements of admiration or concern are thought attractive when understood as an expression of machismo. . . .

In private life, we are free to question the going rate of exchange and free to negotiate a new one. If we are not satisfied, we can leave; many friendships and marriages die of inequality. But in the public world of work, it is often part of an individual's job to accept uneven exchanges, to be treated with disrespect or anger by a client, all the while closeting into fantasy the anger one would like to respond with. Where the customer is king, unequal exchanges are normal, and from the beginning customer and client assume different rights to feeling and display. The ledger is supposedly evened by a wage. . . .

Public Life

The more important service becomes as an arena for competition between airlines, the more workers are asked to do public relations work to promote sales. . . .

Because airline ads raise expectations, they subtly rewrite job descriptions and redefine roles. They promise on-time service, even though planes are late from 10 to 50 percent of the time, industrywide. Their pictures of half-empty planes promise space and leisurely service, which are seldom available (and certainly not desired by the company). They promise service from happy workers, even though the industry speedup has reduced job satisfaction. By creating a discrepancy between promise and fact, they force workers in all capacities to cope with the disappointed expectations of customers.

The ads promise service that is "human" and personal. The omnipresent smile suggests, first of all, that the flight attendant is friendly, helpful, and open to requests. But when words are added, the smile can be sexualized, as in "We really move our tails for you to make your every wish come true" (Continental), or "Fly me, you'll like it" (National). Such innuendos lend strength to the conventional fantasy that in the air, anything can happen. As one flight attendant put it: "You have married men with three kids getting on the plane and suddenly they feel anything goes. It's like they leave that reality on the ground, and you fit into their fantasy as some geisha girl. It happens over and over again."

So the sexualized ad burdens the flight attendant with another task, beyond being unfailingly helpful and open to requests: she must respond to the sexual

fantasies of passengers. She must try to feel and act as if flirting and propositioning are "a sign of my attractiveness and your sexiness," and she must work to suppress her feelings that such behavior is intrusive or demeaning. . . .

Like company manuals, recruiters sometimes offer advice on how to appear.
Usually they presume that an applicant is planning to put on a front; the question is which one. In offering tips for success, recruiters often talked in a matter-
of-fact way about acting, as though assuming that it is permissible if not quite
honorable to feign. As one recruiter put it "I had to advise a lot of people who
were looking for jobs, and not just at Pan Am. . . . And I'd tell them the secret
to getting a job is to imagine the kind of person the company wants to hire and
then become that person during the interview. The hell with your theories of
what you believe in, and what your integrity is, and all that other stuff. You can
project all that when you've got the job." . . .

. . . Some flight attendants could see a connection between the personality
they were supposed to project and the market segment the company wants to attract. One United worker explained: "United wants to appeal to Ma and Pa Kettle. So it wants Caucasian girls—not so beautiful that Ma feels fat, and not so
plain that Pa feels unsatisfied. It's the Ma and Pa Kettle market that's growing,
so that's why they use the girl-next-door image to appeal to that market. You
know, the Friendly Skies. They offer reduced rates for wives and kids. They weed
out busty women because they don't fit the image, as they see it." . . .

Trainees must learn literally hundreds of regulations, memorize the location of
safety equipment on four different airplanes, and receive instruction on passenger
handling. In all their courses, they were constantly reminded that their own job
security and the company's profit rode on a smiling face. A seat in a plane, they
were told, "is our most perishable product—we have to keep winning our passengers back." How you do it is as important as what you do. There were many direct
appeals to smile: "Really work on your smiles." "Your smile is your biggest asset—
use it." In demonstrating how to deal with insistent smokers, with persons board-
ing the wrong plane, and with passengers who are sick or flirtatious or otherwise
troublesome, a trainer held up a card that said "Relax and smile." By standing
aside and laughing at the "relax and smile" training, trainers parried student resistance to it. They said, in effect, "It's incredible how much we have to smile, but
there it is. We know that, but we're still doing it, and you should too."

Beyond this, there were actual appeals to modify feeling states. The deepest
appeal in the Delta training program was to the trainee's capacity to act as if the
airplane cabin (where she works) were her home (where she doesn't work).
Trainees were asked to think of a passenger *as if* he were a "personal guest in your
living room." The workers' emotional memories of offering personal hospitality
were called up and put to use, as Stanislavski would recommend. As one recent
graduate put it:

> You think how the new person resembles someone you know. *You see your sister's eyes
> in someone sitting at that seat.* That makes you want to put out for them. I like to think

of the cabin as the living room of my own home. When someone drops in [at home], you may not know them, but you get something for them. You put that on a grand scale—thirty-six passengers per flight attendant—but *it's the same feeling.*

On the face of it, the analogy between home and airplane cabin unites different kinds of experiences and obscures what is different about them. It can unite the empathy of friend for friend with the empathy of worker for customer, because it assumes that empathy is the *same sort of feeling* in either case. Trainees wrote in their notebooks, "Adopt the passenger's point of view," and the understanding was that this could be done in the same way one adopts a friend's point of view. The analogy between home and cabin also joins the worker to her company; just as she naturally protects members of her own family, she will naturally defend the company. Impersonal relations are to be seen *as if* they were personal. Relations based on getting and giving money are to be seen *as if* they were relations free of money. The company brilliantly extends and uses its workers' basic human empathy, all the while maintaining that it is not interfering in their "personal" lives. . . .

The transmutation is a delicate achievement and potentially an important and beneficial one. But even when it works—when "service ratings" are high and customers are writing "orchid" letters—there is a cost to be paid: the worker must give up control over *how* the work is to be done. In *Labor and Monopoly Capital* (1974), Harry Braverman argues that this has been a general trend in the twentieth century. The "mind" of the work process moves up the company hierarchy, leaving jobs deskilled and workers devalued. Braverman applies this thesis to physical and mental labor, but it applies to emotional labor as well. At Delta Airlines, for example, twenty-four men work as "method analysts" in the Standard Practices Division of the company. Their job is to update the forty-three manuals that codify work procedure for a series of public-contact jobs. There were no such men in the 1920s when the flight engineer handed out coffee to passengers; or in the 1930s when Delta hired nurses to do the same; or in the 1940s when the first flight attendants swatted flies in the cabin, hauled luggage, and even helped with wing repairs. The flight attendant's job grew along with marketing, becoming increasingly specialized and standardized.

The lessons in deep acting—acting "as if the cabin is your home" and "as if this unruly passenger has a traumatic past"—are themselves a new development in deskilling. The "mind" of the emotion worker, the source of the ideas about what mental moves are needed to settle down an "irate," has moved upstairs in the hierarchy so that the worker is restricted to implementing standard procedures. In the course of offering skills, trainers unwittingly contribute to a system of deskilling. The skills they offer do not subtract from the worker's autonomous control over *when* and *how* to apply them; as the point is made in training, "It will be up to you to decide how to handle any given problem on line." But the overall definition of the task is more rigid than it once was, and the worker's field of choice about what to do is greatly narrowed. Within the boundaries of the job, more and more actual subtasks are specified. Did the flight attendant hand out magazines? How many times? By the same token, the task to be accomplished is more clearly spelled out by superiors. How were the magazines handed out? With a smile? With a *sincere* smile? The fact that trainers work hard at making a tough job easier and at making travel generally more pleasant only makes this element of deskilling harder to see. The fact that their training manuals are prepared for them and that they are not themselves entirely free to "tell it like it is" only illustrates again how deskilling is the outcome of specialization and standardization. . . .

A person who does emotional labor for a living must face three hard questions that do not confront others, the answers to which will determine how she defines her "self."

The first one is this: How can I feel really identified with my work role and with the company without being fused with them? This question is especially salient for younger or less experienced workers (since their identities are less formed) and for women (since a woman is more often asked to identify with a man than vice versa). For these groups, the risk of identity confusion is generally greater.

To address this issue successfully, the worker has to develop a working criterion for distinguishing between situations that call on her to identify her self and situations that call on her to identify her role and its relation to the company she works for. To resolve the issue, a worker has to develop the ability to "depersonalize" situations. For example, when a passenger complains about the deprivations of the Friendship Express, a flight attendant who cannot yet depersonalize takes it as a criticism of her own private shortcomings. Or when a passenger is delighted with the flight, such a worker takes the compliments as a reflection on her own special qualities. She would not, for example, take such a compliment as a sign that a strong union stand has improved the ratio of workers to passengers. She interprets events so that they easily reflect on her "true" self. Her self is large, and many events reflect on it.

All companies, but especially paternalistic, nonunion ones, try as a matter of policy to fuse a sense of personal satisfaction with a sense of company well-being and identity. This often works well for awhile. Company emphasis on the sale of "natural niceness" makes it hard for new workers to separate the private from the public self, the "at-ease me" from the "worked-up me," and hard to define their job as one of acting. In a sense, the two selves are not estranged enough. Such workers do not have the wide repertoire of deep acting techniques that would enable them to personalize or depersonalize an encounter at will. Without this adaptability, when things go wrong (as they frequently do), they are more often hurt, angered, or distressed.

At some point the fusion of "real" and "acted" self will be tested by a crucial event. A continual series of situations batter an unprotected ego as it gives to and receives from an assembly line of strangers. Often the test comes when a company speed-up makes personal service impossible to deliver because the individual's personal self is too thinly parceled out to meet the demands made on it. At this point, it becomes harder and harder to keep the public and private selves fused. As a matter of self-protection, they are forced to divide. The worker wonders whether her smile and the emotional labor that keeps it sincere are really hers. Do they really express a part of her? Or are they deliberately worked up and delivered on behalf of the company? Where inside *her* is the part that acts "on behalf of the company"?

In resolving this issue, some workers conclude that only one self (usually the nonwork self) is the "real" self. Others, and they are in the majority, will decide that each self is meaningful and real in its own different way and time. Those who see their identity in this way are more likely to be older, experienced, and married, and they tend to work for a company that draws less on the sense of fusion. Such workers are generally more adept at deep acting, and the idea of a separation between the two selves is not only acceptable but welcome to them. They speak more matter-of-factly about their emotional labor in clearly defined and sometimes mechanistic ways: "I get in gear, I get revved up, I get plugged in." They talk of their feelings not as spontaneous, natural occurrences but as objects they have learned to govern and control. As one flight attendant, who had come to her own terms with this issue, explained: "If I wake up in a sunny mood, I spread it around to the crew and passengers. But if I wake up on the wrong side of the bed, all depressed, I keep to myself on the flight until I'm out of it. The way I think of it, when I'm on, I'm out; when I'm down, I'm in."

Yet workers who resolve the first issue often find themselves brought up more sharply against a second one. While they *have* the skills of deep acting, they can't always bring themselves to use them. "How," the second question goes, "can I use my capacities when I'm disconnected from those I am acting *for?*" Many flight attendants can't bring themselves to think of the airplane cabin as their living room full of personal guests; it seems too much like a cabin full of 300 demanding strangers. The closest they can come to a bow from the heart is to disguise their feelings through surface acting. Many of them want to do deep acting but cannot pull it off under speed-up conditions, and so they fall back on surface acting.

For this reason, a new issue becomes central for them: whether one is "being phony." If a worker wants to put her heart into the work but can only lend her face to it, the risk for her lies in thinking of herself as "phony." Among flight attendants, this word came up with surprising frequency. It was common to hear one worker disparage another for being phony (for example, "She just laid it on in plastic"). But workers also seemed to fear that disparagement themselves; it was common to hear a sentence begin, "I'm not a phony, but. . . ." Talk about phoniness was serious because it was usually seen not merely as an instance of poor acting but as evidence of a personal moral flaw, almost a stigma.

Thus the third issue arises: "If I'm doing deep acting for an audience from whom I'm disconnected, how can I *maintain* my self-esteem without becoming cynical?" There were those for whom the issue of phoniness—and self-esteem—was resolved by redefining the job. Although some blamed themselves for phoniness, others saw it as surface acting necessary and desirable in a job that positively calls for the creation of an illusion. . . .

Both men and women do emotion work, in private life and at work. In all kinds of ways, men as well as women get into the spirit of the party, try to escape the grip of hopeless love, try to pull themselves out of depression, try to allow grief. But in the whole realm of emotional experience, is emotion work as important for men as it is for women? And is it important in the same ways? I believe that the answer to both questions is No. The reason, at bottom, is the fact that women in general have far less independent access to money, power, authority, or status in society. . . .

. . . As for many others of lower status, it has been in the woman's interest to be the better actor. As the psychologists would say, the techniques of deep acting have unusually high "secondary gains." Yet these skills have long been mislabeled "natural," a part of woman's "being" rather than something of her own making.

Sensitivity to nonverbal communication and to the micropolitical significance of feeling gives women something like an ethnic language, which men can speak too, but on the whole less well. It is a language women share offstage in their talk "about feelings." This talk is not, as it is for men offstage, the score-keeping of conquistadors. It is the talk of the artful prey, the language of tips on how to make him want her, how to psyche him out, how to put him on or turn him off. Within the traditional female subculture, subordination at close quarters is understood, especially in adolescence, as a "fact of life." Women accommodate, then, but not passively. They actively adapt feeling to a need or a purpose at hand, and they do it so that it *seems* to express a passive state of agreement, the chance occurrence of coinciding needs. Being becomes a way of doing. Acting is the needed art, and emotion work is the tool.

The emotion work of enhancing the status and well-being of others is a form of what Ivan Illich has called "shadow labor," an unseen effort, which, like housework, does not quite count as labor but is nevertheless crucial to getting other things done. . . .

Wherever it goes, the bargain of wages-for-other-things travels in disguise. Marriage both bridges and obscures the gap between the resources available to men and those available to women. Because men and women do try to love one another—to cooperate in making love, making babies, and making a life together—the very closeness of the bond they accept calls for some disguise of subordination. There will be talk in the "we" mode, joint bank accounts and joint decisions, and the idea among women that they are equal in the ways that "really count." But underlying this pattern will be *different potential futures outside the marriage* and the effect of that on the patterning of life. The woman may thus become especially assertive about certain secondary decisions, or especially active in certain limited domains, in order to experience a sense of equality that is missing from the overall relationship. . . .

There is one further reason why women may offer more emotion work of this sort than men: more women at all class levels do unpaid labor of a highly interpersonal sort. They nurture, manage, and befriend children. More "adaptive" and "cooperative," they address themselves better to the needs of those who are not yet able to adapt and cooperate much themselves. Then, according to Jourard (1968), because they are seen as members of the category from which mothers come, women in general are asked to look out for psychological needs more than men are. The world turns to women for mothering, and this fact silently attaches itself to many a job description. . . .

How, then, does a woman's lower status influence how she is treated by others? More basically, what is the prior link between status and the treatment of feeling? High-status people tend to enjoy the privilege of having their feelings noticed and considered important. The lower one's status, the more one's feelings are not noticed or treated as inconsequential. . . .

Given this relation between status and the treatment of feeling, it follows that persons in low-status categories—women, people of color, children— lack a status shield against poorer treatment of their feelings. This simple fact has the power to utterly transform the content of a job. The job of flight attendant, for example, is not the *same job* for a woman as it is for a man. A day's accumulation of passenger abuse for a woman differs from a day's accumulation of it for a man. Women tend to be more exposed than men to rude or surly speech, to tirades against the service, the airline, and airplanes in general. . . .

. . . [F]emale flight attendants mingle with people who expect them to *enact* two leading roles of Womanhood: the loving wife and mother (serving food, tending the needs of others) and the glamorous "career woman" (dressed to be seen, in contact with strange men, professional and controlled in manner, and literally very far from home). They do the job of symbolizing the transfer of homespun femininity into the impersonal marketplace, announcing, in effect, "I work in the public eye, but I'm still a woman at heart."

Passengers borrow their expectations about gender biographies from home and from the wider culture and then base their demands on this borrowing. The different fictive biographies they attribute to male and female workers make sense out of what they expect to receive in the currency of caretaking and authority. One male flight attendant noted:

> They always ask about my work plans. "Why are you doing this?" That's one question we get all the time from passengers. "Are you planning to go into management?" Most guys come in expecting to do it for a year or so and see how they like it, but we keep getting asked about the management training program. I don't know any guy that's gone into management from here.

In contrast, a female flight attendant said:

> Men ask me why I'm not married. They don't ask the guys that. Or else passengers will say, "Oh, when you have kids, you'll quit this job. I know you will." And I say, "Well, no, I'm not going to have kids." "Oh yes you will," they say. "No I'm not," I

say, and I don't want to get more personal than that. They may expect me to have kids because of my gender, but I'm not, no matter what they say.

If a female flight attendant is seen as a protomother, then it is natural that the work of nurturing should fall to her. As one female attendant said: "The guys bow out of it more and we pick up the slack. I mean the handling of babies, the handling of children, the coddling of the old folks. . . ."

In fact, passengers generally assume that men have *more* authority than women and that men exercise authority *over* women. For males in the corporate world to whom air travel is a way of life, this assumption has more than a distant relation to fact. As one flight attendant put it: "Say you've got a businessman sitting over there in aisle five. He's got a wife who takes his suit to the cleaners and makes the hors d'oeuvres for his business guest. He's got an executive secretary with horn-rimmed glasses who types 140 million words a minute and knows more about his airline ticket than he does. There's no woman in his life over him." This assumption of male authority allows ordinary twenty-year-old male flight attendants to be mistaken for the "managers" or "superintendents" of older female flight attendants. A uniformed male among women, passengers assume, must have authority over women. In fact, because males were excluded from this job until after a long "discrimination" suit in the mid-1960s and few were hired until the early 1970s, most male flight attendants are younger and have less seniority than most female attendants.

The assumption of male authority has two results. First, authority, like status, acts as a shield against scapegoating. Since the women workers on the plane were thought to have less authority and therefore less status, they were more susceptible to scapegoating. When the plane was late, the steaks gone, or the ice out, frustrations were vented more openly toward female workers. Females were expected to "take it" better, it being more their role to absorb an expression of displeasure and less their role to put a stop to it.

In addition, both male and female workers adapted to this fictional redistribution of authority. Both, in different ways, made it more real. Male flight attendants tended to react to passengers *as if they had more authority* than they really did. This made them less tolerant of abuse and firmer in handling it. They conveyed the message that *as authorities* they expected compliance without loud complaint. Passengers sensing this message were discouraged from pursuing complaints and stopped sooner. Female flight attendants, on the other hand, assuming that passengers would honor their authority less, used more tactful and deferential means of handling abuse. . . .

Estrangement from aspects of oneself are, in one light, a means of defense. On the job, the acceptance of a division between the "real" self and the self in a company uniform is often a way to avoid stress, a wise realization, a saving grace. But this solution also poses serious problems. For in dividing up our sense of self, in order to save the "real" self from unwelcome intrusions, we necessarily relinquish a healthy sense of wholeness. We come to accept as normal the tension we feel between our "real" and our "on-stage" selves.

More women than men go into public-contact work and especially into work in which status enhancement is the essential social-psychological task. In some jobs, such as that of the flight attendant, women may perform this task by playing the Woman. Such women are more vulnerable, on this account, to feeling estranged from their capacity to perform and enjoy two traditional feminine roles—offering status enhancement and sexual attractiveness to others. These capacities are now under corporate as well as personal management.

~

CHAPTER FIFTEEN

Robert Bellah et al. on Individualism and Community in America

~ Introduction ~

This chapter concludes *Self, Symbols, and Society* with Bellah et al.'s influential book *Habits of the Heart*. Robert Bellah (1927–) was born in Altus, Oklahoma, and was educated at Harvard University. His research interests then, as now, concerned the sociology of religion. After completing his studies, Bellah stayed at Harvard, conducting research and teaching in the areas of social relations and world religions. In 1967 he became Ford Professor of Sociology at the University of California, Berkeley. Bellah is currently Elliot Professor of Sociology Emeritus there. He received the National Humanities Medal on December 20, 2000, from President Bill Clinton. In addition to being the senior author of *Habits*, he and his coauthors published a sequel entitled *The Good Society* (1992). Bellah's other publications include *Tokugawa Religion* (1957); *Beyond Belief* (1970), which includes a number of his most influential essays including "Civil Religion in America" and "Religious Evolution"; and *The Broken Covenant* (1975), which won the Sorokin Award.

Richard Madsen was educated at Maryknoll College, Maryknoll Seminary, Fujen University (Taiwan), National Taiwan University, and Harvard University. Madsen is currently a professor of sociology at the University of California, San Diego. Madsen's other publications include *China's Catholics* (1998), *China and the American Dream* (1995), and *Morality and Power in a Chinese Village* (1984), which won the C. Wright Mills Award.

William Sullivan earned his doctoral degree in philosophy at Fordham University, and is currently a professor at La Salle University. His other publications include *Work and Integrity: The Crisis and Promise of Professionalism in America*.

Ann Swidler is professor of sociology at the University of California, Berkeley. Her other publications include coauthorship of *Inequality by Design: Cracking the*

Bell Curve Myth (1996), and *Talk of Love: How Americans Use Their Culture* (forthcoming).

Steven Tipton was educated at Stanford University and Harvard University. He is currently professor of sociology of religion and director of the graduate division of religion at the Candler School of Theology at Emory University. His other publications include *Getting Saved from the Sixties: Moral Meaning in Conversion and Cultural Change* (1982).

Habits of the Heart: Individualism and Commitment in American Life (1985) was a national bestseller and winner of the *Los Angeles Times* Book Award for Current Interest. Like Riesman in *The Lonely Crowd*, Bellah et al. examine the issue of character as it relates to changes in society. However, while Riesman suggests that character development should have autonomy as its aim, Bellah et al. suggest that "individualism may have grown cancerous" in America. The reader should understand by now that individualism is not merely a psychological phenomenon existing in a vacuum but rather a product of biological, historical, and social factors that shape its form and prevalence. The authors discuss the benefits as well as the costs to society of placing such a high value on individualism.

In their research Bellah et al. detected the continued existence of the biblical, republican, and individualist strands that have historically shaped American culture. The early influences of the Puritans were significant in the forming of the United States. As a result, Christian strands (containing the ideals of a community spirit) make up a fundamental aspect of the value system of American culture. The political founders of the nation, such individuals as George Washington and Thomas Jefferson, were committed to republicanism; in terms expressed by Bellah et al., "the ideal of a self-governing society of relative equals." And the authors detected the strands of utilitarian individualism (i.e., economic success based upon individual effort) and expressive individualism (i.e., self-discovery as an end in itself). While the biblical and republican strands focus on social relations, both forms of individualism, in varying degrees, emphasize the self apart from others. If it is true that individualism is the dominant value in America, what, then, holds society together? In searching for the answer to this question, the authors take their lead from the keen observer of early American culture, French social philosopher Alexis de Tocqueville. Tocqueville referred to the mores of culture as "habits of the heart." These habits of mind and behavior shape the unique practices that comprise a culture. Such habits take one out of oneself (thereby connecting the individual to something larger than him- or herself) in order to accomplish social goals. Bellah et al. note in the reading, "In Tocqueville's still-agrarian America . . . the competitive individualism stirred by commerce was balanced and humanized by the restraining influences of a fundamentally egalitarian ethic of community responsibility" (38).

A representative character reflects the ideal view of personality for people at a given time and place. The representative character that Tocqueville observed was that of the "independent citizen." Bellah et al. add, "A representative character provides . . . a point of reference and focus, that gives living expression to a vision of life, as in our society today sports figures legitimate the strivings of youth and the scientist represents objective competence" (39). The authors describe the representative character that Tocqueville observed as the "independent citizen" because the reference point of personality, the ideal for personality at the time, was the self-made man who held strongly to biblical and republican bonds.

As the living conditions within a culture change, the representative character also changes. For example, as industrialization began to pervade social life more and more, unique challenges to living a successful life emerged, and this paved the way for changes in representative character: different circumstances required different forms of character. Bellah et al. identify the professional manager and the therapist as the representative characters of twentieth century American culture. These representative characters have much in common: the belief in specialization, self-interest, progress, and the acceptance of the mechanics of industrial society. Together, they reinforce an individualist perspective in a social climate that may be described as a "world of bureaucratic consumer capitalism." Essentially, they establish the ideal for personal character in the prevailing social milieu. While these representative characters continue to reinforce the traditional strand of individualism, the emphasis they place on managing oneself undermines their ability to reinforce the biblical and republican strands embedded in the history of American culture. As a result, the representative characters of the modern period place a heavy burden on the self—in essence, to create a psychologically meaningful life in isolation from others. Achieving such a task is difficult, in part, because it involves a distorted view of the structure of social and psychological life. As explained in our prior readings, the psychological categories in which we think have their origins in social life. The management of the self apart from others means that one has to deny vital parts of oneself—in fact, the parts that are the accomplishment of social relationships. The representative characters have a view of community (based upon biblical and republican strands) that is difficult to accomplish because the categories used to define a successful life are contrary to the personal sacrifices necessary to achieve community. While limited knowledge prevented previous generations from achieving a broadly defined sense of community, in the contemporary period a broadly defined sense of community is undermined by a too narrowly defined sense of self.

Bellah et al. note that such a narrowly defined sense of self must also confront the difficulty of grounding one's beliefs. What is the basis upon which an isolated self makes its decisions? If such a self is not to behave like a leaf in the wind, then personal decision making must be egocentric, because the ego's whims stand as the sole arbiter in orienting one's actions. In the authors' view, "'being good' becomes 'feeling good'" (77). Without a shared grounding to orient the selves that comprise society, each self feels that it must make its own way with only its wit and intuition to guide it. The irony is that this sense of making one's own way is a shared social phenomenon. Our collective definition of self, our representative characters, isolates us from each other, and rather than experiencing the shared acknowledgment of our differences, we place greater emphasis on feeling different. Bellah et al. explain, "our sense of the dignity, worth, and moral autonomy of the individual, is dependent in a thousand ways on a social, cultural, and institutional context that keeps us afloat even when we cannot very well describe it" (84). While people today derive value from both utilitarian and expressive forms of individualism, neither form provides a sufficient "language" to connect individuals to each other. The failure to sustain a viable language that connects the individual's interest to the public's interest, the failure to sustain a viable language that reveals the connections between individual lives and social life, creates a social environment that is not conducive to the preservation of a democratic order.

The lack of social integration manifests itself in a variety of psychological forms. It is partly the function of the therapeutic attitude to manage such conflicts. As Bellah et al. note, however, the tendency of the therapeutic attitude is to either soothe (though not really change) the tensions arising from personal problems associated with bureaucratic structures or to assist individuals in creating a personal space that they can call their own apart from these bureaucratic structures. By dealing with a social problem psychologically, the social problem is not ameliorated, and it becomes the individual's challenge to be strong enough psychologically to endure the social tensions that he or she, ironically, contributes to creating. While a significant part of therapy's role is to assist individuals in finding their own voices, Bellah et al. note in the reading, "Therapy's 'democratic side' lacks any public forum" (127). This results in many of the issues addressed in the previous selection on the management of feeling. For example, Hochschild comments that because of the challenges of achieving a sense of wholeness in a social environment where "success" seems to require carving up the self, social structures maintain an imposing and impersonal presence. Our psychological language—the concepts we use in thinking about ourselves and each other (e.g., egos as islands)—undermines our ability to articulate the social underpinnings of our psychological conflicts.

Bellah et al. suggest that individuals take another look at tradition. However, they distinguish tradition from traditionalism. While traditionalism is the futile effort of transforming the past into the present, the notion of revitalizing tradition suggests examining how the present is adversely tied to the past (that is, an old idea that no longer works or has gone awry), and how elements of the past may be transformed into appropriate, contemporary problem-solving strategies. For example, historically the call for individual liberties was, in part, a response against the constraining forces of tightly knit communities. The contemporary call for community may be the product of individualism gone awry. However, contemporary individuals would likely feel smothered in a community that seriously limits individual thought and expression. Contemporaries may garner from tradition a greater appreciation of where they came from (examining the original goals and determining whether they are still desirable), why their current situation is the way it is (where and when the goals changed or where and when the decision making got off-course), and how problem-solving strategies for balancing individualism and civic responsibility can be obtained. The failure to engage in such cultural reflection can lead to individuals becoming trapped in restrictive conventions.

Today, one type of restrictive convention may be the cultural assumption of the isolated individual. With the ascension of the individualism strand over the biblical and republican strands, the individual has lost important supportive structures in the historical struggle for liberty. As the authors write, "Classical republicanism evoked an image of the active citizen contributing to the public good and Reformation Christianity . . . inspired a notion of government based on the voluntary participation of individuals" (142). Apart from these other strands, individualism may result in more forms of self-mastery as well as more instances of self-preoccupation at one's own, others', and the culture's expense. A part of this expense is the individual's sense of impotence in the face of impersonal social forces, as expressed in such common clichés as "What can I do?" or "How can I fight city hall?" These common responses to the functioning of society's institutions are inconsistent with the society's dominant value that prides itself on individualism. Contemporary individualism does not speak a language that clarifies to itself "the workings of the interdependent American political economy." The failure of citizens to achieve the difficult task of seeing how society is pieced together as a whole, and how they, as citizens, play a role in this (what the authors call "invisible complexity"), prevents the formulation of "a language of the common good." Instead, what is formulated by default is a language of competing needs and wants that are resolved in terms of relative power. As a result, citizens (who are presently called consumers) become mistrustful of the institutions that supposedly represent their interests (e.g., big government, big business, big labor).

Bellah et al. ask readers to consider anew the American strands that reinforce moral obligations and to apply such considerations to the nation's large-scale institutions for the sake of the common good. They note that Martin Luther King, Jr.'s vision in his famous "I Have A Dream" speech encapsulates the ideal to be worked toward in achieving the common good. King is also interesting in that his most autonomously based decisions (such as his position on the Vietnam War) were also his strongest pleas for a more inclusive community. In essence, he demonstrated that autonomy need not be counter to the interests of community, but rather, they may enrich each other. Bellah et al. suggest that greater efforts toward local, national, and global community should be made. However, as long as economic interests (at the expense of other interests) drive individual and collective activities, neither autonomy nor the common good is likely to be achieved, for these depend upon a balancing of interests. Bellah et al. observe, "What we find hard to see is that it is the extreme fragmentation of the modern world that really threatens our individuation; that what is best in our separation and individuation, our sense of dignity and autonomy as persons, requires a new integration if it is to be sustained" (286).

∼ Habits of the Heart ∼

In the 1830s, the French social philosopher Alexis de Tocqueville offered the most comprehensive and penetrating analysis of the relationship between character and society in America that has ever been written. In his book *Democracy in America*, based on acute observation and wide conversation with Americans, Tocqueville described the mores—which he on occasion called "habits of the heart"—of the American people and showed how they helped to form American character. He singled out family life, our religious traditions, and our participation in local politics as helping to create the kind of person who could sustain a connection to a wider political community and thus ultimately support the maintenance of free institutions. He also warned that some aspects of our character—what he was one of the first to call "individualism"—might eventually isolate Americans one from another and thereby undermine the conditions of freedom.

The central problem of our book concerns the American individualism that Tocqueville described with a mixture of admiration and anxiety. It seems to us that it is individualism, and not equality, as Tocqueville thought, that has marched inexorably through our history. We are concerned that this individualism may have grown cancerous—that it may be destroying those social integuments that Tocqueville saw as moderating its more destructive potentialities, that it may be threatening the survival of freedom itself. We want to know what individualism in America looks and feels like, and how the world appears in its light.

We are also interested in those cultural traditions and practices that, without destroying individuality, serve to limit and restrain the destructive side of individualism and provide alternative models for how Americans might live. We want to know how these have fared since Tocqueville's day, and how likely their renewal is. . . .

So long as it is vital, the cultural tradition of a people—its symbols, ideals, and ways of feeling—is always an argument about the meaning of the destiny its members share. Cultures are dramatic conversations about things that matter to their participants, and American culture is no exception. From its early days, some Americans have seen the purpose and goal of the nation as the effort to realize the ancient biblical hope of a just and compassionate society. Others have struggled to shape the spirit of their lives and the laws of the nation in accord with the ideals of republican citizenship and participation. Yet others have promoted dreams of manifest destiny and national glory. And always there have been the proponents, often passionate, of the notion that liberty means the spirit of enterprise and the right to amass wealth and power for oneself. The themes of success, freedom, and justice that we detected . . . are found in all three of the central strands of our culture—biblical, republican, and modern individualist— but they take on different meanings in each context. . . .

Most historians have recognized the importance of biblical religion in American culture from the earliest colonization to the present. Few have put greater emphasis on the religious "point of departure" of the American experiment than Alexis de Tocqueville, who went so far as to say, "I think I can see the whole destiny of America contained in the first Puritan who landed on those shores." . . .

John Winthrop (1588–1649) was one of those "first Puritans" to land on our shores and has been taken as exemplary of our beginnings by commentators on American culture from Cotton Mather to Tocqueville to Perry Miller. Winthrop was elected first governor of the Massachusetts Bay Colony even before the colonists left England. Just over forty years of age, he was a well-educated man of good family and earnest religious convictions, determined to start life anew in the wilderness in company with those of like religious commitment. In the sermon "A Model of Christian Charity," which he delivered on board ship in Salem harbor just before landing in 1630, he described the "city set upon a hill" that he and his fellow Puritans intended to found. His words have remained archetypal for one understanding of what life in America was to be: "We must delight in each other, make others conditions our own, rejoyce together, mourn together, labor and suffer together, always having before our eyes our community as members of the same body." The Puritans were not uninterested in material prosperity and were prone when it came, unfortunately, to take it as a sign of God's approval. Yet their fundamental criterion of success was not material wealth but the creation of a community in which a genuinely ethical and spiritual life could be lived. . . .

The founding generation of the American republic produced so many individuals exemplary of the republican tradition that it is hard to choose among them. George Washington seemed to his contemporaries like some figure out of the early Roman republic. Though he would have preferred to live quietly on his country estate, Washington responded to his country's call to be commander-in-chief of the revolutionary army and, later, first president of the United States. After graduating from Harvard College, John Adams of Massachusetts, a descendant of the Puritans, devoted his talents as a young lawyer to the constitutional defense of the rights of his fellow colonists, and subsequently to the revolutionary cause. Thomas Jefferson (1743–1826), however, as author of the Declaration of Independence and leader of the popular cause, stands out as a particularly appropriate example of republican thinking.

Jefferson came from the planter class of western Virginia. After graduating from William and Mary College, he early took an active part in the politics of the Virginia colony. At the age of thirty-three, he drafted the Declaration of Independence, and with the words "All men are created equal" gave enduring expression to his lifelong commitment to equality. Jefferson did not believe that human beings are equal in all respects. By equality, he meant fundamentally political equality. No man, he believed, is born with a saddle on his back for another man to ride. Therefore, however much he temporized on the practical issue of emancipation, Jefferson vigorously opposed slavery in principle.

Though he held that equality is a universal principle, true at all times and places, Jefferson was a genuine adherent of the republican tradition in believing that it is only effective politically at certain times and places where relatively rare conditions allow it to be operative. Political equality can only be effective in a republic where the citizens actually participate. "The further the departure from direct and constant control by the citizens," he said, "the less has the government of the ingredient of republicanism." Indeed, the ideal of a self-governing society of relative equals in which all participate is what guided Jefferson all his life. . . .

Freedom was not so tightly tied to substantive morality for Jefferson as it had been for Winthrop. Indeed, Jefferson's first freedom, freedom of religion, aimed at ensuring that people like Winthrop would not have legal power to force their views on others. In general, Jefferson favored freedom of the person from arbitrary state action and freedom of the press from any form of censorship. Yet he also believed that the best defense of freedom was an educated people actively participating in government. The notion of a formal freedom that would simply allow people to do what they pleased—for example, solely to make money—was as unpalatable to Jefferson as it had been to Winthrop. However important formal freedom was to either of them, freedom only took on its real meaning in a certain kind of society with a certain form of life. Without that, Jefferson saw freedom as quickly destroying itself and eventuating in tyranny.

Listing the essential principles of government in his first inaugural address, Jefferson began with: "Equal and exact justice to all men, of whatever state or persuasion, religious or political." While he certainly believed in the procedural justice of our legal system, he could not forget that there is a higher justice that sits in judgment over human justice: "the laws of nature and of nature's God." In considering the continued existence of slavery, Jefferson wrote, "Indeed I tremble for my country when I reflect that God is just; that his justice cannot sleep forever." The profound contradiction of a people fighting for its freedom while subjecting another to slavery was not lost on Jefferson and gave rise to anxiety for our future if this contradiction were not solved. . . .

Benjamin Franklin (1706–1790) was long regarded at home and abroad as the quintessential American. Though uncomfortable with the Puritanism of his native Boston, Franklin learned much of practical use from Cotton Mather, whose life his own overlapped by twenty-two years. One of the founders of the American republic, Franklin often gave evidence of his republican convictions. And yet it is finally neither for his Christian beliefs, which he embraced rather tepidly and perhaps more for their social utility than for their ultimate truth, nor for his republicanism, which he more genuinely espoused, that he is best known. Rather he is the archetypal poor boy who made good. It is the *Autobiography* that recounts Franklin's worldly success and the maxims from *Poor Richard's Almanack* advising others how to attain the same that are most indelibly associated with him. . . .

. . . Even more influential than the *Autobiography* are the aphorisms in *Poor Richard's Almanack* which have passed into the common sense of Americans about the way to attain wealth: "Early to bed and early to rise, makes a man healthy, wealthy, and wise." "God helps those that help themselves." "Lost time is never found again." "Plough deep, while Sluggards sleep, and you shall have

Corn to sell and to keep, says Poor Dick." In short, Franklin gave classic expression to what many felt in the eighteenth century—and many have felt ever since—to be the most important thing about America: the chance for the individual to get ahead on his own initiative. . . .

. . . Franklin understood, with Jefferson, that it was only a certain kind of society that was likely to give such scope to ordinary citizens, to protect their rights, and to secure their equal treatment before the law. But for many of those influenced by Franklin, the focus was so exclusively on individual self-improvement that the larger social context hardly came into view. By the end of the eighteenth century, there would be those who would argue that in a society where each vigorously pursued his own interest, the social good would automatically emerge. That would be utilitarian individualism in pure form. Though Franklin never himself believed that, his image contributed much to this new model of human life. Along with biblical religion and republicanism, utilitarian individualism has been one of the strands of the American tradition since Franklin's time.

By the middle of the nineteenth century, utilitarian individualism had become so dominant in America that it set off a number of reactions. A life devoted to the calculating pursuit of one's own material interest came to seem problematic for many Americans, some of them women, some of them clergymen, and some of them poets and writers. The cramped self-control of Franklin's "virtues" seemed to leave too little room for love, human feeling, and a deeper expression of the self. The great writers of what F. O. Matthiessen has called the "American Renaissance" all reacted in one way or another against this older form of individualism. In 1855 Herman Melville published *Israel Potter,* a novel that subjected Franklin himself to bitter satire. Emerson, Thoreau, and Hawthorne put aside the search for wealth in favor of a deeper cultivation of the self. But it is perhaps Walt Whitman who represents what we may call "expressive individualism" in clearest form. . . .

For Whitman, success had little to do with material acquisition. A life rich in experience, open to all kinds of people, luxuriating in the sensual as well as the intellectual, above all a life of strong feeling, was what he perceived as a successful life. Whitman identified the self with other people, with places, with nature, ultimately with the universe. The expansive and deeply feeling self becomes the very source of life, as in "Passage to India":

> Passage indeed O soul to primal thought,
> Not lands and seas alone, thy own clear freshness,
> The young maturity of brood and bloom,
> To realms of budding bibles.
>
> O soul, repressless, I with thee and thou with me,
> Thy circumnavigation of the world begin,
> Of man, the voyage of his mind's return,
> To reasons's early paradise,

> Back, back to wisdom's birth, to innocent intuitions,
> Again with fair creation.

Freedom to Whitman was above all the freedom to express oneself, against all constraints and conventions:

> Afoot and light-hearted I take to the open road,
> Healthy, free, the world before me,
> The long brown path before me, leading wherever I choose.

The frankness of Whitman's celebration of bodily life, including sexuality, was shocking to nineteenth-century Americans and led to more than a few difficulties, though he never compromised the integrity of his expression. His homosexuality, vaguely but unmistakably expressed in the poetry, was another way in which he rejected the narrow definition of the male ego dominant in his day.

For all his unconventionality, there was a strong element of the republican tradition in Whitman, particularly evident in *Democratic Vistas* (1871) and elsewhere in his prose writings. The self-sufficient farmer or artisan capable of participation in the common life was Whitman's ideal as well as Jefferson's and Franklin's. He would thus have shared their idea of justice. But for Whitman, the ultimate use of the American's independence was to cultivate and express the self and explore its vast social and cosmic identities. . . .

. . . Tocqueville . . . saw the great importance, in the American mores of his day, of the continuing biblical and republican traditions—the traditions of Winthrop and Jefferson. He also saw very vividly the way in which Americans operated in the tradition of Benjamin Franklin, and to describe this, he helped to give currency to a new word. "'Individualism' is a word recently coined to express a new idea," he wrote. "Our fathers only knew about egoism." Individualism is more moderate and orderly than egoism, but in the end its results are much the same: "Individualism is a calm and considered feeling which disposes each citizen to isolate himself from the mass of his fellows and withdraw into the circle of family and friends; with this little society formed to his taste, he gladly leaves the greater society to look after itself." As democratic individualism grows, he wrote, "there are more and more people who, though neither rich nor powerful enough to have much hold over others, have gained or kept enough wealth and enough understanding to look after their own needs. Such folk owe no man anything and hardly expect anything from anybody. They form the habit of thinking of themselves in isolation and imagine that their whole destiny is in their hands." Finally, such people come to "forget their ancestors," but also their decendants, as well as isolating themselves from their contemporaries. "Each man is forever thrown back on himself alone, and there is danger that he may be shut up in the solitude of his own heart." Tocqueville mainly observed the utilitarian individualism we have associated with Franklin. He only in a few instances discerns something of the expressive individualism that Whitman would come to represent.

Tocqueville saw the isolation to which Americans are prone as ominous for the future of our freedom. It is just such isolation that is always encouraged by despotism. And so Tocqueville is particularly interested in all those countervailing tendencies that pull people back from their isolation into social communion. Immersion in private economic pursuits undermines the person as citizen. On the other hand, involvement in public affairs is the best antidote to the pernicious effects of individualistic isolation: "Citizens who are bound to take part in public affairs must turn from the private interests and occasionally take a look at something other than themselves." It is precisely in these respects that mores become important. The habits and practices of religion and democratic participation educate the citizen to a larger view than his purely private world would allow. These habits and practices rely to some extent on self-interest in their educational work, but it is only when self-interest has to some degree been transcended that they succeed.

In ways that Jefferson would have understood, Tocqueville argues that a variety of active civic organizations are the key to American democracy. Through active involvement in common concerns, the citizen can overcome the sense of relative isolation and powerlessness that results from the insecurity of life in an increasingly commercial society. Associations, along with decentralized, local administration, mediate between the individual and the centralized state, providing forums in which opinion can be publicly and intelligently shaped and the subtle habits of public initiative and responsibility learned and passed on. Associational life, in Tocqueville's thinking, is the best bulwark against the condition he feared most: the mass society of mutually antagonistic individuals, easy prey to despotism. These intermediate structures check, pressure, and restrain the tendencies of centralized government to assume more and more administrative control.

In Tocqueville's still-agrarian America, as indeed throughout the nineteenth century, the basic unit of association, and the practical foundation of both individual dignity and participation, was the local community. There a civic culture of individual initiative was nurtured through custom and personal ties inculcated by a widely shared Protestant Christianity. The mores Tocqueville emphasized were still strong. Concern for economic betterment was widespread, but it operated within the context of a still-functional covenant concern for the welfare of one's neighbor. In the towns, the competitive individualism stirred by commerce was balanced and humanized by the restraining influences of a fundamentally egalitarian ethic of community responsibility. . . .

A representative character is a kind of symbol. It is a way by which we can bring together in one concentrated image the way people in a given social environment organize and give meaning and direction to their lives. In fact, a representative character is more than a collection of individual traits or personalities. It is rather a public image that helps define, for a given group of people, just what kinds of personality traits it is good and legitimate to develop. A representative character provides an ideal, a point of reference and focus, that gives living expression to a vision of life, as in our society today sports figures legitimate the strivings of youth and the scientist represents objective competence.

Tocqueville's America can be viewed as an interlocking network of specific social roles: those of husband, wife, child, farmer, craftsman, clergyman, lawyer, merchant, township officer, and so on. But the distinctive quality of that society, its particular identity as a "world" different from other societies, was summed up in the spirit, the mores, that animated its members, and that spirit was symbolized in the representative character of what we can call the independent citizen, the new national type Tocqueville described. In many ways, the independent citizen continued the traditions of Winthrop and Jefferson. He held strongly to biblical religion, and he knew the duties as well as the rights of citizenship. But the model of Benjamin Franklin, the self-made man, loomed ever larger in his defining traits. Abraham Lincoln was perhaps the noblest example of the mid-nineteenth-century American independent citizen. In his language, he surpassed the biblical eloquence of John Winthrop and his understanding of democratic republicanism was even more profound than that of the man he always recognized as his teacher, Thomas Jefferson. And yet it was Lincoln the railsplitter who went from log cabin to White House rather than Lincoln the public theologian or Lincoln the democratic philosopher who captured the popular imagination.

In any case, representative characters are not abstract ideals or faceless social roles, but are realized in the lives of those individuals who succeed more or less well in fusing their individual personalities with the public requirements of those roles. It is this living reenactment that gives cultural ideals their power to organize life. Representative characters thus demarcate specific societies and historical eras. . . .

The bureaucratic organization of the business corporation has been the dominant force in this century. Within the corporation, the crucial character has been the professional manager. The competitive industrial order with its sectoral organization and its push toward profitability has been the indisputable reality of modern life for the manager. . . .

Like the manager, the therapist is a specialist in mobilizing resources for effective action, only here the resources are largely internal to the individual and the measure of effectiveness is the elusive criterion of personal satisfaction. Also like the manager, the therapist takes the functional organization of industrial society for granted, as the unproblematical context of life. The goal of living is to achieve some combination of occupation and "lifestyle" that is economically possible and psychically tolerable, that "works." The therapist, like the manager, takes the ends as they are given; the focus is upon the effectiveness of the means.

Between them, the manager and the therapist largely define the outlines of twentieth-century American culture. The social basis of that culture is the world of bureaucratic consumer capitalism, which dominates, or has penetrated, most older, local economic forms. While the culture of manager and therapist does not speak in the language of traditional moralities, it nonetheless proffers a normative order of life, with character ideals, images of the good life, and methods of attaining it. Yet it is an understanding of life generally hostile to older ideas of moral order. Its center is the autonomous individual, presumed able to choose the roles he will play and the commitments he will make, not on the basis of higher truths but according to the criterion of life-effectiveness as the individual judges it. . . .

The American understanding of the autonomy of the self places the burden of one's own deepest self-definitions on one's own individual choice. For some Americans, even 150 years after Emerson wrote "Self-Reliance," tradition and a tradition-bearing community still exist. But the notion that one discovers one's deepest beliefs in, and through, tradition and community is not very congenial to Americans. Most of us imagine an autonomous self existing independently, entirely outside any tradition and community, and then perhaps choosing one.

It is harder for us to see ourselves choosing our families in the same way. We are just born into them. But even here, the work of therapy is often aimed at so distancing us from our parents that we may choose, or seem to choose, freely, which aspects of them we will resemble and which not. Leaving home in a sense involves a kind of second birth in which we give birth to ourselves. And if that is the case with respect to families, it is even more so with our ultimate defining beliefs. The irony is that here, too, just where we think we are most free, we are most coerced by the dominant beliefs of our own culture. For it is a powerful cultural fiction that we not only can, but must, make up our deepest beliefs in the isolation of our private selves. . . .

. . . Breaking with the past is part of our past. Leaving tradition behind runs all the way through our tradition. But how is such a separate self to be shaped and grounded? . . .

If the self is defined by its ability to choose its own values, on what grounds are those choices themselves based? For . . . many . . ., there is simply no objectifiable criterion for choosing one value or course of action over another. One's own idiosyncratic preferences are their own justification, because they define the true self. . . . The right act is simply the one that yields the agent the most exciting challenge or the most good feeling about himself.

Now if selves are defined by their preferences, but those preferences are arbitrary, then each self constitutes its own moral universe, and there is finally no way to reconcile conflicting claims about what is good in itself. All we can do is refer to chains of consequences and ask if our actions prove useful or consistent in light of our own "value-systems." All we can appeal to in relationships with others is their self-interest, likewise enlightened, or their intuitive sympathies. . . .

If the individual self must be its own source of moral guidance, then each individual must always know what he wants and desires or intuit what he feels. He must act so as to produce the greatest satisfaction of his wants or to express the fullest range of his impulses. The objectified moral goodness of Winthrop obey-

ing God's will or Jefferson following nature's laws turns into the subjective goodness of getting what you want and enjoying it. Utility replaces duty; self-
expression unseats authority. "Being good" becomes "feeling good.". . .

Given this individualistic moral framework, the self becomes a crucial site for
the comparative examination and probing of feelings that result from utilitarian
acts and inspire expressive ones. . . .

Clearly, the meaning of one's life for most Americans is to become one's own
person, almost to give birth to oneself. Much of this process, as we have seen, is
negative. It involves breaking free from family, community, and inherited ideas.
Our culture does not give us much guidance as to how to fill the contours of this
autonomous, self-responsible self, but it does point to two important areas. One
of these is work, the realm, par excellence, of utilitarian individualism. Traditionally men, and today women as well, are supposed to show that in the occupational world they can stand on their own two feet and be self-supporting. The
other area is the lifestyle enclave, the realm, par excellence, of expressive individualism. We are supposed to be able to find a group of sympathetic people, or
at least one such person, with whom we can spend our leisure time in an atmos-
phere of acceptance, happiness, and love.

There is no question that many Americans find this combination of work and
private lifestyle satisfying. For people who have worked hard all their lives, life
in a "retirement community" composed of highly similar people doing highly
similar things may be gratifying. . . .

On the other hand, a life composed mainly of work that lacks much intrinsic meaning and leisure devoted to golf and bridge does have limitations.
It is hard to find in it the kind of story or narrative, as of a pilgrimage or quest,
that many cultures have used to link private and public; present, past, and future; and the life of the individual to the life of society and the meaning of the
cosmos.

We should not forget that the small town and the doctrinaire church, which
did offer more coherent narratives, were often narrow and oppressive. Our present radical individualism is in part a justified reaction against communities and
practices that were irrationally constricting. A return to the mores of fifty or a
hundred years ago, even if it were possible, would not solve, but only exacerbate,
our problems. Yet in our desperate effort to free ourselves from the constrictions
of the past, we have jettisoned too much, forgotten a history that we cannot
abandon.

Of course, not everyone in America or everyone to whom we talked believes
in an unencumbered self arbitrarily choosing its "values," "entirely independent"
of everyone else. We talked to Christians and Jews for whom the self makes sense
in relation to a God who challenges, promises, and reassures. We even talked to
some for whom the word *soul* has not been entirely displaced by the word *self*.
We talked to those for whom the self apart from history and community makes
no sense at all. To them, a self worth having only comes into existence through
participation with others in the effort to create a just and loving society. But we

found such people often on the defensive, struggling for the biblical and republican language that could express their aspirations, often expressing themselves in the very therapeutic rhetoric that they consciously reject. It is a rhetoric that educated middle-class Americans, and, through the medium of television and other mass communications, increasingly all Americans, cannot avoid. And yet even those most trapped in the language of the isolated self ("In the end you're really alone") are troubled by the nihilism they sense there and eager to find a way of overcoming the emptiness of purely arbitrary "values."

We believe that much of the thinking about the self of educated Americans, thinking that has become almost hegemonic in our universities and much of the middle class, is based on inadequate social science, impoverished philosophy, and vacuous theology. There are truths we do not see when we adopt the language of radical individualism. We find ourselves not independently of other people and institutions but through them. We never get to the bottom of our selves on our own. We discover who we are face to face and side by side with others in work, love, and learning. All of our activity goes on in relationships, groups, associations, and communities ordered by institutional structures and interpreted by cultural patterns of meaning. Our individualism is itself one such pattern. And the positive side of our individualism, our sense of the dignity, worth, and moral autonomy of the individual, is dependent in a thousand ways on a social, cultural, and institutional context that keeps us afloat even when we cannot very well describe it. There is much in our life that we do not control, that we are not even "responsible" for, that we receive as grace or face as tragedy, things Americans habitually prefer not to think about. . . .

How Americans think about love is central to the ways we define the meaning of our own lives in relation to the wider society. For most of us, the bond to spouse and children is our most fundamental social tie. The habits and modes of thought that govern intimate relationships are thus one of the central places where we may come to understand the cultural legacy with which we face the challenges of contemporary social life. Yet in spite of its great importance, love is also, increasingly, a source of insecurity, confusion, and uncertainty. The problems we have in thinking about love are an embodiment of the difficulty we have thinking about social attachment in general.

A deeply ingrained individualism lies behind much contemporary understanding of love. The idea that people must take responsibility for deciding what they want and finding relationships that will meet their needs is widespread. In this sometimes somber utilitarianism, individuals may want lasting relationships, but such relationships are possible only so long as they meet the needs of the two people involved. All individuals can do is be clear about their own needs and avoid neurotic demands for such unrealizable goods as a lover who will give and ask nothing in return.

Such a utilitarian attitude seems plausible for those in the throes of divorce or for single people trying to negotiate a world of short-term relationships. It is one

solution to the difficulties of self-preservation in a world where broader expectations may lead to disappointment or make one vulnerable to exploitation. Then
love becomes no more than an exchange, with no binding rules except the obligation of full and open communication. A relationship should give each partner
what he or she needs while it lasts, and if the relationship ends, at least both partners will have received a reasonable return on their investment.

While utilitarian individualism plays a part in the therapeutic attitude, the full
significance of the therapeutic view of the world lies in its expressive individualism, an expanded view of the nature and possibilities of the self. Love then becomes the mutual exploration of infinitely rich, complex, and exciting selves.
Many of our respondents stress that their own relationships are much better than
their parents' marriages were. They insist on greater intimacy, sharing of feelings,
and willingness to "work through" problems than their parents found possible. . . .

On the whole, even the most secure, happily married of our respondents had
difficulty when they sought a language in which to articulate their reasons for
commitments that went beyond the self. These confusions were particularly clear
when they discussed problems of sacrifice and obligation. . . .

. . . To reappropriate a language in which we could all, men and women, see
that dependence and independence are deeply related, and that we can be independent persons without denying that we need one another, is a task that has
only begun.

What would probably perplex and disturb Tocqueville most today is the fact
that the family is no longer an integral part of a larger moral ecology tying the
individual to community, church, and nation. The family is the core of the private sphere, whose aim is not to link individuals to the public world but to avoid
it as far as possible. In our commercial culture, consumerism, with its tempta-
tions, and television, with its examples, augment that tendency. Americans are
seldom as selfish as the therapeutic culture urges them to be. But often the limit
of their serious altruism is the family circle. Thus the tendency of our individualism to dispose "each citizen to isolate himself from the mass of his fellows and
withdraw into the circle of family and friends," that so worried Tocqueville, indeed seems to be coming true. "Taking care of one's own" is an admirable motive.
But when it combines with suspicion of, and withdrawal from, the public world,
it is one of the conditions of the despotism Tocqueville feared. . . .

The relevance of therapy is enhanced by the fit of the therapeutic attitude of
self-realization and empathic communication to the increasingly interpersonal
nature of the work we do. As the managerial and service sectors of the economy
gradually take in a wider and wider slice of the U.S. labor force, more of us do
work for which therapy serves as a model rather than a contrast.

Not only is therapy work, much of our work is a form of therapy. Preston, a
human potential therapist, describes how he prepares for work: "Ninety percent
of communication is body, tone, facial expression. It's who you are and how you
sit there and react to someone. So when I prepare to do group therapy, my co-
therapist and I go to dinner before every group. We have an hour-and-a-half

dinner. When we sit down, we don't talk about our clients. Only in the last few minutes do we plan and go into strategy for the session. We talk about each other. We complain, we give each other therapy, we comb each other's feelings. We fall back in love. We need to, because we don't see each other except then. We are in love by the time we go into that group. That is the basic work we need to do, because then when we enter that room, we are a unit." The same sort of interpersonal communication runs the gamut from work to love and back again. Co-workers "give each other therapy" to cement teamwork. Individuals who meet only on the job make use of intimacy as a method to become more effective as a working "unit." Their sensitive and caring conversation is not a break from the job. It's part of the job. Conversely, therapy's fee-for-services exchange and its strict procedural regulation (in which being a few minutes early or late, missing appointments, or forgetting payments all acquire personal significance) tie it into the bureaucratic and economic structure of the larger society. Therapy's stress on personal autonomy presupposes institutional conformity. The modern self's expressive freedom goes hand in hand with the modern world's instrumental control.

The therapeutic attitude shapes itself to follow the contours of both entrepreneurial and corporate work. It encourages adaptation to such work, whether enthusiastic or skeptical. At the entrepreneurial and enthusiastic ends of the spectrum, its effects are much like those lauded by a hard-driving thirty-five-year-old insurance broker reporting on what a year's therapy has meant to him in the wake of his divorce: "It's made me more disciplined. I can handle my feelings better when I'm feeling depressed, anxious, whatever. That's helped me handle my relationships better, too. It's been good for me from a personal standpoint and it's good for business." Asked how, he explains: "I share more of myself now. The more I share and get out and meet people, the better I do. If I'm sharing with people, they know I can take care of their business and look after their interests. If they know who I am, they're gonna care for me for who I am. There's not gonna be any secrets about me." Therapy enables us to "handle" our feelings more effectively and thereby manage others' responses to us more successfully in business and social life. More sensitive self-expression allows more effective self-assertion. "Being sensitive makes you stronger, not weaker," agrees the broker. Yet simultaneously the therapeutic attitude reaffirms an expressive axiom, that such acceptance and success follow on the genuine goodness of the self so revealed. I succeed because others know and care for me "for who I am," not simply because I am more poised.

In larger bureaucratic settings, therapy at its most ambitious seeks to humanize the corporation and, in so doing, to make it more productive. Echoing the human-relations approach to industrial management, therapists attest to the powerful effects of engaging fellow-workers in sensitive and caring communication. One explains how a client, a data-processing manager for the phone company, transforms their "general prescription that you tell people what to do and make sure they do it and just generally act like a horse's ass" into therapeutic terms: "She approaches everybody in a very perceptive manner. There's four or five different people in her group and each one is absolutely different from the other one. And she's approached each one absolutely differently and she's getting that particular group going from the least productive to the most productive in that organization." Recognizing the uniqueness of each individual appears here as an expressive end in itself *and* as a method of putting people to more efficient use as human resources.

More subtly, therapeutic habits of monitoring one's own and others' responses enter bureaucratic work even when self-expression is subordinated to the organization's "bottom line" goals. The county supervisor of a state welfare agency, for example, explains how she relies on therapeutic insights to keep her office "problem-focused and problem-solving": "I've learned to listen to myself and listen to other people, step into their shoes and see it from their perspective. I've also learned not to over-identify, since that gets in my way as a manager." By way of example, she thinks of "a conflict situation, where someone is trying to make you angry." As a sensitive yet efficient manager, "you have to know it's there and behave as though it's not. Don't raise your voice, don't put them down. Don't lose control. Own your own projections, and make them take responsibility for theirs. Don't get hooked into their stuff." Communication and sympathy cannot fully humanize the world of bureaucratic work, but they can make it more comfortable and cooperative. They can smooth conflict between people and help them through the regulated channels they must negotiate to get the job done while looking out for themselves. "It *is* a jungle out there, and you *do* have to look out for number one," concedes the welfare supervisor, "but you can do it without hurting people and creating more jungle."

When the faith that personal authenticity and occupational success fit neatly together begins to falter, therapy assumes another, less optimistic stance toward the world of work. A humanistic psychologist who often works with pressured middle managers, sales directors, and lawyers skeptically assesses such work as a "game" demanding self-concealment if one is to make a living. She advises them to "play the game when you have to, but know it's a game. Don't buy into it. Choose where and when to play it." She sees herself helping her clients make decisions about their lives in terms of the "tradeoffs" between the "money, power and glamor payoffs" of necessary, but personally unfulfilling, work and the genuine joys of marriage, leisure, and home life.

The fit between the therapeutic outlook and the autonomous, yet routine, pattern of bureaucratic life eases the impersonality of corporate settings but does not eliminate the tension between conceptions of people as ends in themselves and as means to organizational ends. So the same welfare supervisor who defended her own therapeutic style of management can also criticize her driving, yet psychologically skilled, boss for much the same sort of approach: "She'll bring in homemade cookies and flowers for your desk [and] at the same time she'll do anything necessary to get the organizational results she wants and advance her career." The welfare supervisor recalls a client's suicide in which all her boss cared about was "whether we were covered legally." Then she sums up her discontent as a therapeutic individual working in a bureaucratic world: "What's so frustrating to me is this confusion between what's personal and what isn't, not being able to sort it out. There's this sense of seduction and feeling scared you're going to be used." Therapeutic techniques and practices lend themselves to working relationships at odds with therapy's own formal ideals but in line with the bureaucratic institutions in which its clients live. "In the system I work in," says the welfare supervisor, "our motto could be, 'If you don't have to report it, it didn't happen.' Appearances and regulations are all that count!" she exclaims. "There's no meaning except what's legal. That devalues the human reality of what is, the human relatedness between people." A sense of conflict between organizational goals and bureaucratic defensiveness may be unusually acute among professional helpers employed in a state agency. But many of us share the cultural conviction that the meaning of our lives lies apart from the rules and regulations that surround us. Ubiquitous, yet purely procedural and institutionally variable, they compel our conformity without capturing our spirit in some larger vision of the good. Social integration by such means remains a tactical effort apart from self-integration.

In response, we may search for friendship at work, free of manipulation. We may play our work roles tongue in cheek, making tradeoffs there for the sake of authenticity at home or leisure. But such juggling of roles and relationships can leave us with the feeling that who we really are lies beyond them all. Preston encourages clients with this familiar feeling to "balance your meal of activities and pace yourself to get more done," while invoking the image of a healthy person as an ever-growing plant: "The image is that a healthy person is a plant, and that you never stop growing. Most of us don't need tomato stakes. We're basically good, and so with enough sunshine and water, we'll grow beautifully. You can grow in any direction and that adds to the variety of the world. That goes counter to the whole puritanical side of America, that there's one way of life and we're gonna fit you into it. Therapy is like the democratic side. If you become a unique person and grow in a different direction, that helps you, everybody, and society, too." Such an ideal self feeds on its role-bound activities to grow beyond them. The belief that personal growth goes on endlessly and in any direction points up the ultimately aimless nature of the organic metaphor in such post-Freudian therapeutic hands. What is not questioned is the institutional context. One's "growth" is a purely private matter. It may involve maneuvering within the structure of bureaucratic rules and roles, changing jobs, maybe even changing spouses if necessary. But what is missing is any collective context in which one might act as a participant to change the institutional structures that frustrate and limit. Therapy's "democratic side" lacks any public forum. Its freedom is closer to the free choice of a market economy than to the shared argument and action of free citizens in a republic. . . .

. . . The complexity of such issues as abortion, welfare, and child abuse is only increased by emphasis on the relativity of individual feelings, values, and priorities with respect to them. Given the objective complexity of the issues and the chaos of conflicting subjective reactions to them, therapy's empathic face-to-face communication can make little headway. It cannot span the gap between the one-on-one situation and the great social scale and bureaucratic density of public life. Even though it might ideally be possible for the highly educated and sensitive to sit down and talk through the issues, the managers and professionals who could are already "reaching burnout" because of overwork, professional commitments, and family obligations. . . .

We have seen that therapy has developed an acute concern for the monitoring and managing of inner feelings and emphasizes their expression in open communication. Therapy thus continues the tradition of expressive individualism that we considered earlier in this book. But we have seen, too, how therapeutic language is preoccupied with strategic considerations of costs and benefits, and has thus also incorporated much of what we have called utilitarian individualism. Indeed, in contemporary therapeutic language, the managerial and the therapeutic modes seem to be coalescing as our professional and economic life involves more and more subtle forms of interpersonal relating. We have, in fact, seen that therapeutic understandings of interaction work best in bureaucratic and market situations where individuals are under pressure and need to coordinate their activities with precision.

The benefits of the increasing importance of therapy in our lives are tangible. Americans today, especially, but not exclusively, middle-class Americans, are more "in touch with their feelings," better able to express them, and more able to seek what they want in relationships. The increase in psychological sophistication has apparently brought an increase in feelings of personal well-being.

But there is a cost. Anxiety and uncertainty about more important and enduring relationships are increasing rather than decreasing. . . .

The contradictions we have described make us wonder if psychological sophistication has not been bought at the price of moral impoverishment. The ideal therapeutic relationship seems to be one in which everything is completely conscious and all parties know how they feel and what they want. Any intrusion of "oughts" or "shoulds" into the relationship is rejected as an intrusion of external and coercive authoritarianism. The only morality that is acceptable is the purely contractual agreement of the parties: whatever they agree to is right. But just as the notion of an absolutely free self led to an absolutely empty conception of the self, complete psychological contractualism leads to the notion of an absolutely empty relationship. And this empty relationship cannot possibly sustain the richness and continuity that the therapeutically inclined themselves most want, just as they want not empty but rich and coherent selves. . . .

In one sense, the therapeutic critique of traditional relationships and their moral basis is legitimate. Where standards of right and wrong are asserted with dogmatic certainty and are not open to discussion, and, even worse, where these standards merely express the interests of the stronger party in a relationship, while clothing those interests in moralistic language, then the criticism is indeed justified. Unfortunately, in all existing societies, traditional social practices and the moral standards that govern them are subject to just these distortions. But the therapeutically inclined are wrong to think that morality itself is the culprit, that moral standards are inherently authoritarian and in the service of domination. . . .

Traditional moral discourse, while subject in particular cases to the distortions the therapeutically inclined fear, is not the monolith of external authority and coercion that they imagine. Whether philosophical or theological, traditional ethical reflection is based on the understanding that principles and exemplars must be interpreted to be applied, and that good people may differ on particular cases. Nonetheless, there is some confidence that a rough consensus is possible so that there can be common understandings of moral obligations. Not everything is up in the air all the time, although there is nothing that is in principle closed to discussion. It is true that in periods of rapid social change, when moral standards seem to be crumbling and relativism seems to be pervasive, some people are tempted to assert a simple and unquestionable morality and, in some circumstances, to force it on their neighbors. But such people deeply misunderstand tradition even when they seek to embrace it. They defend not tradition but traditionalism, and, as Jaroslav Pelikan has said, whereas tradition is the living faith of the dead, traditionalism is the dead faith of the living. A living tradition is never a program for automatic moral judgments. It is always in a continuous process of reinterpretation and reappropriation. Such a process assumes, however, that tradition has enough authority for the search for its present meaning to be publicly pursued as a common project.

It is just that assumption that the therapeutically inclined defenders of expressive and utilitarian individualism challenge. In asserting a radical pluralism and the uniqueness of each individual, they conclude that there is no moral common ground and therefore no public relevance of morality outside the sphere of minimal procedural rules and obligations not to injure. In so doing, they do not realize the degree to which their own individualism has become the common cultural coin. There is no moment when the therapeutically inclined sound more similar than when they are asserting their uniqueness. In thinking they have freed themselves from tradition in the pursuit of rationality and personal authenticity, they do not understand the degree to which their views are themselves traditional. Even being anti-traditional is part of the individualist tradition. Nor do they realize that their minimalist insistence on justice, fairness, and respect for individuals is rooted in a much richer defense of the same things in the religious and civic philosophical traditions. Indeed, by not seeing the extent to which their own beliefs are part of a pervasive common culture, they run the risk of doing just what they attack in the older moral traditions—that is, accepting as literally true what is merely a cultural convention. . . .

Individualism lies at the very core of American culture. Every one of the four traditions we have singled out is in a profound sense individualistic. There is a biblical individualism and a civic individualism as well as a utilitarian and an ex-pressive individualism. Whatever the differences among the traditions and the consequent differences in their understandings of individualism, there are some things they all share, things that are basic to American identity. We believe in the dignity, indeed the sacredness, of the individual. Anything that would vio-late our right to think for ourselves, judge for ourselves, make our own decisions, live our lives as we see fit, is not only morally wrong, it is sacrilegious. Our high-est and noblest aspirations, not only for ourselves, but for those we care about, for our society and for the world, are closely linked to our individualism. Yet, as we have been suggesting repeatedly in this book, some of our deepest problems both as individuals and as a society are also closely linked to our individualism. We do not argue that Americans should abandon individualism—that would mean for us to abandon our deepest identity. But individualism has come to mean so many things and to contain such contradictions and paradoxes that even to defend it requires that we analyze it critically, that we consider especially those tendencies that would destroy it from within.

Modern individualism emerged out of the struggle against monarchical and aristocratic authority that seemed arbitrary and oppressive to citizens prepared to assert the right to govern themselves. In that struggle, classical political philoso-phy and biblical religion were important cultural resources. Classical republican-ism evoked an image of the active citizen contributing to the public good and Reformation Christianity, in both Puritan and sectarian forms, inspired a notion of government based on the voluntary participation of individuals. Yet both these traditions placed individual autonomy in a context of moral and religious obligation that in some contexts justified obedience as well as freedom.

In seventeenth-century England, a radical philosophical defense of individual rights emerged that owed little to either classical or biblical sources. Rather, it consciously started with the biological individual in a "state of nature" and de-rived a social order from the actions of such individuals, first in relation to na-ture and then in relation to one another. John Locke is the key figure and one enormously influential in America. The essence of the Lockean position is an al-most ontological individualism. The individual is prior to society, which comes into existence only through the voluntary contract of individuals trying to max-imize their own self-interest. It is from this position that we have derived the tra-dition of utilitarian individualism. But because one can only know what is use-ful to one by consulting one's desires and sentiments, this is also ultimately the source of the expressive individualist tradition as well.

Modern individualism has long coexisted with classical republicanism and biblical religion. The conflict in their basic assumptions was initially muted be-cause they all, in the forms commonest in America, stressed the dignity and au-tonomy of the individual. But as modern individualism became more dominant in the United States and classical republicanism and biblical religion less effec-tive, some of the difficulties in modern individualism began to become apparent. The therapeutic ethos to which we have devoted so much attention is suggestive of these because it is the way in which contemporary Americans live out the tenets of modern individualism. For psychology, as Robert Coles has written, the self is "the only or main form of reality."

The question is whether an individualism in which the self has become the main form of reality can really be sustained. . . .

America is also the inventor of that most mythic individual hero, the cowboy, who again and again saves a society he can never completely fit into. The cowboy has a special talent—he can shoot straighter and faster than other men—and a special sense of justice. But these characteristics make him so unique that he can never fully belong to society. His destiny is to defend society without ever really joining it. He rides off alone into the sunset like Shane, or like the Lone Ranger moves on accompanied only by his Indian companion. But the cowboy's importance is not that he is isolated or antisocial. Rather, his significance lies in his unique, individual virtue and special skill and it is because of those qualities that society needs and welcomes him. Shane, after all, starts as a real outsider, but ends up with the gratitude of the community and the love of a woman and a boy. And while the Lone Ranger never settles down and marries the local schoolteacher, he always leaves with the affection and gratitude of the people he has helped. It is as if the myth says you can be a truly good person, worthy of admiration and love, only if you resist fully joining the group. But sometimes the tension leads to an irreparable break. Will Kane, the hero of *High Noon*, abandoned by the cowardly townspeople, saves them from an unrestrained killer, but then throws his sheriff's badge in the dust and goes off into the desert with his bride. One is left wondering where they will go, for there is no longer any link with any town.

The connection of moral courage and lonely individualism is even tighter for that other, more modern American hero, the hard-boiled detective. From Sam Spade to Serpico, the detective is a loner. He is often unsuccessful in conventional terms, working out of a shabby office where the phone never rings. Wily, tough, smart, he is nonetheless unappreciated. But his marginality is also his strength. When a bit of business finally comes their way, Philip Marlowe, Lew Archer, and Travis McGee are tenacious. They pursue justice and help the unprotected even when it threatens to unravel the fabric of society itself. Indeed, what is remarkable about the American detective story is less its hero than its image of crime. When the detective begins his quest, it appears to be an isolated incident. But as it develops, the case turns out to be linked to the powerful and privileged of the community. Society, particularly "high society," is corrupt to the core. It is this boring into the center of society to find it rotten that constitutes the fundamental drama of the American detective story. It is not a personal but a social mystery that the detective must unravel.

To seek justice in a corrupt society, the American detective must be tough, and above all, he must be a loner. He lives outside the normal bourgeois pattern of career and family. As his investigations begin to lead him beyond the initial crime to the glamorous and powerful center of the society, its leaders make attempts to buy off the detective, to corrupt him with money, power, or sex. This counterpoint to the gradual unravelling of the crime is the battle the detective wages for his own integrity, in the end rejecting the money of the powerful and spurning (sometimes jailing or killing) the beautiful woman who has tried to seduce him. The hard-boiled detective, who may long for love and success, for a place in society, is finally driven to stand alone, resisting the blandishments of society, to pursue a lonely crusade for justice. Sometimes, as in the film *Chinatown*, corruption is so powerful and so total that the honest detective no longer has a place to stand and the message is one of unrelieved cynicism.

Both the cowboy and the hard-boiled detective tell us something important about American individualism. The cowboy, like the detective, can be valuable to society only because he is a completely autonomous individual who stands outside it. To serve society, one must be able to stand alone, not needing others, not depending on their judgment, and not submitting to their wishes. Yet this individualism is not selfishness. Indeed, it is a kind of heroic selflessness. One accepts the necessity of remaining alone in order to serve the values of the group. And this obligation to aloneness is an important key to the American moral imagination. . . .

. . . Practically all of those we talked with are convinced, at least in theory, that a selfish seeker after purely individual success could not live a good, happy, joyful life. But when they think of the kind of generosity that might redeem the individualistic pursuit of economic success, they often imagine voluntary involvements in local, small-scale activities such as a family, club, or idealized community in which individual initiatives interrelate to improve the life of all. They have difficulty relating this ideal image to the large-scale forces and institutions shaping their lives. This is what creates the pathos underlying many of the conversations about work, family, community, and politics we recounted in the last chapter. Many of those we talked with convey the feeling that sometimes their very best efforts to pursue their finest ideals seem senseless.

Of course, some, particularly the activists, only occasionally see their participation in political and social movements as senseless, while others, often professionals and managers, have definite ideas about why efforts at community involvement turn out to be frustrating. It is rarely "getting involved" as a moral act that is thought to be senseless. Instead, the difficulty has to do with the realm of politics. For a good number of those we talked to, *politics* connotes something morally unsavory, as though voluntary involvement were commendable and fulfilling up to the point at which it enters the realm of office holding, campaigning, and organized negotiating. Their judgments of public involvement and responsibility turn negative when they extend beyond the bounds of their local concerns. . . .

The extent to which many Americans can understand the workings of our economic and social organization is limited by the capacity of their chief moral language to make sense of human interaction. The limit set by individualism is clear: events that escape the control of individual choice and will cannot coherently be encompassed in a moral calculation. But that means that much, if not most, of the workings of the interdependent American political economy, through which individuals achieve or are assigned their places and relative power in this society, cannot be understood in terms that make coherent moral sense. It further suggests why, in order to minimize "cognitive dissonance," many individuals tend not to deal with embedded inequalities of power, privilege, and esteem in a culture of self-proclaimed moral equality.

Lacking the ability to deal meaningfully with the large-scale organizational and institutional structures that characterize our society, many of those we talked to turned to the small town not only as an ideal but as a solution to our present political difficulties. Nostalgia for the small town and the use of its image in political discussion was common regardless of political views. . . .

If the culture of individualism has difficulty coming to terms with genuine cultural or social differences, it has even more difficulty coming to terms with large impersonal organizations and institutions. Politicians are always tempted to personalize and moralize complex problems. The media are much more interested in the charisma of politicians and the dramatic conflicts between them than in their positions on policy issues. Understanding a complex modern society is indeed not easy, particularly when we cannot relate its problems to immediate lived experience.

The tremendous growth of the social sciences in this century, especially economics and sociology, testifies to the widespread desire to understand the complexity of modern social relations. Whatever the achievements of social science (largely, after all, a realm of "experts"), the Americans with whom we talked had real difficulty piecing together a picture of the whole society and how they relate to it. We call this the problem of invisible complexity.

Since, as we have seen, we lack a way of making moral sense of significant cultural, social, and economic differences between groups, we also lack means for evaluating the different claims such groups make. The conflict of interests is troubling when we do not know how to evaluate those interests. In this moral vacuum, it has been tempting to translate group claims and interests into the language of individual rights, a language that makes sense in terms of our dominant individualistic ideology. But if large numbers of individuals and groups or categories of individuals begin to insist, as they have in recent years, that they are owed or are entitled to certain benefits, assistance, or preference as a matter of right, such claims are not readily accepted as matters of justice. They begin to be treated instead as simply competing wants. And since wants cannot be evaluated in terms of the ideology of individualism, the outcome of the political struggle is widely interpreted in terms of power. Wants are satisfied not in terms of their justice but in terms of the power of the wanters. Too many demands can even begin to threaten the legitimacy of the logic of individual rights, one of the few bases for making morally legitimate claims in our society. A conception of society as a whole composed of widely different, but interdependent, groups might generate a language of the common good that could adjudicate between conflicting wants and interests, thus taking the pressure off of the overstrained logic of individual rights. But such a conception would require coming to terms with the invisible complexity that Americans prefer to avoid.

As we have noted before, the image of society as a marketplace of fair competition among roughly equal competitors is an appealing resolution to the problems of understanding the larger society, one that complements the moral balance of consensual voluntary community. But though this model continues to have wide appeal, most Americans know that it is far from descriptive of what really happens. Most are aware to some degree of things that do not fit the market model: large corporations that dominate whole sectors of the market; massive efforts to influence consumer choice through advertising; government programs that subsidize various sectors, such as agriculture; contracts for defense industries that escape reliable cost accounting; technologies that extend and intensify the centralized control of finance, production, and marketing; and so forth.

One long-standing American reaction to such facts is to suspect all groups powerful enough to avoid the operation of the free market. It is not only big government but big business and big labor that have suffered declining levels of public confidence in the past two decades. Such groups in one way or another "go too far" in interfering with market mechanisms for the benefit of special interests. But at the same time, many Americans are aware that large-scale organizations, however distasteful, are part of social reality in the late twentieth century and that trust-busting, union-busting, and the dismantling of government regulative agencies are not really desirable. . . .

To remind us of what is possible, we may call to mind one of the most significant social movements of recent times, a movement overwhelmingly religious in its leadership that changed the nature of American society. Under the leadership of Martin Luther King, Jr., the Civil Rights movement called upon Americans to transform their social and economic institutions with the goal of building a just national community that would respect both the differences and the interdependence of its members. It did this by combining biblical and republican themes in a way that included, but transformed, the culture of individualism.

Consider King's "I Have a Dream" speech. Juxtaposing the poetry of the scriptural prophets—"I have a dream that every valley shall be exalted, every hill and mountain shall be made low"—with the lyrics of patriotic anthems—"This will be the day when all God's children will be able to sing with new meaning, 'My country 'tis of thee, sweet land of liberty, of thee I sing'"—King's oration reappropriated that classic strand of the American tradition that understands the true meaning of freedom to lie in the affirmation of responsibility for uniting all of the diverse members of society into a just social order. "When we let freedom ring, when we let it ring from every village and hamlet, from every state and every city, we will be able to speed up the day when all of God's children, black men and white men, Jews and Gentiles, Protestants and Catholics, will be able to join hands and sing the words of that old Negro spiritual, 'Free at last! Free at last! Thank God almighty, we are free at last!'" For King, the struggle for freedom became a practice of commitment within a vision of America as a community of memory. We now need to look at that national community, our changing conceptions of it, and what its prospects are. . . .

. . . [W]e need to see what we can learn from our traditions, as well as from the best currently available knowledge. What has failed at every level—from the society of nations to the national society to the local community to the family—is integration: we have failed to remember "our community as members of the same body," as John Winthrop put it. We have committed what to the republican founders of our nation was the cardinal sin: we have put our own good, as individuals, as groups, as a nation, ahead of the common good. . . .

. . . The American dream is often a very private dream of being the star, the uniquely successful and admirable one, the one who stands out from the crowd of ordinary folk who don't know how. And since we have believed in that dream for a long time and worked very hard to make it come true, it is hard for us to give it up, even though it contradicts another dream that we have—that of living in a society that would really be worth living in. . . .

. . . What we find hard to see is that it is the extreme fragmentation of the modern world that really threatens our individuation; that what is best in our separation and individuation, our sense of dignity and autonomy as persons, requires a new integration if it is to be sustained.

~

Where Do We Go from Here?
Toward a Theory of the
Cycle of Individualism

After reading the selections in this book, you may be thinking to yourself, "Well, that was interesting, but what can I do with what I've learned?" The goals of this conclusion are: (1) to compare some of the theories that have been presented in this book in terms of individualism, social interaction, and society; (2) to contextualize these theories by reviewing the historical development of individualism; (3) to critique where we are today in terms of individual expression and gender equity; and, (4) to suggest a new direction for social change.

There would appear to be at least three distinct theories concerning the nature of individualism. Theory One suggests that individualism is a product of society, and like society, individualism evolves into a more complex phenomenon over time (see, for example, Durkheim). Theory Two suggests that individualism is a temporary stage that appears when social bonds and norms are weak (see, for example, Thomas). Theory Three suggests that individualism is the product of the relative complexity of social interaction, and its relative development is not necessarily one of continual refinement (see, for example, Simmel). Each of these theories either implicitly or explicitly links individualism to social interaction and changes in society. Divergent theories seem to converge on the conclusion that individualism emerges as a consequence of particular social relations. Individualism emerges, perhaps, as a result of social complexity that may serve to increase the probability of the survival of the group. But once in place within a social group, does individualism continue to evolve or simply change, or does it vanish into communal bonds until some crisis stimulates its reemergence as a type of survival mechanism?

The idea or observation of individualism did not originate with the authors we have encountered in this anthology. In fact, individualism is a very old phenomenon. We know, for example, that individualism was of concern in ancient

Greece. Irving Zeitlin points out that Solon (c. 594/3 B.C.), the Athenian law-giver, was inspired by the teachings of Delphi (which included the message "Know Thyself"). Solon was an important proponent of democracy. However, in democratic Athens, only certain members of society were permitted the enjoy-ment of justice, equality, and individual freedoms. Thurston Davis (1956, 208) points out: "It should, of course, not be forgotten that the circumstances of its [justice] growth in the Greek *polis* automatically set limits to the range of human equality. Slaves, metics, women, and barbarians were in varying ways outside the pale." Knowing oneself appears to have pertained only to those who viewed the structure of reality as destining them for this privilege.

The ideas of democracy and individual freedoms did not remain static throughout Greek history. The Peloponnesian War (a war fought 431–404 B.C. between the cities of Athens and Sparta—Sparta being the victor) undermined the Solonian democratic tradition. Following the Peloponnesian War, Athens struggled to restore a democratic social and political climate. Zeitlin (1993) writes:

> Socrates and Plato [who lived during this time] addressed definite problems . . . in their reflections on society and politics. And there can be little doubt that what gave rise to those reflections was the larger historical context, notably the Greco-Persian wars as a struggle between social systems, and the Peloponnesian War as a political-ideological conflict between oligarchy and democracy. (25)

Plato communicated his philosophy, which was fundamentally based upon the teachings of his mentor, Socrates, in a series of writings called dialogues. In one of these, called *Gorgias*, we encounter a critique of Callicles' philosophy, which says that the pursuit of self-interest is the highest virtue. Regarding the struggle between self-interest and the greater good as it was understood at that time, Thurston Davis (1956, 208) argues that "[t]he ideas of men like Callicles . . . had evidently worked an effective triumph over the old Solonian principles." How-ever, does the position of Callicles reflect individualism or alienation? Individual expression cannot occur without the consent of others. Even the mightiest can prosper only so long as others choose to allow or endure them to do so. The pur-suit of individual freedoms that are blind to the fact of mutual consent represents a type of individual expression that exists in an alienated state. The pursuit of self-interest at the expense of others can only be maintained as long as the self-interested party is alienated from his or her interdependence. Such alienation becomes the driving force behind self-interest. Self-interest is not a product of individualism per se; rather, it is one form of the degradation of individualism. Callicles' philosophy represents the demise of democratic principles and indi-vidualism as it was represented over two thousand years ago.

The seeds for the development of democratic principles and individualism were also sown by the religious faiths of Judaism and Christianity. Within Ju-daism, the belief in a monotheistic, transcendent God contributed to the growth of personal contemplation. The focus on the written word and humanitarian principles in Judaism also contributed to the refinement of a standard moral code. Regarding the development of individualism, these beliefs and practices were taken to a different level in Christianity, with its tenet that Jesus was God made flesh; this truly sanctified the person. Colin Morris, in a remarkable book called *The Discovery of the Individual 1050–1200* (2000), says, "Ultimately a Christian origin can be found for many of the elements in the European concept of the self" (11). While the Italian Renaissance of the fifteenth century is usually discussed among scholars as a significant period for the growth of individual expression, Morris demonstrates that the French Renaissance of the twelfth century contained many of the elements of individualism and humanism that would flourish during this later period. The French Renaissance was the result of the growth of cities, a knightly class that valued stories of individual heroism, and the growth of a large class of educated men. Morris comments, "new social and cultural circumstances were forcing upon the individual choices in important areas of consciousness where previously they had scarcely existed" (45). In order to try to make sense of the changing times, many turned to the past for guidance. The result was a rediscovery of important elements in Greek thought—perhaps most notably, the Delphic "Know Thyself." The combination of rediscovering classic literature, along with advances in logic, led to interesting questions concerning self-knowledge. For example, Aelred of Rievaulx (d. 1167) inquired: "How much does a man know, if he does not know himself?" Peter Abelard (d. 1143) wrote *Ethics: or, Know Yourself*, a work on intention and sin based on the principle of knowing oneself. What is interesting to note here is that self-discovery, as with the Greeks, applied mainly to those within privileged classes. During this time, self-discovery also assumed a Christian guise. Self-discovery operated within culturally defined economic and ideological categories, with the exception of the adoption of individual confession, which became widely practiced at this time.

Progress in humanist and individualist thought in the early Renaissance was dampened by the resurgence of the authority of Church and State and the rise of the professionally minded who were in line with the changing thought of the times. These factors coincided in creating a social order for the elite that was simultaneously self-interested (in terms of securing status) and authoritarian. Critics of these developments at the time (for example, medieval satirists) focused on, among other things, the vision of Jesus as the man of humanity and the poor as juxtaposed with the impersonal, authoritarian structure of the Church. The legend of Narcissus (the story of a boy who fell in love with his own image), which was of interest among the ancient Greeks as well as among the leading figures of the twelfth century French Renaissance, held a lesson that was apparently not heeded.

Although modern individualism has its roots in the traditions that we have been exploring, the series of events that transpired after the Renaissance fueled the conditions necessary for a more widespread call for the freedoms associated with individual rights. These events included the Reformation (which facilitated the privatization of beliefs), the printing press (which made reading and education more widespread), advances in science (which competed successfully against the authority of religious dogma and facilitated a more atomistic approach to knowledge and understanding), the Enlightenment (an eighteenth-century movement that celebrated human reason), and the American Revolution. Thomas Jefferson in "The Declaration of Independence" echoed some of the important themes to come out of these historical developments: "We hold these truths to be self-evident, that all men are created equal, that they are endowed by their Creator with certain unalienable Rights, that among these are Life, Liberty, and the pursuit of Happiness." Through these developments (and others, such as the Industrial Revolution), Americans acquired a greater consciousness of their rights as individuals.

What progress has been made in the United States since the turn of the century (or, since the development of microsociology) concerning the implementation of this greater consciousness of the freedom and equality of the individual? To begin to answer that question, we will now look at observations of the individual woman that were made by some of the social psychologists in this anthology.

In 1923 William Thomas observed that mechanical inventions, diffusion of print, the growth of cities, the capitalist system, scientific research, doctrines of freedom, and the proliferation of consumer products were stimulating the imaginations of people beyond their capacity to grasp all that they could see and hear. Thomas (72) noted that this was particularly true for women because they had "heretofore been most excluded from general life." (You will remember, for example, that women in the United States had only been granted the right to vote three years previously.) While social conditions for women in the United States have changed since Thomas's day, how much have they changed fundamentally? In Garfinkel's case study of Agnes in the 1950s, we observe an individual acquiring the social practices of gender in order to be accepted as a woman. Among other things, these social practices entail a certain quality of passivity—a quality of passivity unique to women in their relations with men. In the 1980s Hochschild reported that in the airline industry, women tended to be viewed with less authority than their male counterparts. She observed that women were more willing to choose a nurturing and passive role than men if it would help them get their job done. A number of things are going on here: (1) women and men are succumbing to roles that define for them their sense of individual expression—and this is occurring in a culture that explicitly expresses valuing individualism; and (2) while there can be no question that women have achieved much in the course of the twentieth century, there is nevertheless some continuity in the roles of inequity assigned to women as compared with men. While more women actively participate in the economy today than ever before, it is also the case that women and children represent a majority of those living in poverty. Moreover, in the last quarter century there has been a steady rise in the operations of sweatshops and people sold as commodities—both trends disproportionately affecting women. In many ways, these trends reflect Simmel's observation that objective culture moves at a faster pace than subjective culture, that the appearance of progress is deceptive.

Let us now explore this discrepancy between the external appearance of change and the lack of fundamental change in human relations. Garfinkel states that norms represent a grid from which individuals choose in order to get a desired effect. He emphasizes the individual's choice in following or not following norms in social interaction in order to argue that individuals actively participate in the maintenance or modification of social practices. Garfinkel's position contrasts with that of Talcott Parsons, who argues that individuals internalize the norms of culture (thereby conveying a more passive role for individuals in the maintenance of social practices). But do individuals really choose courses of action in social interactions that result in a desired effect? In her study, Hochschild observed women actively adapting in passive ways in order to get a socially desired effect—getting the job done. Actively adapting to passive roles can reinforce a perception of women that undermines their individual authority in status positions. While Hochschild points out that women actively choose such roles (and therefore are not simply passive, nurturing beings), does the selection of passivity result in a personally desirable effect? Certainly a woman could choose to engage in a breach in the standard practice of the situation, but how often will she be willing to do this in a place of business in order to demonstrate an important point? In choosing courses of action, individuals in social interaction tend not to focus on the historical and cultural factors that shape the normative options that they sense are available to them. When a job needs to get done, it is more likely that individuals will think about the normative options available to them and choose a course of action that gets the desired effect as defined by the normatively defined definition of the situation. In Hochschild's example, a stewardess is not likely to consider the historical and cultural factors impinging upon her selection of a more passive role. If she does consider such factors, and if she clearly understands the paradox of social existence, she might choose a different course of action, one ultimately more empowering though this could endanger her employment status. Individuals frequently choose courses of action from a normative grid that do not serve to empower them or help them to establish mutually satisfying and respectful social roles and interactions, particularly in situations involving the reification of social phenomena (such as money). To apply Karl Mannheim's perspective to this issue, the failure to take into consideration the historical and structural factors that impinge upon the dynamic of symbolic interaction undermines the potential of individuals in social interaction to modify their social conditions in a more intentional way.

Value systems tend to change very little while other aspects of culture may seem to change a great deal. This point is made clear in a collection of essays by Parsons (1964) published under the title *Social Structure and Personality*. Parsons argues that despite the apparent rapid changes taking place in the United States, the value system of the nation remains relatively stable. He describes the economic aspect of American society as one that highly values productivity, the free enterprise system, and private consumption. Parsons characterizes the underlying value pattern in America as being one of instrumental activism (though derived from the Puritan traditions, this value pattern need not be religiously grounded). Instrumental activism is reflected in the value of individual achievement as it tends to be defined within the normative order. For example, many of the "countercultural" practices of the youth in the 1960s actually reflected historically consistent patterns of activism, materialism, and conformity. In regard to this cohort, Parsons states:

> Clearly, American youth is in a ferment. On the whole, this ferment seems to accord relatively well with the sociologist's expectations. It expresses many dissatisfactions with the current state of society, some of which are fully justified. . . . Yet the general orientation appears to be, not a basic alienation, but an eagerness to learn, to accept higher orders of responsibility, and to "fit," not in the sense of passive conformity, but in the sense of their readiness to work within the system, rather than in basic opposition to it. (182)

Indeed, while this cohort has introduced some changes concerning social arrangements, these changes have generally been consistent with the value system of the nation. Echoing Robert Nisbet (1969), persistence rather than change tends to be the norm of social behavior through time.

Yet, how are we to explain that some things seem to "progress" as other things progress more slowly or not at all? Frederick Teggart (1925), who was a mentor to Robert Nisbet, has illuminating observations on this issue:

> To reach an understanding of "how things work" in the course of time, we may envisage the facts of experience as arranged conceptually in a series of concentric circles. Outermost, we would have the stellar universe; within this, the physical earth; within this, the world of organic life; within this, again, the world of human activities; within this, the larger group or nation; within this, the local community; and, finally, within this, the individual. In such a series, it is obvious that change in any outer circle will affect all that lies within it. We may, then, define an "event"'as an intrusion, from any wider circle, into any circle or condition which may be the object of present interest. (148)

Teggart's illustration is useful but limited. In the social world, each circle represents a different layer of social reality, each manifesting its own pace of social change. While the outer layers may have an impact on the inner layers (and vice versa), these impacts are not going to define the relative pace of change within each layer. In addition, these intrusions are less likely to have an impact the more one penetrates into the inner circles that constitute what it is to be human. For example, the technology of a culture (such as computer technology) may change; this may alter some social roles, but the underlying value system of the culture, which tends to participate significantly in defining the arrangements of social power within a situation, may change little.

Basic patterns of social inequality are not altered by changes in the superficial levels of social interaction, although it is at these levels that most social interactions pertaining to economic exchange occur. It is the impersonality of the ("outer circle") market that gives the impression of its being a free market, yet this superficiality prevents the intrusion of "inner circle" mechanisms to humanize its processes. This is the issue that concerns Parsons (164) when he notes that "the great problem has come to be, what to do with all these advantages."

Have people taken advantage of the insights garnered from the hundreds of years of political struggles for freedom and a hundred years of empirical research concerning the relationship between self and society and the mechanisms guiding social interaction? While more people today live within an elite condition of enjoying freedoms, it must be noted that many of these enjoyments stem from the proliferation of working conditions for the majority of people in the world that are deplorable. And yet, within social interactions the circumstances that impinge upon the social arrangements of power may be circumvented. An individual today, man or woman, may feel a sense of individual empowerment due to a "flexible" economy that prevents him or her from coming to terms with the fact that his or her individual freedom is the product of literally enslaving others (see Richard Sennett, *The Corrosion of Character*, 1999, and Kevin Bales, *Disposable People*, 2000). Historically speaking, there is nothing new about this, and that is the point.

This brief analysis of a hundred years of social psychological research demonstrates that social changes pertaining to individual freedoms are hard won and tend to be quite modest—inequalities tend not to disappear but rather are continually displaced. Inequalities are displaced because fundamental changes in social arrangements rarely occur. We may also wonder if Christopher Lasch's *The Culture of Narcissism* is not only a commentary on late twentieth century culture, but also a repetition of history. If so, then the continuing displacement of social inequalities would also be the product of modern individualism falling, once again, into a state of narcissism.

Some readers may note that the position expressed here is reminiscent of Friedrich Nietzsche's theory of the eternal recurrence of the same. In Volume II of Martin Heidegger's four-volume set of the philosopher's writings, *Nietzsche* (1991), he clearly explains the central position of this theory:

> The eternal return of the same is to prove to be the fundamental determination of the world totality. . . . [E]ternal return of the same is to prove to be the *way in which* being as a whole *is*. . . . [T]he world's becoming runs backward and forward in endless (infinite) time. . . . Because no homeostasis or equilibrium prevails, it is clear that it never was attained, and here that means that it never can come to prevail. The world's becoming, as finite, turning back on itself, is therefore a *permanent* becoming. . . . Since such cosmic becoming, as finite becoming in an infinite time, takes place continuously, not ceasing whenever its finite possibilities are exhausted, it must already have repeated itself, indeed an infinite number of times. And as permanent becoming it will continue to repeat itself in the future. (109)

Though this (metaphysical) statement takes us beyond the realm of analysis intended, the central argument is consistent with this brief historical conclusion. Heidegger states that the eternal return of the same is the way in which "being" (existence–life–human existence–human organization) "is." He states that the world's "becoming" (emerging being–change–social change) "runs backward and forward" endlessly through time. Because there is never stasis (or the attainment of some end point of development), there are no grounds upon which to suggest that humankind, in the past as well as in the future, has or can attain a point beyond where it continuously circles.

Heidegger's statement that "The world's becoming, as finite, turning back on itself, is therefore a permanent becoming" suggests that finite beings, human beings, never attain insight into the conditions that repeat themselves; human beings may interpret superficial change as progress. For example, each age looks back upon another with the judgment: "How could they have thought that way?" "How could they engage in such practices?" The members of the present age are generally good at ignoring the barbaric consequences of some of their current practices. The failure to recognize the repetition of human existence demonstrates its inevitable recurrence. The point of the cliché, "Those who don't learn from the mistakes of history are doomed to repeat them," is an admonition in this regard. But the recognition that history may repeat itself does not seem to be translated into fundamental changes concerning social practices. As Yukio Mishima expresses in *Spring Snow*: "To live in the midst of an era is to be oblivious to its style." Finally, Heidegger's statement, "Since such cosmic becoming . . . takes place continuously, not ceasing whenever its finite possibilities are exhausted, it must already have repeated itself" suggests that when humankind (as a part of existence) exhausts a path of potential development, a process occurs whereby developments are started seemingly anew.

What could be the beginning point of individualism in demise? The appearance of narcissism as a norm would seem to signal both the demise of individualism as well as the intimation of the eventual repetition of individualism. Individualism thus appears as a self-limiting process sparked by the human desire to break free from restrictive communal or social bonds. Individualism at this point represents an emancipatory act by a self-conscious social animal. At this point physical developments (such as population growth and density, and technological innovations) and social interactions create individual needs and wants that supercede the prevailing norms of the community. Though some would refer to this as "cultural lag," that term suggests that one aspect of culture must catch up to other aspects of culture; but since there is no fundamental progress, we are not describing cultural lag, but rather, one point in a circle. Finally, the emancipatory act of individualism is eventually followed by a regressive act into narcissism, which is only quelled by the desire for strong communal or social bonds (thereby completing the circle or recurrence of the same). While individualism emerges out of the social conditions and interactions that spur its growth and depth, historically speaking, at least in Western civilization, we cannot conclude that individualism is a progressive phenomenon. Indeed, just as the growth in the social value of individualism does not guarantee its continuation (nor can we necessarily conclude that the potentialities of individualism are more fulfilled at a later period than at an earlier time in history), the yearning for community is an indication that the potentialities of individualism at a given time are perceived by the population as being exhausted.

Synthesizing Teggart's theory of concentric circles with that of the eternal recurrence of the same contextualizes individualism even further. The human being in social interaction represents the beginning. From this relationship emerge communal developments such as institutions, rules, and technologies. Once established, the circles representing technologies and social institutions act back upon their creators—persons in social interaction. While these intrusions alter, perhaps refine, human relationships (as in language), they do not fundamentally change the social tendencies of human beings. Hence, for example, refinements in the outer circle of technology do not change the tendency of modern humankind to create an economy that includes more slaves today than those who were stolen from Africa in the time of the transatlantic slave trade (Bales 2000). While we may hold onto the possibility of humankind's being affected by and effecting significant change in the outer circles that comprise its institutions, for this to be a meaningful hope, humankind would have to learn fundamentally from the mistakes of history. But in order for this to happen, a fundamental shift would have to occur in the constitution of individualist strivings. Historically, the ideas of freedom and individualism have been wed; it has been assumed that equality would follow. However, when the freedoms of individualism have occurred, equality has endured a rough ride at best—always fighting to survive. It is possible that equality requires a different sort of individualism than does freedom. The marriage of individualism and equality seems to be the peak of the historical circle of individualism. If the repetitions that have been described here are not inevitable, and if humankind truly values equality, then humankind must engage in activities that break this cycle. Equality as a byproduct of individual freedom fails. Perhaps freedom could be a successful byproduct of individual equality. Individual equality would entail both self-confidence and self-sacrifice. At the nation-state level, this utopian vision would undermine self-interest in deference to the promotion of democratically arrived-at goals common to the survival of human existence. In many ways there is nothing to risk; the present pattern ultimately results in the fear of individualism, the yearning for collectivization, and the deaths of countless individuals.

Glossary

Addams, Jane (1860–1935)   Sociologist and leader in social reform. Addams co-founded the famous settlement house, called Hull House, for Chicago's urban poor.

a priori (Latin)   Proceeding from a known or assumed cause and not from experience.

anomie   Social condition characterized by individual wants outpacing available means. According to Emile Durkheim, norms should govern or limit wants to attainable levels.

collective or common consciousness   The overarching system of beliefs of a particular social group. According to Durkheim, as the members of the social group engage in increasingly specialized activities, the guiding force of the common consciousness weakens, thereby reflecting a new form of solidarity based upon individual differences.

comparative sociology   Denotes an interest in institutional factors analyzed comparatively across different societies.

Comte, Auguste (1798–1857)   French social philosopher who coined the term "sociology."

cultural lag   Inconsistent levels of development among the institutions and norms of society.

Darwin, Charles (1809–1882)   British naturalist who developed the idea that evolution is a product of natural selection in *On the Origin of Species* (1859).

Dewey, John (1859–1952)   U.S. philosopher and educator. Along with colleague George Herbert Mead, he furthered the philosophical and social reform movement known as pragmatism.

dialectic   The art or science of arriving at the truth by drawing rigorous distinctions between differing points of view and then overcoming them through a transformational process.

differentiation   Process in social interaction whereby individuals become more distinct from one another.

division of labor   Concept developed by Adam Smith in *The Wealth of Nations* to describe specialization in the process of production that results from subdividing work performed by separate workers. The division of labor forms the basis of modern industrial

355

production. The concept was developed further by the founders of sociology: Karl Marx, Emile Durkheim, and Max Weber.

Enlightenment, The A philosophical movement of the eighteenth century that utilized the point of view of rationalism to examine critically previous and existing doctrines and institutions. Often referred to as "The Age of Reason."

epistemology Pertaining to the nature and origin of knowledge.

ex nihilo (Latin) Out of, or from, nothing.

externalization In social interaction, the acknowledgement by the receiver (via expression) that information has been effectively communicated.

generalized other Expression used by George Herbert Mead to convey the prevailing ideas of the culture that reinforce the socialization of the individual.

Goethe, Johann Wolfgang von (1749–1832) German Romantic poet, dramatist, and philosopher who espoused the value of holistic and intuitive thinking over rationalist thought.

Gresham's Law First promulgated by Sir Thomas Gresham (1519–1579), the theory states that if two kinds of money have the same denominational value but different intrinsic values, the money with higher intrinsic value will be hoarded and eventually driven out of circulation by the money with lesser intrinsic value.

"grown old together" Term used by Alfred Schutz to describe the phenomenon of the We-relationship.

habitualization The behaviors and attitudes that become a part of the taken-for-granted that function in the social roles comprising social institutions.

Hall, G. Stanley (1844–1924) Pioneer in American psychology, founded the *American Journal of Psychology*, and served as the first president of the American Psychological Association.

ideal type A term used by Max Weber to formulate general, abstract concepts of social phenomena.

inter alia (Latin) Among other things.

internalization In social interaction, the incorporation of information from external sources.

James, William (1842–1910) American philosopher and psychologist who furthered the philosophical movement known as pragmatism. His works, which include *The Principles of Psychology* and *The Varieties of Religious Experience*, are considered to be classics in the field.

Kant, Immanuel (1724–1804) German philosopher who was one of the founding fathers of the Enlightenment.

legitimate order Refers to social conditions that have the presumption of legitimacy or authorization.

leveling The reduction of social values and individual qualities to a quantifiable average.

modo praeteritus (Latin) Just recently gone by.

money economy An economy that uses money as its currency rather than using bartering or other nonmonetary means of exchange.

moral order A socially established set of obligations to which people in a society are expected to conform.

Nietzsche, Friedrich (1844–1900) German philosopher whose work reflected the primacy of the individual and an existential critique of morality.

objectification Reflects one of the moments in the process of internalization and externalization, whereby what one learns takes on the quality of objective reality.

objective culture   Pertaining to the development of the objective (i.e., material) aspects of culture.

ontology   Pertaining to knowledge of being or existing.

papyri   Documents written on a kind of paper made from the stems of an aquatic plant called *Cyperus papyrus*.

phenomenology   The philosophical study of appearance, developed by Edmund Husserl around 1905.

Parsons, Talcott (1902–1979)   Sociologist at Harvard University, greatly influenced by the work of Durkheim and Weber, Parsons's thoughts on social systems were a powerful force in the United States for many years.

pragmatism   Philosophical movement of the late nineteenth and twentieth centuries that emphasized interpreting ideas through their consequences.

reciprocal typifications   Social behaviors operating in consort that produce the social roles comprising social institutions.

reflexivity   Capacity of the human mind to reflect upon itself.

romanticism   A literary, artistic, and philosophical movement originating in late eighteenth century Europe that developed in reaction to the Enlightenment and emphasized emotion and imagination rather than reason.

routinization   The application of formal principles in the production process, resulting in the maximization of efficiency.

Royce, Josiah (1855–1916)   U.S. philosopher and educator who was the primary representative of idealist philosophy between the Civil War and World War I.

Schiller, Friedrich von (1759–1805)   German poet, dramatist, and philosopher who was a friend and collaborator of Goethe.

Schlegel, Friedrich von (1772–1829)   German philosopher, poet, and critic who was the leader of the Romantic movement in Germany.

Schleiermacher, Friedrich (1768–1834)   German philosopher and theologian who, rather than defining religion in terms of reason or morality, stressed the importance of subjective feeling.

significant symbol   The gestures, objects, and expressions used by persons in interaction that reflect the norms of the generalized other.

sociability   Human proclivity for social feeling and social relations.

social character   Concept used to describe the prevailing character of persons at a given period in society.

socialization   Social means by which society teaches its young and other new members its ways.

solidarity   Term used by Durkheim to explain social cohesion. He described two forms of solidarity: mechanical solidarity, which is based upon strong social bonds; and organic solidarity, which is based upon modern, complementary social relations.

Smith, Adam (1723–1790)   Scottish political economist and philosopher. Advocated the position that people could compete freely with minimal government intervention in the economy. Smith is the author of *The Wealth of Nations*, which strongly influenced capitalist theory and practices in the West.

Spencer, Herbert (1820–1903)   English social philosopher who adopted ideas from such men as Charles Darwin and Adam Smith to develop a unique functionalist sociology. Spencer's work is often associated with Social Darwinism or the application of Darwinian principles (i.e., survival of the fittest) to human relations and social development.

subjective culture   Pertaining to the development or cultivation of the person.

sublimation   Presentation of a socially unacceptable behavior in a socially acceptable form, for example, that sports is a socially acceptable outlet for aggressive behavior.

sui generis (Latin)   Of one's own making.

symbols   The gestures, objects, and expressions that form the basis of human communication.

symbolic universe   The outskirts of understanding and meaning for a given society at a particular time and place.

taken-for-granted   The assumed knowledge base of social interaction in a given society.

utilitarianism   Philosophical doctrine, proposed by Jeremy Bentham and John Stuart Mill in the nineteenth century, that values usefulness and espouses the importance of achieving the greatest amount of good for the greatest number of people.

world-openness   The human capacity for flexible learning and skill as opposed to being determined by instinct.

Wundt, Wilhelm (1832–1900)   German philosopher who is generally acknowledged as the founder of experimental psychology.

Bibliography

Bales, Kevin. 2000. *Disposable People: New Slavery in the Global Economy*. University of California Press.

Bellah, Robert, Richard Madsen, William M. Sullivan, Ann Swidler, and Steven M. Tipton. 1996. *Habits of the Heart: Individualism and Commitment in American Life*. University of California Press.

Berger, Peter L., and Thomas Luckmann. 1967. *The Social Construction of Reality: A Treatise in the Sociology of Knowledge*. Doubleday Anchor Books.

Blumer, Herbert. 1966. "Sociological Implications of the Thought of George Herbert Mead." *American Journal of Sociology* 71:535–44.

———. 1986. *Symbolic Interactionism: Perspectives and Method*. University of California Press.

Buber, Martin. 1970. *I and Thou*. Charles Scribner's Sons.

Cooley, Charles Horton. 1922. *Human Nature and the Social Order*. Charles Scribner's Sons.

Davis, Thurston N. 1956. "Justice as the Foundation of Human Equality in Ancient Greece." Pp. 207–20 in *Aspects of Human Equality: Fifteenth Symposium of the Conference on Science, Philosophy and Religion*, edited by Lyman Bryson, Clarence H. Faust, Louis Finkelstein, and R. M. Maciver. The Conference on Science, Philosophy and Religion in their Relation to the Democratic Way of Life, Inc.

Durkheim, Emile. [1893] 1984. *The Division of Labor in Society*. Translated by W. D. Halls. The Free Press.

Fromm, Erich. 1965. *Escape From Freedom*. Avon Books.

Garfinkel, Harold. 1996. *Studies in Ethnomethodology*. Polity Press.

Goffman, Erving. 1959. *The Presentation of Self in Everyday Life*. Doubleday Anchor Books.

Heidegger, Martin. 1991. *Nietzsche*. Volume I: *The Will to Power as Art*; Volume II: *The Eternal Recurrence of the Same*. Translated by David Farrell Krell. HarperCollins.

Heritage, John. 1996. *Garfinkel and Ethnomethodology*. Polity Press.

Hochschild, Arlie Russell. 1983. *The Managed Heart: Commercialization of Human Feeling*. University of California Press.

Lasch, Christopher. 1991. *The Culture of Narcissism: American Life in an Age of Diminishing Expectations*. W. W. Norton & Company.

Mannheim, Karl. 1936. *Ideology and Utopia*. Translated by Louis Wirth and Edward Shils. Harvest Books.

Mead, George H. 1908. "The Philosophical Basis of Ethics." *International Journal of Ethics* 18:311–23.

——. 1909. "Social Psychology as Counterpoint to Physiological Psychology." *Psychological Bulletin* 6:401–8.

——. 1910. "What Social Objects Must Psychology Presuppose?" *Journal of Philosophy* 7:174–80.

——. 1912. "The Mechanism of Social Consciousness." *Journal of Philosophy* 9:401-6.

——. 1913. "The Social Self." *Journal of Philosophy* 10:374–80.

——. 1922. "A Behavioristic Account of the Significant Symbol." *Journal of Philosophy* 19:157–63.

——. 1923. "Scientific Method and the Moral Sciences." *International Journal of Ethics* 33:229–47.

——. 1925. "The Genesis of the Self and Social Control." *International Journal of Ethics* 35:251–77.

——. 1929. "National-Mindedness and International-Mindedness." *International Journal of Ethics* 39:385–407.

——. 1967. *Mind, Self, and Society from the Standpoint of a Social Behaviorist*. Edited by Charles W. Morris. The University of Chicago Press.

Morris, Colin. 2000. *The Discovery of the Individual, 1050–1200*. University of Toronto Press.

Nisbet, Robert A. 1953. *The Quest for Community: A Study in the Ethics of Order and Freedom*. Oxford University Press.

——. 1969. *Social Change and History: Aspects of the Western Theory of Development*. Oxford University Press.

Parsons, Talcott. 1964. *Social Structure and Personality*. The Free Press.

Riesman, David, with Nathan Glazer, and Reuel Denney. 1954. *The Lonely Crowd: A Study of the Changing American Character*. Yale University Press.

Scheler, Max. 1992. *On Feeling, Knowing, and Valuing: Selected Writings*. Edited by Harold J. Bershady. The University of Chicago Press.

Schutz, Alfred. 1942. "Scheler's Theory of Intersubjectivity and the General Thesis of the Alter Ego." *Philosophy and Phenomenological Research* 2,3:323–47.

——. 1946. "The Well-Informed Citizen: An Essay on the Social Distribution of Knowledge." *Social Research* 13,4:463–78.

——. 1950. "Language, Language Disturbances, and the Texture of Consciousness." *Social Research* 17,3:365–94.

——. 1953. "Common Sense and Scientific Interpretations of Human Action." *Philosophy and Phenomenological Research* 14,1:1–37.

——. 1956. "Equality and the Meaning of the Social World." Pp. 33–78 in *Aspects of Human Equality: Fifteenth Symposium of the Conference on Science, Philosophy and Religion*, edited by Lyman Bryson, Clarence H. Faust, Louis Finkelstein, and R. M. Maciver. The Conference on Science, Philosophy and Religion in their Relation to the Democratic Way of Life, Inc.

———. 1967. *The Phenomenology of the Social World*. Translated by George Walsh and Frederick Lehnert. Northwestern University Press.

———. 1970. *On Phenomenology and Social Relations: Selected Writings*. Edited by Helmut R. Wagner. The University of Chicago Press.

Sennett, Richard. 1999. *The Corrosion of Character: The Personal Consequences of Work in the New Capitalism*. W. W. Norton & Company.

Simmel, Georg. 1978. *The Sociology of Georg Simmel*. Translated and edited by Kurt H. Wolff. The Free Press.

———. [1907] 1990. *The Philosophy of Money*. Translated by Tom Bottomore and David Frisby. Edited by David Frisby. Routledge.

Teggart, Frederick J. 1925. *Theory of History*. Yale University Press.

Thomas, W. I. 1923. *The Unadjusted Girl*. Little, Brown and Company.

Weber, Max. [1956] 1978. *Economy and Society*. Two volumes. Translated and edited by Guenther Roth and Claus Wittich. University of California Press.

Zeitlan, Irving M. 1993. *Plato's Vision: The Classical Origins of Social and Political Thought*. Prentice-Hall, Inc.

Index

acting: deep, 298, 305–7, 310–13; surface, 305, 307, 312–13

action: joint, 250–52, 255–56, 258–59, 261–62; rational, 27, 29–33, 39–42, 45–46, 48–50; social, 4, 25–51, 143, 250, 252–62, 277–78, 280, 293

Adams, John, 323

Addams, Jane, 117

adjustment, character or social, 188–89, 194–98, 201, 203–4, 206, 208

Agnes (Garfinkel's study subject), 266–67, 280–92, 348

alienation, 52

alter ego, 153, 156, 166

American Revolution, 26

anomie, 10, 188–89, 196–98, 201, 206, 208

associations, 327

audience, 212, 214, 218–20, 222, 226, 228

autonomy, 188–90, 194–96, 198, 200–208

back region performance, 211, 224–25

Bales, Kevin, 351, 353

Bellah, Robert, 5, 317–43

behavior, crowd, 43–44

Beauvoir, Simone de, 220–21

Berger, Peter, 2, 5, 230–48

biblical religion, 318–19, 321–22, 325–28, 331, 338, 342

Blumer, Herbert, 5, 249–63

bureaucracy, 25

ceremony, 217, 224

character: representative, 318–19, 327–28; social, 187–88, 190–91, 193, 195–96, 199–201, 204–5

character type: inner-directed, 187–88, 193–94, 196–97, 199–207; other-directed, 187–88, 193–97, 201–3, 205–7; tradition-directed, 187–88, 193–94, 196–97, 199–200, 207

Christianity, 55, 96, 174–76, 346–47

collective consciousness, 10, 12, 14–19, 21, 23

common consciousness. See consciousness

common good, 321, 341, 343

communication, 86, 89, 91–92, 93–94, 97, 265, 279

community, 318–21, 323, 327, 329–30, 332, 339–40, 342–43, 352–53

Comte, Auguste, 1, 9, 22

conduct, social, 121–26, 128, 131–32

conformity, 187–89, 191, 193–94, 196, 206, 261

consciousness: collective, 10, 12, 14–19, 21, 23; individual, 14–15, 18, 20–21,

23–24; stream of, 153–54, 156, 158, 160, 164–65
conversation analysis, 265–66
Cooley, Charles H., 4, 85–102, 116, 126, 146, 232
crowd behavior, 43–44
culture: objective, 75–82; subjective, 75–82

Darwin, Charles, 10, 19, 85, 116–17
Declaration of Independence, 323, 348
deep acting, 298, 305–307, 310–13
definition of the situation (term of William I. Thomas), 4, 104–5, 108–14, 147, 149, 155, 170, 178, 211–12, 219, 221, 226, 229, 242–43, 349
democracy, 120, 320, 327, 346
demography, 192–93
Descartes, René, 176
despotism, 327, 342
deviance, 104, 261
deviation, 196, 201–2, 206
Dewey, John, 116, 148, 205
differences in stimulus, 68
division of labor, 9–24, 73–74, 76, 79–80, 115, 199, 244
documentary method, 265–66, 270–71, 275, 279
dramaturgical approach, 5, 209–10, 212, 221, 228
Durkheim, Emile, 1, 4, 9–24, 217, 220, 281, 345
dynamic density, 10

ego, alter, 153, 156, 166
Emerson, Ralph Waldo, 325, 329
emotion work, 298–300
Enlightenment, the, 54, 72
equality, 54–55, 61–63, 65–70, 73, 322–25, 341–42, 346, 348, 351, 353
ethics, 135–37
ethnomethodology, 5, 264
evolution, 135, 137–39
exchange, gift, 301
expressive individualism, 318, 320, 325–26, 330, 332, 336–38
externalization, 232, 236, 238, 241–42

face-to-face situation, 145, 156, 159–63, 166–67
feeling rules, 298, 301–2
Fichte, Johann G., 60, 71
Franklin, Benjamin, 324–26, 328
fraternity, 61
freedom, 52–55, 60–70, 73, 89, 91, 101–2, 147, 149, 181, 202, 205–6, 322, 324, 326–27, 329, 333, 335, 338, 342–43, 346–48, 351, 353
French Revolution, 9, 26, 60
Freud, Sigmund, 292, 301, 303–4
Fromm, Erich, 191, 202, 205
front (in performance), 210–16, 218, 224–25

Garfinkel, Harold, 5, 264–93, 348–49
gender, 207, 267, 281–92, 298–300, 302–3, 308, 311, 313–16, 348
generalized other, 119, 133–34, 233
gestures, 117–19, 121–24, 127–28, 131–32, 134, 169
gift exchange, 301
Goethe, Johann W., 57, 61, 71–72, 74
Goffman, Erving, 5, 209–29, 305
Greek culture, 173, 200, 346–47
group size, 52

habitualization, 231–33, 236–37
Hall, G. Stanley, 116
Hegel, G. W. F., 125
Heidegger, Martin, 351–52
Heritage, John, 265
Hochschild, Arlie, 5, 297–316, 320, 348–49
Hull House, 103, 117
humanism, 347
Husserl, Edmund, 5, 143, 156–57, 270

"I," 92–95, 97
"I" and "me," 118, 124–27, 133, 169
ideal type, 27, 30–31, 33, 35, 39, 41–42, 165–67, 188, 193, 197, 214
identification, 243–44, 247–48
ideology, 168, 171
imagination, 88–89, 95, 98–100
imitation, 43–44, 89–90
independent citizen, 328

indexicality, 265, 278
individual consciousness, 14–15, 18, 20–21, 23–24
individualism, 1–3, 26–27, 53–74, 87–90, 92–93, 96, 98–101, 105, 107–10, 112–15, 118–19, 124, 126–27, 131–32, 134–40, 147, 152, 154, 165, 169–72, 176–77, 179–81, 183, 189, 195, 199–200, 202, 204–7, 233, 240–42, 244, 246–48, 318–22, 325–27, 329–31, 335, 337–43, 345–53; expressive, 318, 320, 325–26, 330, 332, 336–38; utilitarian, 318, 320, 325–26, 330–32, 336–38
Industrial Revolution, 1, 25–26, 105, 111, 248
industrial society, 100, 319, 328
inequality, social, 5–6, 99–100, 102, 207, 298–303, 308, 313–15, 346, 348, 351, 353
inhibition, 108, 119, 122, 131, 169
inner-directed character type, 187–88, 193–94, 196–97, 199–207
institutionalization, 231–33, 237, 239
instrumental activism, 350
interaction, 209–13, 226–27, 229; non-symbolic, 254–55; social, 52–53, 231–33, 237, 249–52, 254–57, 259, 262, 264–66, 269, 345, 349, 351–53
internalization, of social processes, 232, 238, 242–45, 247–48
intersubjectivity, 5, 143, 145, 162, 242, 264
invisible complexity, 321, 341–42

James, William, 116, 125, 127, 219
Jefferson, Thomas, 318, 324–28, 330, 348
joint action, 250–52, 255–56, 258–59, 261–62
Judaism, 346–47
justice, 322, 324, 326, 337, 339–41, 346

Kant, Immanuel, 13, 53–54, 59–60, 63, 65–66, 125
King, Martin Luther, Jr., 321, 342–43
knowledge: sociology of, 5, 169–70, 173, 181, 231, 239; stock of, 144, 146, 236, 244

labor, division of, 9–24, 73–74, 76, 79–80, 115, 199, 244
language, 118, 145, 231, 233, 244–45, 265–66, 278–80, 320–21, 328, 331–32, 336, 340–41
Lasch, Christopher, 351
legitimate order, 50–51
liberty, 320–22, 348
lifestyle enclave, 330
Lincoln, Abraham, 328
Locke, John, 338
looking-glass self, 4, 95, 98
love, 331–33
Luckmann, Thomas, 5, 230–48

macrosociology, 1
Madsen, Richard, 317
manager (professional), 319, 328, 332–36
Mandela, Nelson, 189
Mannheim, Karl, 5, 168–84, 270, 349
Marx, Karl, 201, 203, 205
Mead, George Herbert, 5, 103, 116–42, 169, 199, 232, 249–51, 254–56, 258–63
mechanical solidarity, 10, 14, 19
Melville, Herman, 325
microsociology, 1
Mill, John Stuart, 11, 204–5, 207
morality, 22–23, 104–5, 108–10, 112, 114, 119, 128–30, 136–42, 152, 182, 321, 324, 328–30, 332, 336–42
moral order, 227–28, 266–67, 270, 275, 282, 285, 288–90, 292, 347
Morris, Colin, 347

narcissism, 347, 351–52
narrative, 330
natural attitude, 145, 154
negative solidarity, 13
Nietzsche, Friedrich, 53, 57–59, 205, 351
Nisbet, Robert, 350
non-symbolic interaction, 254–55
norms, 264, 266–67, 272–77, 290–91, 293, 345, 349–50, 352

objectivation, 238–42
objective culture, 75–82
objects, 252, 256–57, 259–60

oligarchy, 346
Oracle of Delphi, 346–47
order: legitimate, 50–51; moral, 227–28, 266–67, 270, 275, 282, 285, 288–90, 292, 347
organic solidarity, 10, 15, 19
orientation: they, 146, 164, 166–67; thou, 145–46, 164, 166–67
Orwell, George, 225
other-directed character type, 187–88, 193–97, 201–3, 205–7
outside region, 226

paradox, social, 2–4, 349
Parsons, Talcott, 4, 5, 256, 264, 267, 271, 275, 281, 349–51
performance, 209–29
personality and social structure, 2
phenomenology, 143, 231
Plato, 346
play, 119, 133
population density, 52, 55
positive solidarity, 13
pragmatism, 85, 117, 120, 137
propaganda, 189
psychological social psychology, 1
Puritans, 318, 323–24, 338

rational action, 27, 29–33, 39–42, 45–46, 48–50
reciprocal perspectives, 155, 265, 269–70
reciprocal typifications, 231, 237–39
reflexive self, 250, 252–53, 259–60
reflexivity, 266–67, 275, 277, 292
region: back, 211, 224–25; outside, 226
reification, 232, 239–40, 349
relevances, 144–47, 151–53, 155
religion, biblical, 318–19, 321–22, 325–28, 331, 338, 342
representative character, 318–19, 327–28
republicanism, 318–19, 321–26, 328, 331, 342–43
Revolution, American, 26
Revolution, French, 9, 26, 60
revolutions, 192
Riesman, David, 5, 187–208, 318
Romanticism, 72
Rousseau, Jean-Jacques, 60, 64

routine (performance), 210, 212, 214–18, 222–23, 228, 236, 241, 245
Royce, Josiah, 116, 126

Santayana, George, 220
Sartre, Jean-Paul, 224
Scheler, Max, 154
Schutz, Alfred, 5, 143–67, 169, 231, 264–65, 267, 269, 279
script, 211, 222–23
S-curve, 192–93
Sennett, Richard, 351
setting, 213–14, 216–17
sign-equipment, 215–18
significant others, 243–44
significant symbol, 119, 132–34, 242
Simmel, Georg, 1, 4, 25, 52–82, 147, 345, 348
slavery, 324
Smith, Adam, 10, 11
social action, 4, 25–51, 143, 264, 277–78, 280, 293; types of, 44–46
social change, 112–14
social character, 187–88, 190–91, 193, 195–96, 199–201, 204–5
social conduct, 121–26, 128, 131–32
social inequality, 5–6, 99–100, 102, 207, 298–303, 308, 313–15, 346, 348, 351, 353
social institutions, 280
social interaction, 52–53, 231–33, 237, 249–52, 254–57, 259, 262, 264–66, 269, 345, 349, 351–53
socialism, 54, 61, 66–69, 139
sociality, 88, 91–92
socialization, 195, 210–11, 220, 222, 231–33, 238, 243–48, 263
social paradox, 2–4, 349
social psychology: psychological, 1; sociological, 2–6
social relationship, 46–48
social structure, 147, 174, 181, 195, 233, 243, 245, 248, 256, 261, 264, 281
sociological social psychology, 2–6
sociology of knowledge, 5, 169–70, 173, 181, 231, 239
Socrates, 346

solidarity: mechanical, 10, 14, 19; negative, 13; organic, 10, 15, 19; positive, 13
specialization, 10–11, 22–24, 56, 58, 74, 76, 79, 236
speech, 122, 124–25, 127–28, 132
Spencer, Herbert, 9, 13, 21
stage production, 210
Stanislavski, Constantin, 305, 309
stimulus, differences in, 68
stock of knowledge, 144, 146, 236, 244
stratification, 218
stream of consciousness, 153–54, 156, 158, 160, 164–65
subjective culture, 75–82
sublimation of the wish, 105, 114
Sullivan, William, 317
surface acting, 305, 307, 312–13
Swidler, Ann, 317
symbol, 92–93, 118–19, 125, 127; significant, 119, 132–34, 242
symbolic interactionism, 2, 249–50, 254–56
symbolic universe, 232–33, 240–41

taken-for-granted, 144, 147–48, 153, 155–56, 160, 169, 232–33, 236, 241, 244–45
Teggert, Frederick, 350, 353
therapist, 319–20, 328, 331–37
they-orientation, 146, 164, 166–67
Thomas, William I., 4, 103–15, 211, 345, 348
thou-orientation, 145–46, 156–57, 159, 162, 164–66
Tipton, Steven, 318
Tocqueville, Alexis de, 205, 318–19, 322–23, 326–28, 332

tradition, 320, 322, 329, 336–37, 343
tradition-directed character type, 187–88, 193–94, 196–97, 199–200, 207
transmutation, 298–99, 302–3, 310
Tufts, James H., 117
types of social action, 44–46
typifications, 144–47, 150–52; reciprocal, 231, 237–39

"us," 146, 155
usage, custom, and self-interest, 48–50
utilitarian individualism, 318, 320, 325–26, 330–32, 336–38
utopia, 168, 171

Veblen, Thorstein, 107, 201

Washington, George, 318, 323
"we," 154–55, 158–61
Weber, Max, 4, 5, 25–51, 85, 143, 165, 197, 264
we-relationship, 145–46, 157–59, 161–63, 166
Whitman, Walt, 325–26
Winthrop, John, 323–24, 326, 328–29, 343
wish, sublimation of the, 105, 114
wishes, the, 104, 106–15
words, 182
work, 139, 142
world-openness, 231, 234–35, 241
Wundt, Wilhelm, 116, 131

Zeitlin, Irving, 346
Znaniecki, Florian, 103
zones of relevance, 144, 148–49

~

Credits

Chapter 1

Reprinted with the permission of The Free Press, a Division of Simon & Schuster, Inc. from *The Division of Labor in Society* by Emile Durkheim, translated by W. D. Halls. Introduction by Lewis A. Coser. Introduction, copyright ©1984 by Lewis A. Coser. Translation, copyright © 1984 by Higher & Further Education Division, Macmillan Publishers Ltd. Selection from pages 1–2, 17, 22, 38–39, 61, 75–76, 83–85, 117–23, 217–18, 220–21, 232–33, 306–8, 332–34, 335, 336.

World rights, excluding North America, for publication of *The Division of Labour in Society* by Emile Durkheim, are held by Palgrave Publishers Ltd.; reproduced with permission of Palgrave.

Chapter 2

From Max Weber in *Economy and Society*, 2 volumes, translated and edited by Guenther Roth and Claus Wittich. University of California Press, 1978. Selection from volume 1, pages 4–15, 17–32. Reprinted with permission.

Chapter 3

Reprinted with the permission of The Free Press, a Division of Simon & Schuster, Inc., from *The Sociology of Georg Simmel*, translated and edited by Kurt H. Wolff. Copyright © 1950, copyright renewed 1978 by The Free Press. Selection from pages 58–84.

From Georg Simmel in *The Philosophy of Money*, translated by Tom Bottomore and David Frisby, edited by David Frisby. Routledge, 1990. Selection from pages 448–50, 453–54, 460–63, 467–70. Reprinted with permission.

Chapter 4

From Charles Horton Cooley, *Human Nature and the Social Order*, Charles Scribner's Sons, 1922. Selection from pages 36–37, 40–42, 45–47, 56–57, 65–68, 71–74, 83–87, 127, 130–31, 168–71, 177–78, 180–86, 196–97, 199, 217–18, 256, 258–62, 288, 309, 422–23, 425–26, 431–32.

Chapter 5

From W. I. Thomas, *The Unadjusted Girl*, Little, Brown and Company, 1923. Selection from pages 2–6, 9, 11–12, 17–18, 31–32, 38–44, 50, 68–72, 78, 81–82, 228–35, 242–44, 254, 256–57.

Chapter 6

In order of appearance:
George H. Mead, "The Mechanism of Social Consciousness," *Journal of Philosophy* 9 (1912): 401–6.
George H. Mead, "The Social Self," *Journal of Philosophy* 10 (1913): 374–80.
George H. Mead, "A Behavioristic Account of the Significant Symbol," *Journal of Philosophy* 19 (1922): 157–63.
George H. Mead, "The Philosophical Basis of Ethics," *International Journal of Ethics* 18 (1908): 311–23.

Chapter 7

First, fourth, and fifth selections in chapter:
From Alfred Schutz, "Equality and the Meaning of the Social World," in *Aspects of Human Equality: Fifteenth Symposium of the Conference on Science, Philosophy and Religion*, edited by Lyman Bryson, Clarence H. Faust, Louis Finkelstein, R. M. Maciver. The Conference on Science, Philosophy and Religion in Their Relation to the Democratic Way of Life, Inc., 1956, 33–78. Reprinted with permission by the Jewish Theological Seminary of America, New York, N.Y.

Second selection:
From Alfred Schutz, "The Well-Informed Citizen: An Essay on the Social Distribution of Knowledge." *Social Research* 13, 4 (1946): 463–78. Reprinted with permission.

Third selection:
From Alfred Schutz, "Language, Language Disturbances, and the Texture of Consciousness," *Social Research* 17, 3 (1950): 365–94. Reprinted with permission.

Sixth selection:
From Alfred Schutz, "Scheler's Theory of Intersubjectivity and the General Thesis of the Alter Ego," *Philosophy and Phenomenological Research* 2, 3 (1942): 323–47. Reprinted with permission.

Seventh and ninth selections:
Alfred Schutz, *The Phenomenology of the Social World*, translated by George Walsh and Frederick Lehnert. Northwestern University Press, 1967. Selection from pages 108–9, 163–71, 176–78, 180–81, 183–85, 194–95, 202–4. Reprinted with permission.

Eighth selection:
From Alfred Schutz, "Common Sense and Scientific Interpretations of Human Action," *Philosophy and Phenomenological Research* 14, 1 (1953): 1–37. Reprinted with permission.

Chapter 8

From Karl Mannheim, *Ideology and Utopia*, translated by Louis Wirth and Edward Shils. Harcourt, Inc.; Routledge, 1936. Selection from pages 3–6, 9–24, 28–30, 47–50, 82–85, 95–96, 100, 105–7. Reprinted with permission.

Chapter 9

From David Riesman, Nathan Glazer, and Reuel Denney, *The Lonely Crowd: A Study of the Changing American Character*, Yale University Press, 1954. Selection from pages 17–23, 40–41, 275–98. Reprinted with permission.

Chapter 10

From *The Presentation of Self in Everyday Life* by Erving Goffman, copyright © 1959 by Erving Goffman. Used by permission of Doubleday, a division of Random House, Inc. Selection from pages 15–16, 22–30, 33–36, 41–42, 48–49, 51, 55–58, 70–76, 111–12, 121–22, 124, 126, 134–35, 229, 248–51, 254–55.

Chapter 11

From *The Social Construction of Reality* by Peter L. Berger and Thomas Luckmann, copyright © 1966 by Peter L. Berger and Thomas Luckmann. Used by permission of Doubleday, a division of Random House, Inc. Selection from pages 47–49, 51–55, 60–61, 74–75, 78–79, 88–89, 96, 99–102, 104, 129–32, 134–35, 138, 143–44, 152–55, 163–64, 171, 173, 176–79, 183.

Chapter 12

From Herbert Blumer, "Sociological Implications of the Thought of George Herbert Mead," *American Journal of Sociology* 71 (1966): 535–44. Reprinted from *The American Journal of Sociology* by permission of The University of Chicago Press.

Chapter 13

From John Heritage, *Garfinkel and Ethnomethodology*, Polity Press, 1996. Selection from pages 76, 78–82, 84–86, 90, 92–96, 106–10, 115–17, 128–29, 139–41, 144–49, 154, 180–98, 308–9. Reprinted with permission.

Chapter 14

From Arlie Russell Hochschild, *The Managed Heart: Commercialization of Human Feeling*, University of California Press, 1983. Selection from pages 17–21, 24–25, 29–31, 33–35, 42–44, 46–49, 76, 83–86, 92–94, 96–98, 104–6, 119–20, 132–34, 162–63, 167, 169–70, 172, 174–78, 183–84. Reprinted with permission.

Chapter 15

From Robert Bellah, Richard Madsen, William M. Sullivan, Ann Swidler, and Steven M. Tipton, *Habits of the Heart: Individualism and Commitment in American Life*. University of California Press, 1996. Selection from pages xlii, 27–35, 37–40, 45, 47, 65, 75–78, 82–84, 107–9, 111–12, 123–27, 132, 138–43, 145–46, 199, 204, 207–8, 249, 284–86. Reprinted with permission.

About the Editor

Nathan Rousseau is assistant professor of sociology at Jacksonville University.